For PETER
BEST WISHES,

f.f. Bll

Advance Praise for *Cowboys Over Iraq*

"What does it take to fly and fight with America's Air Cavalry? That's the story of *Cowboys Over Iraq*. You'll meet bold personalities right out of a Hollywood movie. You'll be right there as Jimmy Blackmon and his fellow Cavalry troopers track down and tangle with determined foes. You'll experience the highs of triumph and the lows of bitter loss. Most importantly, you'll see how and why Jimmy Blackmon learned hard-won leadership and battle lessons in the deadly skies of Iraq. Strap in. Hang on. Get ready to go hunting with the Air Cav."

—DANIEL P. BOLGER; *Lieutenant General, US Army (Retired),*
Commander, 1st Cavalry Division 2008–2010

"A *great* read by an exceptional combat aviator, leader, *and* writer! Jimmy Blackmon captures brilliantly the enthralling story of the air cavalry unit that was the eyes and ears of the 101st Airborne Division (Air Assault) during the fight to Baghdad and throughout the first year in Iraq—when I was privileged to command the division. He captures vividly, as well, the courage, skill, and feel for the battlefield of the gifted pilot and commander of the squadron, Lieutenant Colonel Steve Schiller, to whom we turned repeatedly when the missions were the toughest."

—GENERAL DAVID PETRAEUS; *US Army (Retired),*
Commanded the 101st Airborne Division (Air Assault), Multinational Force-Iraq,
US Central Command, and coalition and US forces in Afghanistan

"Jimmy Blackmon has done it again! Another great book that captures the essence of the United States Cavalry in battle. Having personally served in Iraq during that initial year of combat in Iraq, Jimmy's colorful writing style instantly transported me back in time. This page-turner is of unparalleled value to leaders of all organizations."

—DR. MARK GREEN; *US Army (Retired)*

"In the spring of 2003, I was privileged to accompany the famed 101st Airborne Division during the invasion of Iraq. As an NBC Correspondent, I enjoyed unparalleled access to the division's leadership as well as their soldiers. It was there, in the skies over Najef, Hillah, and Karbala that I was introduced to Lieutenant Colonel Stephen Schiller. A fearless leader with an ample amount of cavalry swagger, Schiller led from the front on every mission from Kuwait to Mosul. *Cowboys Over Iraq* paints a reflective and sobering portrait of decisions made under pressure, and literally in the face of blowing sandstorms and haze of the battlefield. It's a must read! Well done, Jimmy Blackmon."

—DANA LEWIS, *Freelance TV Journalist based in London and former NBC War Correspondent*

"Master story-teller and noted Air Cavalry-man Jimmy Blackmon's *Cowboys Over Iraq* is an exhilarating tale of modern day combat leadership and follow-ership seen through the lens of the U.S. Army's invasion of Iraq in 2003 and its first year of an extended counter insurgency few saw coming. Spotlighting the 101st Airborne Division's (Air Assault) Air Cavalry Squadron Commander, legendary Lieutenant Colonel Steve Schiller—Stetson on his head, pistol at his side, his steed the well-armed OH-58D Kiowa Warrior—Blackmon focuses on the triumphs of close quarters combat, but pulls no punches on the inevitable losses of life and the grief and longing that war brings to the home front and families. If you served in Iraq or know someone who did, this book is for you. Never served but want to learn from experts about tough but charismatic, and ultimately extremely effective leadership? Read *Cowboys Over Iraq!*"

—MAJOR GENERAL JEFF SCHLOESSER; *US Army (Retired), Commanding General, 101st Airborne Division (Air Assault) 2006–2009*

"Trust and common purpose are woven into the social fabric of teams—particularly in military units facing combat. Jimmy Blackmon's *Cowboys Over Iraq* at once tells the compelling story of America's first engagements in Iraq, while simultaneously reminding us that relationships, above all else, define who we choose to become."

—GENERAL STANLEY McCHRYSTAL; *US Army (Retired)*

"*Cowboys Over Iraq* is a detailed, compelling, and intimate portrait of the men and women who served in the air cavalry in the early stages of Operation Iraqi Freedom; Jimmy Blackmon's insightful and fascinating storytelling brings to life the trials and tribulations of this unit...the training, the skill, the courage, the life-long relationships established and the sacrifices endured are uniquely portrayed in this first-rate account. Jimmy puts a human face on the ugliness of war. A great read—a riveting story, this unit and those that served with it made extraordinary contributions for our Nation."

—JOHN F. CAMPBELL; *General, US Army (Retired), Former Commander, 101st Airborne Division (2009–2011), Vice Chief of Staff, Army (2013–2014) and Commander of US and NATO Forces, Afghanistan (2014–2016)*

ALSO BY JIMMY BLACKMON

*Pale Horse: Hunting Terrorists and Commanding Heroes
with the 101st Airborne Division*

COWBOYS
OVER IRAQ

LEADERSHIP FROM
THE SADDLE

JIMMY BLACKMON

Post Hill
PRESS

A POST HILL PRESS BOOK

Cowboys Over Iraq:
Leadership from the Saddle
© 2020 by Jimmy Blackmon
All Rights Reserved

ISBN: 978-1-64293-398-7
ISBN (eBook): 978-1-64293-399-4

Cover art by Cody Corcoran
Cover photo by John Giaquinto
Interior design and composition, Greg Johnson, Textbook Perfect

Post Hill Press
New York • Nashville
posthillpress.com

Published in the United States of America

This book is lovingly dedicated to the cavalrymen of 2nd Squadron, 17th United States Cavalry Regiment, and in particular to Captain Matthew "Bubba" Worrell, Chief Warrant Officer Two Michael Blaise, Chief Warrant Officer Four James "JC" Carter, and Chief Warrant Officer Four Michael Slebodnik, our brothers who made the ultimate sacrifice.

Until we meet at Fiddler's Green.

Major General David H. Petraeus
Commanding General, 101st Airborne Division (Air Assault)

Brigadier General Benjamin C. Freakley
Assistant Division Commander for Operations

Brigadier General Frank Helmick*

Brigadier General Edward J. Sinclair
Assistant Division Commander for Support

Brigadier General Jeffrey Schloesser*

Colonel Ben Hodges, 1st Brigade "Bastogne"

Colonel Joseph Anderson, 2nd Brigade "Strike"

Colonel Michael S. Linnington, 3rd Brigade "Rakkasan"

Colonel Gregory P. Gass, 101st Aviation Brigade "Destiny"

Colonel William H. Forrester, 159th Aviation Brigade "Thunder"

Colonel William L. Greer, 101st Division Artillery "Glory"

Colonel James E. Rogers, 101st Division Support "Lifeliner"

Colonel Gerald A. Dolish, 101st Corps Support Group*

*Assistant Division Commanders changed out in Mosul, Iraq, in the summer of 2003.

101st Aviation Brigade "Destiny"
Colonel Gregory P. Gass
Commander

2nd Squadron, 17th Cavalry "Saber"
(Division Cavalry Squadron)
Lieutenant Colonel Stephen M. Schiller

1st Battalion "No Mercy"
(AH-64 Apache Attack Battalion)
Lieutenant Colonel Douglas Gabram

2nd Battalion "Eagle Warrior"
(AH-64 Apache Attack Battalion)
Lieutenant Colonel Stephen Smith

3rd Battalion "Eagle Attack"
(AH-64 Apache Attack Battalion)
Lieutenant Colonel Jim Richardson
Lieutenant Colonel Grady King

6th Battalion "Shadow of the Eagle"
(General Support Aviation Battalion)
Lieutenant Colonel Chuck Fields

8th Battalion
(Aviation Intermediate Maintenance)
Lieutenant Colonel Joseph Jellison

2nd Squadron, 17th Cavalry Regiment "Saber"

Lieutenant Colonel Stephen M. Schiller
Commander

HEADHUNTER TROOP

Squadron Executive Officer	**Captain Thomas Petty**	Command Sergeant Major
Major Kenneth "Todd" Royar	**Captain Reginald "Reggie" Harper**	**CSM Jeff Troy**
Major Kenneth Hawley*		**CSM Mark Herndon***

ANNIHILATOR TROOP

Squadron Operations Officer	**Captain Matthew "Bubba" Worrell**
Major Kenneth Hawley	**Captain Marcus Ritter***
Major Jimmy Blackmon*	

BAN'SHEE TROOP

Captain John Cowan
Captain Adam Frederick*

CONDOR TROOP

Captain Mark Faulkner
Captain Richard "Boomer" Arnold*

MUSTANG TROOP

Captain Krista Bonino
Captain Daryl Gilbert*

*All of the majors, the command sergeant major, and the troop commanders changed out after the squadron arrived at Q-West.

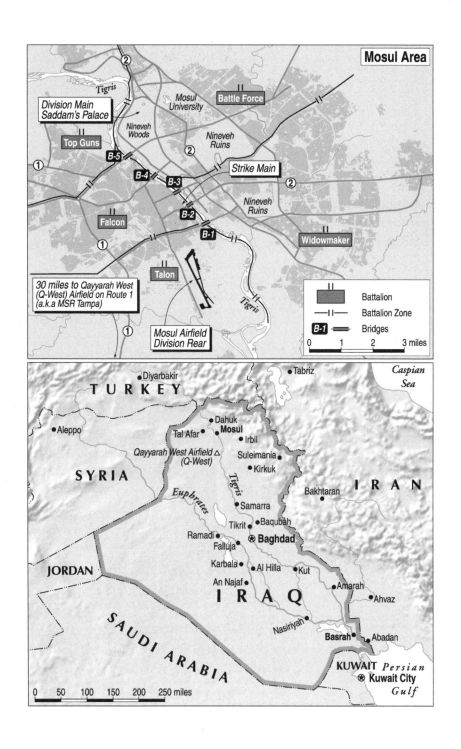

Mosul Area

Tigris

②

Division Main
Saddam's Palace

Mosul
University

Battle Force

Nineveh
Woods

Top Guns

Nineveh
Ruins

B-5

①

②

B-4 B-3

Strike Main

②

Nineveh
Ruins

B-2

Falcon

B-1

①

Widowmaker

30 miles to Qayyarah West
(Q-West) Airfield on Route 1
(a.k.a MSR Tampa)

Talon

Tigris

①

Mosul Airfield
Division Rear

Battalion
Battalion Zone
B-1 Bridges

0   1   2   3 miles

Diyarbakir

Tabriz

*Caspian
Sea*

T U R K E Y

Aleppo

Dahuk

Tal Afar **Mosul**

Irbil

Qayyarah West Airfield △
(Q-West)

Suleimania

Kirkuk

S Y R I A

Tigris

Bakhtaran

I R A N

Euphrates

Samarra

Tikrit Baqubàh

Ramadi

⊛ **Baghdad**

Falluja

JORDAN

Karbala Al Hilla Kut

An Najaf

I R A Q

Amarah

Ahvaz

Nasiriyah

SAUDI ARABIA

Basrah Abadan

KUWAIT *Persian*
⊛ **Kuwait City**
Gulf

0   50   100   150   200   250 miles

CONTENTS

FOREWORD

It is a military axiom that no plan survives contact with the enemy or reality. That truism was revalidated many times during my nearly four years in Iraq and throughout several additional years in the greater Middle East and Central Asia.

This book captures vividly many of those occasions during the invasion of Iraq and the rest of the first year there, focusing on the operations of the 101st Airborne Division (Air Assault) and, in particular, the operations of its air cavalry squadron.

I was privileged to command the 101st Airborne Division throughout that period. Predictably, I guess, we had to deal with many unpredictable developments. We had to respond to a variety of unexpected enemy elements, as well as enemy tactics beyond those on which we had focused. We also had to deal with an epochal sandstorm—during which torrential rain turned the sandstorm into an extraordinary mud storm—as well as increasing heat and logistical challenges beyond even the considerable ones for which we had planned. During that first year, we came to expect that we would frequently encounter the unexpected.

It is another military axiom that the key to swiftly adapting plans and operations to enemy actions and other developments is great leaders, highly proficient staffs, and great soldiers. The 101st Airborne Division was blessed with substantial quantities of each of those ingredients—and the Division's achievements were a testament to them and to the U.S. Army's training and leader development programs.

Leading the Air Assault troopers of the 101st was a group of the best and brightest commanders in the United States Army. The men and women who led the units assigned to the 101st—the brigades, battalions, squadrons, companies, batteries, platoons, and squads—were selflessly and relentlessly committed to accomplishing every objective despite the ever-changing operating environment in Iraq. Many of those leaders have prominent roles in this book. And many of them achieved further prominence in the subsequent sixteen years of war since we invaded Iraq. In fact, each of our three Infantry Brigade commanders earned three stars before retiring in recent years, and many of our other commanders earned multiple stars as well. The same was true for the exceptional assistant division commanders I was fortunate to have.

Inevitably, a few individual leaders stood out during various phases of the fight to Baghdad and the rest of our year's operations in Iraq. One of those is the most prominent figure in this book, Lieutenant Colonel Steve Schiller. Steve was truly exceptional. Indeed, the Army had chosen brilliantly when it selected Steve for command of the 101st Airborne's Air Cavalry Squadron. With considerable experience in special operations aviation, including leadership in combat as a "Little Bird" commander and pilot, Steve had a rare combination of extraordinary skills as an aviator and equally extraordinary skills as a commander. He had a considerable degree of self-confidence and willingness to take calculated risks, but these qualities were justified by his ability and informed by his previous combat experiences. In many respects, he was cut from the same cloth as those chronicled by Tom Wolfe in his classic book, *The Right Stuff.* Steve was, in many respects, the Army version of the legendary Air Force pilot Chuck Yeager. But Steve's confidence in his and his unit's abilities was also tempered by his keen awareness of the perils posed by the enemy's capabilities and the limitations to man and machine posed by Iraq's crushing heat, ever-present dust, and relentless desert winds, as well as by sheer human fatigue and endurance.

As we advanced into Iraq in late March 2003, Steve came to be one of my principal "go-to guys." And his unit, the only light attack and reconnaissance helicopter capability (24 OH-58D Kiowa Warriors) in the Division's armada of 258 helicopters, proved to be an invaluable asset throughout the push to Baghdad, during our subsequent large air assaults to Mosul, and in our eventual counterinsurgency campaign in northern Iraq.

When, for example, the Mechanized Infantry Division that led the U.S. advance up the west side of the Tigris River reported to us that the landing zones we had selected based on a map reconnaissance and imagery analysis were too dusty to safely land helicopters, it was to Steve we turned. He and his assets launched rapidly, flew hundreds of miles to the locations we had designated, verified their suitability, and radioed back their assessment. And with that information, I decided that the launch of the first of our massive air assaults should go forward as planned. It succeeded.

When, several days later, during the Battle of Najaf, I needed to see the fighting for myself from a better vantage point than that afforded by standing on the hood of my HMMWV and looking through binoculars, it was with Steve and his team that I flew over the battlefield, gaining invaluable perspective and a much improved sense of the situation on the ground as we whirled around in the sky at very low altitude to keep from being shot down. When, in each of our subsequent major fights—at Karbala and Hillah and beyond—we needed reconnaissance and attack assets ahead of or "over the shoulder" of our lead units, it was to our Air Cav Squadron that we turned, and its aircraft often led the way for our seventy-two exceedingly lethal Apache attack helicopters (AH-64Ds) that tended to stand off while unleashing their arsenal of weaponry (which had greater range, accuracy, and explosive power than the weapons on Steve's light attack aircraft). Later, in a variety of different missions during our time in northern Iraq, it was to Steve and the intrepid aviators of the 2nd Squadron, 17th Cavalry Regiment that we often turned for hunting the increasingly lethal insurgents, scouting various far-flung areas, and responding on short notice to developing missions. Indeed, it was flying in the left seat with Steve at the controls, this time over Mosul, that he and I encountered a substantial weapons cache being looted by possible insurgents—which Steve made short work of in the course of numerous plunging attacks during which he fired our full load of rockets and machine gun rounds. (It was also during that encounter that I learned how physically draining repeated high G-force dives, turns, and climbs in a helicopter were on one's body.)

While there were innumerable "heroes of the battlefield" in the 101st Airborne during the offensive to Baghdad and the takedown of the Saddam Hussein regime, and then during the rest of our year in Iraq, Steve Schiller and his Air Cavalry men and women certainly stood in the front ranks of the groups that merited recognition. And Steve himself earned multiple medals for valor and combat aviation operations, as well as a Purple Heart; I was privileged to pin most of those on him myself.

Through it all, Steve displayed a truly unique quality. Perhaps because of his background in Special Ops and his previous combat experience, he was more comfortable than most in responding to unexpected enemy situations. He also repeatedly demonstrated impressive initiative, creativity, innovativeness, and courage. And in some cases, he was also comfortable operating outside institutional norms—after conducting careful assessments of risk. The other aviators and members of 2-17 CAV broadly shared these qualities and demonstrated them repeatedly as we recognized that the war in Iraq was steadily invalidating many of the assumptions and assessments made at higher levels before the decision to invade—and as the consensus emerged that serving in Iraq was "all hard, all the time."

Several years later, after my three-star tour in Iraq, it was Steve and the Division's many other intrepid and creative leaders I had in mind when, among the 14 observations I distilled for an article published in *Military Review*, was observation #13: "*There is no substitute for flexible, adaptable leaders.*" He and innumerable others in the early years were the basis for that reflection.

Steve was, in short, a commander with an unrivaled blend of audacity, skill, and tenacity in the face of the enemy. And this mentality was echoed by every trooper in his squadron. The men and women of 2-17 Cavalry Squadron sacrificed selflessly, performed admirably, and, perhaps most importantly, adapted swiftly and smoothly. In an ever-changing, often perilous environment where one quick decision could be the difference between life and death, the soldiers of 2-17 Cavalry were an extraordinary reflection of Steve Schiller's unique, impressive leadership. Like their commanding officer, they were very technically proficient and never afraid to respectfully challenge orthodoxy or doctrinal norms in order to accomplish the mission. Steve Schiller sought to develop a climate of independent, thoughtful risk-taking in his squadron, and it worked.

Like Steve Schiller, Jimmy Blackmon knows what it takes to be an extraordinary aviation leader. Jimmy was at Fort Leavenworth, Kansas—a student in the Command and General Staff Course—when we went there to plan the invasion of Iraq. Colonel Greg Gass, the 101st Aviation Brigade Commander, hand-selected Jimmy to join us in Iraq as soon as he graduated. Jimmy arrived in early June and went to work as Steve Schiller's operations officer, remaining in that position for the rest of our time in Iraq and then back at Fort Campbell, Kentucky, as well.

Jimmy later commanded both an air cavalry squadron and an aviation brigade in the 101st in combat, as well. During his career, Jimmy developed a deep understanding of the risks, difficulties, and opportunities of aviation operations against tough enemies in challenging weather and environmental conditions. He also developed a nuanced understanding of the human dimension in war—of the privileges and burdens of leadership in combat, and of the bonds that tie soldiers together during the toughest of combat operations. As a writer, he has shown to be a keen observer of human nature and one who also appreciates the emotions on the battlefield. In this book, he captures for the reader the words that pass between soldiers during the tension-filled hours before missions and the flood of emotions that follow combat operations. His experience and understanding, together with his exceptional ability to tell a story, make him the ideal observer to provide a wonderful account of 2-17 CAV's first year in Iraq.

There have, of course, been many exceptional books written about the Iraq War. Very few, however, capture so accurately and forthrightly the experiences of airmen, ground crews, and their leaders as does this one. Jimmy describes all of this, as well as the bonds that form during long combat deployments and the qualities that have long distinguished America's men and women in uniform. And he tells this story the way it should be told, bluntly, honestly, and accurately—and also in wonderfully readable prose. His account deservedly recognizes—and honors—those who sacrificed so much early on in Iraq, painting a vivid, clear-eyed picture of what Iraq was like for those of us privileged to serve our country during our first year in the Land of the Two Rivers. It also conveys why those who have served our country in the wars of the post-9/11 period have rightfully earned recognition as America's "New Greatest Generation."

As I have often observed to those with whom I was privileged to soldier while "Eagle 6," as commander of the 101st Airborne Division during the first year in Iraq, we were part of something very special. Jimmy Blackmon captures why that was the case, and he does so brilliantly.

General David H. Petraeus (US Army, Ret.)
Arlington, Virginia
June 2019

PREFACE

I was playing with toy soldiers before I could ride a bicycle. To the rhythm of rain falling on the tin roof of my mother's little country store, I plotted the downfall of the Soviet Union well before the Berlin Wall came tumbling down. Through the black and white tones of a Zenith television, I imagined Hawkeye Pierce and B. J. Hunnicutt patching my men up at the M*A*S*H 4077. Still, no matter how hard I played, no matter how vivid my imagination, I could not have possibly evoked the emotions of war—until I was in one.

At that time, I could not have dreamt what it might feel like for someone to try to kill me. Nor could I have anticipated the heart-wrenching emotions I would experience when men begged me not to kill them. No book, no movie, no childhood imagination could have prepared me for the searing pain of loss when a fellow soldier was killed. I never imagined I would one day stand numb in a foreign land as I witnessed a woman being told that her husband was not coming back from a mission. Sadly, I would come to understand that some of this life's most extreme and painful emotions are reserved for those who have gone to war.

I have been asked, "Did your experiences in combat change you?"

Simply put, war changes all of its participants. While war is common, it is not natural. If taking life did not adversely affect each of us, we would have reason to be gravely concerned. War is a costly endeavor. Loosely, we say that the price of war is a nation's blood and treasure, but after a decade and a half of war, I have become convinced that it is soldiers and their families who pay the greatest price.

While I had twice participated in operations in the Balkans, 2003 was my first combat experience. In retrospect, it was a gentle beginning to my twelve-year affair with the wars in Iraq and Afghanistan, soft notes that would reach a crescendo, a climatic emotional experience—an experience that, strangely enough, I would not trade for anything in the world. That seems to be the ironic dichotomy of war. It rips our hearts to shreds with pain and fear and loss, yet it binds us like nothing else can. It produces unparalleled bonds—a brotherhood—forged in the heat of combat.

I do not begin to suggest that my experiences are unique, nor do I propose that they are equal in intensity to others'. My experiences were simply mine. Through hundreds of interviews with soldiers in writing this book and my previous work, *Pale Horse: Hunting Terrorists and Commanding Heroes with the 101st Airborne Division*, I came to realize that everyone copes differently. Some soldiers compartmentalize the pain, others rely on their faith; some turn to drugs, others to alcohol; some seek counseling, while others use their family to anchor them. Sadly, some are unable to cope and lose hope. They choose to end the pain. I hope those who still struggle to survive today can take some degree of comfort in knowing that they are not alone, and that war affects us all, but there is no reason to give up. It's okay to reach out for help, as so many others have.

But it is important to note that this story takes place before my generation slowly and sadly realized the extreme emotional and psychological price of war. There were a few soldiers who had deployed to Operation Desert Storm, but for most of us, Iraq was our first time in combat. At the writing of this book, most people, conservatives and liberals alike, consider the Iraq War a mistake. With the benefit of hindsight, it has become a very unpopular war. Yet in 2003, the vast majority of our country supported the decision to go to war in Iraq. Saddam Hussein was a tyrant. The atrocities against the Kurds and Shia Muslims were sickening and unquestionable. We had been convinced that he possessed weapons of mass destruction (WMD). To that end, in October 2002, the U.S. Senate passed the *Authorization for Use of Military Force Against Iraq Resolution of 2002* with a 77–23 vote. It passed in the House of Representatives 297–133, with three representatives not voting.[1] In March 2003, 72 percent of Americans polled by the Pew Research Center said that the decision to use military force in Iraq was the right decision.[2]

Soldiers envisioned an opportunity to do what they had trained for their entire careers. They would destroy the Iraqi Army and depose

Saddam Hussein, and the Iraqi people would celebrate our triumph and embrace our way of life. It would be only a matter of time before a McDonald's and a Walmart opened in every Iraqi city. "No two countries that both had McDonald's had fought a war against each other," soldiers joked, quoting Thomas Friedman's 1999 book, *The Lexus and the Olive Tree.*

Like most of my peers, my point of reference for war was World War II, Korea, and Vietnam. The movies and television programs we watched as children portrayed those wars. I joined the army, hoping that I would never have to fight a war yet vowing that if the time ever came, I would be prepared.

In February 1986, an army recruiter knocked on my raggedy screen door in Ranger, Georgia, and asked me to enlist in the army. It took me about ten seconds to answer that question. Instantly, I envisioned myself standing tall and proud in my father's old Eisenhower jacket—Corporal Blackmon. I happily accepted his invitation.

In the seventeen years following that cold February day, I trained to go to war, but I had not experienced war; nor had I been near one, smelled one, heard one, or tasted one.

The year I spent in Iraq with 2nd Squadron, 17th Cavalry Regiment laid the foundation for how I would lead soldiers in combat for the next twelve years, and the most influential figure during that year was our squadron commander, Lieutenant Colonel Stephen M. Schiller.

Innovative, determined, and focused, Stephen Schiller was General John Buford, dismounting his cavalrymen at Gettysburg, vowing to hold the high ground until the main force could arrive. He displayed the daring, gutsy traits of General Nathan Bedford Forrest, who had thirty horses shot out from under him during the American Civil War and killed more men in combat than any other general officer. Colorful and charismatic, Schiller was also Colonel Bill Kilgore of *Apocalypse Now* fame, who stood fearless on a Vietnamese beach wearing a yellow neckerchief and a Stetson hat asking his troopers[3] if they wanted to surf or fight. Stephen Schiller was considered fearless by most, reckless by some; he was loved by many and envied by more than will admit it.

"Steve was crazy," one of his peers once told me. "It was like he wanted to die. He's lucky he didn't."

Schiller was candid, confident, controversial, and a little cocky—sometimes all at once.

It would take a man with a personality like Schiller's to shape an organization in such a way as to do the things you are about to read. It would require a bold and audacious leader, one who was willing to assume risk and lead from the front.

In Tolstoy's classic *War and Peace*, Nikolai Rostov, a young cavalryman recently returned from war, is asked when and where he received his wound. Tolstoy wrote,

This pleased Rostov and he began talking about it, and as he went on became more and more animated. He told them of his Schon Grabern affair, just as those who have taken part in a battle generally do describe it, that is, as they would like it to have been, as they have heard it described by others, and as sounds well, but not at all as it really was. Rostov was a truthful young man and would on no account have told a deliberate lie. He began his story meaning to tell everything just as it happened, but imperceptibly, involuntarily, and inevitably he lapsed into falsehood... He could not tell them simply that everyone went at a trot and that he fell off his horse and sprained his arm and then ran as hard as he could from a Frenchman into the wood... His hearers expected a story of how beside himself and all aflame with excitement, he had flown like a storm at the square, cut his way in, slashed right and left, how his saber had tasted flesh and he had fallen exhausted, and so on. And so he told them all that.[4]

This scene in Tolstoy's work burned in my mind as I tried to accurately capture our experiences and portray the characters who lived them. I love the soldiers in this work. The daily task of writing about them never ceased to produce a smile on my face. However, at the writing of this book, my memories have lain dormant for fifteen years. Despite my best efforts to confirm each recollection with that of others who shared these experiences, I am confident that I erred in some small way. For this, I apologize. I have done my very best to bring our experiences back to life with accuracy and color.

From the start, I felt that this story was important to tell. From intense episodes of hardship and pain to relaxing moments with cigars and laughter, we formed lifelong bonds. That brotherhood forms the backdrop of this story. The vast majority of war stories are recounted as graphic depictions of battles won and lost. Rarely does the reader get to step into the space between fights. I have tried to bring those moments alive here, giving the reader a campstool at the fire and a cigar at the table, as we forged bonds which time has no power to diminish.

This is our story.

The finest people I ever met
were those with whom I carried a rucksack
and slept in a mud puddle.

—First Sergeant (Ret.) John Price

GOING TO WAR

At first, I couldn't breathe. I stepped off the airplane in Kuwait and felt like I had walked into an oven. Never before in my life had I experienced such stifling heat. It was difficult to draw a full breath of air. It took me by surprise because I thought I was used to the heat. Having been born in Georgia, I came out of the womb sweating, but "Georgia hot" paled in comparison to "Kuwait hot." I had heard people from the Southwest talk about a *dry* heat, but I had never been both dry and hot at the same time until Kuwait. The sweat evaporated before it could wet my skin, leaving me encrusted in a thin layer of salt, which made my T-shirt feel prickly like wool.

Squinting through dark sunglasses, I made my way down the airstairs and onto the tarmac at Ali Al Salem Air Base. A fine, powdery dust filled the air, limiting visibility to less than a mile. Still, seeing one hundred meters in Kuwait was as good as seeing forever in my estimation. Pancake-flat desert lay to the north and west for as far as the eye could see, even on a clear day.

Our gear had been dumped into a pile adjacent to an open-faced tin building. An air force sergeant with a clipboard soon appeared and barked over the sound of jet engines roaring in the distance. "Welcome to Kuwait! Once you secure your bags, you will be palletizing them for onward movement. If you are going to Balad, you need to take your gear to that stall," he said, pointing to an area at the end of the tin building. "If your destination is BIAP [Baghdad International Airport], palletize your bags over there. All of you who are going to Mosul, you're over there. When you are finished, someone will come by and inspect your pallets." Then he turned and disappeared into a large festival tent.

1

Everything I had brought was stuffed into a rucksack, a duffel bag, and an aviator kit bag. I dug through the mountain of green and brown gear until I found the ones stenciled, "BLACKMON, JIMMY F., MAJ. 2-17 CAV." Some of the soldiers had been issued the newly fielded desert brown gear before deploying, but several of us still carried equipment camouflaged in the woodland green pattern.

With my rucksack on my back and a bag in each hand, I waddled over to the area designated "Mosul," and along with several other soldiers, I began neatly stacking bags on wooden pallets. I knew that it was in our best interest to stack them perfectly. Having played this game before, I knew that if the bags were not tight and neat, the sergeant would tell us to re-palletize them, which would mean starting over. Once the bags were stacked, we secured them to the wooden pallet with a nylon cargo net. When our C-130 Hercules arrived, the pallet would be loaded into the belly of the airplane.

Before long, the sergeant with the clipboard returned to announce what time the airplanes would arrive to transport us to our final destinations. He glanced down at the clipboard. "If you're going to Balad your manifest time is nineteen hundred hours [seven p.m.]. BIAP, you'll manifest at twenty hundred [eight p.m.]. Mosul, you're not leaving until ten hundred hours tomorrow morning," he said. "Now, I need all of you to file into the tent behind you for a mandatory briefing."

Once seated in the tent, we watched a video that explained General Order #1, which directed us not to drink alcohol, gamble, have sex, or take war trophies. Following the video, we were released until our designated manifest times. I found an open cot in the corner of the sleep tent and struggled to get comfortable. The tent was large and dark. A sea of headlamps cast the only visible light inside the massive structure. Looking in from the door, I saw headlamps flashing back and forth as soldiers fished through their bags or read books. It reminded me of spelunkers spread out in a spacious cave. I adjusted my own headlamp and began writing in my journal.

So many thoughts raced through my mind that first night in Kuwait. I wondered how my unit would receive me after having already forged tight bonds in combat. Would it be difficult to earn their respect? How would my new boss treat me? I had only briefly met Lieutenant Colonel

Stephen Schiller at Fort Leavenworth, Kansas, while the 101st Airborne Division planned for the invasion of Iraq.

I had been impressed with Schiller, but I really did not know him yet. A former boss of mine, Colonel Mark Landrith (Ret.), had served with Schiller during Desert Storm. While at Fort Leavenworth, I was on my way to meet Schiller for the first time when I ran into Mark Landrith in the hallway.

"What's up, wild man?" he had inquired with a scratchy, smoke-scarred voice.

"Not much, sir. It's good to see you again," I replied, genuinely happy to see him. "How have you been?" I asked, with a nod to his civilian attire.

"Not bad," he answered, and then grasping the lapels of his brown suit coat, the old colonel stood tall and leaned back slightly. "As you can see, I'm a civilian now," he said with an air of pride. "Say, where are you headed after you finish the Command and General Staff College, Jimmy?"

"I'm going to the 101st Airborne Division," I said, knowing he would approve. He had previously commanded an Apache attack battalion in the 101st Aviation Brigade, where I was headed. "I'll be the operations officer for Lieutenant Colonel Stephen Schiller, in the 2nd Squadron, 17th Cavalry Regiment," I said, trying to conceal a smile. I was proud to be going to 2-17 CAV.

"I'll be damned," he said, with a bright smile on his face. "Steve Schiller was a lieutenant in my outfit during Desert Storm. He's a damn good officer. At least he was then. I assume he still is. As I recall we made him a company commander while he was still a lieutenant, ahead of his peers. He went on to the 160th Special Operations Aviation Regiment (SOAR) after he left our outfit. I heard he kicked ass over there too. I really think you'll like working for him."

"Well, I'll get to meet him today," I replied. "The 101st is here at Fort Leavenworth planning a major exercise," I said.

"Is that right?" Landrith replied.

"Rumor has it they are actually planning for the invasion of Iraq, but no one will confirm it," I said. "I'm having lunch with Lieutenant Colonel Schiller and my future brigade commander, Colonel Greg Gass."

Greg Gass was the reason I was going to the 101st Airborne Division. He and I had served together in Virginia. He was kind enough to submit a request to Human Resources Command for me to be assigned to his brigade.

"I'm a little surprised the special ops boys let Steve go," Landrith said. "I figured he would stay over there the rest of his career."

"Talking to some of the guys in the 160th, they say he will almost certainly go back and command 1st Battalion, 160th after he finishes this command. 1st Battalion is only selected as a second battalion command. No one gets it as a first command," I said.

"Well, Steve Schiller'll do well wherever he commands. You'll like him," he said.

Recognizing that it was time to link up with Schiller and Gass, I extended my hand to Mark Landrith. "Sir, I have to go meet these guys. It was good seeing you again."

He grasped my hand firmly, looked me dead in the eye, and said, "You take care, wild man."

Landrith's positive endorsement of my future boss was comforting. I respected Mark Landrith, and I knew that if he approved of Schiller, then he was most likely a warrior because that's what Landrith liked—warriors.

I turned toward the food court that morning at Fort Leavenworth and immediately saw Colonel Gass already standing in line ordering food with two other men. One of them was Lieutenant Colonel Schiller; the other was my peer, Major Kenneth Hawley.

"Hey, Jimmy," Colonel Gass said, as I approached.

"Hello, sir. It's good to see you again."

"You too," he replied, and then, turning to the other men, said, "This is your future boss, Lieutenant Colonel Steve Schiller, and this is his operations officer, Ken Hawley."

Schiller was about my height with a lean, athletic build, thinning sandy blond hair, and pale blue eyes. I immediately noticed the 160th SOAR ring adjacent his wedding band on his ring finger, indicative of 160th alumni.

He had begun his career at Fort Riley, Kansas, where he met and served with then Major Mark Landrith. As Landrith had noted, the command had recognized Schiller's strong leadership ability, so after his unit returned from Desert Storm, they placed him in command of A Company, 1-1 Aviation.

Schiller was thrilled to serve as a company commander. He had joined the army for an opportunity to lead soldiers, but the attack mission did not overly excite him. He felt that the leaders within that community were far too risk averse. One of the warrant officers in Schiller's unit had tried out for a secretive unit called the 160th Special Operations Aviation Regiment.

Back then, before internet and cell phones, it was hard to find information about the special mission units assigned to the Joint Special Operations Command (JSOC). Schiller had heard other pilots talk about 160th SOAR's "Little Birds," and what little he heard appealed to him. So, after returning from Desert Storm, he began preparing himself to try out for the highly selective special operations unit. He submitted an application to the unit's recruiting team and patiently waited. His opportunity came in 1993. Steve's tryout went favorably, so soon thereafter he and his wife, Rhonda, moved to Fort Campbell, Kentucky, to begin a new journey in life.

Schiller progressed through the ranks as an AH-6 "Little Bird" gun pilot in B Company, 1st Battalion, 160th SOAR. On September 11, 2001, he was in Hungary participating in a Joint Special Operations Exercise. Upon being notified about the tragic events of that fateful day, the JSOC commander cancelled the exercise. Steve returned to Fort Campbell and immediately began planning for an altogether different mission. Just three weeks later, on October 7, 2001, he deployed to Afghanistan as the operations officer of Task Force 1–160.

By that time, Schiller had been promoted to lieutenant colonel and was slated to take command of 2nd Squadron, 17th Cavalry Regiment in the 101st Airborne Division. He returned from Afghanistan in January 2002, to learn to fly the OH-58D Kiowa Warrior. In June of that same year, Schiller took command of 2-17 CAV. His new call sign was "Saber Six," but everyone referred to him as "the SCO" (pronounced sk-ō), which was short for squadron commander. By fall of that same year, yet again, Schiller was preparing to deploy to southwest Asia to face Saddam Hussein's Iraqi Army.[1]

As we sat eating lunch at Fort Leavenworth, Schiller asked me questions about my family and hobbies. He told me about his children, Calvin and Courtney. A hint of laughter persisted in his blue eyes. I don't know what I expected of this Special Operations Aviator, but I found myself somewhat caught off guard with his engaging and personable demeanor. He struck me as a leader who truly understood the importance of people and relationships. He also emitted an air of confidence and pride. My first encounter with Steve Schiller left me eager and excited to work for him. I only hoped that the feeling was mutual.

After lunch, we shook hands and parted ways, not knowing what the future held. War was on the horizon, a long war that would forever shape our lives. The next time I would see Greg Gass, Stephen Schiller, and Ken Hawley would be in the deserts of Iraq, and that's where I was finally headed. Barring any issues, I'd join my unit in Iraq the following morning.

I felt a strange, uncomfortable sense of insecurity. The question that lingered in my mind was, *Am I good enough? Will I measure up?* I didn't like that feeling. I had always excelled in the army. I had been the corps commander at North Georgia College, hero of the battle at the National Training Center multiple times, early for promotion to major—still, I was now in the 101st Airborne Division. The division where the best of the best aviators went to serve, and I could not help but doubt myself. Was I now a small fish in a big pond? That thought made me queasy, so I forced it from my mind.

After a long journal entry that evening in Kuwait, I curled up on the cot with a poncho liner and fought for a few hours of sleep. The next morning, I awoke to the sound of an airman yelling. Bright light flooded the tent as he burst through the door. Standing in the light, he looked like I had always imagined an angel. He glowed in the sunlight, making it impossible to look directly at him without shielding my eyes.

"If you're going to Mosul," he bellowed in a deep baritone voice, "you need to move to the passenger terminal now!"

Not knowing exactly how much time we truly had, several of us raced to prepare ourselves. I ran to the latrine and dragged a dry razor across my face. Quickly, I brushed my teeth and laced up my boots. Then in true military fashion, we waited in the terminal for three hours. Eventually, they called us forward, and another airman walked us out on the tarmac to an airplane. Approaching the rear of the C-130 was like walking into a giant hair dryer. We leaned into the blast of hot air generated from the propellers as we walked up the ramp and strapped ourselves into red nylon seats. Within minutes of boarding the airplane, we were on our way.

Having previously flown on many C-130s, I prayed that no one would get sick. When the pilots fly tactically, it's not uncommon for the passengers to become violently ill. Hot air, the inability to see outside, and a bumpy ride are a nasty combination that can humble the toughest iron-gut soldiers. You know it's only a matter of time when men begin pulling their airsickness bags from their cargo pockets, or a soldier holds his patrol cap in front of his face. Multiple people usually get sick all at once. They hold off puking until one finally pops. Once the first one blows, the others follow in rapid succession. Even the strongest-willed soldiers can't hold it back once the smell fills the airplane. Thank goodness, that day we made it to Mosul without anyone becoming sick.

As I walked off the aft ramp of the C-130 at Mosul airfield, a strange feeling came over me. Our nation was at war, and I was quite literally in harm's way—in a combat zone. It seemed like only yesterday that I had sat in my father's lap, in a rickety, old recliner in Ranger, Georgia, and watched men whistle the "Colonel Bogey March" as they walked to a bridge over the River Kwai. My experience was quite different from anything I'd seen in the movies, of course, but still, our nation was at war and I was there. Better yet, I was in the famed 101st Airborne Division and from that moment until the end of my career, I'd be able to wear Old Abe, the 101st Airborne Division patch, on my right shoulder.[2]

Mosul is the former biblical town of Nineveh, where Jonah was commanded to preach. Looking out across the airfield, I could see the Tigris River, which had previously been nothing more than a page in a middle school social studies book. I could not help but wonder how that whale swam up the Tigris to spit Jonah out in Nineveh.

After securing my gear, I made my way to the Division Rear (DREAR) command post. Bedraggled soldiers smoked cigarettes just outside the building, their appearance a start contrast to the clean, pressed uniforms I'd seen in Kuwait. One young private's boot was wrapped with tape to keep the sole intact. *Now there's a soldier who has earned his stripes in combat,* I thought.

A sergeant called my unit and told them I had arrived. 2-17 CAV was located at Qayyarah West, which we simply called Q-West. As the crow flies, it sat approximately thirty miles south of Mosul. I figured it would take them at least an hour to make the drive to Mosul, so I sat down on my duffel bag, leaned back against a wall in the shade, and waited.

About an hour later, a master sergeant and several soldiers from 2-17 CAV pulled up in two Humvees. While in Kuwait, they had issued me one ten-round magazine of 9mm ammunition for my Beretta pistol, enough firepower to protect myself from a good-size snake. After introductions, I asked the sergeant if he had more ammo.

"No sir," he said. "All we have is M4 ammo."

I had never felt quite as vulnerable as I did when we drove out the gates of Mosul airfield, worked our way through dense traffic to Highway 1, and headed south. I un-holstered my pistol and kept it in my hand, but even that seemed somewhat comical to me. Being the new guy, I tried to hide my concern, but concerned I was. I was about to spend an hour on the roads in Iraq with nothing but a pistol and ten rounds of ammunition. To my surprise, the other soldiers did not seem at all concerned. Two Humvees with a total of six soldiers and no crew-served weapons seemed like a soft target to me.

What I did not know was that things had been relatively calm since 2-17 had arrived in northern Iraq. The soldiers commonly drove into Iraqi towns to purchase rugs, chairs, and other creature comforts aimed at making life in a bombed-out Ba'ath Party headquarters building a little more comfortable. At one point, they had even bought a coop full of chickens from local Iraqis to kill and cook. After three months of nothing but dehydrated army rations, anything was better than MREs (Meal, Ready-to-Eat).[3] They purchased everything with cash, which the Iraqis were more than happy to accept. Soldiers found millions of American dollars in the walls of Saddam's palaces. In turn, they were told to put the money back into the Iraqi economy.

After a long, straight stretch of road south, we turned west and then south again into Q-West airfield. We entered the main gate on Old Bill Avenue. We then drove to Fiddler's Green Street and turned right. I saw the red-and-white striped curb over two hundred meters out, and knew I was nearing the home of the cavalry, which caused me to chuckle to myself. They had purchased paint and turned their little corner of Q-West into "CAV Country." The street signs had been painted red and white and given cavalry names. Dating back to at least the 1830s, the dragoons' guidon was red and white. Thus, the color of the cavalry became red and white.

I felt more than a little nervous anticipation as we approached the headquarters. It wasn't that I was scared; I simply wanted to make a good impression. The SCO and Ken Hawley were sitting on the front stoop in red plastic chairs when we pulled up. As soon as they saw us, they stood and started for the Humvee. There was a cement arch in front of the headquarters building with a life-size painting of Saddam Hussein on it. The CAV troopers had painted a Stetson hat on Saddam's head and bored a hole through the cement where his hand hung by his side. Through the hole, they placed the squadron guidon. Saddam Hussein had become the 2-17 CAV guidon bearer, no doubt the greatest honor ever bestowed upon him by an American. Schiller and Hawley met me at the truck.

I saluted and said, "Out Front, sir." I held my hand to my brow until Schiller returned my salute. While some units do not salute in combat for fear of a sniper picking the officers off, I was told before I boarded the plane for Iraq that the 101st Airborne salutes in the field and in combat.

Schiller smiled broadly and threw his hand up to his brow in a quick salute. "Welcome, Jimmy! No one is happier to see you here than Ken," he said. "He's been playing X3 for way too long."

At the start of the war, Ken had been the operations officer (S3), and Major Todd Royar had been the executive officer (XO). Colonel Greg Gass chose Todd to move up and become the Brigade Operations Officer, so Ken was left to cover both jobs until I arrived, thus the SCO's reference to X3.

The soldiers unloaded my bags from the Humvee, set them on the curb, and drove off. I shouldered my rucksack while Ken grabbed my other two bags and showed me to our room. He and I would be room-mates. Kenneth Hawley was lean and wiry with a thin face and a visible Adam's apple. Flecks of gray mixed with dark hair that was closely cropped in a flattop, presenting a dark silvery appearance. A native of Ludlow, Massachusetts, Ken had been in the Civil Air Patrol, which spurred his desire to fly. He first received an appointment to the United States Military Academy at West Point, which he accepted, but later also received an appointment to the Air Force Academy. "Congressman Paul Tsongas called to tell me that I had been accepted to the Air Force Academy," Ken said. "Not thinking, I told him that I'd already accepted an appointment to West Point so that's where I'd be going to school. Desperately wanting to fly, I regretted the decision the second I hung up the phone."[4]

Nevertheless, aviation was still an option at West Point. "I knew that if I graduated in the top fifty percent of my class, I could most likely branch aviation, which I did," he later told me. Ken graduated in 1990 and departed for flight school right away.

Despite both of us serving as air cavalrymen our entire careers, I had not met Ken prior to our assignment in 2-17 CAV. Ken was easy to laugh and almost always smiling. I liked him from the start.

Saddam Hussein had not fully trusted his military leaders, so Ba'ath Party members, whom he did trust, closely monitored the military. Our command post was established in the Ba'ath Party building on Q-West, which one might expect to be a relatively nice residence, but that was not the case.

US forces had bombed the building during the early stages of the war, so when 2-17 arrived, they had a lot of work to do. The building was square with the center left open like a square doughnut and a court-yard in the middle. Before 2-17 CAV arrived, locals had looted Q-West, taking everything usable, including the wiring inside the walls. Looters cut the copper wires, bundled them together, and then tied them to the bumper of a truck. Once the signal was given, the driver sped away from the building, gutting the wiring right out of the walls. Then they melted the wires and sold the residual copper on the market.

Ken walked me around the squadron area, introducing me to the team that afternoon. At long last, I was the operations officer (S3) of 2nd Squadron, 17th Cavalry Regiment.

My first meal with my new unit was served out of the squadron's Mobile Kitchen Trailer (MKT). The MKT was a kitchen on wheels that folded up like a pop-up camper. Soldiers grumbled as they liberally doused Texas Pete hot sauce on white rice and beef tips, and subsequently chewed until their jaws cramped.

"Can't they find anything other than beef tips and rice?" one of the captains said aloud to no one in particular.

The meal cycle was M-M-T, which meant an MRE for breakfast, an MRE for lunch, and T-rations, cooked out of the MKT for dinner. T-rations were tins of food that were warmed over steaming water inside the mobile kitchen. The problem was that the only T-rations available were beef tips and rice. While the soldiers were grateful for a hot meal, they were sick of the same menu served over and over again. However, they did serve marble cake for dessert, which quieted a handful of complaints. It was far from flavorful, but a welcome change of taste.

We ate standing by trucks, our plates and a Styrofoam cup of sugary Kool-Aid resting on the hood. Ken looked over and stared at me as I wolfed down the plate of food. "Have you not eaten today?" he asked.

"I ate breakfast," I said. "No lunch. Why?"

"You suddenly stopped talking and started acting like somebody might steal your plate," he said.

"Sorry man. I eat fast."

Eating, where I grew up in the South, was something of a cultural pastime. My mother and grandmother cooked throughout most of the day. When they were not preparing a meal, they were cleaning up after one and planning for the next. For most of her life, my mother rose at 5:00 a.m. and rolled out biscuits with a rolling pin. Since the matrons of our family spent an inordinate amount of time laboring in the kitchen, it should come as no surprise that they hovered over us as we ate, urging us to "have another biscuit, honey. You want another piece of chicken? Here, take this thigh."

A man who could put away far more food than any one person should was oddly celebrated, his talent for eating being akin to playing a banjo or the guitar. I had a neighbor who bellowed in laughter as he frequently recounted the story of being asked to pay again at an all-you-can-eat catfish buffet. After his fourth heaping plate of catfish and hushpuppies, the manager visited his table. "Son, I know it says that it's all you can eat, but if you load up one more plate, you're gonna have to pay again," he said.

We grew, butchered, caught, or killed most everything we ate, and we never lacked for food. Meat and cornbread were staples, and we always had a variety of vegetables on our table. Meals were social events where we shared gossip infused with politics, religion, and police radio calls intercepted with a scanner. We never rushed while sitting at the dinner table.

For me, the speed did not come until I attended Ranger school. When I attended the course in 1992, it was sixty-eight days in duration. Hailed as the toughest combat course in the world, the elite leadership school tests and stresses Ranger students both mentally and physically. Sleep is limited to a few precious hours here and there, and students are issued one MRE per day. As my old college roommate, Fred Wintrich, likes to say, "There is only one reality at Ranger school: when the sun goes down, you'll be walking, and when the sun comes back up, you'll still be walking." And, I would add, you'll be hungry while you're doing it.

When I was in mountain phase of Ranger school, at Camp Frank D. Merrill, I witnessed the power of hunger in a fellow Ranger student. A small group of us had been walking nonstop for three days, it seemed. We passed through Penitentiary Cove, where people sometimes camp. I watched the Ranger student walking in front of me reach down and pick up a banana peel. The very tip of the banana remained in the peel. It had probably been lying on the ground a full day or more, but that did not deter the starving Ranger. He swallowed it and threw the blackened peel back on the ground before an instructor could see him. I was hungry, but not to that point yet.

I weighed 185 pounds when I reported to Fort Benning, Georgia, in 1992. The day I received the coveted black and gold Ranger tab, along with only 53 of my original 352 classmates, I was down to 158 pounds. From that point forward, I ate at full speed, fork in my right hand and left arm arching around my plate, prepared to defend my chow should someone reach for it. My mother-in-law, Lois, observed it first. Now, Ken Hawley had picked up on it.

"There's one thing about eating food that sucks," Ken said.

"Oh yeah. What's that?" I asked.

"There's always plenty left over," he said shaking his head.

STOGIES AND STORIES

That evening, after dinner, several of the senior warrant officers and troop commanders gathered around two picnic tables inside the courtyard of our headquarters building. Their uniforms were well worn and dirty. Their boots were scuffed up, some to the point of being almost completely worn out. It was obvious that they had been roughing it for quite some time. I was suddenly self-conscious of my clean uniform. My appearance screamed new guy.

Ken Hawley walked out of the Tactical Operations Center (TOC)[1] with a wooden box filled with an assortment of cigars. "Gentlemen," he announced, "choose your poison." And he set the box on the table.

Each man methodically sniffed and rolled cigars between his finger and thumb until he found one that called out to him. Despite cigars being a tradition in the cavalry, I was not a smoker and had no desire to puke on the first day with my new unit, so I stuck to sipping bottled water.

"Gotta love a good Cuban," one of the warrant officers said, holding it out in front of his face, admiring the one he'd chosen. Then he began licking it from one end to the other.

"This would be illegal in the States," another warrant officer said.

"Good thing we're not in the States," another replied.

Tempered pride and cigar smoke hung thick in the air that evening. Justifiably, they were proud of all that they had achieved thus far in the war. I detected a strong sense of camaraderie among the men. I was sad that I had missed so much, disappointed that I could not join in their stories, and envious of the obvious bonds that they had forged through shared hardship. Additionally, their respect for Stephen Schiller was evident. His willingness to step forward and convince the division commander, Major

General David Petraeus, that his cavalry outfit could fight over the cities had earned 2-17 CAV a prominent role in each battle as the 101st made its way north through Iraq. As I learned that evening, the pivotal moment came at An Najaf.

2nd Brigade "Strike" had the mission to clear the city of An Najaf. It was the first battle of the war for the 101st. Strike soldiers were moving slowly and methodically.

"It was everyone's first crack at urban fighting," Schiller told me later. "From our helicopters, we could see the battlefield well, but we weren't at a point yet that the ground forces trusted our read of what was happening. I understood how they felt. They were walking down streets, waiting for the enemy to shoot at them any second, and this guy in a helicopter is telling them to move faster because he doesn't see enemy in front of them. That takes some significant trust, faith. I decided to land so that I could speak with Major General Petraeus.

"I laid my map out on the hood of his truck and pointed out where we'd found the enemy and where we hadn't seen any enemy fighters at all. I told him we could and should move faster. We had to, in order to capitalize on the gains we'd made. He thought about the situation for a minute then wanted to see it for himself from a helicopter, so we took him up in a Kiowa."

Since Petraeus was not an aviator, he did not own a flight helmet. Schiller looked at Ken Hawley's head and judged it to be about the same size as Petraeus's head. "Grab your helmet," Schiller told Ken. "Let the boss wear it."

Without a word, Ken handed Petraeus his flight helmet and he and Schiller departed, almost immediately being shot at by the enemy. The flight not only enabled the division commander to better understand the enemy situation at Najaf, but it demonstrated how maneuverable the Kiowa helicopter was and just how well Steve's pilots could see the battlefield.

"It was a pivotal moment. From that day forward, the infantry brigade that was assigned the mission to root the enemy out of a given city got the CAV,"[2] Schiller said.

Schiller's flight with General Petraeus put 2-17 CAV squarely in the middle of every fight for the remainder of the war, but that took place after the epic sandstorm, which the men lamented about over cigars that evening.

Chief Warrant Officer Two Tim Slifko looked cross-eyed at the cigar in his mouth, trying to see if it was properly lit. Finally giving up, he pulled it out of his mouth and looked at the end of it. Seeing that it was indeed lit, he began the story.

"We were at FARP [Forward Area Arming and Refueling Point] Shell. The winds began to pick up about twelve hours prior to the storm of all storms, crushing us," he said.

Heads nodded up and down, confirming the validity of Slifko's story and providing encouragement for him to continue with the telling. Despite having heard them hundreds of times, soldiers love telling and hearing war stories in which they play a prominent role. They all knew the story of the sandstorm—heck, they lived it—but they would take turns telling it over and over.

Slifko continued. "The visibility began to decrease quickly. We started taking precautions. Everyone tightened up their equipment and gear; we tied down the aircraft rotor blades and put pillows in the exhaust to try and keep as much sand as possible out of the engines,"[3] he said.

Schiller and his cavalrymen set up small pup tents beside their Kiowas that night. "The quick set-up and tear-down of those compact little tents made it easy for us to jump around the battlefield," Slifko said. "They were perfect for our small aircraft. We could stuff them in the back compartment and still have room for a sleeping bag, food, and some water. I had a simple fifty-dollar Coleman two-man tent. I was a big fan of Mr. Coleman after the war."[4]

The pilots took shifts pulling security around the small perimeter that night. Fortunately, they did not encounter any enemy forces, but they did awake the following morning to much worse weather conditions.

The lead elements, including Petraeus himself, arrived on that second day. After a scary flight in horrid conditions, Petraeus called back to Colonels Greg Gass and Bill Forrester and told them not to send any more helicopters forward.[5] Conditions were too difficult for flight. Over the next seventy-two hours, the soldiers endured the worst storm any of them had ever encountered.

Shaking his head gently side to side with a soft but serious expression on his face, Slifko looked directly at me and said, "Sir, you should have been there."

"It was a bitch," another warrant added in a low somber tone as if he had survived Armageddon.

"When it hit, it was a monster," Slifko said. "We all ran to our tents and buttoned up for the fun that we were about to experience. It was like that sandstorm in the movie *The Mummy.* I know that sounds crazy, but I'm serious. It was no joke—literally, a wall of sand came straight at us," Slifko said, and then spit a stream of Copenhagen juice into the dirt.

"For the next seventy-two hours, the winds maintained a steady sixty to seventy miles per hour," he said.

"He's not shittin' you," the other warrant said with his eyebrows held high.

Having a deep appreciation for good storytelling, I recognized that we had clearly shifted gears. The story had begun to crescendo. With increased tempo, Slifko continued.

"The visibility was reduced to zero," he said, meaning that they could not see one meter in front of their faces. "In those seventy-two hours, the only time I left my tent was to go pull my one-hour guard duty or to go to the latrine. I would have pissed in a bottle, but I only had one.

"Hell, I pissed in a bottle the whole night," the other warrant said, shaking his head and laughing at himself. "I emptied it the next morning and used it again the next day. We were dehydrated by that point anyway, so we didn't pee much. Hell, you could get three pees in a two-liter bottle."

Sensing he was at risk of losing control of the story, Slifko cut back in. "The winds were so strong that it folded the entire roof and sides of the tent vertical on itself and on top of me. The fiberglass dome supports bent, but they never broke! The entire nylon tent acted as a weathervane in the strong winds. I used my arm to keep the tent from rubbing my face. I split my gear up to use as weights in each corner of the tent. My rucksack was at my feet and held down the right corner of the tent. My flight gear and armor vest and duffel bag secured the opposite corners on the left, and my body, shoulder, and head, literally held down the remaining corner. I lay there spread-eagle for all of it, keeping the corners of the tent and my gear in place with a foot or hand for hours and hours.

"We wore our 'earth, wind, and fire'[6] goggles and wrapped scarves around our heads and faces. No matter what we did or how well we were buttoned up, sand still got in everywhere. I remember after each nap, because I never really slept, having to remove my goggles and physically pull my eyelids apart. They were glued together from the sand and crud," Slifko said.

"He's not shittin' you, sir," the other warrant said, resuming his supporting role in the story.

Slifko continued, "My eyes reminded me of those nasty feral barn cats that lived on my grandfather's dairy farm when I was a kid. They always had some type of conjunctivitis in their eyes that glued them shut.

"Guard duty was a nightmare. A bit scary actually, not because of the enemy threat—no human, good or bad, was moving in that storm—but attempting to find our assigned fighting positions in zero visibility was quite an undertaking. I remember someone screaming for me outside my tent. It sounded like he was miles away, but in reality, he was right outside my tent. I unzipped the tent, stepped outside, and had to yell at the top of my lungs to communicate with him. He was there to tell me that it was my turn to head out to the fighting positions.

"I secured my tent from the outside as best as I could. I zipped it up and stomped on the stakes, praying it would still be there when I returned. Then I headed out in the general direction where I thought the aircraft was, about one hundred meters to my south. It took me a few minutes to get out there. I had to physically reach out with my hands and feel for a helicopter to know I had reached my destination. Once I found one, I used my hands to keep in contact with it, and then I eased my way around it to look for the appropriate tail number, to make sure I was at the right helicopter. I ended up one aircraft over from mine and had to move to my right to what should have been mine. I finally found it and lay down in the fighting position for the next fifty minutes or so.

"I lay there and wondered how I was going to do anything if something bad happened. Then I realized that nothing on earth could navigate that storm, so the chance of enemy contact was not likely.

"Anyway, I did my time out on the perimeter and then began the adventure of returning to my tent. It took me about thirty minutes to find it. You don't know how happy I was that it was still there.

"When the sun set that day, it was a complete blackout. I'm not kidding. It was utter darkness, period. Everything was exactly like if your eyes were closed; no trace of any visible illumination. You could barely see the light from a flashlight twelve inches away," he said.

"That's no joke," the other warrant added, hanging on Slifko's every word as if to both relive that moment and ensure that Slifko told the story with the appropriate drama and detail.

"When it was finally over, everything was completely covered in a layer of sand 'crud.' Because there was some moisture at times during the storm, it was stuck like glue to our helicopters and trucks,"[7] he concluded.

Just telling the story, and reliving those events, seemed to amp up all of them. Schiller's crew buddy, Doug Ford, jumped in. "The day after the storm passed, the SCO wanted to go fly, get out and do some reconnaissance," he said.

I did not know Doug, but I detected a touch of sarcasm. I sensed that he was a colorful character who, being crewed with the SCO, was allowed to mock the boss a bit, so long as he didn't cross the line.

He continued, "The troop commanders were having their guys clean the helicopters up when I went out to preflight mine and the SCO's. We flew an Annihilator Troop bird," Doug said. "I noticed that our aircraft needed transmission fluid, so I told the crew chief to go find some, but Schiller had already arrived at the bird.

"He said, 'Let's go,' and I told him we had to wait to get transmission fluid. Suddenly, he was pissed. The storm was over and he was antsy, ready to go fly. We were at war, and he figured the enemy might be moving since the storm was over. So, he did what he does best when he's pissed off: he chewed the troop commander's ass right in front of me,"[8] Doug said.

I looked over at Schiller to judge his response. He rolled his eyes and smiled, then took a drag on his cigar. Doug looked at me and lowered his voice as if he didn't want Schiller to hear him. "He is a hard ass on the troop commanders. Especially when it comes to keeping the birds combat ready. I was sitting there in the helicopter while he chewed the troop commander's ass. I was stuck in the middle of the ass chewing with nowhere to go. It was an awkward moment.

"Finally, he finished, and we launched," he said, and then he raised his voice so that Schiller was sure to hear him. "Like dumbasses, we went out SINGLE SHIP!"

He let that statement hang in the air a moment for effect. Then he rendered judgment. "I thought that was stupid, but Doug doesn't get a vote. Doug just goes where the SCO goes."

I looked over at Schiller again. He was leaning back against the wall, feet crossed. Smoke drifted up out of his mouth, one eye closed and the other squinted as he took another drag of the cigar, which was now only three or four inches long. I did not yet know what kind of a sense of humor he had. He lowered the cigar, blew the smoke out, and gently shook his head at Doug. Feeling it was safe to continue, Doug spoke again.

"We flew out alone, scouting and looking around. Eventually, we found what we were looking for—Fedayeen guard forces. When they saw us, they immediately began running to their fighting positions, where their weapons were lying. I told the SCO we needed to get the hell out of there, and he agreed. That was some crazy shit!"[9]

Schiller seemed happy that they had such stories to share, almost as if he planned to operate on the edge just to give them something exciting to talk about, stories to tell their children and grandchildren one day.

Eventually, the rapid-fire, colorful war stories that had burned hot with the embers of their cigars began to slow their pace. Stogies were reduced to butts, and long, silent pauses filled space previously occupied by laughter, but thin smiles endured. I could sense how proud they were of what they had accomplished. Slowly, one by one, they began to wander off into the night.

Schiller snubbed his cigar out and looked at me. "Jimmy, I'll sit down with you in the morning," he said. "We'll talk," he added and turned to walk away.

"Yes sir," I replied, and went to my own room.

I unrolled a Therm-a-Rest sleeping pad that I had bought when I deployed to Bosnia and began to inflate it. It was the best piece of equipment a man could own if he intended to sleep on the ground or an army cot for a year. Ken walked in, sat down, and began unlacing his boots.

"It's going to be hot," he said. "It cools off as the night goes on, but the air doesn't circulate in this building, so it sucks," he added.

"Yeah, I can tell," I replied.

As Ken prepared for bed, I saw dog tags swing from his neck. I noticed a medallion that appeared to be a St. Michael, who is the patron saint of airborne and aviation. "Where did you get that St. Michael?" I asked.

"Someone was giving them out as I boarded the plane to deploy," he said. "It has the 101st patch on the back of it."

"That's pretty cool. Are you Catholic as well?"

"Not yet," he said, then paused to consider the question. "It's complicated."

"How's that?"

"I was born and raised Protestant. My wife, Grace, is a good Catholic girl. I have attended mass with her for quite a while, but I asked her not to push me too fast. Now, here we are in the middle of Iraq, and we have a Catholic priest as a chaplain. I've been talking to him casually for a while now. He says that he can take me through the Rite of Christian Initiation of Adults while we are over here, so I have begun. I guess it will be my surprise for Grace when I return home."

"Well, I'm sure life in the Hawley home will be much easier. A home divided in faith is tough," I said.

"Yeah. She's been patient with me, but it took me a while to truly understand the Catholic faith," he said, then set his boots under the end of his cot, adjusting them so that the boots, his shower shoes, and tennis shoes were all neatly aligned under his cot. I looked under my own cot to confirm that the toes of all my shoes were perfectly in line as well. Both of us were products of military schools. We had been forever shaped by four years of uncompromising obsessive-compulsive behavior and rigid rules. Despite no one checking or even caring, it would have eaten at both of us if our foot gear was not perfectly aligned.

"Well, what do you think so far?" Ken asked, referring to the unit in general.

"I'm just happy to be here. It was fun listening to all the war stories. I wish I had been with you guys to experience them," I said, feeling as if I had made it to the party just as everyone was getting ready to go home.

"Well, there's plenty left to do," Ken said. "It's not over yet."

"Is that your wife?" I asked, pointing to a picture taped to the wall over his cot.

"Yeah. That's Grace. And those are my four kids," he said, pointing to another picture. "That's Kaitlyn, Sarah, Nick, and that is little Hannah."

"Wow, was that picture taken right before you left?" I asked.

"Yeah. The SCO let me deploy on the final flight to Kuwait and Hannah was nice enough to come into the world a little early, so I got to be there for her birth and then take her and Grace home before flying out," he said.

I still didn't know Ken well, but I recognized that I could not have picked a better roommate and fellow major. There are two majors in a squadron, the executive officer and the operations officer. Since they are peers, sometimes the majors feel that they are competing with one another, which makes for an unhealthy environment within the squadron. I got no sense of competition whatsoever from Ken.

With a sheet spread over my sleeping pad, I lay down on my back and stared at the ceiling, thinking about my own wife and kids. Finally, I broke the silence. "The guys seem to really like the SCO."

"Yeah, well, he's different. That's for sure," Ken said. "He led from the front on every fight we fought in. And if you got into a fight and he wasn't in the front, you'd better watch out. He'd come flying in and cut you off on the way to the target to get a shot.

"There were times he dodged RPGs [rocket-propelled grenades] in flight while he was in the middle of a gun run. Most men would follow their instincts and break off the attack, but not him. It just pissed him off that somebody had the audacity to shoot at him. He'd dodge the RPG in flight and keep barreling in on them, guns ablaze.

"At Najaf, several enemy fighters went into a massive graveyard. They hid among the tombstones. These two guys made a run toward a ZPU-2 antiaircraft gun, but Doug and the SCO saw them. The dudes knew they had been caught, so they ducked into the doorway of a tomb. The SCO put a rocket through the doorway and hit them. Ask Doug about it. He flew with the SCO the whole time."

I was excited just listening to Ken tell the stories. Countless questions flooded my mind, but I waited too long. With no more than thirty seconds' pause in our conversation, I heard Ken's deep rhythmic breathing. He was sound asleep. As for me, I had far too many things on my mind to sleep.

Gradually, my thoughts traveled from Iraq, the war, and my new boss to a place much farther away. I wondered what my wife and kids might be doing. I wondered how they were.

I had graduated from the Command and General Staff College on June 6, 2003, seventeen years to the day after I had reported to basic training as a brand-new army recruit. Following graduation, we drove direct from Kansas to Kentucky, where I immediately signed into the 101st Airborne Division. There were no houses available on post, so we purchased a home in Clarksville, Tennessee. Then, seventeen days later, on June 23, I boarded a bus bound for Baltimore, Maryland, where I caught a plane to Kuwait.

Meanwhile, my wife, Lisa, and three children began plowing through boxes, making new friends, and establishing a home. Having watched Desert Storm while sitting in the Gaillard Hall dayroom at North Georgia College with fellow cadets, I had been anxious to join my unit in Iraq as quickly as possible. I recalled how envious I had been when soldiers returned from Desert Storm and told their war stories. Not wanting to miss the next one, all I could think about was joining my unit before the war was over; however, the deployment was open ended. We went with no idea when we'd return. That made it extremely difficult for those being left behind—our families.

Like most Americans, I had watched President George W. Bush address the world from the USS *Abraham Lincoln* as he stood beneath a banner that read "Mission Accomplished." At that point, I thought the war was over, that I had already missed another one. Our president had been wrong, and so had I. We had uncorked the bottle of war and, if history has taught us anything, it's that once you uncork that bottle, war soon takes on a life of its own.

Nevertheless, as I lay there on my cot, I found myself excited, eager to begin the next day. I looked forward to my initial counseling with the SCO. He seemed to be an exceptional leader. I already felt like I was a part of something very special. I couldn't wait to begin flying missions, so I would have my own stories to share.

THE SCO

Having passed through eight time zones, I had not yet adjusted to my new environment. After only a couple of hours of sleep, I woke at 4:00 a.m. Trying not to wake Ken, I rolled out of my squeaky army cot. As quietly as I could, I got dressed in my physical training uniform and slipped out of the room. It was already getting light outside, so I was eager to get out and run on Q-West, to see as much as possible on foot.

Standing in front of the headquarters, I stretched for a few minutes. I noticed that there was no dew on the ground. Dew reminded me of home, of my childhood, of a time when my grandfather would holler out the window of his old Ford truck before going to town, "Mow the yard once that dew dries!" It's amazing how a simple memory can transport you back in time. It was a pleasant thought, one that left me with a smile.

I ran the perimeter road, and once I was out of earshot of the steady hum of generators, it was quiet and peaceful. That morning I saw my first spectacular Iraqi sunrise. The massive orange ball appeared to be just over the horizon. It was unlike any sunrise I had ever seen. I stopped running and stood on the side of the dusty road to take it all in. For a moment, before the dogs and birds awoke, before the sound of day began and life began to stir, the quiet seemed louder than the noise.

The next mile was peaceful. The steady rhythm of my breathing and the soft touch of running shoes to the pavement was all that I heard until a convoy of trucks passed me. They blew by at a high rate of speed, clearly expecting me to get the heck out of the way or be run over. A cloud of dust boiled up at the rear of the convoy, choking me half to death. I pulled my shirt up and tried to breathe through it, using it as a filter, but it was no use. Snorting and coughing, trying to keep from going blind, I stopped running and waited for the dust to clear. It took a good three or four minutes. By the time I got the dust out of my nose and eyes, I was ready to be done, so, like a tired and sweaty horse, I headed for the barn and called it good.

I returned to my room, sponged off with a bottle of water, and put on my uniform. As I stepped into the hallway outside my room, I heard a female soldier yelling outside the logistics bay. It seemed strangely out of place, so I went to investigate. As I turned the corner on the western side of the building, I saw ten Iraqi men standing in a row, shoulder to shoulder. Each wore the traditional *dishdasha*,[1] or "man dress," as we called them. On the ledge of the building, towering over the men, stood a female African American sergeant. Her hands were on her hips and she leaned slightly forward at the waist as she addressed the men. With a mean scowl on her face, she barked, "You will not enter anyone's room!" Then she turned and walked along the ledge staring at the ground, hands still on her hips and a snarling scowl plastered to her face.

"You will not go anywhere without an escort. Not even to the latrine!" she barked. "Do you understand?" to which the men just stared at her.

The local Iraqi men had been hired to work around our squadron area, cleaning up, painting, and doing whatever chores the soldiers could think up. The sergeant in charge of the local worker program was intent on making sure that they clearly understood what they could and could not do, although I'm not sure any of them comprehended a single word she said. They did not speak English. Nevertheless, you could see by their body language that they understood one thing: she was the boss, and she meant business.

She spoke to the men as a drill sergeant would address new army recruits, and the men stood rigidly in formation, just as new recruits would stand, fixated on, and a little frightened of, the authority figure addressing them. In a male-dominated society such as Iraq, I could not help but wonder what was going through their minds.

I was not the only one wondering. "I'll bet they're pretty excited," a soldier with a smirk on his face said to me. Then he lifted his eyebrows and in a hushed voice said, "I guarantee you they have never had a woman talk to them like that before," he said. "Hell, I bet it's strangely exciting for them."

I shook my head and headed for the TOC.

It must have been difficult for the men to take such forceful orders from a woman, much less an American woman they did not know. When American soldiers entered Iraqi villages, their women veiled their faces and ran inside their homes. These men had come to work for us, and we put a woman in charge of them. I was left to assume that they must have desperately needed the money. Otherwise, why would they do it? I wondered if they viewed her differently since she was American.

Schiller was reading as I entered his office. I knocked on the open doorway to let him know I was there. "Morning," he said, looking up. "Come on in."

"Morning, sir."

Schiller got up from his desk and walked around to two chairs that sat facing each other. He sat down in one and pointed to the other. "Sit down. How did your run go this morning?"

"Good. It will take some time to adjust to the time zone changes. I was up early," I said.

"Yeah, it'll take a few days," he said, then held up my Officer's Record Brief (ORB), which is a single-page document that chronicles an officer's career. "I've seen your ORB, so I know where you've been assigned and in what jobs you've served, but why don't you start by telling me a little bit more about yourself—your family, why you joined the army, stuff like that."

"Okay," I said, thrilled to tell the story. I loved sharing my story because I felt that it was proof that the American Dream still existed. Only in America could you go from the factory to field-grade officer. "Well, I grew up the son of a mill village worker in northern Georgia. My father's family moved to Calhoun, Georgia, during the Depression because my great-grandfather was offered a job at Echota Cotton Mill. My mother's family moved there in the late 1830s," I said.

"Really?" he said, clearly surprised that I knew so much about my family's history. "How do you know that?"

"I've researched my family, done a lot of genealogy work," I said. "Because my ancestors fought in the Revolutionary War and later the War of 1812, they were eligible to enter the Cherokee Land Lottery. The last Cherokee Indian Nation capital was in my hometown, New Echota."

"That's fascinating," he said, genuinely interested.

"My family drew land in the 1829 Cherokee Land Lottery, but they did not move to Calhoun until several years later, because the Indians didn't take kindly to being driven out," I said. "Some of the Indian women married white men. I am an eighth Cherokee myself," I said.

Keeping his eyes focused on me, Schiller got up and retrieved a bottle of water. He held one out to me without saying a word, so as not to interrupt my story. I took the bottle and kept talking as he sat back down.

"My mother and father met in Calhoun and were married right after high school. My father was drafted during the Korean War. After his enlistment was up, he returned to Calhoun, and the cotton mill. He was proud of his service. He kept his wool Eisenhower jacket hanging in his closet, but he never urged me to join or anything like that. I just assumed I'd work in the cotton mill. The only thing I ever debated in school was which shift I'd work. The mill was a foregone conclusion. But, one day, an army recruiter showed up and asked me if I wanted to join the service. I saw it as a chance to change my future, go somewhere, and do something different, so I jumped at the offer.

"I joined the Army Reserves and took advantage of the Montgomery GI Bill. That, and a boatload of school loans, allowed me to attend North Georgia College, where I was commissioned," I said.

"I saw that you went to North Georgia on your ORB. I've known some North Georgia guys. That place produces some good officers," he said.

"Yes sir. I loved North Georgia."

"That's pretty cool that you know so much about your family history," he said.

As I told my story, Schiller had been glued to me, genuinely interested. "What about you, sir?" I asked, eager to learn more about him.

"Well, I grew up in Missouri. I went to Missouri Western State University on a baseball scholarship," he said. "While I was there, I met Rhonda and we started dating." His wife, the former Rhonda Piveral, was a petite blonde.

"We dated throughout college, but after that everything happened rather quickly. I graduated from Missouri Western on May 14, 1986. I was commissioned a second lieutenant on May 15, and we got married on the seventeenth," he said.

It wasn't that uncommon for cadets to marry quickly. In fact, because North Georgia was a military college, I'd seen multiple couples' transition from college to army life in a matter of weeks.

"I think you told me at Fort Leavenworth that you've got two kids, right?"

"Yes. Calvin and Courtney," he said. "You?"

"I have three: Kasey, Austin, and Madison," I said.

"Are they settled in in Clarksville?" he asked.

"They're working on it," I said.

"Moving's a bitch," he said. "Tell Lisa to call Rhonda if she needs help."

"Thanks, I will."

Eventually, Schiller transitioned to business. He showed me several training plans he had either written himself or directed others to write.

One document explained the standards for shooting M4 rifles out the door of a Kiowa while in flight. He had developed a training program for operating helicopters over cities, and several other initiatives that he sought to pursue further when time permitted. For our helicopters to become more agile over cities, he was working on a plan to take the Mast Mounted Sites (MMS)[2] off the Kiowas. It was hot in Iraq, and the helicopter was heavy, operating near maximum gross weight. He knew he could shed almost four hundred pounds from the helicopter by taking the MMS off. He did not want us to shoot Hellfire missiles, which weighed ninety-six pounds each and required the MMS. He preferred 2.75-inch rockets and the .50-caliber machine gun, neither of which required the MMS. By reducing the weight of the Kiowa, it would increase our power margin, thus the aircraft would maneuver with much more agility over the cities. He seemed to be filled with innovative ideas for how to create a more effective organization, and he expected his soldiers to think the same way.

Just listening to him think out loud set lights off in my own mind. Most aviation leaders would never consider altering the helicopter to conform to the mission profile. Even if they did think that it would be nice to have more power, they would not consider altering the airframe because the military industrial complex would get upset that their technology was not being used or proven in combat.

In Stephen Schiller, I saw a very methodical and calculated leader. He was a rare breed. His clear excitement and enthusiasm for innovation—how we could transform not only our aircraft, but also our tactics—was infectious. I found myself thinking about what we might do differently to become better at our mission. Then I realized that was his intent. He was intent on deliberately shaping the culture of the organization. If Schiller could inspire his subordinates to think more like him, there was no telling how effective we might become. We would no longer be limited by his innovation. With a culture of innovation, we'd tap into the collective potential of our squadron. That was important to him because Schiller knew that the collective potential of any organization is greater than the leader's potential alone.

Training and disciplined execution were his forte. He was demanding in terms of flight procedures. He expected his cavalrymen to know the standards and to devoutly enforce them. It was through disciplined and consistent execution of standards that confidence and trust grew within the unit. As I would soon discover, if 2-17 CAV planned it, briefed it, and rehearsed it, you could damn well bet they would execute it with precision.

"Jimmy," he said, "it has been my dream since flight school to do what we have done so far this year. Honestly, this has been a dream come true for me."

"What do you mean by that?" I asked.

Schiller leaned forward in his seat and placed his elbows on his knees. I saw the passion in his face, and I knew that he was about to share his convictions.

"I believe that cavalry is a mentality," he said.

I began smiling, because I had always thought the same thing. I interrupted, "It's a way of thinking," I said.

"You damn right, it is. You can teach it to a degree, but honestly, I think the mentality is inherent in one's personality. Since taking command of 2-17, I have tried to bring that mentality out in our troopers. I can look at what we've accomplished already in this war and know that we've made a difference. I've seen it come out in battle—how the guys thought and fought."

Then he pointed at the ground between his feet to indicate 2-17 CAV and said, "This is where I've wanted to be my entire career. Right here. In the United States Cavalry, surrounded by bad asses who are tough and rugged. Men who look forward to taking the fight to the enemy, who race to the sound of the guns in battle, sleep in the dirt with their head on a rock, and get up every day excited to go kick some ass all over again!

"I believe in investing in soldiers with the right mentality. Hire the right people, give them simple, capable tools they can use in a broad range of environments, and give them exceptional leadership, and they will succeed," he said.

"So here is your guidance. I want you to lead from the front. Set the example. Push your people and encourage them to make us better. Now, what are your questions?"

"Ha. I don't have any questions about that. I like the trust and latitude, but I do have other questions."

"Fire away," he said.

"What's up with that holster?" I asked, pointing at it.

He leaned back in his chair. "When I got to the unit, the soldiers didn't seem to have the cavalry spirit, so to speak. I let them wear their Stetson[3] hats at first, to try to motivate them, but it wasn't long before a few of them began wearing their *unauthorized* hats all over post. We were only allowed to wear them in CAV Country.

"It pissed the division sergeant major off that my guys violated the rule, so I got grief about it, not from him, mind you, but from others he complained to. I told the soldiers that since they were not responsible with their Stetsons, they'd have to earn the right to wear them. At that same time, I was radically changing how the unit trained. I had them wearing all of their combat kit [equipment] when they flew. I forced them to fly with the doors off the aircraft on every flight. Many of them were naturally resistant to change. I wanted them to embrace very demanding training and exude confidence, but it was challenging. I was trying to shape the culture and that is a tall order.

"I told them they could wear their Stetsons in the squadron area only, but nowhere else. Then the deployment came. We were going to war, and I wanted my troopers to have that cavalry mentality. I have always believed that effective leadership is a little bit of theatre anyway. Not that one has to *act* in a way that isn't who they are, but playing a role that gives your soldiers some degree of confidence in your ability can also enable you to get some things done more easily, push some limits. Soldiers like the persona. So, after having restricted the Stetson and pushing the unit to be a 'real cavalry' unit in mentality, I felt I had to do something different. So, when we actually deployed, I told them that the Stetson was authorized for wear everywhere and decided on the holster as my part of the 'theatre' that I thought fit well with a Stetson hat and spurs."[4]

I was instantly reminded of George Custer's buckskin jacket, white-handled pistols, and Bowie hunting knife. Schiller's theatrics worked. By the time I arrived in June, he had become central to something of a cult of personality. He had demonstrated in combat that he was a fearless leader who would share hardship with his troopers. He would fight to ensure they were at the forefront of every mission in the division, and he filled the role as their leader. They deserved an iconic SCO, and Schiller gave it to them.

"I see," I said.

"What else? I'm in no hurry," he said, leaning back in his chair, sensing that I had more questions.

"Last night, when the guys were telling war stories, you didn't say much," I said.

"I love listening to them tell their stories. I am proud of them. I'd rather listen to them talk than tell my own stories," he said.

"I'd be interested in your perspective of how the war unfolded. I'm just trying to piece it all together in my own mind," I said.

"Well, that will require a stogie," he said as he rose to his feet. He walked to a small wooden humidor and fingered through several cigars before finding the one he was looking for. He chose a dark, chocolate-colored cigar, removed the wrapper, and snipped the end off with a piercer. "Let's go out to the picnic table," he said.

THE STORM:
UDAIRI TO AN NAJAF

Schiller walked to the far side of the picnic table and sat down straddling the bench, as if he was about to ride a seesaw. He wore an army
physical training uniform with a well-worn pair of black Adidas combat
boots. Special Operations Command (SOCOM) is unique in that they
can independently contract specialized gear. The Adidas boots were one
of the few things Schiller held on to from his years in the 160th.

"So, the first months of the war," he began, then raised the cigar to
his mouth with his left hand while holding a cigarette lighter to the end
of it with his right. For the first time, I realized he was left-handed. He
squinted as he drew short, choppy breaths through the cigar, lighting it.
Once the end glowed red, he leaned back, took a deep draw from the
cigar, and then opened his mouth and huffed a breath of air out of pursed
lips. A perfect ring of smoke floated out of his mouth. He exhaled the
remainder of the smoke out of the corner of his mouth so as not to disturb
the ring that hung, spinning in the air, in front of his face. I wasn't sure if
this was part of the theatre he'd told me about, or if he had become somewhat of a cigar aficionado.

"Out of the blue, General Freakley called me to his command post,
which was set up in a tent just big enough for him to work with his small
staff. They had a few tables, folding chairs, and maps inside. Just enough
to monitor the war and give guidance. That's why he called me there—to
give me guidance," he said.

Brigadier General Benjamin Freakley was the Assistant Division
Commander for Operations (ADC-O). He was responsible for the

31

ongoing operations, or the current fight, as we called it. Based on the approved war plan and Major General Petraeus's guidance, Ben Freakley's job was to conduct the 101st Airborne Division's orchestra of destruction in combat. Sometimes Freakley operated from a ground command post, but he also coordinated the fight from a consortium of Black Hawk command and control helicopters, which were equipped with a suite of communications equipment.

"When I got there, he was standing in front of the map studying it and looking somewhat perturbed," Schiller said. "He told me that he had been in contact with the 3rd Infantry Division and that they had reported that the area we had selected to set up FARP Shell was not usable, which was a bit confusing to me. Hell, the entire desert could be used as a FARP. It might be dusty, or there might be powerlines we'd have to avoid, but all you had to do was move a few hundred yards in any direction and you'd find more open desert."

The 3rd Infantry Division was attacking into Iraq on the eastern flank of the 101st Airborne. FARP Shell was an area in the desert south of the Iraqi city An Najaf. That area had been selected as the location where the division would set up a massive FARP designed to provide fuel and ammunition for all the division's helicopters.

Freakley continued, "3rd Infantry's lead forces are rolling north up Highway 1, to their intermediate staging base. I'm not sure why the area we chose for FARP Shell would not be suitable, but that's what they are reporting. Steve, I need you to go up there and confirm or deny that report as soon as possible."[1]

Taking another long drag from the cigar, Schiller then told me, "Jimmy, I'm sure you've used plenty of FARPs in your time as an aviator, but I doubt you've seen one quite like these massive FARPs in the 101st. They are huge, and they scare the hell out of me. We are the smallest bird in the fleet, and these big-ass FARPs get dusty and windy. We were planning to fly 258 helicopters north, all using the same series of FARPs as we moved."

"Two hundred fifty-eight helicopters. Wow. There are more helicopters in the 101st Airborne Division than most nations own," I said.

"Absolutely," he replied, then returned to the story. "So, General Freakley sent us north to reconnoiter. The only units from the 101st that crossed the berm into Iraq in front of us were those that that moved forward to set up FARP Exxon. Because we had so far to fly, we leap-frogged using the FARPs. FARP Exxon's purpose was to provide a refuel point about two hundred miles north of Kuwait, so that we could refuel the helicopters there and then move on, another two hundred-plus miles north to establish FARP Shell. Shell would then enable us to attack farther north with our Apaches.

"Shell would not only serve as a FARP, but it would also become a forward operating base," Schiller said. "We didn't know how long we'd have to fight from there before we could push on to Baghdad, because at that point we had no idea how hard the Iraqis would fight."

The TOC door swung open, and Ken Hawley emerged, squinting from the sudden brightness of the sun. Seeing Schiller and me sitting at the picnic table, he approached. "Morning," Ken said.

"Morning," Schiller and I replied in unison.

"I'm just catching Jimmy up on the initial push through Iraq," Schiller said. Then, patting the bench beside him, he said, "Sit down and help me out."

"I have to run up to brigade," Ken said. "But I've got a few minutes. What have you told him so far?" he asked, as he sat on the bench beside Schiller.

"Just getting started actually. We're standing in General Freakley's little tent they set up for a command post at FARP Exxon," Schiller said.

"Oh, gotcha," Ken said, shaking his head, as if he was recalling the Spartan accommodations in his mind.

"Do you remember?" Schiller asked. "That's where General Freakley told me to go reconnoiter Shell to see if it was suitable for a FARP. He sent us up there to confirm or deny the report by 3rd Infantry that it was unusable." Schiller turned his head to the side and spit into the rocks.

Since I was not a smoker, I never fully understood the spitting thing, but the guys certainly spit a lot when they smoked. I was left to assume that there was something in cigars that increased saliva production.

"Oh, I remember it well," Ken said.

Schiller turned his attention back to me. "I told General Freakley that I understood the mission he'd given me. I told him that I had one cavalry troop of Kiowas with me as well as a FATCOW Chinook. You know what a FATCOW is, right?" he asked me.

"Yes sir," I said. "A Chinook with fuel cells and pumps inside the cargo bay that you use to make a small FARP."

"Yep. I wasn't sure if other units use them as much as we do in the 101st," he said. "Anyway, I told Freakley that we'd head up there once the Chinook finished refueling. I told him I'd report back to him as soon as I could find a way to call him because we didn't have a satellite radio. I'd have to find someone in 3rd Infantry with one I could use."

Since the Kiowas did not consume much fuel, a Chinook FATCOW FARP was convenient for OH-58 operations. The Chinook has the capability to transport, and to pump, up to 2,320 gallons of aviation fuel. The fuel is contained in 600-gallon tanks carried inside the belly of the helicopter. Each tank has only 580 usable gallons, hence the 2,320 gallons' available total, but that is sufficient fuel to keep a Kiowa troop flying for quite some time.

"I told him that I'd figure it out, but it might be helpful if he called the 3rd Infantry and let them know that I was coming—pre-coordinate it. I asked him if he would not mind doing that," Schiller said.

"Freakley said he'd call them; then he asked me what else I needed. I told him I was good to go, had everything I needed. I turned and left the command post. As I walked out of the tent, I saw Captain Matt Worrell and several of his pilots standing around smoking cigars. They were dirty and sweating, yet ready to get moving north into Iraq. Matt saw me walk out of the tent, so he walked straight to me."

Schiller told me that he had selected Matt's troop [Annihilator Troop] as the lead troop to take forward across the berm. Matthew Worrell was a Texas A&M grad who everyone affectionately called "Bubba." Matt had been Schiller's most aggressive troop commander thus far. Schiller felt that if he was personally forced out of the fight for any reason, he could count on Matt to successfully continue the mission.

"What's up, sir?" Worrell asked.

"Well, we're on to FARP Shell," Schiller had told Matt that March morning. "The 3rd Infantry Division has reported that Shell is unusable as a FARP. We need to fly up there and confirm or deny that report, so the division can either continue as planned or find a new location for the FARP. If Shell isn't suitable for a FARP then we'll need to find a new spot. Fair enough?" Schiller asked Worrell.

"Fair enough, boss," he said. "We are refueled and ready to go. I just need to check with Pachyderm to make sure they've got that Chinook ready and then we can get moving," Worrell said.

Pachyderm was the call sign of the Chinook FATCOW, commanded by Captain John Knightstep.

Schiller continued, "Then I turned to the small group of Matt's pilots that had gathered around me to hear the plan. I looked at them and, Jimmy, I was proud as hell. They were sweaty and dirty, had no idea what we were about to fly into, but they were ready to go. Ready to follow me. That was humbling. Those were my guys, and I was proud of them.

"It was already hot as hell, so the MOPP suits we wore made it miserable, but we all knew that was going to be a reality for the foreseeable future," Schiller said, then spit in the rocks again.

The MOPP suit is a thick jacket and trousers designed to protect soldiers against chemical, biological, radiological, and nuclear weapons. All soldiers were required to wear their MOPP suit during the initial stages of the war because we expected the Iraqis to use chemical weapons; after all, that's the main reason we were there—Saddam's WMD. Soldiers carried the protective mask, gloves, and boots in a carrier on their side, but the jacket and pants were worn at all times.

"That's when you called me," Ken said, inserting himself into the story.

"Yeah, right after I got the mission from General Freakley, I called you," Schiller confirmed.

Ken looked up at the sky and squinted his eyes as if he were trying to remember, "It was March 19th, as I recall. I was back at Camp Virginia, in Kuwait. You told me that we were moving out earlier than expected, so I was to get the Ground Assault Convoy [GAC][2] ready to move out that night. I had coordinated with Mike Getchell. He was the 1st Battalion, 187th Infantry executive officer—1st Battalion of the Rakkasans. He said we could join their convoy. He told me to fall in behind their forward support battalion. I had fuel trucks, ammunition, and our Tactical Command Post [TAC]. John Rowell, our Australian exchange officer, and Captain Candy Smith, our S2 [Intelligence Officer], were with me as well."

"So, the 1-187 Infantry guys were providing your security?" I asked.

"Sort of. They had gun trucks, so they spaced them throughout the convoy. It was comforting to have those guys there," he said. "We were

35

about to drive into Iraq in light-skinned vehicles. Naturally, we were worried about ballistic protection, so we filled sandbags and put them in the floorboards of our trucks. We must have added one thousand pounds of weight to every truck," he said, laughing.

Content to listen for a spell, Schiller used his left index finger to hook his dog tag chain, which hung around his neck. In a looping motion, he pulled the chain up over his head. The dog tags rattled as he stuck his hand out to the side of his body and began to spin them. Rotating his hand in small circles, the tags spun freely on his index finger. Then he clamped his thumb down on the chain, stopping it from spinning, and it began coiling around his finger. Once it was completely wrapped around his finger, he reversed the motion until it had unwound itself and once again spun freely.

The story then began to leapfrog, Ken telling what happened on the ground as they moved north and Schiller telling what happened in the air.

"We drove up to the border that evening," Ken said. "I remember seeing Brigadier General E. J. Sinclair, the Assistant Division Commander for Support [ADC-S], who was already at the border waiting on us. He had been my brigade commander in the 6th Cavalry, so I knew him well. We dug fighting positions there and spent the night sleeping in our trucks or on the ground. Early the next morning, we crossed the border into Iraq. I remember seeing General Sinclair standing at the border saluting the soldiers as they crossed into Iraq that morning. It was like something you might see in a movie."

"So, let me get this straight in my mind," I said, interrupting. "The SCO took a troop of Kiowas and the FATCOW Chinook forward to reconnoiter FARP Shell?"

"Yes."

"You guys, along with 3rd Brigade 'Rakkasans,' had driven from Kuwait up to FARP Exxon. You got fuel and spent the night there."

"Yes."

"Then you planned to cross into Iraq and drive up to FARP Shell, wherever that might be."

"Roger."

"The rest of the Division's helicopters would fly from Kuwait up to FARP Exxon and wait there until Shell was ready, and then they'd fly forward to Shell?"

"Exactly."

"Okay," I said. "I'm just trying to keep up with all the moving pieces." Ken continued, "We had a couple of trucks break down right away. It was nothing major, but we had brakes seize up on some of our trailers. We cross-loaded the equipment into other vehicles and kept on moving north."

"You just left the trailer sitting in the desert?" I asked.

"Yeah. It was interesting. Since 3rd Infantry Division had already moved up that route, we saw broken-down vehicles strewn across the desert everywhere. I assumed that they could not wait and planned to come back and get them later," he said.

"We drove all day. That night we stopped and set up a perimeter for security. It was by some ruins and a bunch of Iraqis came over to meet us. They wanted food or anything else we'd give them. We had to pull security to keep them from stealing our stuff, more so than out of fear of the enemy," Ken said.

"The second day we drove in dust all day. It sucked! Literally, the desert floor was, like, eighteen inches deep in a loose dirt that was like talcum powder. It was so soft and deep that we buried a couple of vehicles along the way.

"For the next two days all we did was drive. We began seeing burning enemy vehicles along the route that second day, so we knew we were getting closer to the action, but the soldiers were really beginning to tire. We had driven for two straight days and only got a couple of hours of rest the night prior to that. Every time we stopped, John Rowell and I would walk the line of vehicles and the drivers would all have instantly fallen asleep. It was crazy. We'd walk the line to tell them to wake up and move out, but as soon as we stopped again, they were asleep. I worried that we would have wrecks, but we never did," he said.

Schiller picked the story back up with the helicopters. "Once all the helicopters were ready to go, we took off ahead of the division. Now that felt pretty cool, the cavalry leading the charge into Iraq for the 101st Airborne Division," he said. "We flew as low as possible to minimize our signature across the desert, yet we flew at an altitude that would keep us safe above wires. There are electrical wires all over this country, so I wanted to ensure that we'd pass over any wires we didn't see in time to avoid them. We passed over herds and herds of camels and goats. I remember thinking that that part of Iraq seemed to be completely unaffected by the twenty-first century. It was primitive.

"Of course, I was flying with my crew buddy, Doug Ford," Schiller said, as if noting that his flying with Doug meant so much more than he simply *flew* with him.

I had only briefly met Doug, but watching him interact with the rest of the guys and picking up on their comments about him led me to believe that he was a colorful character.

Chief Warrant Officer Douglas Ford was the squadron safety officer. It was something of a tradition in army aviation at that time that the safety officer fly with the squadron commander. When they first deployed, Doug was a chief warrant officer three, but he had been selected for promotion to chief warrant officer four, so Schiller promoted him in the middle of the Iraqi desert, during the war. Of medium stature, Doug wore a thick black mustache that Schiller said made him look like Adolf Hitler, but Hitler would have ruled the world if he had had Doug Ford's personality, which was enough for any two people. I thought Doug's toothbrush moustache made him resemble Charlie Chaplin more than Hitler and, like Doug, Chaplin had enough personality to make an entire movie without speaking. However, Doug Ford was anything but silent.

Doug grew up in Pickerington, just outside Columbus, Ohio. He joined the army in 1987 and went straight to flight school, what we call a high school to flight school pilot. His first assignment in the army was Annihilator Troop, 2-17 CAV at Fort Campbell. He later moved to 3rd Battalion, 101st Aviation Brigade as an AH-1 Cobra pilot and deployed to Iraq for Operation Desert Storm with them.

After Desert Storm, Doug went to Korea for a year, then back to Fort Campbell. He became a Cobra Instructor Pilot in 1993, then moved to Fort Stewart, Georgia, for two years. He learned to fly the OH-58D Kiowa Warrior in 1997, then headed back to 2-17 CAV, where he would remain for the rest of his career. Armed with a quick wit, Doug was commonly sarcastic, and his well of insults never ran dry. An equal opportunity insulter, Doug distributed jabs and prods across all ranks, making sure to add the proverbial *sir* when making fun of a senior officer. He kept everyone on their toes.

"I flew us out of Kuwait, but then I quickly transferred the flight controls to Doug, so he could fly," Schiller told me. "Right after we crossed the berm into Iraq, Doug said, 'I hate this fucking country!'"

It wasn't that Doug hated the Iraqi people. Far from it. He was willingly there to help them. Nor did Doug hate that he was deployed to a war. That was his profession. It was just that Doug had deployed to Southwest Asia before, so he already knew how challenging life was going to be in the desert. He knew that he was going to have to burn his own feces; eat dehydrated food for months on end; savor every drop of water he could find; live sweaty, dirty, and stinky; and to make matters worse, the enemy was going to try to kill him. It was as though everything in the desert—the wind, dust, electrical wires, towers, storms, and enemy forces—was united to try to kill him, and Doug took that personally. Until Saddam Hussein was removed and the Iraqi people liberated, life was going to suck. *I hate this fucking country* was simply Doug's way of summing all of that up.

"Like me, Doug was a Desert Storm veteran," Schiller said. "He had seen this desert before.

"Doug flew for a little while," Schiller said. "Then, out of the blue he says, 'I'm hungry. Do you mind taking the controls?'"

"'No, I don't mind flying, Doug,' I told him. He reached up on the dashboard and grabbed an MRE. He fished through the brown bag like he was searching through his kitchen pantry, not sure what delectable dehydrated delight he wanted to devour at the moment," Schiller said, shaking his head. "Doug is a good officer. He is perfect for me." Then Schiller paused, as if reflecting on his cockpit time with Doug, "Although, he did draw the short straw."

"What do you mean by that?" I asked.

"He had to fly with *me* throughout the initial stages of the war, and that meant doing a lot of things *for* me that I could not do for myself. My responsibilities lie with the squadron. While everyone else was getting their helicopters ready to fly or setting up their tents for the night, I had to walk around and talk with them—keep their morale up and be there for them. Meanwhile, Doug did all the work of preparing our helicopter for the next mission and setting up our tent. Quite often, I returned after a walkabout to find everything done, even my gear neatly placed on my bedroll. I felt guilty," Schiller added.

As they flew north into Iraq on that first day, Doug cautiously peeled the top off a packet of beef stew, careful not to spill it on his MOPP suit, a garment he knew that he'd have to wear for months without a wash. "Do you think this war will be as anticlimactic as the first one?" he asked Schiller.

"I don't know, Doug. I would suspect that Saddam will resist a little harder now that he knows we're coming for his ass."

"I just hope we don't have to spend another hot-ass summer in this shithole," Doug said, then looked over at Schiller with a cheesy grin on his face that seemed to accentuate his dark mustache.

"Doomsday Doug," Schiller said.

"What's that supposed to mean?" Doug asked, surprised.

"You've never been one for silver linings, have you?"

"You see silver linings? Where? I just see a miserable, hot-ass desert," he said, staring into the distance. "Somewhere out there, there's a bunch of dudes that would like to try and kill us, but they may decide to just give up like last time instead. I'd rather they do that and get this over with quickly, so we can go home."

Doug's question was apropos. Saddam had once again been unable to stop America and its partners from assembling their military might just south of his border. The truth was that no nation on earth could have stopped the force that was then preparing to race through his country. Some might intuitively say that it would have taken another Goliath to challenge such a military giant as the US, but soon an unconventional threat would emerge from the ashes, a threat more like a virus than a beast of war—an asymmetrical menace that would put us to the test.

The US had prepared itself for the clash of great armies. For the most part, we had flushed the tactics used in Vietnam, but the war we were embarking upon was to be more akin to Vietnam than Desert Storm. Another counterinsurgency war lay in wait for us, but this time it would be fought in cities instead of jungles.

The two-hour flight across the barren desert went quickly. Schiller told me that the proposed location for FARP Shell was adjacent to a two-lane highway dubbed ASR Denver, south of An Najaf. The 3rd

Infantry Division had secured their own forward operating base about ten miles north of Shell. He described how he and his cavalrymen had taken a close look at the area once they got there and deemed it suitable, but did have some concerns that the helicopters might "brownout" when they landed.

When a helicopter lands, the wind vortices change. The helicopter's rotors force the wind downward, which blows the sand up in a desert environment, causing what we call a brownout condition. In many cases, the pilot can't see the ground. It is a tricky and dangerous situation, particularly at night.

"By the time we took a good look around the area, we were running low on fuel," Schiller told me. "I told Matt Worrell to begin refueling his helicopters once Pachyderm got the FATCOW FARP set up and ready to start pumping fuel.

"As we circled Shell, I told Ford, 'I've got to piss.'

"'Me too!' Doug replied.

"'Let's fly up north a little and see if we can find someone from 3rd Infantry. If we can find a vehicle, we'll land and ask to use their satellite radio. That way, we only have to land once. We can make the call back to General Freakley, tell him Shell is good to go, and piss too.'

"'Sounds good,' Doug said, 'but we can't screw around too long. We're getting low on fuel.'"

"Doug and I started looking for an American vehicle with a bunch of antennas sticking out of it. The vehicle with all the antennas would most likely be a command and control vehicle, so it would be the one most likely to have a satellite phone or radio," Schiller said. "It only took a few minutes until we found a convoy pulled over on the side of the road, so I landed.

"As I got out of the helicopter, I saw something move behind a small bush," Schiller said. "I took a closer look and found a soldier squatting to take a crap. I thought to myself, *I could have gone all day without seeing that!*"

Schiller picked another bush, well away from the soldier answering mother nature's call, and took a leak. Then he walked over to the vehicle. It belonged to an infantry battalion S3, the operations officer. "He let me use his phone to call Freakley and tell him Shell was suitable for the FARP.

As soon as I hung up with General Freakley, I walked back to the helicopter, where I received a severe ass chewing from Doug," Schiller said, rolling his eyes. "Doug was shaking his head and poi   g his finger at the fuel gauge as I buckled into the aircraft. Once I got my helmet plugged into the helicopter and could hear him, he started in on me.

"'Sir, we really don't have enough gas to fly much longer. We can't be screwing around.'

"But I knew what Doug was really saying to me," Schiller said.

"What's that?" I asked, not completely sure what he might say.

"'*You took too damn long—now hurry your ass up and get in this helicopter before we run out of gas and you get both of us killed*,'" Schiller said, laughing and shaking his head.

"Anyway, as we took off, heading to the FARP, I was reminded of an incident that occurred years earlier to a colleague of mine at the National Training Center in 1992," Schiller said, much more serious now. "He took off low on fuel and crashed. The idea of running out of fuel in flight scared the hell out of me, but I knew that the FATCOW was only a little over a mile away. I knew we could make it.

"The terrain changed significantly in the short distance we flew to the FARP. The Euphrates River Valley was on the east side of the highway. That area was lush and green. Farmers had clearly been irrigating the land by the river for centuries, but as we flew west, the land became dry and just as rocky as it was sandy."

"Really?" I asked, trying to picture it in my mind.

"Yeah, and there also seemed to be a contrast in the people who lived near the river versus those who dwelt in the rocky desert," he said. "The homes near the river were nicer. Many of them had satellite receivers on their roofs. They were neat and clean, a stark contrast to the sheep and goat herders who lived farther west. Gently rolling folds in the terrain gave little relief to the wide-open expanse of desert, though enough to conceal parked helicopters and a few pup tents."

Schiller had continued smoking the stogie as he told the story. It was no more than two inches long by the time he asked me, "Do you want something to drink?

"I believe I will take one, if you don't mind. Thanks, sir," I said.

"Ken, you want one?" he asked.

"No. I'm good," Ken answered.

Schiller rubbed the end of the cigar on a rock to extinguish the remaining embers, then laid it on the picnic table, being careful to place it so that it would not roll away. I had visualized the entire story as he and Ken told it, wishing I had been there.

"What are you thinking about?" Ken asked.

"Nothing," I said.

"Yeah, right," he said. "I can see it on your face."

"I've just been imagining the whole thing as you guys have told it," I said. "I knew I was coming to this unit before you guys deployed, but I was still in school at Fort Leavenworth. Every day I would watch the news and try to visualize what you guys might be doing. Now, here I am in Iraq, listening to you guys tell what really happened. It's kind of surreal."

"I guess the most interesting part of the whole experience was not knowing exactly how things were going to go," Ken said. "You start a war with a plan. You have doctrine, so that forms the basis for what you intend to do, but then you just make it up as you go based on the environment. The cool thing about working for Schiller is that nothing is off the table with him. There is no limit to the possibilities. He might not want to do what you come up with, but he's open to considering anything and everything."

"There aren't that many leaders in our army like that," I said. "We've become slaves to our doctrine or procedures. That stagnates growth."

"Yep."

"I am just surprised that the senior leaders turned him loose. Essentially, they let him do what he wanted," I said.

"Well, he didn't exactly ask, but Petraeus loved him, and for the most part, Colonel Gass did let him run free," Ken said.

"Okay, where was I?" Schiller said, sitting back down at the table and handing me a soda. "The first night at Shell, I guess."

"Yes sir," I answered, eager for him to continue the story.

"And at that time, I was still droning across the desert in a convoy," Ken said, rolling his eyes. "The boss was heeerrre." Ken held his hand out flat and above the table about a foot. "And I was heeerrre." He placed his other hand behind the first and placed it flat on the table. "Eating dust and chasing the boss," he added. "It must be good to be king."

Schiller laughed at him. As he popped the top on his drink, he said, "Worrell and his guys had already refueled and shut down in the ravine while Doug and I had made the call to General Freakley. We got gas, then parked our steed with the rest of the Annihilator Troop birds."

He employed the cavalry vernacular with ease. Schiller had completely bought into the cavalry mentality, and his troopers loved him for it. He never went anywhere without his Stetson hat. He wore spurs at all formations and called the helicopter a steed, and he did not get in and out of the steed. Rather, he mounted and dismounted.

Schiller continued.

"We unloaded our gear; then I went over to speak with Worrell about establishing a security plan for the night. We were on our own in Indian country, and I didn't want to get surprised by the enemy. After speaking with Worrell, I returned to the helicopter to find Doug bent over, driving a tent stake into the rocky ground.

"He looked up at me with sweat running down his forehead and reiterated, 'I hate this fucking country.'

"'Doug, thanks for setting the tent up. I'm sorry I wasn't here to help,' I told him, in genuine appreciation of what he had done for me.

"'No problem, sir. The aircraft is good to go, now!' Doug said. Then he added, 'You over-torqued it when you landed. Don't worry—I got Tom Castagna to come do the visual inspection. It's okay to fly,' he concluded."

Doug was happy at the opportunity to jab Schiller a bit, which demonstrated that Schiller was anything but sensitive to sarcasm and criticism. He could take it as well as he dished it out.

Despite reducing some of the Kiowa's weight, Schiller had not been able to put his complete weight-reduction program into place yet. The helicopter was heavy and power was limited. Landings required more power, especially in brownout conditions. The pilot had to finesse the bird to remain within the torque limitations in that environment. Fortunately, Schiller just barely exceeded the power limit, so it only required a visual inspection of the drive train by a maintenance test pilot. The Annihilator Troop maintenance officer, Tom Castagna, took a look and deemed it good to go.

Picking up the story, Schiller returned to the conversation between Doug and him.

"'Tom said to tell you to just let me fly and all will be okay,' Doug lied, and snickered.

"'Yeah, and if we had to shoot something, we'd never kill it,' I shot back.

"Doug rolled his eyes at me and drove the final tent stake into the ground.

"It was late afternoon by that point, and the sun was beginning to near the western horizon.

"We gathered all the pilots together and reviewed the security plan for the night," Schiller continued. "We were well out of contact with the rest of the division. I knew 3rd Infantry was about ten miles up the road, which was somewhat comforting, but if we were attacked on our perimeter, we'd be on our own. I wanted all the men to clearly understand their responsibilities for the night. As the sun went down, the temperature dropped with it. It had been scorching hot all day, but it was cold as hell once the sun went down. It was time for a cigar."

Schiller carefully spread his jacket out on the ground so he could safely lay his pistol parts out on it. He planned to clean his pistol, eat an MRE, and smoke a stogie.

"'Doug, did you check the .50 cal.?' I asked him.

"'Yes, sir. It was dirty as hell. I did what I could to clean her out, but you know how that goes in this dusty-ass environment,' Doug replied.

"'Yep.'

"We spent that night wondering how the war would proceed," Schiller said. "We really had no idea how hard of a fight the enemy would put up."

That night was peaceful. The men slept well, getting some much-needed rest in the utter silence of the desert. In contrast, the next day FARP Shell became as busy as a metropolitan airport. "The next morning, the rest of the squadron began to arrive," Schiller said. "It was awesome to stand there and watch our cavalrymen fly in."

"Yep. That's when we rolled in as well," Ken said, "filthy and exhausted!"

"And then seventy-two Apaches descended upon us—all three battalions' worth," Schiller said.

Throughout the day, helicopters and vehicles swarmed FARP Shell. Once the division tactical command post arrived, they set up their radios and equipment, and word began to spread that a storm was brewing.

"We got there just ahead of the Apaches. They flew right over us as they came in," Ken said.

"Yep," concurred Schiller, "and right after you guys arrived, the sky began to slowly change colors. By late afternoon, the sun seemed to just disappear, though not behind any visible clouds. It just seemed to dissipate and was suddenly gone. The sky was opaque and the winds carried sand with them to the east. Once we finalized the security plan for that second night, we walked out of our command post and discovered a sky unlike anything I've ever seen before in my life. It had a burnt orange hue and visibility was quickly deteriorating. The sky appeared to be descending upon us like a sheet that had been thrown up into the air and was slowly floating down on top of us. Soldiers stood out in the desert in groups, pointing at it. No one had ever seen anything like that. Within minutes, a westerly wind began to beat the rotor blades of the parked helicopters. They flopped up and down with the gusts. We knew we were in for a long night.

"As Slifko told you last night, we had bought small pup tents, which were really nice to have. With darkness came winds like I had never felt before. Doug and I huddled together in our tent, literally holding it down with our bodies. We weathered the storm in our tents for three days. We only left the tent to check the helicopters and each other.

"Every time we'd get a really heavy blast of wind, Doomsday would say, '*I hate this fucking country.*' Once the storm cleared, the skies opened up, and a light breeze accompanied sunshine. Every crevasse in every helicopter was filled with sand. We spent the entire day recovering from the storm, and that night was the night of the disastrous 11th Regiment deep attack; the one in which they were shot to pieces.

"But we weren't immune to mishaps and accidents in the 101st either. We had two hard landings and several other incidents. By the second night at FARP Shell, Major General Petraeus restricted our night flights. Fortunately, no one was killed, but General Petraeus wasn't going to keep risking it. It was an embarrassing predicament," he said. "I felt like our commanding general had lost confidence in his aviation units. We were crashing helicopters landing and taking off in the desert sand under night vision goggles. Restricting us to only flying during daylight hours put us at higher risk to being shot by the enemy because they could see us in the daytime."

Schiller had just left the 160th, which proudly proclaimed, "We Own the Night." They prided themselves in using the cover of darkness as an advantage over the enemy. Now, justifiably so, our own leaders were limiting night flights. The night was our friend, but could also be our enemy. Relatively speaking, we did own the night. No army in the world could do what we did at night, but it had killed a lot of aviators over the years and scared the rest half to death. Combine the desert sand and dust with a moonless night and you get a scary situation, but it can be conquered. Schiller knew better than anyone that the only way to truly own it was to get out there and fly in it, but that option had been taken away for the time being.

Schiller continued. "The next morning, March 27th, I guess it was, Ban'shee Troop was first out the door, doing reconnaissance. They pushed up near An Najaf that morning, and just before noon, Ken came to find me."

"Yeah, Ban'shee Troop had just had a couple aircraft shot up," Ken said. "You said, 'Bummer! Is everyone okay?' like it was no big deal."

"I was concerned, but I didn't want anyone to think that I was risk averse. I certainly didn't want anyone to get shot, but I also wanted our cavalrymen to know that I understood that there was a price to aggressively hunting and attacking the enemy," Schiller said.

"I told you that the Ban'shees were out doing reconnaissance. They were over to the east, in a small village just south of An Najaf, and they ran into a Fedayeen paramilitary force. Jeff Cowan and Tim Merrell were on their way to brief you, and I wanted you to know what was up before they got there," Hawley said.

Captain Jeff Cowan was the Ban'shee Troop Commander. A very competent officer, Jeff was a graduate of North Georgia College, my alma mater. Chief Warrant Officer Four Timothy Merrell was Jeff's troop standardization instructor pilot.

"You asked me what I thought we should do next," Hawley said to Schiller.

"And what did you say?" Schiller said.

47

"I told you that I wanted your approval to continue conducting reconnaissance in that area, to see if we can flush them out," Hawley said.

"Right, and I told you that I got the impression that you had already given the troop commanders that very guidance," Schiller said.

"Weeellll," Hawley said. "Technically, I had, but you are the boss and you really needed to approve it."

"But you knew that I trusted you and had empowered you to make decisions. You know that I want you, and you too, Jimmy," he said, turning his attention to me, "to act without hesitation based on my intent.

"I completely agreed with you that morning. We needed to press hard and not let up. Our mission was to protect the FARP, and those enemy forces weren't too far from Shell. The bad guys had to know that we weren't afraid of a fight. So, I wanted to go flush them out," he said.

Schiller turned to me, then spoke of Ken as if he weren't there. "Ken really got it," he said. "I knew he did, but I wanted to reiterate my aggressive philosophy to him, especially since we'd just had a few helicopters shot up. The guys needed to know that that would not intimidate me. I knew that my reaction would permeate through the rest of the squadron. If I was timid then, they would be timid as well. If I was aggressive, they would be aggressive."

"Oh, I knew you were aggressive," Ken said. "No doubt about that."

Schiller then described how Jeff Cowan and Tim Merrell had approached him that day. Cowan reached out to shake Schiller's hand. Schiller grasped his hand with his arm fully extended. Then, when they clasped hands, Schiller pulled Cowan toward him. Cowan awkwardly stumbled, almost falling into Schiller. Schiller burst out laughing. The event clearly demonstrated that Schiller was not upset or concerned with a troop commander who had just gotten several of his helicopters shot up. His joking around at that moment was purposefully done.

Jeff Cowan placed a tattered map down and said, "Sir, we were conducting reconnaissance right over here," pointing to a spot on the map.

Schiller acknowledged the location, then grabbed a campstool and sat down. "Great work, Jeff. How bad are the airplanes shot up?"

"Not bad, sir. We'll need a little time to patch them up, replace a few rotor blades, track and balance them, and we'll be ready to go," Jeff said.

"Are the men shaken up?" Schiller asked.

"No, not really," he said. Then holding his hands up and making air quotation signs, he added, "It was their first encounter with *real* combat."

"Did you shoot back?" Schiller asked.

"No, sir," Jeff responded sheepishly as if he already knew where Schiller was going with the question.

"You know you have the inherent right to self-defense within the rules of engagement, right?" Schiller said, desiring that Cowan clearly understood that that's what he expected.

"Yes, sir."

"Okay," Schiller said, having made his point. "Let's continue to press the enemy. Now, you know where they are. Get your next team out there and don't let up. Major Hawley will make sure Condor Troop is ready to go when your shift is over. He'll brief them up on everything you guys have seen. Now, let's go kick some ass."

"Roger, sir," Cowan said, folding his map.

"That afternoon, we received a warning order that the division was going to put us under the operational control of 1st Brigade 'Bastogne,'" Schiller told me.

Colonel Ben Hodges commanded Bastogne. Only six days prior, Hodges had been injured in Kuwait when one of his own soldiers, Sergeant Hasan Akbar, threw grenades into sleeping tents, and fired his rifle at fellow soldiers in the ensuing chaos. Akbar fatally shot Captain Christopher Seifert in the back, and a grenade killed Air Force Major Gregory Stone. Fourteen other Bastogne troopers were injured, including Hodges and his brigade executive officer. The fragging attack was felt throughout the entire division.

"Once we got word that we were about to be cut to Bastogne, we sent a liaison officer," he said, then looked me directly in the eye. "You really need to understand how I feel about liaisons, Jimmy. They are crucial to our success and our reputation. I believe that we *must* send our best officers to represent our unit. I let Ken pick them," he said, nodding at Ken, "but I watched who he chose very carefully. For Bastogne, we sent Captain Marek Wiernuz.

"Marek is an exceptionally talented young officer who had just been recently promoted to captain when we sent him to Bastogne. He has the brass balls of a feisty seasoned captain. I like him because he doesn't take crap from anyone, and he's a warfighter. He's my kind of officer.

"We sent John Rowell, our Australian exchange officer, to Strike. Rowely, as we call him, is another great officer. When he came to us, he needed to go to Fort Rucker and get a transition to the Kiowa Warrior helicopter. I told him that he could go to war with us and worry about flying later or he could remain back in the States and go to Rucker to get the aircraft transition. He said, *'I'm going to war with you!'*

"We sent Captain Adam Frederick to the Rakkasans. Adam came to us out of the advanced course, ready to take troop command. Of course, he is now commanding Ban'shee Troop, but he was our liaison to 3rd Brigade Rakkasan. Adam is a stud," Schiller said.

Ken broke in. "We have a stable of very good captains," he said. "Studs."

I completely understood Schiller's point. Over the course of my career, I had seen units send weak officers to serve as liaisons because they wanted to keep their best talent in their own headquarters.

"So, we sent Marek up to Bastogne to start planning with them, and Ken and I flew up there the following day to check in with Colonel Hodges and get his intent for the fight," Schiller said. "After speaking with Colonel Hodges, I left Marek with my intent; then Ken and I flew back to Shell. We were to begin taking An Najaf the next morning.

"The battle for An Najaf began on March 31st. We divvied up the squadron. Each of our air cavalry troops was assigned to each of their battalion task forces, of which there were three: 1-327th Infantry 'Bulldog,' 2-327th 'No Slack,' and 3-327th 'Battle Force.' I used my team as a swing team, capable of going wherever I needed to go, versus fighting with a specific troop. That gave me the flexibility to see the whole battlefield, as well as conduct reconnaissance of the surrounding terrain in order to influence future operations. I could move ahead and find the enemy, so we'd know what was next.

"An Najaf was densely populated, but it wasn't a huge town, so we had to establish strict graphic control measures to keep the troops separated," Schiller said.

Graphic control measures were labeled lines on a map that could be used as a quick reference in order to coordinate and synchronize operations.

"All the aircrews launched with a common set of graphics on their maps. I went out a little bit later because I wanted to let the troop commanders get out there and do their job. It was important that they know I had confidence in them. Ban'shee Troop made contact with the enemy right away. They didn't hold back either. I guess they were pissed off from being shot up the previous day," he said, then paused. "It was a thing of beauty. They were aggressive. They took it to the enemy.

"Over the radio, I heard General Petraeus taking reports and giving guidance. He was on the move, so I decided to get up in the air. I told Doug to gather his gear and meet me at the aircraft. It was anyone's guess what General Petraeus might ask over the radio, so I wanted to be in a position to answer any questions he might have about the fight. Each of Bastogne's battalions had a mission to seize an objective in and around An Najaf. They fought their way to those objectives with our air troops over their heads, clearing rooftops, streets, and alleyways as they went. We served as their eyes from above.

"One of the Ban'shee Troop lieutenants called me on the radio," Schiller said.

"'Saber Six, this is Ban'shee 2-6, sport report, over,' he said.

"'Ban'shee 2-6, this is Saber Six, send your report,' I answered.

"'Saber Six, I have multiple weapons caches, two ZU-23 antiaircraft guns, and several technical vehicles located at…,' and he gave me the grid coordinates. 'Request permission to engage.'

"Thrilled that they were doing exactly what Bastogne needed them to do, I cleared him to shoot the caches and destroy the guns," Schiller told me.

"Suddenly, the radios buzzed with traffic. Our cavalrymen were finding enemy forces everywhere. I remember hearing someone transmit over the squadron net, 'Taking fire!' so I knew that the enemy was fighting back as well.

"The teams were doing great, so I decided to conduct reconnaissance around the periphery of the town. Doug and I found huge caches of weapons and munitions on the outskirts of town. I was amazed at how many and how large they were. There were literally piles of stuff stacked up everywhere," he said.

"Like, how big?" I asked him.

"They were too big to fit into an American two-car garage, floor to ceiling," he said.

"Wow," I responded.

"Some of them were guarded by a couple of guys, others were completely unmonitored. We began sending grids to their locations to Bastogne and asking permission to blow them up. They told us to go ahead, so we shot them with rockets and .50 caliber. It wasn't long before there were numerous streams of black smoke billowing into the air hundreds of feet high. It looked like something you'd see in a movie after a battle.

"We found Roland radar dishes and Frog missiles, large-caliber artillery guns, vehicles with antiair guns mounted on them. The country was set for a war, but it didn't seem like their soldiers were overly committed to the fight," Schiller said.

"Battle Force was moving slow, very deliberate, but we didn't see significant enemy forces in front of them. I felt like they could move faster, and if they did, it would enable us to envelop the town rather quickly. As we flew over Bastogne's tactical command post, I saw Major General Petraeus's vehicle. Ken and Tracy Owens were flying as my lead, so I told them I was landing to speak with Petraeus. Doug looked over at me and rolled his eyes, pissed off that I wanted to stop fighting to talk with the general.

"With my map in hand, I dismounted the helicopter, left it at idle, and told Doug that I would be right back. I took my helmet off, put my Stetson on, and walked over to Petraeus's vehicle. He was hunched over a map that covered the entire hood of his Humvee. Several officers and a civilian were gathered around the map. Seemingly impervious to the battle raging around us, General Petraeus turned and smiled broadly, which made me feel good.

"'Saber Six, I am glad you're here. Tell me, what are you seeing out there?' Petraeus asked.

"Before I could answer the question, Petraeus stopped me, 'I'm sorry Saber Six. This is Rick Atkinson from the *Washington Post.*'

"'Sir, it's nice to meet you. I read *Crusade* and the first part of *An Army at Dawn*, but the war interrupted me,' I said. 'I look forward to finishing it.'

"Atkinson was a small man, about Petraeus's size, carrying a simple little notepad and a short, tattered pencil. I couldn't help but think, if this guy can write as well as he does under these circumstances with such diminutive resources, he's pretty damn impressive," Schiller told me.

"Turning back to Petraeus, I told him that we could speed up our movement through the city. I explained that there was really nothing between us and the eastern edge of town. We had conducted reconnaissance all the way to the river, I told him, pointing at the map.

"'There are virtually no enemy forces to the north, on the east side of the town,' I told Petraeus. 'I can increase the pressure with my Kiowa teams to facilitate the ground movement.'

"As I spoke to him, we could hear secondary explosions going off. It sounded as if we were taking artillery fire. From where we stood, you could see smoke billowing up where we had blown caches, so Petraeus asked me if there were more caches out there.

"'Sir, we're destroying each one we find,' I told him. 'I think it's better that we blow them up as we go, so the enemy can't come back and use them later.'

"'Good,' he said, agreeing yet looking off into the distance as if pondering what to do next. He seemed somewhat vexed as to what to say or where to go at that time.

"'Sir, I know we can move faster and get this job done. I'm not convinced our guys are moving at the pace they should. We can keep the Fedayeen off balance if we can secure the city quickly,' I told him.

"'Steve, I want to take a look,' Petraeus suddenly said. 'Can I go up in your helicopter?'

"'That's a great idea, sir. I'll keep Ken here and you can go up with Tracy Owens, my instructor pilot. He's the best pilot in the squadron,' I said."

I could see Ken shaking his head and smiling as he sat beside me. Schiller continued.

"I knew that if we could get him up in a Kiowa, so he could see the battlefield from our vantage point, he would press the fight. Petraeus and I didn't really have a relationship at that point. It was like we were two dogs sniffing each other out. I was careful to try and read his body language and responses as I offered advice. I think he was trying to figure out how much he wanted to trust my advice. I say two dogs sniffing each other out, but he was a much bigger dog," he said, laughing.

"As Ken handed his helmet to Petraeus, he looked at me with a funny look as if to say, *Why the hell are you leaving me here, boss?* No aviator wants to be left behind," Schiller said.

"Ohhhh, noooo," Ken interjected, "I was thinking, *Who better than me to be left standing in the desert with no helmet.* Seriously, I was thinking, *He's the commanding general. Doesn't he have a flight helmet of his own in his vehicle? He does fly in a Black Hawk a lot.*"

"Anyway," Schiller continued. "General Petraeus strapped into the helicopter with Tracy Owens, and we took off. We flew all over town. We probably flew for well over an hour. I got the impression that he was gaining a much better perspective of the fight from the air. He asked a lot of questions and freely shared his insights with me. To me, it was exactly what he needed. The flight truly enabled him to see what a valuable asset we were to the ground forces. Our eyes and ears, our perception, was perhaps our most lethal weapon system. It also helped our relationship with the boss. We were gaining his trust. I saw a smile on his face when he got out of the helicopter and handed Ken his helmet.

"Ken got back into his Kiowa and, as soon as we took off, Ban'shee Troop called for us. They had been in a serious fight and had taken a lot of small arms fire. The team that called us needed to land and check the aircraft out; they asked if we could come relieve them, so we hauled ass over there.

"As soon as we took the fight from them, we began taking fire. Ken and Tracy took several rounds to their avionics compartment, near the tail boom and through their rotor blades as well. Doug and I took fire too, but they didn't hit us because I fly much more tactically than Tracy and Ken," Schiller said and bellowed out in laughter.

"Noooo," Ken said. "We were your lead, flying into the battle in front of you, and lower to the ground. It was our job to find the enemy and hammer them. Your job, as our wingman, was to cover us."

Then Ken looked at me and said, "You see how well he covered us. We were nearly shot down."

"Bullshit," Schiller said, still laughing at Ken. "You guys flew right into that mess."

Ken rolled his eyes.

"Doug was dying to kill the guys shooting at us," Schiller said. "He kept pointing all over the place and saying, 'Shoot them fuckers! Over there, down there, shoot them fuckers!' but they were in the city, so it was hard to find them. It was late afternoon by that point anyway. We'd been flying all day, and Bastogne had been fighting hard on the ground throughout the day. I had been listening in on their radio, so I knew they had decided to hold up where they were for the night. Ken's airplane was all shot up, Bastogne was stopping for the night, so I told Ken to head back to the assembly area. It was time to call it a day and check to see how much damage had been done to our helicopters."

"Quite a few of the helicopters had bullet holes that night," Ken said, "but nothing so bad that our sheet metal guys couldn't patch them up."

"How many rounds hit you?" I asked Schiller.

"I don't recall exactly. Most of the airplanes had eight or ten bullet holes in them," he said.

"Well, gents, that's it for me," Ken announced, getting up from the table. "I've got to head up to brigade. I'll see you at lunch, hopefully."

"Oh yeah, wouldn't want to miss sharing an MRE with you," Schiller said.

"I think we have some Scooby snacks that will get me by until dinner. No MRE for me today," Ken said and turned.

Schiller continued. "The following morning, April Fools' Day, we were up early and pressing on to the north. The fighting sort of picked up where we left off the previous evening," he said. "We had made it up to the huge graveyard. You've already heard the guys talk about that graveyard, I'm sure."

"Yes, sir," I replied. "I've seen pictures of it too."

"It was unbelievable, over five kilometers across," he said. "Anyway, Annihilator Troop got the mission to conduct reconnaissance of that cemetery. It was not like an American cemetery with headstones. It was complex terrain. There were structures all over the cemetery where enemy forces could hide. I decided to fly that mission with Annihilator. You met Curtis Phipps last night too. He's the Annihilator Troop Standardization Instructor Pilot. He flew as my lead that day. Do you remember Curtis?" he asked.

"Yes, sir," I said.

"You'll like him," Schiller said. "Curtis is a lean, mean fighting machine. Seriously, he's a commander's dream. I love a guy like Curtis. He's soft-spoken, but he's tough and aggressive. He maintains this perfect balance between ferociousness and modesty."

Curtis flew with one of the Annihilator Troop platoon leaders, Lieutenant Matthew Green. Curtis and Matt—a man crowding middle age, seasoned and shrewd, and a young lieutenant, raw and green, yet eager to learn—were a great pairing.

Returning to the fight, Schiller said, "As soon as we got to the cemetery, Doug and I saw some guys huddled around a small truck. I called Curtis, whose call sign was Annihilator 21, and said, 'Annihilator 21, this is Saber Six. I have several personnel to our ten o'clock in the vicinity of a pickup truck. It looks like they're loading something in the bed of the truck.'

"Curtis banked left to take a look and immediately located the enemy.

"When they saw that we were coming for them, two of the guys took off running for another truck," Schiller said. "It was a technical vehicle, a pickup sporting weapons. It had a big-ass ZU-23-2 antiaircraft gun mounted in the bed. That dang thing was a problem.

"Seeing the men running, Curtis called to me over the radio. 'I've got two guys running for that gun. I'm inbound!' he said, letting me know that he was going to shoot the two men.

"I radioed back to Curtis, '*Get 'em! I'll move to cover you.*'

"Curtis bumped and dove at the men. He let loose with the .50 caliber and killed both men instantly. Then before he broke off of the gun run, he shot a rocket and hit the truck dead center of the hood. It was an amazing engagement," Schiller added, clearly proud of his cavalrymen.

The weapon systems on an OH-58D Kiowa Warrior are fixed forward. To shoot a target, the pilot uses "Kentucky windage." The aircraft is manipulated in flight to aim the weapon systems, so Curtis had to put the helicopter in a position to shoot the two running men, and then quickly orient on the vehicle and shoot the rocket before getting too low to the ground. It took both agility and great marksmanship to execute the gun run.

"Then the philosopher, Dr. Doug, spoke up," Schiller said.

"'Sir, have I told you lately,' he paused for effect, 'I hate this fucking country!'

"While Curtis shot those two guys and their truck, the other two knuckleheads sprinted for cover. Curtis quickly spun back around and took a shot at them, but he wasn't in a good position to shoot. I had time to line up, so as soon as Curtis broke off the target and was out of the way, I was ready to shoot. The guys dove into the doorway of a crypt. This is the shot that everyone told you about last night. Just as they entered the door, I punched two rockets off, and the rockets followed them into the crypt. They never knew what hit them," Schiller said.

"Throughout the rest of the day, over seven hours of fighting, we fought with Fedayeen fighters in trucks with machine guns. It was as if they were sitting there waiting to shoot at Bastogne who was moving through the city, but they didn't expect us to show up to cover Bastogne's movement from the air. We'd fly right up on them and surprise them. They would try to shoot us, and we'd kill them. That went on all day long.

"Finally, that afternoon, I returned to FARP Shell for an update briefing with the staff," he said. "It gave me time to think. An Najaf had revealed three major lessons. First, we were shooting triple the amount of ammunition we initially thought we would. We needed to get ahead of this and find more ammo before we ran out. Second, the closer our FARP was to the fight, the quicker we could make turns between fighting and refueling and rearming. We needed to move our bivouac site closer to the fight to increase our response time. Third, maintenance was critical. We had to have a plan to keep the airplanes ready to fight. When I returned to the TOC, I made my priorities clear to the troop commanders and my staff: One) maintenance; Two) move the assembly area; Three) find more ammunition."

In the heat of battle, junior leaders and the staff often become completely focused on the current fight. They tend to get so caught up in trying to keep up with ongoing operations that they do not look ahead. Schiller understood that it was his role as the commander to assess their current situation and anticipate future requirements. That assessment enabled him to provide clear guidance and priorities to his staff and troop commanders.

"Helicopter maintenance was kicking our ass," he said. "We had two aircraft out of the fight due to the hard landings the day of the storm. Four helicopters were down due to combat damage, and components began to fail due to the harsh desert terrain—sand and dust," Schiller said.

"The guys were doing everything they could to stay in the fight despite damage to their helicopters," he said. "For example, during the battle that day, the enemy had shot a mortar round directly under Curtis Phipps and Lieutenant Green's helicopter. It blew the Plexiglas chin bubbles out, but that didn't stop them. Curtis flew back to the FARP, and he and Tom Castagna, the Annihilator Troop Maintenance Pilot, taped it up with 100 mph tape (duct tape); then he went right back into the fight.[3]

"Our machine guns were failing too, but we had spare parts and a .50 caliber is a simple gun, so we were able to keep repairing those. We established a twenty-four-hour maintenance cycle. Crew chiefs and maintenance pilots never stopped turning wrenches.

"Each night, we conducted an update briefing to review everything that had happened that day. Since the junior leaders, noncommissioned officers, and staff folks were not forward in the battle, they were only able to see the fight through a narrow lens. I felt that it was important to make sure everyone understood the big picture—knew exactly what was going on on the battlefield. I wanted them to know that our guys were kicking ass and making a difference in the fight. I wanted them to know that *they* were a huge part of that larger effort.

"I told my executive officer, Todd Royar, to find us another assembly area, closer to the fight and in a position that would serve us well in the coming days. Todd told me that he had already conducted a map reconnaissance based on what he believed the division had planned. All he needed to do was conduct an aerial reconnaissance to confirm the suitability of the proposed location," Schiller said. "Todd is one of the best officers in our army, the epitome of a great executive officer, anticipating the next move and taking action."

Todd Royar was a small, thin man. An introvert in a world of loud, often obnoxious cavalrymen. A meticulous planner, Todd had the tiniest handwriting I'd ever seen. Many aviators are somewhat obsessive-compulsive when it comes to their gear, notes, and workspaces, but Todd was a bit more extreme. He took meticulously neat notes and anticipated future requirements better than any staff officer I'd met. It's very difficult for a staff officer to get ahead of the commander, who is constantly out on the battlefield in the fight, consulting with other commanders. The commander has a firsthand view of operations. The staff, on the other hand, is in the rear trying to discern what is happening over the radios. It's difficult to pick up on the details and remain abreast of everything that is happening, but Todd did that amazingly well.

That night in the TOC, Schiller visualized the plan with his staff:

"I see us continuing up the highway. Most likely Al Hillah will be next and then Karbala," Schiller had said, pointing to a map. "Ken, which brigade will get the next fight?"

"Sir, I am not sure yet. It makes sense that Al Hillah will be next, but Strike is already planning for an attack on Karbala. I should know for sure tonight. I suggest we focus on the fight in Al Hillah and begin taking a cursory look at Karbala, but I'm going to get everyone ready to move the assembly area by the day after tomorrow. Oh and, sir, you have an Associated Press interview in the morning."

"You've got to be kidding me!" Schiller groaned. "Thanks a lot, Ken."

Schiller explained to me, "I didn't really want to do an interview. The timing wasn't great, but I had planned to fly out to the fight a little later the following morning, so I had time to do it. I wanted the troop commanders to get to fight their teams without me hovering right over their shoulder. They needed to know that I trusted them implicitly. Going out later in the morning would also allow me to spend some time with our planners going over the order of battle for the upcoming fights."

"How did the interview go?" I asked.

"Great, actually. It was Dana Lewis with NBC. We really hit it off and have since kept in touch. He's a super guy. NBC did a piece on the squadron that was very well done. We have a copy of it on the computer. You can watch it later," he said.

What Schiller didn't know is that I had watched the news piece on television before deploying. It captured the cavalry mentality perfectly. "Cowboys over Iraq," Dana Lewis had called 2-17 CAV. "They know the deal," Schiller had told Mr. Lewis in the interview, referring to Iraqi forces. "We're gonna wreak havoc on them."

Schiller resumed his story. "The next morning, I took a close look at the work our planners were doing. The Rakkasans were planning an operation to take Baghdad International Airport. I thought the 3rd Infantry Division or the Special Forces might get that mission instead of the 101st, but either way, once it came to it, I didn't think that mission would be a lot of drama. What did concern me was Objective Bears."

"What was Objective Bears?" I asked.

"Objective Bears was an area near Taji. It was a very complex, built-up urban area, and intelligence suggested that it was heavily defended with a concentration of enemy fighters all over it. If the division was tasked to seize Objective Bears, I knew they would send us in first. I wanted to make sure we planned that mission right," he said.

"Over the next two days we cleared Najaf out," he continued. "Then we moved the squadron to a bivouac site that Todd Royar and Ken had picked just south of Najaf. I moved the squadron up there to live alone, detached from the rest of the division."

"Did you like being away from everyone else?" I asked. "Didn't you worry about security?"

"Yes and no, but hold that thought. I've got to piss," Schiller said, and stood up. "I'll be right back."

As I sat there, digesting everything he'd told me, John Rowell emerged from the TOC.

"Morning, sir," he said.

"Hey, Rowely."

He tapped a pack of cigarettes, preparing to smoke. "Saw you with the SCO," he said. "You talking shop? I don't want to interrupt."

"No. The SCO did my initial counseling earlier this morning, then I asked him to talk me through the ground war from his perspective, so we've been out here talking ever since," I said.

"Mind if I join you, mate?" he asked.

"No. I don't care."

I had heard a great deal about John Rowell through the men. He had a tremendous reputation. With sandy blond hair, standing over six feet tall and fit, he was a handsome man with an accent everyone enjoyed hearing. For whatever reason, I viewed his personality as a stereotypical California surfer dude, completely laid back and unexcitable; only, John Rowell was capable of becoming G.I. Joe at a moment's notice. John was indeed a type B personality, which gave great balance to our team of heavily weighted type As. He smiled and laughed easily, and rarely showed anger or frustration, despite Doug Ford's incessant attempts to get under his skin.

Everyone called him Rowely, except Schiller, who called him Johnny. Rowely grew up in poverty. His parents divorced when he was three. His mother did the best she could, but when Rowely turned twelve, his mother and stepfather sent him to a boarding school. Much like the American army for me, the Australian military was a way out for Rowely. Both of us were also enlisted as soldiers before we received a commission. Rowely and I hit it off from the start.

"So, Rowely, have you enjoyed your assignment with the CAV?" I asked him.

"Bloody hell. It's been amazing," he said, eyebrows lifted high. "Incredible!"

Having relieved himself, Schiller walked back into the courtyard. "Johnny Rowell," Schiller announced as he approached.

"Hello, sir. Mind if I join you? I don't want to intrude."

"Not at all," Schiller said, sitting back down, straddling the bench. "I was just about to get to the part about you anyway."

Rowely raised his eyebrows, "About me. What's that?" he asked.

"Strike and Karbala," Schiller said.

"Oh, bloody hell. That's one for the history books," Rowely said.

"You tell Major Blackmon about it," Schiller said.

THE BATTLE OF KARBALA

"Well," Rowely said. "The fighting in Hillah was dying down, and I was at the ruins by the car park, outside the Ba'ath Party officers' mess. We had split the tactical command post up at that point. Major Hawley was at another location, up the road a bit.

"He called me on the radio and told me to get my shit together. He said you were coming to get me in twenty minutes,"[1] Rowely said, nodding to Schiller.

"Major Hawley told me that you needed me at Karbala, the following day. I thought, *what the hell?*" Rowely said, his eyes wide open. "I was excited to be in the mix and thrilled that you were happy to count on me to be your eyes and ears in the forward battle, but hell's bells, mate. I knew that Karbala was going to be no small deal. In the back of my mind, I was wondering what the hell I was going to be faced with. I knew that the town was right by the Karbala Gap, where the intel lads had said we were likely to get chem'ed and hit with Frog missiles. It was also the place where the 11th Regiment had their arses handed to them," he said, then tapped a pack of cigarettes against the palm of his right hand.

"I packed my shit," he said, then lit a cigarette. He squinted as he blew smoke out of the side of his mouth, then looked at Schiller, and continued. "Sure enough, I saw you flying in, coming to get me in a Kiowa."

Then Rowely turned directly toward me and winked. "I could tell it was him by the way he came flying in. It was more aggressive than most. Then this figure dismounted the helo like John Wayne, spoke with some lads, and patted some backs. Finally, he made his way over to me, stuck his hand out to shake, and I fell for it. I grasped his hand, and he snatched me into him. I fell forward, looking like a jackass, and he laughed at me. We're on the eve of a major battle, and the SCO is horsing around."

Rowely reached over and slapped the SCO on the shoulder. "You've got to love the man. Anyway, he told me that he needed me at Karbala with Strike the following day.

"Fucking tomorrow!" Rowely said in a high-pitched tone, as if it still surprised him. "It was nearly lunch that day, and Strike was told to take Karbala the next day."

I am not sure why, but it struck me as interesting that our Australian exchange officer was so close to everyone in the unit, particularly Schiller, whom he obviously admired. Were it not for his uniform and Aussie accent, one would never know that he was not American. We treat our imbedded allies well, but they generally stick together when serving in a larger headquarters. Rowely was the only one in our unit, but he wasn't merely accepted by the team. He was one of our best—a go-to guy for the commander.

"The boss," Rowely said, nodding to Schiller, then trying to speak with an American accent while emulating Schiller, "'Johnny,' he told me, 'it's gunna be a big fight. I need you up there on the ground, managing the battle, telling our boys what they need to know as they enter the fight.'"

Returning to his own voice, Rowely continued. "Then he looked me in the eyes with this serious look on his face and said, 'You know the deal.'"

"Sir," Rowely said, turning his attention to me. "You have to understand what *you know the deal* means."

Schiller watched him with a thin smile, obviously enjoying the story.

"*You know the deal* is Saber Six's way of giving guidance. He is never short on mentoring, providing direction, or leading. In fact, those are some of his greatest strengths. Perhaps it's because he does so much of those things that we all know what *you know the deal* means. It means to get beside the ground force commander and his planners and make damn sure they use us right from the get-go. Get us, the CAV, as far forward in the battle as you possibly can. Make bold decisions early, just make them—you know what to do! Lean forward in the saddle and design the most aggressive air cavalry plan in the history of modern warfare. Then get out there and execute it with panache. That's what *you know the deal* means," he said, content with himself. He took another draw of the cigarette, looked at the end of it, rubbed it out on the table, and began fieldstripping it.

Schiller was laughing at this point. He appeared almost embarrassed. Rowely continued.

"Saber Six dropped me off at the assembly area, and one of the pilots from Ban'shee Troop flew me up to join Strike. We flew on the western side of An Najaf, then up the river. I was going to Al Kifl, which was north of An Najaf and just east of the Euphrates River.

"We called Strike's TOC on the way up there and requested coordinates for their exact location," he said. "They seemed uninterested when we told them we were coming in to land. I saw where their headquarters was set up, in this industrial complex, so we shot an approach beside the highway, in a large green field.

"As soon as our skids hit the ground, I was out of the helicopter and heading toward their TOC. We landed across the road, so I had to cross a field, then cross the road, and walk across yet another open area to get to them. They were set up in a rather large group of buildings.

"I took my flight helmet off, so I could hear. My M4 was slung across my body, at the ready. I got to the berm of the highway and saw a car still burning. It appeared that a tank or something had actually driven over the top of it and then through some barriers that had been set up to block the road. The thing that stuck with me, and always will, is the smell. I could still smell cordite in the air, but I also smelt something else," he said.

"What's that?" I asked.

"It was the smell of a significant gun battle still lingering in the air—flesh, bone, and blood mixed together with the smell of cordite.

"I will never forget that smell," he said. "As I began across the road, I saw a severed foot still inside a shoe on the side of the highway. I figured, or hoped, that the shooting had stopped, since I was out in the open and quite vulnerable. Still, I began jogging across the road. I didn't want to look like a clown to the Joes [young soldiers] across the road, but deep inside, I wanted to sprint like hell to their location.

"I tried to lock eyes with the guys on the perimeter across the road, because I was wearing an Australian uniform. Bottom line: I was armed, and I was coming at them in a uniform that the dudes at the gate, behind an M240B machine gun I might add, had never seen before. To make matters worse, it was not as if the guy on the radio, the one that I had spoken to as we flew in, alerted them that an Aussie was coming in. In fact, I was sure that he had not. These lads had just fought their way all the way through An Najaf.

"Fortunately for me, they could not have cared less if an officer in a funny-looking uniform or otherwise was being dropped off in a helo. I looked at the two blokes, changed the grip on my M4 from the pistol grip to the stock so I looked less threatening, and made sure my other hand was visible as well. They looked at me, but I didn't see their heads or the barrels of their weapons move as I got closer to them, so I was relieved."

"Did you really think they'd confuse you with an Iraqi and shoot you?" I asked.

"I didn't want to find out. As I walked up, I could see that they weren't fussed with me at all. I kept jogging until I was inside their perimeter. Then I could hear music. I couldn't believe what I was hearing, what I was experiencing. It was AC/DC, an Australian band, mind you, and the music was blaring out of speakers set up in the back of a truck."

"Sounds like something you'd see in a movie," I said.

"Exactly! I had just jumped out of an American helo in an unsecure landing zone, rifle at the ready," he said excitedly. "I had jogged through the smell of burning vehicles, flesh, and fuel. Bits of someone lay on the road. I was waiting for bullets to continue flying through the air at any second. Then I ran into a group of American lads lying about on their trucks guzzling cans of Kufa Cola while AC/DC blared off the back of a truck. It was insane. Oh, and it was the second time I'd heard Americans listening to AC/DC. The 101st lads seemed to like that Aussie band.

"What a scene. I saw soldiers walking out of a large building with cartons of Kufa Cola on their shoulders and then loading them into their vehicles. The compound the 101st had selected for their temporary head-quarters turned out to be the abandoned factory of the largest soft drink company in Iraq, Kufa Cola.

"There are many things in life that you can't quite describe," Rowely said. "At least not adequately. Going for months on end drinking nothing but water, in the midst of a war no less, and happening upon a soft drink factory is one of them. Those lads needed some time out, and they deserved every one of those dozen or so cans of cola they drank. What a scene," he repeated.

"I went straight to the command post and found the operations officer. Petraeus had just ordered these lads to attack Karbala, the third largest city in Iraq. I rolled up my sleeves and went to work. Because the city was so large and complex, we needed good graphic control measures— common graphics—off which to fight. We divided the city up by grid and numbered the sections on a map—a horse blanket, as we call it. It was classic 101st, American style, no fanfare, no bullshit, just the basics of combat planning," he said. "But everyone had the same graphics, and it worked like a charm.

"And that's how I made linkup with Strike," Rowely said.

Priding myself as somewhat of a connoisseur of storytelling, I was impressed with Rowely's storytelling ability. He was a colorful, charismatic guy.

"Speaking of soft drinks, I think I'll have one. How about you lads? Sir? You want one?" Rowely asked as he rose from the picnic table.

"No. I'm good," I said.

"No, thanks, Johnny," Schiller said.

It was noon and shadows were dwindling. The heat was already bearing down on us, but Schiller pulled his shorts up a few inches and extended his leg out on the bench to get some sun, so I assumed we were committed to the rest of the story.

"He seems like a really good dude," I told Schiller as Rowely walked out of earshot.

"He's shit hot," Schiller said. "As good as they come." Then he straightened his back and sighed, flexing his shoulders to stretch his cramped muscles. Many of the guys called Schiller "the Old Man," as soldiers often call their commander. He was only thirty-nine, but I suppose that's old to a seventeen-year-old private.

"Strike briefed their mission in the Kufa soda factory on the evening of April 4th," Schiller said, continuing with the story. "Ken and I flew up there to receive the briefing with all of the other battalion commanders in the brigade. 9th battalion, 101st Aviation Regiment was Strike's habitually aligned assault battalion, but for some reason 5th battalion, one of the other assault battalions, was tasked to support them for the Karbala fight."

"So that was Lieutenant Colonel Laura Richardson's battalion?" I asked.

"Yep," he said.

Laura Richardson commanded 5-101 Aviation, which was composed of three Black Hawk companies. Her husband, Lieutenant Colonel James "Jim" Richardson, commanded 3-101, an Apache attack battalion.

"Strike planned to conduct an air assault as a part of their mission to seize Karbala," Schiller said. "I took a look at the landing zones they had selected and told Colonel Anderson that we should look at some alternate ones closer to the city. Laura shot me a stern look and then said that the landing zones were outside of small arms and RPG range."

"So, you pissed her off," I said.

"It's not the first person he's pissed off, mate," Rowely said, returning to the table. "The boss has a knack for candid feedback. Sometimes the truth hurts."

"I was very professional," Schiller said, defending himself. "In no way did I intend to embarrass her in front of Colonel Anderson. I told her that I understood her logic. A Black Hawk from another unit had been shot down just two days prior; however, I told her that if I sent my scouts in first and they determined that the edge of town was secure, free of enemy forces capable of repelling the assault force, then we should land her Black Hawks closer to the edge of town. Then I pointed to an area close to town and said, 'Like right here.'"

"What did she say to that?" I asked.

"She told me that she didn't intend to land her helicopters anywhere near that town,"[2] Schiller said. "I thought the landing zones her guys had selected were good as a backup. If the enemy on the edge of town proved formidable, they would be fine, but I felt like we needed to have a plan to land the Strike soldiers as close to town as possible. Landing them several hundred meters outside town in the middle of the desert would mean that they would have to cross that open space in the face of the enemy. I planned to take my Kiowas in first to see if there were enemy forces there. If so, we'd kill them. If not, then we could land the Blackhawks right by the city wall, so that Strike soldiers could run fifty meters or so and get behind cover, gain a toehold on the city right away."

"Did you push the issue?" I asked.

"No, because I thought I could convince her once we got out there," he said.

"I see."

"The battle for Karbala began the following morning at 9:00," Schiller said.

"So that was April 5th, right?" I asked.

"Yeah, the fifth. I gave Annihilator Troop the air assault security mission. They were to go in ahead of the Black Hawks and recon the landing zones, then push into the edge of the city and find the enemy. I decided to fly with them because I still felt like I could convince Laura to land closer to the city if we determined that there were no enemy forces near the landing zones. And if there were enemy forces, we could kill them and then I'd have her land them closer.

"We got in there early, well ahead of the air assault, and we couldn't find any enemy on the edge of town. While Annihilator pushed deeper into the city searching for the enemy, I called Laura on the radio and told her that there were no enemy forces near the edge of the city. Hell, there weren't any people there at all. It was a ghost town on that side of the city," Schiller said.

"What did she say?"

"She acknowledged my radio call, but her Black Hawks landed almost two miles from town. It took several hours just to get the entire battalion task force on the ground. They had to make several trips with the Black Hawks, and then we watched them slog across the hot-ass desert with heavy loads in near one-hundred-degree heat. I was furious," Schiller said.

"Wow," I said, surprised that the air commanders weren't able to work it out on the radio and land the Strike soldiers closer.

"It's our job as aviators to help our ground forces out," Schiller said. "We watched Strike soldiers just sit down in the desert and do the ruck-sack flop on the ground. They looked like turtles, belly side up, as they lay back on their rucksacks. Strike wound up with several heat casualties. The whole day was spent trudging across the desert just to get to the edge of town."

"You're kidding," I said.

"No. I'm not kidding. That movement sucked. We're lucky that they didn't have to fight their way into town," he said. "Meanwhile, Annihilator was getting after it deeper inside the city. They found a military compound with antiaircraft guns, trucks with machine guns mounted on them, and several ammunition caches. I could see them diving and shooting. Then I'd hear the explosions."[3]

"I'm sure you were tempted to go over and help them out," I said.

He smiled. "I took a peek a few times, but I needed to be there to cover Strike's movement to the city. I also tried to resist taking things away from my troop commanders. They needed to know that I trusted them," he said.

Doug seemed to indicate that Schiller was tough on the troop commanders; perhaps he was, but he clearly empowered them.

"It was hot as hell that day," Schiller said. "In fact, we had the FARP set up on a farm just outside town, and while Doug and I were filling up with gas, we took turns getting IVs just to replace the fluids we were losing."

"Seriously?" I asked.

"Yeah. Remember now, we were still flying in our MOPP suits at that point. We had all of our gear on, our body armor over that, and the MOPP suit over the body armor," he said. "It was hot as balls.

"After getting fuel and ammo in the FARP, Doug and I were flying back to the fight when suddenly we started taking small arms fire from some rooftops. It was over 3-502nd Infantry Battalion, Widowmaker's, area," Schiller said. "It was clear that there were a lot of enemy forces there because we took machine gun fire from everywhere all at once."

"Did any hit your helicopter?" I asked.

"Not that we could tell," he said and then began to describe the area. "Karbala runs generally from southeast to northwest with a natural break in the middle of town."

"What do you mean *break?*" I asked.

"Just a big open area with a water tower. The open area was a dump, where it appeared everyone in the city took their trash. It provided us with an area inside the town where there were no houses. It was some-what of a safe haven in the middle of an otherwise contested area. Doug and I flew in there, into the open area, so we wouldn't be shot while we tried to determine where the guys were that had shot at us."

"Weren't you restricted in that little area?"

"No. It was big enough to fly around in. It was actually ideal for what we needed to do," he said.

"About that time, we got a call from someone in Widowmaker," Schiller said. "I don't know who it was, just a guy on the radio with a Widowmaker call sign. He said that they were taking a lot of machine-gun fire from the buildings to their front. I saw the Widowmaker soldiers on the edge of the city, so immediately I knew that they were describing the same general area where we had taken fire as we flew over. I had my map out studying it as they described the area. Doug was flying at that time, but I folded my map up and placed it on the dash, then told him to give me the controls so I could fly. He did, and then he took the map and grabbed a pack of MRE crackers and peanut butter, which he had stashed on the dash when we took off that morning. On the verge of a major fight, Doug is squirting peanut butter on crackers and stuffing them into his mouth. I laughed and shook my head at him. You've gotta love Doug."

"I suppose he didn't want to go into a fight on an empty stomach," I said.

"That or he didn't want to go down hungry," Schiller said, rolling his eyes.

As I listened to the rest of the story, I could picture it all unfolding in my mind's eye:

"What are you going to do?" Doug asked Schiller when he took the flight controls.

"Arm me," Schiller said, meaning to ensure that his gun and rockets were ready to fire. "I'm going to fly in there fast and low. You know those guys can't stand it. They will shoot at us, and we'll find them so we can kill them."

"Sir," Doug said, looking straight at Schiller as he armed the .50 caliber. "Don't get me killed. I have a wife and kids at home," he added, and then prepared to bite into the peanut butter cracker. But he stopped just before the cracker entered his mouth and said, "Have I told you lately that I hate this fucking country?"

"Doug, I have no intention of dying today," Schiller said, then banked the helicopter hard left and prepared to fly low and fast into a storm of bullets.

Schiller began dipping and diving, juking and jiving the helicopter—banking hard left and right, zigzagging, trying not to provide the enemy with an easy target. Schiller and Ford did not make it very far into the built-up area before all hell broke loose. Fire erupted all at once and from every direction.

"There's enemy everywhere in here!" Doug said, spinning his head, darting his eyes from one building to the next. "I can't plot a grid for all of this shit. They are everywhere."

It seemed that every rooftop and every window in every building had an armed fighter in it, and the focus of their fury was Doug Ford and Steve Schiller's Kiowa helicopter.

"Widowmaker, this is Saber Six," Schiller called to the unknown voice on the radio. "We are taking fire from multiple locations in the vicinity of sector Juliet," he said, using the grid system that Rowely had designed with Strike before the battle began. "We are unable to pinpoint the locations. We'll make another pass to try and verify," he said.

Doug snapped his head toward Schiller when he heard him say, *"We'll make another pass."*

"You're not serious, are you?" Doug asked.

"Well, Doug. What should we do? Fly away scared and hide? Lob a few rockets into town?" Schiller asked sarcastically.

"No! But make damn sure we don't get hit," Doug said.

"Roger. I'm heading in," Schiller said, scanning the rooftops for fighters.

As Schiller and Ford plunged back into the fray, the city erupted in gunfire once again. They were able to note a couple of areas where fighters seemed to be concentrated. Suddenly, there was a bright flash to their front and a loud concussion. "What the hell was that?" Schiller asked, as if only mildly concerned.

"THAT was an RPG," Doug said dryly. "I don't much care for those."

"Yeah. That'll leave a mark," Schiller said, remaining calm and focused.

"It looks like most of these jackasses are in that area right over there," Doug said pointing toward a group of three-story buildings.

"Can you get a grid?" Schiller asked.

"Roger, stand by."

Plotting a grid on a map while orbiting in circles and dodging bullets was not an easy task for Doug. He needed to focus all his attention on the map to try and make sure he read the right grid coordinates, but it was hard to focus inside the helicopter when everyone outside was trying to kill him.

To make matters worse, the maps were not overly accurate, so Doug had to try and terrain-associate to narrow the area down as best as he could. As he flew the bird, Schiller looked out across Karbala. He saw smoke rising from the city in numerous locations. He saw his cavalrymen swarming like tiny mosquitos above the billowing smoke, and he realized that his other Kiowa teams were experiencing the same thing as he and Doug. He smiled to himself, proud of his cavalrymen. They were making a very meaningful difference in the fight. *That's the cavalry mentality*, he thought.

Doug wrote the grid out on his kneeboard so that Schiller could read it off his leg. "There," Doug said to Schiller, pointing to the grid.

Schiller passed the grid to Widowmaker. "We're pinned down over here," the soldier replied, yelling into the radio. Schiller could tell that the stress level was high on the ground as well. "Every time we try and gain a better foothold, we take significant fire from the rooftops and windows," the soldier said.

In an urban environment, particularly in a flat desert, the buildings become decisive terrain, high ground. In this case, the enemy held the high ground. They could shoot down on the soldiers from the roof and upper stories of the buildings, and they had great visibility of the streets below. Schiller was frustrated. As he and Doug discussed what to do next, another RPG exploded in the air beside them. A bullet cracked in the air right by Schiller's head, causing him to jump in his seat. "We've got to do something here, Doug," he said. "We've got to make something happen."

"Artillery!" Doug said.

"What?" Schiller asked.

"Use someone else's bullets. We're never going to root them out. Let's pound the shit out of them with artillery."

Just as the words left his mouth, another crack seemed to emanate right by Schiller's head. "These guys are pissing me off!" he exclaimed, gritting his teeth. "Fortunately, they don't seem to be great shots."

"It's only a matter of time. If you keep giving them something to shoot at, they'll eventually hit us," Doug said, then stuffed the remainder of the peanut butter cracker into his mouth.

"Widowmaker, this is Saber Six, over," Schiller called.

"Saber Six, Widowmaker, over."

"Request a fire mission, over."

Schiller agreed with Doug. The only way to kill the enemy in the buildings was to pound them with artillery. There was a long pause on the other end of the radio, and then the voice returned.

"Saber Six, Strike Six wants to use precision munitions against that target. Is that feasible?"

"It's feasible; however, I recommend we take out the whole damn block. They are not in one spot. They're everywhere, in multiple locations," Schiller said, noting that a precision munition would only take out one specific fighting position. He needed to level several buildings to free Widowmaker up to maneuver.

"Okay, stand by," came the reply.

"Roger," Schiller answered.

Schiller visualized Colonel Anderson consulting with his staff trying to decide what to do. Schiller assumed that Anderson didn't want to level the town if he could avoid it. "Saber Six, Widowmaker, over."

"Saber Six, over."

"Saber Six, we're coordinating for fast-movers with precision munitions. Can you stand by, over?"

"Standing by," Schiller answered, thinking to himself, *What choice do I have?*[4]

"Doug, get the sight up. We may have to lase the target for the bomb this jet is about to drop."

Meanwhile, Schiller flew back through the gauntlet to try to determine the best location to drop the bomb. Once again, the city erupted in small arms and RPG fire. *Doug's right. We're going to get shot down if we keep doing this,* Schiller thought to himself.[5]

"Saber Six, this is Strike. You have two F-18s in an orbit overhead. Call sign is Flimsy on the close air support frequency, over."

The Strike soldier calling Schiller was the Strike brigade fires officer. He was co-located with Colonel Joe Anderson.

73

"Roger," Schiller answered.

As Doug dialed the close air support frequency into their radio, Schiller realized that he was soaked in sweat. He was roasting. The outside air temperature gauge read thirty-eight degrees Celsius—one hundred degrees Fahrenheit.

Schiller made radio contact with Flimsy and gave him his laser code. Doug lased the building, and Flimsy said he could see the laser but the weapon would not lock onto the laser energy. It seemed to take forever. Back and forth, they struggled to lase and lock the target up. Soon, Schiller heard Anderson's voice on the radio asking why they hadn't dropped the bomb yet.

"Strike Six, Saber Six, our laser is on. Flimsy is having difficulty getting the bombs away," Schiller told Anderson.

"Roger, Saber Six. Abort that mission. Engage with artillery," he said.

Finally! Schiller thought.[6]

"Roger, fire mission, over," Schiller called.

"Saber Six, Strike send the mission," came the reply.

Top Gun, Strike's artillery battalion, prepared to fire a single round for Schiller. He would observe the round as it impacted, and then he would adjust to get them on target, or if the round hit the right spot, he'd tell them to "fire for effect," meaning shoot all the guns at that same grid location. Once the firing solution was set and Top Gun was ready to shoot, they pulled the lanyard on the artillery piece and Strike called Schiller. "Saber Six, shot, over," came the call, meaning that the round had left the gun and was on its way to the target.

"Shot, over," Schiller replied, acknowledging that the round was in the air.

"Splash, over."

"Splash, out," Schiller acknowledged, noting that within seconds, the round would impact. The splash call gave the observer warning, so he could observe the impact.

The round landed long. "Strike, drop one hundred, left fifty, fire for effect," Schiller called.

"Drop one hundred, left fifty, fire for effect," came the reply.

Schiller adjusted the rounds. He needed them to shoot the rounds one hundred meters shorter, and move them to the left fifty meters, but he wanted them to shoot all the guns on the next volley.

"This should be interesting. Those jackasses are going to get their bells rung," Doug said.

"Yep," Schiller replied.

"Shot, over," came the call from Strike.

"Shot, out," Schiller replied.

"Splash, over."

"Splash, out."

The infantrymen on the ground, also listening to the fire mission over the radio, took cover wherever they could find it. Soldiers have confidence in the artillery, but it's still a scary proposition to fire long-range artillery in close proximity to ground forces. Schiller and Ford watched as the steel came raining down from the sky. The artillery rounds obliterated the intended city block. Schiller and Ford beamed as they watched rounds exploding right on top of the locations where they had taken fire.

"Strike, perfect shot, brother. Repeat, over," Schiller said, ordering up another round of similar treatment.

"Repeat, out."

Once again, the rounds exploded right on the intended target. Schiller and Ford observed buildings crumbling under a huge cloud of smoke. Multiple people began to scramble in all directions from the buildings.

"Saber Six, Strike Six," Anderson called to Schiller.

"Saber Six, over."

"Saber Six, can you fly back over the area and assess the damage, over?" Anderson asked.

"Roger, over."

Schiller flew over the crumbling buildings. He saw groups of women and children leaving the area. One old woman walked out of a building and looked up at him. Despite him being over one hundred feet above her, she seemed to make eye contact with him. With rage in her face, she looked up at him and shook her fist, cursing him.

Another RPG exploded near the helicopter. "They're still shooting at us," Doug said.

At that moment, the cockpit went completely blank, and both men felt a shocking thud in the helicopter. The collective control jolted in Schiller's hand, and he felt a significant impact directly under his seat, like a sledgehammer hitting a board held against his butt. All the digital screens and gauges in the cockpit went blank. The radios were suddenly silent. Schiller tried to talk to Ford, but the intercom system was dead.

"Sir! Land the helicopter. We've been hit!" Doug screamed out to Schiller while pointing at the ground.

But the Kiowa was still flying. Schiller wiggled the controls, and the helicopter responded normally. He scanned every instrument and realized that they had a complete electrical failure, but he also knew that the Kiowa was designed to maintain one operational FM radio in the event of an electrical failure. He went to that radio.

"Strike niner-five, Saber Six. We've been hit and sustained some damage. I'll get back with you once I determine the severity of the situation, over."

"Sir, land the helicopter!" Doug yelled out again to no avail. Schiller could not hear a word Doug was saying.

Doug also could not hear the radio call Schiller had made to Strike. "The helicopter flies just fine!" Schiller yelled to Doug, exaggerating every word with his lips and mouth, hoping Doug would understand.

Reliving it as if it were yesterday, Schiller smiled and leaned forward, putting his arms on the picnic table in front of me. "Doug and I could no longer talk. You know the importance of crew coordination. We really needed to be able to communicate, but Strike also needed us in the fight at that time. A thousand things went through my head. I knew Doug would be pissed off and miserable as hell sitting there in the blind like a sandbag in the seat, but I decided to stay in the fight and keep fighting with that one radio. We didn't have a fuel gauge, so we had to trust the time hacks for when we'd need to go get fuel," he said.

"After a while, Doug screamed out to me that we had thirty minutes of fuel left. I called Ken Hawley at the command post and told him to send another team our way to take over the fight. I told him we were coming in for fuel, so I needed him to have a maintenance team ready to fix my aircraft."

To Doug's relief, another Kiowa team soon showed up and took over the fight. Schiller flew them back to the FARP, where they discovered significant damage to the helicopter. The maintenance team concluded that 7.62mm bullets, likely from AK-47s, had hit them numerous times. The round that did the most damage penetrated not only the belly of the aircraft, but the four wire bundles running from the computers in the back of the aircraft to the cockpit, and punctured a hole in the collective lever. The round eventually lodged in the armor panel under Schiller's seat. Schiller had felt the thud directly under him. Doug quickly dug the round out of the armor and took it to Schiller.

"Sir, check this out," Doug said. He held the bullet up with his thumb and index finger. "This could have been knee-deep in your ass!"

"Funny, Doug. Really funny."

"I'm just saying, sir. This was potentially your Forrest Gump wound."

Schiller and Doug found another steed and headed back to the fight, but by the time they arrived in downtown Karbala, the fight was winding down for the day, 2-17 CAV having once again made a profound impact on the fight.

That night, Schiller gathered his leaders together to review the day's events and plan for the following day's fight. After comparing notes, they concluded that they had killed over forty enemy fighters, they had destroyed over a dozen armed trucks and several air defense vehicles, and they had blown up more weapons caches than they could recall.

The maintenance teams turned wrenches throughout the night to patch up the Kiowas as best as they could. Late that evening, Schiller and Hawley received orders from the division headquarters to link up with the Rakkasans, who were planning to take Al Hillah next.

The next morning, Ken and Todd called Rakkasans to make initial coordination for Hillah, but there was still some cleanup work to be done with Strike at Karbala. It would be another day before Schiller could meet with Rakkasan 6, Colonel Mike Linnington.

The second day of fighting at Karbala mirrored the tough street-to-street fighting of the first day. Fortunately, Strike progressed through the city at a steady pace throughout the day and seized the town by sunset. That evening, Schiller and his men concluded that they had destroyed a radar, three huge KS-19 100mm antiaircraft guns, seven BMP [Boyevaya Mashina Pekhoty in Russian] infantry fighting vehicles, two Roland air defense systems, several command and control vehicles, and a huge cache of SA-7 surface-to-air, heat-seeking missiles. The squadron only sustained minor damage to a few aircraft that day.

"That second day in Karbala, the maintenance team worked on my helicopter and got #177 back up and flyable," Schiller said. The tail number of the Kiowa that Schiller and Ford flew was #177. "You get used to a helicopter. After flying it a while, you learn its personality. That was #177 for me and Doug.

"The following day, April 7th, I reported to the Rakkasan assembly area, which was about twenty kilometers west of Hillah, on the eastern side of Highway 9. I landed in a small green field by a palm grove, adjacent to the Rakkasan TOC. When I walked up, Colonel Mike Linnington was leaning over his Humvee eating an MRE. He looked dirty and tired."

"Hi, Steve," Linnington said as Schiller approached. "You ready for tomorrow?"

"Roger, sir. We'll do what we can for you and your men," Schiller said.

"Great. We'll wait 'til everyone gets here before we start. It may take a while," he said.

Soon Humvees began to roll in from all directions. Commanders stepped forth from their trucks and the assembly quickly resembled a family reunion as men slapped backs, hugged, and shook hands with one another.

Once everyone was assembled, the Rakkasan staff officers briefed the mission and each battalion commander explained what they planned to do during the fight. Schiller briefed two tasks for his cavalry squadron: conduct reconnaissance forward of the Rakkasans as they moved to their objectives, and conduct close combat attacks once they found the enemy. It was a classic cavalry mission: locate the enemy and kill as many as possible with organic weapons and artillery, all the while serving as Mike Linnington's eyes and ears forward in the battle.

Al Hillah is adjacent to the ruins of the ancient city of Babylon, where King Nebuchadnezzar once ruled. To its east, dikes supplied water to lush green fields that had been toiled over for centuries. The Babylonians, world superpower of their day, could not have imagined that twenty-six hundred years later, the modern-day world superpower would send the rugged troopers of the 101st Airborne Division across the globe to liberate the Iraqi people.

But that was exactly what was about to take place.

Babylon: The Fight
for Al Hillah

Hillah (ancient Babylon) was equidistant from the Euphrates River to the east as Karbala was to the west, and near the same latitude. Only forty miles separated them. Karbala lay on the edge of an ever-present barren desert while Hillah seemed to sit as a focal point of Mesopotamia.

"Babylon gave me the impression that it was no longer a part of the Middle East," Schiller said. "Manicured dikes and hedgerows gave way to green grass, horticulture, and palm groves. The morning drew a haze that seemed to blanket the Euphrates River Valley. The humidity was high, but there was a cool breeze blowing that morning. The weatherman's guess was that we'd have a high around ninety degrees with winds out of the north at about fifteen miles per hour, gusting to thirty. That concerned me a bit."

Then he furrowed his brow. "You know how tough the wind is for a Kiowa. The weather alone could make for a challenging day," Schiller said.

Weighing in at just over five thousand pounds, the Kiowa is a light-weight helicopter. Given the lack of power in the hot desert environment, a strong wind could easily cause an accident or, worse yet, a crash. The pilots would have to remain vigilant to avoid slowing down with a tail-wind. Like a bird, helicopters fly best with their nose in the wind.

"We initially took off with two teams to begin our reconnaissance through the breadth of Hillah," Schiller said. "We planned to use six Kiowa teams in all, rotating between the fight and the FARP, but I wanted to send two teams out first to try and find out what we were up against. Including ancient Babylon, which is actually adjacent to Hillah proper, the city spans twelve miles north to south. It didn't take long for us to find a fight."

It should be noted that one of the principles of reconnaissance is to gain and maintain enemy contact. Good, aggressive cavalrymen get out on the battlefield and quickly find the enemy, usually by getting shot at. Then they do not let go. They use everything at their disposal to disrupt the enemy and develop the situation.

Shortly after the teams began their reconnaissance that morning, Captain Matt Worrell called Schiller on the radio.

"Saber Six, Annihilator Six, over."

"Saber Six, over."

"We're taking fire from a building complex. It looks like the enemy has a significant stronghold here. This position gives them control of the road, MSR Aspen," Worrell said.

MSR was an acronym for main supply route—a prominent highway. MSR Aspen was the road that led to Hillah from the west. It was about five miles west of 2-70 Armor's objective. 2nd battalion, 70th Armor Regiment was a tank battalion assigned to the 101st for the ground war. Petraeus used it to weight the main effort: whichever infantry brigade had the mission to take a city also got the battalion of tanks and 2-17 CAV.

Schiller's story continued.

"'Annihilator Six, Saber Six,' I called to Worrell. 'Those guys will have to be dealt with because they could impede 2-70 Armor's movement. Can you develop the situation and attempt to call for artillery on them?'

"I wanted to eliminate the enemy so that 2-70 Armor could move unimpeded.

"'Roger,' Worrell replied, happy to oblige.

"Doug and I flew single-ship that morning," Schiller told me. "Our wingman had maintenance problems when he cranked, so Doug and I took off without him."

Then Schiller rolled his eyes. "I know, it might sound risky, but I didn't really think it was at the time. I had two teams already working forward of the main attack with two more teams ready to reinforce the fight, giving me helicopters all over the battlefield. The birds of prey were circling," he said, smiling.

We always flew and fought in teams of two. Schiller was technically not flying with a wingman, thus he violated the unwritten rule, but he was far from alone in the fight. He and Doug would have to stick relatively close to other teams in case they were shot down or got into a significant fight, but he felt the risk was acceptable.

"It was foggy. I could not see all of the teams that morning, but I had radio contact with each of them," Schiller said. "We were unable to find a good place to put the ground command post that day, so Ken, who had orchestrated the rotation of teams and had actually controlled the previous fights from the tactical command post while on the ground, had to go airborne for the fight at Hillah."

"I'm sure that broke his heart," I said sarcastically.

"Oh, he was thrilled to be in the air," Schiller said. "He and I tried to flip-flop to command and control the teams. I would be forward in the fight while he was in the FARP getting more gas and bullets, and vice versa. What worried me most was all the high-tension wires east of Hillah. There were towers and power lines everywhere. Over and over, I kept telling the guys to remain vigilant. Ken had planned a couple of air corridors to serve as aerial highways. That helped. We knew that if we flew at a certain altitude in those corridors, we would not fly into wires or a tower."

"Suddenly, a voice burst onto the radio. 'Saber Six, Annihilator Six, we're taking RPG fire from both sides of the road up here. This appears to be some sort of a military complex. A heavily fortified one,' Matt Worrell said, now seeming a bit more concerned with the situation than he was initially.

"'Roger, Annihilator Six, break…Saber Three, this is Saber Six, we're going to need another team of Kiowas up here to replace Annihilator Six's team, or you need to get your ass up here to go into the fight with me. At the rate Matt's team is shooting, they will be out of ammunition soon,' I told Hawley.

"'Roger,' Hawley answered, not indicating if he was coming or if he intended to send another team.

The ammunition situation was also beginning to concern Schiller. The pilots were shooting so much each day that the division could not keep them resupplied with ammunition. Simply put, if they didn't find ammunition elsewhere, they were going to run out.

The executive officer, Major Todd Royar, spent his time, day and night, managing the heavy maintenance load and trying to find ammunition. He called every unit in Iraq asking if they had ammo they could spare but didn't have any luck, so he decided to assign the mission to a noncommissioned officer (NCO). Royar told Staff Sergeant Mike Beran, a sergeant in the FARP platoon, to take the Chinook and fly to other units all over Iraq. "Your mission is to find .50-caliber ammunition and 2.75-inch rockets," he had told Beran. "Just go find us some ammo."

Royar knew that it's easy to decline a request over the radio, but face-to-face interaction almost always yields better results. Plus, a good sergeant will often make things happen that officers cannot. Beran took off in the Chinook and, sure enough, when he returned the helicopter was filled with pallets of .50-caliber ammo, rockets, mail, and Jimmy Dean meal rations. Jimmy Deans are packaged food rations, but they are a significant step above MREs.

"Because we were having so much success in the battles, morale was really high. The guys were so proud that they were making such an impact, but when Staff Sergeant Beran showed up with mail and Jimmy Deans, morale went through the roof. I seriously think that it was the single-most-important morale-boosting moment of the war for the squadron," Schiller said.

"We fought at the military compound for the better part of two hours," Schiller said. "Initially, we thought it was an Iraqi stronghold, but as it turns out, it wasn't. It was Syrian fighters. Between 2-70 Armor and us, we demolished just about every structure in that compound. Using our helicopters, the tanks, artillery, and jets, we pounded them.

"But, at the end of that day, our maintenance guys had their hands full. One aircraft had a bullet hole in the compressor section of the engine; another bird took rounds in two rotor blades and one through the tail boom. A third aircraft sustained one round in a rotor blade and another in the fuel cell. My helicopter needed more work on the electrical system, as well as a new torque tube. First Lieutenant Matthew Green's helicopter was a complete mess. He was very fortunate to still be with us. His bird took multiple rounds, damaging his main rotor blade hub and swash plate. He had holes in the avionics compartment, and numerous bullets entered the cockpit itself. One bullet hit his multifunctional display, the computer screen right in front of him, stopping the bullet before it hit his chest or face," Schiller said.

"Seriously?" I said.

"Yeah, we got shot up pretty bad that day," he said. "But no one was injured, thank goodness. That night, we sat down to figure out how many helicopters would be flyable the following day. Annihilator Troop had three airplanes, Ban'shee Troop had five, and Condor Troop had seven. Only fifteen of our twenty-four helicopters were operational. That equated to a lot of frustrated cavalrymen. Not everyone had a bird to fly and fight in the following day," Schiller said.

Every pilot wanted to fight, but you had to have a helicopter to fight. Sitting around the command post, listening to the radio in an attempt to follow the fight, left pilots frustrated.

"The next day almost mirrored the previous," Schiller continued. "We destroyed multiple antiair systems and blew up countless weapons caches. Oh, and that's where Curtis Phipps and his team found about twenty guys hiding in chest-high elephant grass and called for artillery on them."

"What?" I asked.

"Curtis found them trying to hide in tall elephant grass, so he called for artillery. He and Matt Green ended up killing sixteen enemy fighters that day.[1]

"That evening, we received word from the division staff that we were headed to Baghdad next. They sent orders chopping us from the Rakkasans back to Strike, and we got word that President Bush had announced the fall of Baghdad," Schiller said.

"Sounds like things progressed pretty nicely," I said. "I bet morale was high."

"Through the roof," he said. "The next day, April 11th, I wanted to find Colonel Anderson and get his intent for the fight in south Baghdad. I also wanted to find us a new bivouac site closer to Baghdad. Johnny Rowell had already moved out to link up with Strike the previous evening."

"So, he didn't remain with them after the fight at Karbala?" I asked.

"No. He came back to help us plan as we moved on to Hillah," he said.

"I see."

"Strike had set up a command post in a chicken factory south of Baghdad," said Schiller.

"They know how to pick 'em, don't they?" I said.

"What do you mean?"

"Well, they set up in a cola factory first. Then they move to a chicken factory," I said.

Schiller laughed. "I guess you're right. Colonel Anderson knows how to keep morale up in Strike.

"Johnny made it up there and sent word back, giving us their exact location, so early that morning, Doug and I saddled up and launched."

"Alone?" I asked.

"Yeah," he said, grinning. "But we weren't trying to pick a fight. We were just going up there to talk to Strike Six."

"And I'm sure you would have passed a fight up if it had presented itself," I said, already feeling more comfortable to chide him.

The grin transformed into a broad smile. "I would have radioed back for help and then tried to kill the bastards before help arrived. Anyway," he said, proceeding with the story. "It didn't take long to find Strike. We circled around and found a spot to land, then headed in. As I mentioned earlier, I told our guys that they could wear their Stetsons everywhere, so after we shut the helicopter down, Doug and I put our Stetsons on and began walking toward Strike's tactical command post. Almost immediately, I saw Colonel Anderson poring over a map laid out on the hood of his Humvee, but he wasn't alone. Once I got a bit closer, I realized that Major General Petraeus was there with him, as well as Lieutenant General William Wallace, the corps commander. I knew Wallace had commanded the 11th Armored Cavalry Regiment, so I knew he was well acquainted with the Stetson hat. Colonel Bill Greer, the division artillery commander, was also there with them.

"As I approached them, I saluted and said, '*Out Front, gentlemen,*'" Schiller said. [2-17 Cavalry Regiment's call sign is Saber, but their motto is "Out Front"; thus, when saluting senior officers, the troopers say, "*Out Front.*"]

"'Saber Six, great to see you,' Petraeus said, returning the salute and extending his hand. 'I'm glad you are here. This is General Wallace,' he added, turning to Wallace. 'This is Lieutenant Colonel Steve Schiller, our cavalry commander who's been in every fight from Najaf to here.'"

Wallace shook Schiller's hand, and then General Petraeus continued explaining his intent for the upcoming battle to Wallace and Anderson. Following their discussion, Doug took a photo of Anderson, Schiller, Petraeus, Greer, and Wallace. Doug showed the photo to all the troopers that evening. The CAV troopers loved seeing Saber Six standing in the midst of the general officers wearing his Stetson hat.

"Doug and I flew from the chicken factory to Iskandariyah, a small town with an airstrip about twenty miles south of Baghdad," Schiller said.

Brigadier General E. J. Sinclair, also an aviator, had chosen the location.

"When I got there, it was very difficult to land."

"How so?"

"Well, it was congested and dusty as hell. In my opinion, it was dangerous. After we finally found a spot to land, I went and found my boss, Colonel Greg Gass, in his command post. We discussed everything that had happened in the previous battles and what was coming up in the days ahead.

"After talking to Gass, I walked out of the command post and looked around. Adding another twenty-four helicopters to the already over-taxed air strip seemed crazy to me, and especially dangerous to our Little Birds. We were a damn hummingbird in a world of eagles. Just cranking a Chinook beside a Kiowa might turn it over," Schiller said.

"So, what did you do?" I asked.

"I turned around and walked back into the command post and told Colonel Gass that, since the CAV would be fighting with Strike in the next battle, I planned to find a bivouac site closer to them."

"What did he say?"

"He seemed preoccupied," Schiller said.

Schiller's relationship with Colonel Greg Gass turned out to be somewhat difficult to cultivate. It was not due to a personality clash. Schiller liked and respected Greg Gass. Their relationship just never seemed easy; it was always a bit awkward.

Being assigned to Gass's aviation brigade meant that Colonel Gass was responsible for 2-17. He was Steve Schiller's boss, but by design, the CAV worked directly for the infantry brigades in combat.

"I tried to keep him informed of what we were doing," Schiller said later. "But he seemed preoccupied with the Apache battalions and their challenges. He was always stoic and unemotional with me, difficult to read. Sometimes, I never truly knew where I stood with him."

Still, Gass gave Schiller the freedom to command 2-17 CAV as he saw fit. "He could have shut me down, but he didn't, and I am grateful for that," Schiller said.

"The mission to secure southern Baghdad turned out to be relatively uneventful. Iraqi fighters, who no doubt knew the fate of Najaf, Karbala, and Hillah, began quickly disappearing. The most obvious thing we saw, sadly, was looting. Local Iraqis began looting everything they could find," Schiller said.

Schiller went on to relate how, on April 16th, they had received a warning order that the next mission was going to be Mosul. Strike intended to brief their plan on April 19th, with mission execution planned for the 20th, but everything had been pushed twenty-four hours to the right for some reason.

The break in fighting happened to coincide with Easter. "You've met our chaplain, Mike Albano, right?" Schiller asked me.

"Yes, sir. I briefly met him," I said.

Captain Mike Albano was a tiny Filipino Catholic priest. "Mike conducted a beautiful and stunning Easter Vigil mass on Saturday night, as well as a sunrise service on Sunday morning. Attendance was high at both events, and Mike initiated two Catholic converts that night in the fields south of Baghdad," Schiller said. "Sergeant Brackenberg and Specialist Robinson both took their baptism and first communion rites that windy evening.

"We patrolled the skies of southern Baghdad for ten days before flying to Mosul on April 21st," Schiller said. "The plan was for us to fly up there and link up with Marines from the 26th Marine Expeditionary Unit [MEU] and 10th Special Forces Group, both of which were already at Mosul airfield, so that's what we did.

"We flew to Mosul airfield and linked up with the Marines. We offered to get out and conduct reconnaissance that night over Mosul, but they told us not to. They said it was too dangerous. They were incredibly skittish. In fact, that night, two Marine squads opened fire on one another inside the perimeter at the airfield. Fortunately, no one was hurt. Truly, I was never quite sure why they were so nervous, but they were more than ready to turn the airfield over to the 101st.

"The following day, the big air assault arrived. Colonel Bill Forrester's 159th Aviation Brigade went to work. By midday, Chinooks and Black Hawks began piling into the airfield with Strike soldiers onboard, and it went on all day long," Schiller said. "The sky was filled with helicopters throughout the day. It seemed that you could never look at the horizon without seeing a steady flow of helicopters flying in and out of Mosul airfield."

Colonel Joe Anderson had flown in a day ahead of the air assault. He met with the Marine leadership. Years later, Anderson told me, "The Marines told me that the city was hostile and they were pretty much hunkering down on the airfield. I spent the day driving around the city to get the lay of the land and to figure out which unit should go where.[2]

"I called General Petraeus on the radio and told him that we would land the battalions at the airfield and have them drive directly into Mosul," Anderson said.[3]

The following day, Chinooks and Black Hawks from the 159th Aviation Brigade flew in with Humvees and containers slung underneath them. Anderson gave guidance to his subordinate leaders while their soldiers prepared their equipment. "The intent was to get into town peacefully and start rebuilding the city with the Iraqis. We put the Civil Military Operations Center [CMOC] in the city hall and immediately began to partner with former Iraqi military forces, the police, and firemen,"[4] Anderson said.

Schiller told me, "The Rakkasans headed out to Tal Afar and Sinjar, west of Mosul. Colonel Bill Greer established his artillery headquarters up on the hill south of Mosul airfield, and Bastogne set up at Q-West airfield, along with the 101st Aviation Brigade. Initially, I took our squadron up to a bivouac site on a hill southwest of Mosul. We camped there for several weeks, so we would be close to the city, but once it was clear we were going to be staying in Iraq for a while, we moved to Q-West. That's how all the units got where they are today, Jimmy. That's how I remember it anyway," he said.

"Those first few weeks were certainly action packed," I said, rising from the picnic table.

"Well, I suspect a lot more is going to take place while you're here," he said, as if to try to provide me some degree of comfort.

Then, placing his hand on my shoulder and smiling gently, he said, "We'll make a lot of history together yet."

"I hope so," I said. "I've kept you long enough. I know you need to get some work done, so I'll leave you alone."

"Anytime you want to talk, I'll make time," he said. "An old boss of mine once told me that the most important thing I could do as a commander was to make myself available. Some leaders seem to always be too busy to spend time with their folks. That's a mistake. Always make time, no matter what your soldiers want to talk about. Make time!"

"I appreciate that," I said as we walked into the TOC.

"Hey, why don't you go to Stayla with me tomorrow? You can meet the locals," he said, laughing as if there were some inside joke. "It'll be a good cultural experience for you. I'm going to fly out there and speak with the *mukhtar.*"

"Sure," I said. "I'd love to."

Once the division had settled in northern Iraq, Major General Petraeus had assigned 2-17 CAV to Strike for the remainder of the deployment. He also directed that each battalion-level unit partner with an Iraqi village. The tiny hamlet of Stayla was 2-17 CAV's village. We had no idea what a cultural experience that would turn out to be.

THE LOCALS: STAYLA

Since I had yet to fly with an instructor pilot, I could not fly with anyone else and perform pilot duties. I could ride in a helicopter, but I could not log time as a pilot until an instructor pilot signed me off, or validated my license, so to speak. Therefore, Schiller flew single pilot that morning. I didn't even enter my name in the helicopter logbook. "It's only about three miles from the front gate of the airfield to the village," Schiller said as we prepared to get into the helicopter. "Omar is going to drive over. He'll meet us there."

Omar, whose real name I will not use, was our interpreter. He worked for us throughout that year in Iraq, but tragically, enemy forces have since attempted to kill everyone who supported US forces in Iraq. At the writing of this book, Omar has been a refugee in hiding for eight years. His brother and father-in-law were shot, and there have been five attempts on Omar's life. He has tried everything under the sun to flee to the US, but for unknown reasons, the embassy in Baghdad has yet to approve the action.

In 2003, Omar lived in Mosul with his wife and two children. Having been educated in the United Kingdom, Omar speaks impeccable English. A portly man with a round face and neat appearance, Omar sports a thick black mustache and parts his jet-black hair on the side. I have never seen him dress in traditional Arab attire; rather, he wears cotton slacks and collared shirts.

As a young man, Omar was a gifted student, which earned him the privilege to attend Queen's College of London, where he earned a degree in engineering. After receiving his degree, Omar returned to Iraq and was commissioned an officer in the Air Force. His posting was Q-West. "We knew it was over when US forces invaded," Omar later told me. "I went home and waited for American soldiers to arrive in Mosul."[1]

As soon as the 101st began flowing into Mosul airfield, Omar approached the leaders. Since US forces were in desperate need of Arabic interpreters, hiring Omar was a no-brainer. He interviewed first with Captain Chris Petty, who served as our logistics officer at the time. Chris was thoroughly impressed, so he hired Omar as the 2-17 CAV interpreter. Omar and the SCO hit it off from the start. Later Omar would tell me, "Steve's a wonderful man and leader. I've been impressed since the day I met him."

Each morning, Omar drove his little white pickup from Mosul to Q-West to spend the day with us. Our interaction with local Iraqis was significant that year, and very few of them spoke English, so Omar was invaluable. To ensure that he understood the purpose of the visit, Omar arrived early that morning. "We've been told to partner with them," Schiller told Omar. "Let's just go meet them and see how they think we might be able to help them."

Omar looked down at the ground, chuckled, and shook his head. "They'll have many ideas for how you can help them, Steve," he said. "They'll ask for everything!"

"Well, they won't get *everything*," Schiller said. "But I'm sure we can help them out in some way. We'll bring the doc with us. Maybe he can hand out some Tylenol or clean up a scrape. That should get us some instant cred. Chris Petty is coming as well. I'm sure they'll want jobs around Q-West. Chris can explain how the process works and see what projects we might be able to support in their village."

"They will want access to the airfield," Omar said. "They will want to work here, come and go as they please, but they will also want handouts, anything you will give them. Be careful what you agree to," he added.

"I will," Schiller said. "Okay, it's time to roll. See you over there."

With that, Omar turned and walked to his truck. "See you there, boss," he said over his shoulder.

As Schiller and I donned our flight gear that morning, I felt self-conscious about my black boots. Everyone in 2-17 CAV wore desert tan boots with their brown uniforms, but by the time I went through the Central Issue Facility (CIF), they were out of my size. I thought the supply sergeant might be able to find a pair in my size if he was properly motivated, so after thinking about it for a while, I decided to apply one of Dale Carnegie's principles, outlined in *How to Win Friends and Influence People.*

The supply sergeant was a good ole Southern boy who had managed to get an assignment back in his native Kentucky. "Howdy, sir. What can I do for you?" he asked as I approached the counter.

I have shed much of my Southern accent, but when I need to, I can blink my eyes, reach back into my North Georgia roots, and come out with a deep Southern drawl. I wield that good ole boy persona like a weapon when the situation calls for it. "I need some tan boots, sergeant. They didn't give me any when I got my issue."

"What size you wear?" he asked.

"Ten and a half," I said.

"We ain't had no ten and a halves in a month, but lemme go look—just to make sure ain't nothing come in that I don't know 'bout," he said and walked into the back.

In a few minutes, he returned, shaking his head. "Sir, we ain't got none. Hell, I don't know when we'll get 'em in."

"Well, sergeant, I sure appreciate you lookin'," I said.

"You got your whole issue, didn't you, sir?" he asked. "They didn't short you nothin', did they?" His sincerity confirmed that we had connected. He wanted to take care of me, but as is often the case, the thing I needed most, he did not have.

"Naw, they didn't short me nothin'," I said. "I got more'n I need. I just didn't get no tan boots."

"Sorry I can't help you. I just don't have none in your size." Then he hesitated, as if he was searching for a possible solution to my dilemma, "Say, if you wanna wear some thick socks, maybe two pair, you can take a pair of twelves with ye. I got plenty 'a twelves," he said.

"No, that's too big, sergeant, but I do appreciate you," I said.

That left me standing by a Kiowa, in front of my new squadron commander, looking like a clown, wearing a tan flight suit and black, spit-shined boots. Of course, Schiller, who took great pride in his appearance, didn't act as if he even noticed my boots. Still, it bothered me.

By 2003, boots had become a funny thing with soldiers. For the first decade plus of my career, a soldier's choice in boots consisted of jungle boots, which were leather boots with green canvas uppers; jump boots, which we wore primarily for parades; or simple army-issue black boots, which we called leg boots. Those were the three options. When the army went to the brown desert uniform post-9/11, commercial companies began flooding the market with a wide array of brown boots. To our astonishment, army leaders allowed soldiers to purchase and wear commercial off-the-shelf boots; however, none of them were authorized for flight personnel, so that didn't help my situation.

After we cranked, Schiller and I took off from Q-West and flew south over the main gate. We had climbed to no more than five hundred feet above the ground, and Stayla was already in sight. "See that village?" Schiller asked, pointing to a small group of mud brick houses.

"Yes sir."

"That's it," he said.

Below us, on a pitiful dirt road, we could see Omar bouncing along in his little truck, leading three Humvees to the village. As soon as we began our descent to the village, children and men began to gather out in front of the houses. The women all veiled their faces and ran for their homes, not to be seen again.

There were a few scrawny hens and a couple of roosters in the yard, but once they realized the big metal bird was headed for them, they ran off as well. "It'd be nice to have some hens to lay a few eggs at Q-West," I told Schiller.

"It wouldn't take long until someone killed and cooked the hens," he said.

"That's true, but fresh eggs sure would taste good for breakfast," I said.

"Yeah," he agreed, focused on where he planned to land.

As we neared the ground, fine dust boiled up and engulfed the helicopter. Schiller landed right in front of the villagers, who now shielded their eyes and faces with their arms. As soon as we touched down, he rolled the throttle off to reduce the wind from the rotors as quickly as possible. Still, they were engulfed in a cloud of dust for several minutes.

Before the rotors stopped turning, the villagers flocked us. The children were fascinated with the helicopter. The men gathered around us to shake our hands and welcome us to their village. Their hospitality was admirable, but I would soon learn, just as Omar had warned us, that they were all about themselves. We represented the United States of America—money and power—and their desire was a liberal handout.

Once the excitement died down, the village elders escorted us to the mukhtar, who stood at the entrance to his house. The mukhtar[2] appeared to be in his late fifties. In a society in which the life expectancy of a male was sixty-five years, that made him relatively old. He was dressed in a white *dishdasha* that was much cleaner than those of the other men. It was clear that the mukhtar supervised the labors of the village, giving orders and guidance, but did very little manual labor himself. His head was draped in a red and white keffiyeh, which is a square scarf held in place with a circular cord called an *agal*. He was a small man, standing half a head shorter than Schiller. On a particularly straight day, he may have stood five feet, six inches tall.

The mukhtar's skin was a deep bronze. His hair was black as onyx, shiny with oil. His thick black mustache curled ever so slightly at the corners of his mouth. His eyes were dark brown at the outer portion of the iris but transitioned to dark green near the pupil. The whites of his eyes were yellowed like phlegm. I'd seen those eyes before, the eyes of an alcoholic set on pickling his liver. But alcohol was shunned in Muslim society. That didn't mean it did not exist; in fact, we knew that it did, but it wasn't likely that the mukhtar drank enough to get cirrhosis. *Hepatitis*, I thought. *Maybe that's what it is. Could it be contagious?*

I shook the mukhtar's hand, which was moist and unusually supple for a man living such a tough existence. I realized that he was a soft man. Nothing about him indicated that he did any physical labor. After shaking hands, he placed his right hand over his heart, dipped his head as if bowing ever so slightly, and said, "*As-salamu 'alaykum*," which translates, Peace be upon you.

He held a riding crop in his left hand, the purpose of which I'd soon discover. In his right hand, he held a handkerchief, which he used to dab at the incessant perspiration on his forehead. After welcoming us to Stayla, he turned and led us into his home. Young boys crowded the doorway, equally excited and curious to witness everything that would take place on the day the Americans flew to their village in a helicopter.

As we entered the room, the mukhtar struck two boys with the riding crop, quick as a rattler. They recoiled with a loud squeal and let us pass.

He led us into a long, narrow room. A rug ran the length of the room. Tattered wallpaper, carelessly matted together in large sheets, covered the far wall, presenting a mural of a bright orange and brown tree in autumn. Leaves covered the lush forest floor around the trunk of the massive oak in the foreground. *How interesting, yet out of place,* I thought. *Perhaps, a people that only know sand, dust, and rock dream of such a scene.*

The mukhtar walked about halfway down the length of the room and sat down on the floor. We filed into the room and sat down around the periphery of the rug. Once Schiller, Omar, and I were seated, the village men filled the remaining space, each fighting to sit as close to Schiller as possible. He was the boss. He represented power and authority in their eyes. Young boys in common street clothes crawled all over one another to try to position themselves so they could see and hear everything. The younger men, appearing to be in their mid-twenties, wore jeans and button-up shirts versus the traditional Arab dress. The younger they were, the farther they sat from the mukhtar and his guests.

As soon as we were all seated, the mukhtar pulled out a cigarette and began to light it, but Schiller stopped him. He pulled a Ziploc bag from his pocket and opened it. He removed a light brown Cuban cigar from the bag and handed it to the mukhtar. He then took one for himself and handed the bag to Sammy, the mukhtar's brother, who had sat down beside Schiller. The eldest men quickly lit their cigars and began to smoke.

Steve Schiller could not verbally communicate with the village men. He had to speak through Omar, but nevertheless he understood how to connect in a meaningful way. The gesture of sharing a cigar with the men was his way of beginning their relationship on the right foot.

I had been told that it was rude to show the soles of one's feet. I give new meaning to the word stiff, so I awkwardly struggled to find a comfortable position while trying to conceal the bottoms of my feet. It was not an easy task.

After a few draws on the cigar, the mukhtar looked at the SCO, raised the cigar, and nodded his head, acknowledging his appreciation of the stogie. We were off to a good start.

Next, the young boys brought kettles of piping hot tea called *chai* into the room. Two boys, walking barefoot on the center carpet, placed small cups in front of each of us while two other boys began pouring the chai. I noticed one young girl standing in the door staring at the boys as they poured the chai. She appeared to be about ten years old. It struck me as odd because she was the only girl who had not run to hide when we arrived. All the boys had short, straight black hair, but her hair was long, curly, and brown. She watched the boys intently as they served the chai, not saying a word to any of the others crowded in the doorway who had whispered, pointed, and laughed incessantly since we arrived.

"That's a beautiful little girl," I told Omar. "Why did she get to stay out here while all the others had to get out of sight?" I asked.

Omar burst out laughing.

"What?" I asked, confused at his reaction.

Omar shook his head.

"What is it?" I asked.

"She *is* pretty, isn't she?" he said.

"Yes, very."

"That's not a girl," he said. "*He's* pretty, but *he's* a boy."

I looked closer. "You're kidding?" I said. "I would swear that's a girl."

I had heard of "house boys" who looked very feminine, but the whole idea made me sick to my stomach. I didn't want to know more, so I dropped it.

After the men had their fill of chai and smokes, the boys began serving food. They ate community style. Large trays of rice, small fried vegetables, vats of broth, and flat bread were placed on the rug in front of us. I followed suit as they tore off pieces of bread and then began digging into the bowls with their hands.

It wasn't until that moment that I was truly appreciative of our doc. Just before I departed Q-West, Doc had handed me a small Ziploc bag containing white pills. "What's this?" I asked.

"Take one now and take another one tonight," he said.

"What is it?"

"Cipro," he said. "You'll need it. It will kill everything you put in your system at that village."

I observed the boys standing by the door, almost salivating as they watched us dig in with our hands. I would learn later that once we left, the children got to eat what remained.

After a long lunch, we finally got down to business. It was rude in their culture to talk business before the social formalities were concluded, which would later become a challenge when we didn't have half a day to devote to them.

Through Omar, Schiller told the mukhtar how happy we were to partner with them. He informed the mukhtar that he would like to know what they needed most. The mukhtar dabbed at his forehead with the handkerchief and nodded his head as Omar translated. Then, in Arabic, the mukhtar spoke to the other elders. Each of them responded to the mukhtar, sometimes all at once. Sammy was the most vocal. Sammy clearly had his brother's ear. Finally, the mukhtar spoke to Omar.

Omar interpreted, "He says that they would like gravel on their road, and they need a bridge over the big ditch in front of the village."

Sammy then spoke directly to Omar. "He says they need jobs. They have heard that the Americans are paying for work on the airfield. They want to work on Q-West," Omar told Schiller.

"Tell him we have set up a CMOC [Civil-Military Operations Center] at the airfield to hire people. They can go there and apply for jobs. There is a screening process, but it's fair."

Omar told Sammy. He shook his head, noting that he understood, then resumed speaking. "He says that there is a lot of scrap metal on the airfield, old tires as well. He wants to come get those things. He says he can sell them. He says the Americans can't use them anyway," Omar said.

"Tell him to go to the CMOC," Schiller said.

Attempting to gain control of the conversation, Schiller spoke. "We want to build a school so your children can get an education," he told them through Omar.

The room erupted in chatter. They made faces as they spoke on top of one another. I could not tell if they thought it was a good idea or not. The mukhtar did not speak. He just sat there, stoic, and listened. Every few minutes he would raise the handkerchief and blot the sweat from his forehead. He was sweating more than everyone else. It was almost as though he had a fever.

Eventually, he did speak, and the sidebar discussions instantly ceased. Through Omar, he said a school would be good. "We will need a teacher and materials," he said. "And a generator for electricity," he quickly added.

Schiller told him that we would begin working on it but warned him that the schoolbooks would require scrutiny, as would the teacher. The mukhtar agreed.

I could tell that Schiller was ready to leave, but the Iraqis seemed happy to continue laying all their burdens at his feet. Several of them had lit cigarettes and were smoking again. "Tell him we will return to check in on the village," Schiller told Omar.

"When do you plan to return?" Omar asked Schiller.

"They do not need to know that," Schiller said. "It will be a surprise for them, not me."

Omar told the mukhtar, who nodded in approval. With that, Schiller stood. Then he looked at me, "Go ahead and get the helicopter ready. Look it over really good. There is no telling what switches they've flipped," he said.

I squeezed my way by the men and walked out to the Kiowa. Several of our soldiers stood by the helicopter, guarding it. "Did they mess with anything, sergeant?" I asked, referring to the pack of kids.

"I'm not sure, sir. They were all over it at first, but once you all walked into the house, we told them to get away. We told them they could look but not touch," he said, grinning.

"Well, I suppose I'd better check it out pretty thoroughly then," I said.

"I reckon you'd better," he said. "Are we leaving?"

"Yeah, the SCO is trying to get out of there now," I said.

I inspected the Kiowa from one end to the other, then got in the cockpit and checked every switch to make sure everything was set appropriately. Men and boys began pouring out of the door; then finally the SCO and the mukhtar emerged. By that time, I already had my helmet on and seatbelt fastened. We were ready to crank once the SCO got in.

Schiller stuck his hand out to shake. The mukhtar took his hand and nodded his head as if to show his approval of their visit. Schiller turned and walked to the helicopter. "Go ahead. Start cranking," he said, as he pulled his flight helmet over his head.

"Clear!" I shouted.

"Clear!" came the reply of the two soldiers keeping everyone back from the helicopter for me to crank.

The turbine engine began to spool up. I could hear the ignitors popping as they sparked a flame. Then I cracked the throttle, dumping fuel across the flames, and a fire caught out in the engine with a dull controlled explosion, and the rotors began to turn. The crowd stood just outside the rotors until the RPMs increased and dust and loose pebbles began to fly. They pulled scarves up over their faces, covering everything but their eyes, which they shielded with their hands. Yet they did not look away. They wanted to see the bird lift off. "As soon as you're ready, let's go," Schiller said as he buckled his seatbelt.

I pulled in power and came to a hover, then quickly turned into the wind and nosed the helicopter over. The children waved as we flew away. The whole visit had taken about three hours.

From that point forward, we visited Stayla every week or two. We paid a local Iraqi construction team to improve their road and build a bridge over the small wadi that ran in front of their village. In summer, it was hard to imagine that water might flow through the dry creek bed, but Omar assured us that all the wadis would flow with water once the rainy season arrived. We hired a teacher and gave them a generator. I told my own kids about the village and the children I'd met there. My oldest daughter, Kasey, sent packages of candy and gum, which I delivered to the grateful children.

Several weeks later, Schiller and I returned to visit and check on the school's progress. When we arrived, we noticed that the generator had been moved to the mukhtar's house. It powered lights and an air conditioner unit. The teacher was living in the school. We were paying him, but we had no proof or confidence that any of the children were going to school.

After a firm tongue-lashing, Schiller made good with the mukhtar and gave him another Cuban cigar. "Let's smoke," Schiller said. The whole scene reminded me of the white man's interaction with early nineteenth-century Native Americans.

The mukhtar put the cigar in his pocket and lit a cigarette instead. Confused, Schiller turned to Omar and said, "Ask him why he's not smoking the cigar," but before Omar could speak, Schiller turned directly to the mukhtar and said, "Don't you like it?"

98

The mukhtar said something to Omar in Arabic. Omar smiled. "He says, thank you. He really likes the cigar. It's strong and he enjoys the way it makes him feel." Then Omar giggled slightly. "He says he wants to smoke it with his wife tonight in the bedroom."

Schiller burst out laughing, and for the first time I saw a bright smile on the mukhtar's face.

After half a day visiting with the mukhtar and his villagers, Schiller and I began to try to break contact, work our way back to our vehicles. It was a laborious task to say goodbye. We left them with a promise that we'd return to check in on them in a week or so.

The following morning, I woke rather abruptly. Feeling a churn in my stomach like a volcano about to erupt, I made a run for the outhouse. I returned to my room with my hand gently resting on my stomach and a concerned look on my face. "What's up?" Ken asked.

"I don't feel so well," I said. "Diarrhea."

"It's the crud. Jimmy's got the crud," he sang loud enough for Doug to hear next door.

"Ohhh baby," Doug said. "Do you prefer that I tell you what's about to happen to you or do you want to experience it blindly? I suggest blindly. Knowing ahead of time means you'll have to deal with the pain of anticipation."

"I'm not up for your humor right now, Doug."

"Well, for whatever it's worth, I'm sorry," he said with clear concern in his voice, which, coming from Doug, worried me even more.

I had heard them talk about "the crud" as if it were a near-death experience; it was something to be avoided at all costs. At the same time, I got the sense that one should be proud, even honored, to have experienced it—a rite of passage of sorts.

"You better go see Doc right now," Ken said.

"I'm okay. I just have diarrhea. It's probably from that food we ate at the village yesterday," I said.

"Did you take the Cipro?' he asked.

"Yeah," I replied.

"Then it's not the food. You've got the Iraqi crud," he said matter-of-factly.

I made it until just before lunch with nothing more than a queasy stomach. By noon, I felt like a freight train had hit me. I began sweating profusely, then shaking with chills. I sat on my cot in misery.

Doc came to see me just after lunch. "Major Hawley said you were sick," he said.

"I think I'm dying, Doc," I said. "I don't think I've ever felt this bad."

"You're not dying, but over the next forty-eight hours or so you're going to wish you were dead," he said, laughing.

He listened to my heart and lungs, checked my pulse, and took my temperature. "Okay, it's going to be essential that you drink as much water as you can. Have you started puking yet?" he asked.

"No."

"Well, that will probably come next. You'll lose a lot of fluids, so you have to drink," he said. "I want you to go ahead and take Tylenol now. Every six hours take Tylenol and every eight hours take Motrin. Come get me if you need anything."

"Okay," I said, and he left.

As predicted, the puking began around two in the afternoon. I alternated throwing up and having diarrhea, and on some trips to the outhouse, I got a two for one. Thank goodness for care packages filled with baby wipes. I was too scared to lie down for fear of not being able to get up and make it to the latrine in time, so I sat sideways on my cot, elbows on my knees and chin resting on the heels of my hands. My stomach churned, and I was soaked in sweat, roasting hot for an hour or so and then freezing. My head felt like there was a little man inside my skull using a jackhammer. Weak and feeble, I dragged myself to the aid station around six in the afternoon and found Doc. "Can you give me something to sleep?" I asked.

"Yeah, but let's check your vitals again," he said and began listening. "You're already dehydrated. Let's put some fluids in you."

Without a word, one of his medics retrieved an IV and began preparing to stick me with a needle. After two bags of fluids, he handed me three Ambien pills. "Go lie down on your cot. Take one and sleep. When you wake up, drink as much water as you can, a full canteen, and then take another Ambien," he said.

"Okay. Thanks, Doc," I said and returned to my room.

I lay down and swallowed the pill. In seconds, I began to feel groggy, and then the lights went out. Six hours later, I woke up. My mouth was dry, and I felt like I should quickly make my way to the outhouse. A miscalculation would be messy and embarrassing. Having done the death march to the outhouse themselves, soldiers stared at me in pity as I passed.

Once inside, I began expelling the demon that was in me. I threw up until I didn't have anything left to throw up but my guts. After several minutes of heaving, I half expected to see them come up. Once I was back in my room, I took another Ambien and slept. I repeated the process three times. Forty-eight hours passed before I awoke and noticed a difference. I was far from normal, but I could tell that I was improving. The worst was behind me. Feebly, I stood and looked at myself in the mirror for the first time. A shadow of whiskers gave contrast to my fish-belly-white skin. Pale, peaked as my mother would say, my face reflected how I felt—frail, or puny, my father would say.

Carefully, I made my way to the TOC, feeling like Sampson after a fresh haircut. "Well, hello roommate," Ken said. "Glad to see you're still alive, mister."

"For the first time in three days, I think I am going to survive," I said. "But it was questionable there for a while."

"It's unavoidable. Everyone gets it," he said. "You don't even have to eat anything or come into contact with anything bad. Just breathing the air here seems to give it to you. This environment is different from anything we've ever encountered, so our bodies revolt. Then, after a violent reaction, our systems seem to adapt."

"Like a dog and ticks, I suppose," I said.

Improving the Foxhole

Qayyarah Airfield West had previously been an Iraqi Air Force Base that was home to MiG-25s and -27s, respectively called the "Foxbat" and "Flogger." By the time the 101st Airborne Division arrived, the Foxbats and Floggers were long gone, so, like the WMD that we were supposed to find, everyone wondered where they had gone. Local Iraqis suggested that the soldiers look underground, so 2-17 CAV took to the skies while Bastogne soldiers searched the terrain around Q-West. It didn't take very long until pilots reported what appeared to be freshly dug tank fighting positions, minus the tanks. Further investigation revealed carefully buried jets. The Iraqi Air Force had wrapped the engines in plastic, heavily greased the mechanical parts to minimize rusting, and buried approximately twenty jets.

A small paved road traced the perimeter of the air base, which was just over twelve miles in circumference. There was no perimeter wall, and the fence that paralleled the perimeter road had multiple spots where a grown man could walk through unimpeded. There were two 11,000-plus feet runways that the US Air Force cratered during the initial stages of the war; however, once we occupied the airfield, the holes were quickly patched and the runways put back to use.

Two large Iraqi weapons storage areas sat approximately seven miles to the north of Q-West. An explosive ordnance disposal (EOD) unit secured the storage sites and named the entire area Objective Jaguar. Almost immediately, the EOD unit began systematically destroying large caches of munitions. Throughout the following year, we would remove as many munitions as possible from the battlefield and transport them to Jaguar for destruction to prevent the enemy from stockpiling them.

There was a semicircle of tank fighting positions that arched for miles and miles around the entire eastern side of Mosul. Saddam's forces had prepared the defensive positions in anticipation of fighting Iranian forces. It was not uncommon to fly over those fighting positions and find a dozen or more tank and artillery rounds stacked up, ready for use. From the air, we snapped digital photos and recorded grid coordinates. We shared those grids with Colonel Bill Greer's division artillery, who sent ground forces out to retrieve the rounds and transport them to Jaguar or another disposal area adjacent to Mosul airfield. The EOD site at Mosul was easily identifiable due to a large water tower that 101st soldiers painted orange with a big "T" for the University of Tennessee.

I had not yet truly settled in before I experienced the first controlled detonation. Like an adolescent boy with a bag full of firecrackers, the mission at Objective Jaguar was a demolition specialist's dream come true. Nothing could be more fun than blowing things up for a year; however, there were many times that we legitimately worried that the EOD team may have perished in the blast. Despite being seven miles away, several explosions blew our makeshift windows completely out of the building. Thinking we were being attacked, I vividly recall diving under my desk after one unanticipated explosion.

"Are you okay?" Ken asked me.

"Yeah," I said, laughing. "But I think I wet myself a little."

Eventually, the men repaired the intercom system at Q-West (the Big Voice, it was called), so the EOD soldiers could announce when a controlled detonation was scheduled to take place. But prior to that, there were random explosions throughout the day that sent everyone diving for cover.

By the time I arrived, 2-17 CAV had improved living conditions in CAV Country considerably. They had hired local Iraqi men to clean out the debris in the buildings. Sheets of plastic covered holes that were once windows. Because no air circulated, it was unbearably hot in the structures. We did not have enough power generation to run fans in every soldier's room, so we lay on cots in our underwear and endured the heat. The SCO slept on the roof. He said it was cooler up there. I woke up sweaty and irritated several nights, so I decided to climb up on top of the roof to try it, but mosquitoes swarmed me. If their constant biting and buzzing around my ears were not enough to keep me awake, the fear of malaria certainly was.

The bombs had ruined the pipes in the building, so we used gravity-fed showers. We placed barrels on the roof, let the sun warm the water throughout the day, and showered at night. In July, a local Iraqi man came by and asked if we wanted him to go buy us anything. Through Omar, we did our best to explain what we wanted him to bring back. I drew a picture of a weight set on a piece of paper, so that he could understand that we wanted to build a gym. Perhaps the most difficult thing to explain was that we wanted to cool the air. We wanted air conditioners. Ken and I worried that power generation would become an issue. Still, we wanted to improve living conditions as much as possible for the soldiers. In the end, the Iraqi man seemed to somewhat understand what we desired. The man told us that he would have to travel to Syria to buy everything. He said to expect him back in a week or so.

That night, Ken and I sat up late trying to figure out ways to further improve the quality of life for the soldiers on Q-West. We knew that if we could improve the basic creature comforts of life, morale would increase correspondingly. Cool air, mattresses, a means to wash clothes, a gym, and rugs were at the top of our list. We didn't get to bed until after midnight. Next morning, after a run, I sat at my desk reading reports about the previous night's operations in Mosul. Boomer Arnold, the Condor troop commander, walked into the TOC. "Sir, you seen Major Hawley?" he asked.

"He's flying," I said. I had rolled over in my cot as Ken quietly slipped out before daylight that morning.

"Well, what I want to talk about is really in his lane, but do you have a minute to hear me out?" he asked.

"Sure, Boomer," I said. "What's on your mind?"

He appeared to be a bit agitated, which was uncommon for Boomer. Ordinarily, he was high energy and very positive. He wore a bright smile, even when Schiller was chewing his butt, but something seemed to be bothering him.

Born to a nineteen-year-old single mother, Boomer had quickly learned to take care of himself. He and his mother bounced around, place to place, throughout his early childhood. Eventually, they settled just outside Eugene, Oregon, which suited Boomer. He loved sports and the lush green forests of Oregon. After a couple of failed attempts, Boomer's mother landed a decent husband, one worth keeping, I suppose. He liked to hunt and fish, which Boomer also enjoyed. Fishing quickly became Boomer's obsession. By the time he was ten, he'd have fished a mud puddle if he thought there was a minnow in there big enough to swallow a hook.

As he grew older, Boomer began to wonder how he might go to college. After speaking with an army recruiter, he realized that the G.I. Bill was as good of an option as any, so he enlisted in the army right out of high school. He got off to a rather rocky start. "I never got in serious trouble, but I know I was a pain in the ass and a little on the immature side for my sergeants,"[1] he later told me.

It took him two full years to obtain the rank of specialist, but after that, he got with the program. Boomer graduated as the distinguished honor graduate of his primary leadership development course. He was also the honor graduate of his air assault school class. Once he made sergeant, Boomer was quickly promoted to staff sergeant and was soon inducted into the coveted Audie Murphy Club, which is a special organization for NCOs who have demonstrated excellence in their profession. By that time, Boomer realized that he was going to make the army a career. He had also decided that he wanted to fly helicopters, so after returning from Operation Desert Storm, he applied for warrant officer candidate school.

Boomer became a scout pilot, flying the OH-58. His first assignment was in Korea. Flying came easily for him, but Boomer didn't like being a warrant officer as much as he thought he would. He wanted to be in charge and make decisions like his company and battalion commanders, so he applied for Office Candidate School (OCS).[2]

After successfully completing OCS, Boomer was commissioned a second lieutenant and headed back to Korea, where he served as a platoon leader for Captain William "Hank" Taylor, who became a powerful influence in his life. "He was the best officer I had met to that point in my career," Boomer later told me. "He was your brother from another mother,"[3] Boomer said, indicating how alike Hank and I were, and he wasn't far off. My best friend in the world, Hank Taylor would later follow me as the operations officer and executive officer in 2-17 CAV.

Having served as an enlisted man and a warrant officer before being commissioned as an officer, Boomer was older than his peers. In fact, Boomer was five months older than I was, but he ı nicely with his fellow troop commanders. Also, having been an enlisted soldier, Boomer seemed to go out of his way to try to take care of his young troopers. To that end, he was at the TOC to plead his case.

"Sir, we're killing our night crews," he said. "It's too hot to sleep when the sun's up."

"I know it's hot, Boomer, but there's not much we can do about it right now. Major Hawley and I asked an Iraqi guy to try and find some air conditioners, but we're not sure he'll be able to deliver on that one," I said.

"Yesterday I went to the helicopter to preflight. It was about four o'clock in the afternoon. The temperature gauge read fifty degrees centigrade, sir," he said.

Then Boomer raised his eyebrows, and his voice went up an octave. "That's like 122 degrees Fahrenheit! That's Tarzan hot, sir!"

"Boomer, I understand," I said. "We'll try to get some air conditioners, but I can't promise anything."

"It's not that bad for the guys flying days," he said. "They are sleeping on the roof at night."

"I tried it," I told him. "The SCO sleeps up there, but I can't handle the mosquitoes. Your guys are taking their doxycycline, aren't they?" I asked.

"Yes, sir," he said, then lowered his voice and looked away. "Most of them," he said under his breath, to keep from lying.

"Hey! You don't want malaria," I said.

"I know, sir. I know."

The docs issued each of us a huge bottle of doxycycline before we deployed. We were supposed to take it daily to prevent malaria, but doxy is tough on the gut. I didn't realize just how bad it was until I took it on an empty stomach. Of course, some soldiers handled it better than others. One day, I took my doxy before I was ready to eat. I'd been told to take it with a meal, but no one told me to take it *after* I ate. I swallowed the pill on an empty stomach and ten minutes later, I was out back puking my guts out.

Returning to his dilemma, Boomer said, "We can handle sleeping at night, but the night crews don't get to bed until dawn and by ten o'clock in the morning, it's too hot to sleep. My cot is solid white from salt because I sweat so much in my sleep."

I knew that Boomer was aware that we would do our best to make the situation better, but he felt obligated, as the troop commander, to try to speed the process along. "Sir, I'm gonna tell you, last week I went three days without sleep. It was so damn miserable I could not sleep at all, and on the third day it began to affect me in the cockpit," he said.

"Boomer, if you're not fit to fly a mission, then you need to make the right call," I said.

"I told Lou," he said. Chief Warrant Officer Three Lou Papesca was Boomer's troop standardization instructor pilot. "I told him I was going to have to take myself off the flight schedule if I didn't get some sleep soon. I planned to go to the doc the next day, but that night I crashed from complete exhaustion. I slept about six hours and felt like a million bucks."

"Well, be smart about who is flying what missions. If you're tired, I'm sure all your guys are as well. Keep an eye on them," I said. "Major Hawley and I will see if we can't find some air conditioners."

"Okay, sir," he said, standing to leave.

Then he stuck his hand out to shake. "Thanks for listening," he said.

"Anytime, Boomer."

True to his word, the Iraqi man returned in a large truck with weights for our gym, huge plastic barrels for water storage, rugs for our rooms, plastic chairs, tables, fans, and, perhaps most importantly, swamp coolers, which we issued to each troop, praying the generators could handle the load.

We placed the barrels on the rooftops of our buildings and filled them with water. The sun warmed the water throughout the day. We put a valve on the end of a hose and ran it from the barrel, so we could stand on a wooden pallet and take a warm shower. We bought buckets, so that we could hand wash our clothes with the detergent we received in care packages from home.

As I sat down with two buckets of water and a box of powder detergent, my mind drifted back in time. I recalled my mother, a Depression-era child, telling me about washing her clothes in an aluminum tub full of spring water. By the time I was born, the old washboards adorned walls of homes as decorations. The ribbed-steel boards, across which people rubbed clothes to help clean them, served as a reminder of a more primitive time in our history. It was a nostalgic moment that made me smile, but once I began washing, the smile quickly vanished, and nostalgia gave way to frustration.

The process of washing clothes took the better part of a day. One garment at a time, I dunked the clothes in soapy water and rung them out, twisting and squeezing over and over until the water squeezed from the clothes slowly transformed from black to clear. When it looked as though the soap was removed from the garment and the water relatively clear, I transitioned to the rinse bucket and continued the process until the soap and dirty water were completely gone. Finally, I hung the garment on a line and moved to the next item.

Once the bucket of wash water was black, I emptied the bucket and replaced it with clean water. The only fast thing about the process was drying. The hot desert air quickly evaporated the water. Because my hands were submerged in water all day, they pruned up quickly, so about an hour into the washing process, blisters formed between the thumb and forefinger. From that point forward, washing clothes was a painful process. Every time I would get to feeling sorry for myself, I'd picture my mother as a little girl, a child whose mother died when she was eight, leaving her with a toddler brother and a father to look after. That image seemed to help somewhat, for an hour or so anyway.

Because washing was so laborious, I found myself getting as much mileage as possible out of my clothes. Sweating all day was unavoidable, but stiff, brittle, salty clothes softened up as soon as the next day's sweat began. We got used to the salt in our uniforms, but juice from an MRE ham slice was sticky and nasty, so we ate our meals carefully, making sure not to spill anything on our clothes.

Our urinal consisted of two large lengths of PVC pipe buried in the ground—a two-urinal latrine that we called "piss tubes." We built an outhouse out of wood. Underneath the seat, we placed a fifty-five-gallon barrel that we cut in half and filled partially with diesel fuel. There was a hinged door in the rear of the outhouse that provided access to the barrels. Each evening, we took turns burning the day's deposits, a memorable experience to be sure.

I hadn't been there long before I joined in the daily chores. Seeing two soldiers headed to the outhouse with bandanas over their noses and mouths, I decided to go assist them with their duty. "What do you want me to do, guys?" I asked as I approached.

They looked at me strangely. They knew I was the new major, but they hadn't gotten to know me yet. "Really, sir?" one of them said, clearly surprised that I had offered to help with such a disgusting task.

"Sure. Give me that hook," I said, pointing at the steel rod that the motor pool soldiers had fashioned into a hook with a long handle on it.

"Pull it out slowly," the soldier instructed as he handed me the hook. "The more you slosh it around, the worse it stinks. Slide it out nice and easy," he said.

Then he pointed to an area about fifteen feet behind the outhouse. "Pull it right over there and we'll burn it."

They had also welded handles onto the barrels. I used the rod to hook the handle and then, as they held the door open, I carefully began pulling the barrel out from under the outhouse. I did not have a bandana to put over my nose, so as I slid the barrel out from under the outhouse, inevitably sloshing the excrement, I received a full-face whiff and almost gagged. The smell was putrid. Once I pulled the barrel out away from the outhouse, one of the soldiers immediately poured several gallons of diesel fuel into the barrel.

"You want to light it, sir?" the other soldier asked.

"Why not?" I said, and he handed me a box of matches.

Having used diesel before, I knew that I could not just throw the match into the mixture. The diesel and urine would extinguish the match if I did. I would have to hold it on the surface of the sludge until it lit, which meant leaning in right over the barrel. I struck the match, took a deep breath and held it, and then leaned in. A flame ignited on the surface and then consumed the top of the barrel. Black smoke billowed up into the sky.

It took the better part of an hour to completely burn the waste. Meanwhile, the thick black smoke billowed out of the barrel and into the sky high above. If the enemy was trying to target us, all they had to do was watch for the smoke signal each evening. With an observer, they could have walked mortar rounds right in on top of us. Fortunately, they never did, but that did not mean that they did not plan to hit us with rockets and mortars later in the year. At that time, we had no idea what fate awaited us.

By the time our Iraqi merchant returned with the initial order, we had already compiled a second list. We asked him to find us a ping-pong table, a pool table, and a couple of televisions with satellite receivers. He said that there were different chips for the satellite receivers, each of which provided different channel options. "Which chip do you want?" he asked through Omar.

"I want Fox News and sports," the SCO said.

"I want BBC and Eurosport," I told him.

The man seemed to understand and departed with a promise to return in another week. Sure enough, he returned with everything we had asked for. He brought another man with him who set the satellite up outside the building and ran the cables in through the window. We wanted to have a television in the TOC so that we could watch the news. We set another, larger television up in the area Ken and I shared as an office, so that we could watch football once the season started.

After several hours of adjustments, the man said the television was ready. He stood proudly in our TOC and fished the remote control out of his bag. Everyone in the TOC watched, excited to have television for the first time in months. He pointed the remote at the television and turned it on. A red light on the bottom of the set turned green and the first channel popped up—gay porn!

"Whoa! Turn that off," I told him.

He quickly turned the channel, but it was another Arabic-speaking station. He then cycled through all the channels. No Fox News, no BBC, no English.

"Wrong chip," he said.

Once again, he promised to return in a week with the proper chip, which he did. Thus, morale increased a bit more. Though our television reception had gotten off to a rocky start, we soon found ourselves thoroughly enjoying the twenty-four-hour news cycle and Sunday football, of course.

It was amazing how much a little cool air and a television could lift morale. It wasn't long before Boomer came back around. "Sir, I want to thank you and Major Hawley for the swamp cooler," he said.

110

"I'm just glad that guy was able to find them, Boomer," I said.

Boomer sat down in a chair beside me and leaned forward with his forearms on his thighs. "Sir, you wouldn't believe what a difference it has made," he said. "We got some plywood and nailed it up to divide a sleeping room off for the night crews. That swamp cooler is blowing cool air in there, and it's awesome. It's called the morgue now," he said, laughing at himself.

"Why's that, Boomer?" I asked.

"Well, we built the room, sealed it up completely so that no light shone in during the daytime, and then we put cots in there for the night crews to sleep on. You know Al Mays, sir? He's our junior warrant officer."

"Yeah, I know Al," I said.

"Well, Lou, my senior warrant officer, told Al, my junior warrant, that he had to take one for the team," Boomer said, using the quote signs with his fingers and bobbing his head as he said *take one for the team*. "He told him to put his cot down at the end of the room by mine. Then Lou announced to all the pilots, 'I'm not putting up with Captain Arnold's snoring and those nasty-ass feet of his.'"

I laughed at Boomer. His animation and persistent smile were always entertaining.

"I asked him what he meant by that," Boomer said. "I wasn't sure if I should be offended or not. Then in true Lou Papesca fashion, he told me that my feet smell worse than the shithouse."

"Well, Boomer, do you need some new insoles in your boots, some foot powder maybe?" I asked.

"They don't smell that bad, sir," Boomer said, defensively, almost as if his feelings were hurt. "Lou just likes to pick at me. Al Mays laughed at Lou's little smart-ass comment, but then he busted on Lou."

"What'd he say?" I asked.

"He told Lou that the place would smell like a morgue by noon if he started busting ass," Boomer said.

"Boomer," I said. "That place is going to stink no matter if Lou busts ass or not. All y'all stink."

"No more than you guys," Boomer said, referring to me, Ken, and the SCO. "Anyway," Boomer said, returning to his story. "The next day I walked to the door of our new sleeping area and there was a sign hanging on the door that read, The Morgue," he said and bellowed in laughter.

"Well, Boomer, I'm happy to hear that morale is clearly on the rise in Condor Troop," I said.

"Me too, sir," he said as he stood up and began walking toward the door. Then he stopped and turned around. "Hey, sir. Have you started flying yet?" he asked.

"Tomorrow is my first day," I said. "I flew out to Stayla with the SCO, but tomorrow is my first day up for a training flight with an instructor pilot."

"Awesome. Who are you flying with?" he asked.

"Annihilator Troop," I said.

"That's too bad. You know Condor is the best," he said.

"Well, Boomer, once I get up and flying I'll be sure to come fly with Condor as well," I said.

"Once you try it, you'll never go back," he said, and walked out the door. "Nothing like Condor," I heard him say as the door shut.

That evening I studied the OH-58D Kiowa operator's manual, our Standard Operating Procedures (SOP), and everything else I could get my hands on. I wanted Curtis Phipps to go back to the troop bragging about the new operations officer. I wanted nothing more than to impress him.

AT LAST, FLYING

Having worked a desk for three years, I could not wait to get back in the saddle. After leaving troop command in 1st Squadron, 1st Cavalry Regiment in Germany, Lisa and I moved to northern Virginia, where I served as the operations officer in 12th Aviation Battalion. It was a unique and exciting assignment where I flew UH-1 Hueys at low level between the Lincoln Memorial and Washington Monument one day and up and down the Shenandoah Valley the next.

In July 2000, I was selected to serve as a board recorder in the Department of the Army Secretariat for Promotion and Selection Boards. As a recorder, I was charged with guiding senior officers through the promotion and selection board process. This posting was an educational experience that I thoroughly enjoyed, but the Secretariat was about as far removed from a helicopter cockpit as one could get.

In 2002, we moved to Fort Leavenworth, Kansas, where I attended the Command and General Staff Officers College. So, with Washington and Fort Leavenworth combined, I'd not flown a helicopter in over three years. I was both excited and nervous. Flying, or "wiggling the sticks" as we say, is like riding a bicycle. It comes back rather easily, but the Kiowa had undergone several digital upgrades since I had last flown it. The technical, button-pushing part of flying would take time to learn.

To be designated as a pilot-in-command means that a pilot has demonstrated mastery of all tasks associated with flying the helicopter. More subjectively, it also means demonstrating good judgment. Chief Warrant Officer Four Curtis Phipps, the Annihilator Troop senior instructor pilot, was my instructor pilot. He was charged with getting me back up as a pilot-in-command. A forty-four-year-old man whose body had forgotten to age, Curtis maxed the physical fitness test in the young man's category (seventeen–twenty-one-year-olds). He did push-ups nonstop for the allotted two minutes, cranked out sit-ups like a piston, and ran like the wind.

A mere thirty days after the squadron settled at Q-West, the SCO directed the troop commanders to conduct physical fitness tests for all the troopers. 2-17 CAV had been deployed to Iraq for about six months at that point, with no ability to conduct organized physical training. However, by July we were operating on a fairly predictable schedule. We had a weight room and there was abundant space on the airfield to run, so Schiller wanted the troopers to understand his expectations—physical fitness was a priority.

I vividly recall going out for a run the day Annihilator Troop took their first physical fitness test at Q-West. They had already begun the two-mile run on an out-and-back course when I saw them. I ran by their starting line, at which point I could see the men strung out along the road in the distance. Most of them had already hit the one-mile turnaround point and were coming back toward me. As I met those leading the pack, I saw that Curtis Phipps, the oldest man in the troop, was running alongside a thin, wiry, and much younger warrant officer named Matt Harris. The two of them led the troop. Tall and strong, Curtis hammered down the road. As he passed me, he grinned and effortlessly said, "Morning, sir." Curtis Phipps held on to a young man's game with an iron grip.

As one might imagine, a commissioned officer's reputation as a pilot is extremely important. No different than the horsemanship of our cavalry predecessors. Aviation warrant officers are subject matter experts. They specialize in one of four career fields: maintenance officer, instructor pilot, safety officer, or tactical operations officer. It's a given that all warrant officers are exceptional pilots. Commissioned officers, however, must become excellent organizational leaders while simultaneously developing as a pilot. Many officers accept that they will never equal their warrant officer counterparts as pilots. While that reality is true for the vast majority of pilots, I will never forget the sage counsel my first commander, Captain Karl Kearney, gave me as a young lieutenant. "Your warrant officers will respect and follow you because you demonstrate competence. Bust your ass to be as good or better than them at everything. Then they will point you out to their peers and say, 'That's my lieutenant.'" Or at least that's how I chose to remember it.

So, as I said, I was both excited and nervous to fly. I was eager to fly the helicopter, but more importantly, I wanted to make a positive impression.

On the day of our first flight, Curtis met me in our headquarters building. We methodically planned our mission and then headed to the flight line. After a thorough inspection of the aircraft, we donned our gear and prepared to go flying. At no point did Curtis try and stump me with nitpicky questions. Instead, he told me that he had reviewed my records and realized that I had not flown in a long time. "Let's just go fly and brush up on things," he said. "The aircraft has changed quite a bit since you last flew it. Today, I'll do a lot of talking and teaching. I just want you to relax, enjoy it, and soak up as much information as you can."

Instantly, I was at ease.

Curtis walked me through the starting procedures step-by-step. With the press of a button, ignitors clicked, emitting sparks in the combustion section of the engine. With a twist of the wrist, fuel flowed across the sparks, creating a controlled explosion—a deep thud that transitioned to a whine as the turbine engine began producing power. Rotor blades began to turn with increased speed and energy until they reached 393 rpm. Four blades rotating at a speed of 491 mph. At full throttle, they sent a high-frequency buzz throughout the airplane—and you. I could literally feel the power of that machine flowing through my body. It was intoxicating.

I took control of the harnessed power, and with the gentle pull of the collective control lever we took to the skies, and the worries of the world vanished with the wind. Primitive accommodations, unbearable heat, and a formidable adversary remained only seven hundred feet below us. They were very real, yet with some wrinkle in reality, they seemed to me a world away.

Curtis and I flew a few standard approaches to the runway at Q-West, then a shallow approach to a running landing. Finally, we conducted autorotations, which simulate an emergency landing with no operational engine.

I could not have written the flight any better. It felt wonderful to fly again. After two hours, Curtis suggested we get fuel and call it a day. I would need several flights to demonstrate proficiency in all the required flight tasks in both daytime and nighttime, under night vision goggles.

I walked back into the TOC invigorated, and then I opened the TOC door. Unexpectedly, I found Doug Ford sitting at my desk filling out a risk assessment for his flight later in the day.

"Doug, you trying to take my job?" I asked.

"Someone needs to," he quipped, then looked up. "Actually, no. I don't want to take your job because then you'd fly more and I'm sure we are all safer with you sitting right here at this desk."

"Funny guy, Doug. You're a funny guy."

Doug resumed filling out the forms and then under his breath said, "Shavetail."

Shavetail was a term used to identify young, inexperienced cavalrymen. When new recruits reported to the cavalry, they would shave their horses' hindquarters to make them easily identifiable. Experienced cavalrymen would give a shavetail more room to maneuver when riding. While the horse was actually shaved, the young cavalryman was known as a shavetail. This label persisted until the young trooper earned his spurs.

"Oh, Doug. I can always count on you," I said, downplaying the insult. "Hey, I was looking through some pictures on the computer yesterday, and I saw this picture with two big spiders attached to one another. What's up with that?" I asked, changing the subject.

"Spiders! Thank goodness. I thought you might say you found porn," he confided. "Whew, what you found was the Arena of Death!"

"The Arena of Death. What's that?" I asked.

Doug placed his pen on my desk, sat back in the chair, kicked his feet out in front of him, and folded his arms across his chest. "Early in the war we started finding camel spiders and scorpions everywhere. Seriously, they were everywhere. One day someone decided to see if they would fight each other. We put two camel spiders in a bucket and it was game on," he said.

"They fought?" I asked.

"Hell yeah, they fought each other. To the death!" he said. "It wasn't long until someone decided to catch a scorpion to see if it would fight."

"Did it?" I asked.

"Absolutely. So, people started finding their entrant into the Arena of Death. We held the fights after the commander's update briefing most of the time. When we got weathered in at FARP Shell, right after we crossed the berm, I found a lizard. It was big, about a foot and a half long. I thought I had found my ticket into the Arena of Death," he said.

"Was it hard to catch?" I asked.

"I had to chase it around for about thirty minutes, but I finally caught it. I put it in an ammo can, and the first time I opened that ammo can, I cleared the tent," he said, laughing.

"Did it win?" I asked.

"No," he said, sadly. "It was too cold at night. I'd put my lizard in the arena, and it would just lie there. It didn't even want to move."

"Did the spiders or scorpions attack it?" I asked.

"No. They just looked at it. I think if it had been warmer, he would have fought," Doug said. "I finally just let it go, but we found it later. It had crawled under Greg Cooper's pup tent to keep warm.

"During the war, the games stopped for a while, but once we got to the hill above Mosul, we started it back up. The artillery guys had a spider that was badass. I forget what they named it, but it killed everyone else's spider," he said.

"How about the scorpions?" I asked.

"The scorpions were tough. It wasn't even a match between them and the spiders. They would sting a camel spider about ten times before it could even move. The best fights were spider on spider," he said.

"The SCO came to me one day and said, 'Okay, Mr. Safety, do we really want guys running around catching spiders?'" Doug said, imitating the SCO.

"What did you say to that?"

"I asked him if he really wanted all those spiders running around in our tactical assembly area."

"What'd he say?"

"Of course, he said, 'Doug, you've got a point.' I was right as usual."

"Were they easy to find?" I asked.

"Yes. Up there at Mosul they were all over the place," he said. "But I haven't seen many since we've been here at Q-West."[1]

"That doesn't bother me at all. I don't like spiders," I said. "Especially, spiders that are as big as my hand."

"Hey, did you hear about the sulfur fire?" Doug asked, changing the subject.

"No. What sulfur fire?"

"If you fly up the river to Mosul, before you get to the city, on the right side of the river, there is a huge mountain of sulfur," he said.

"Mountain of sulfur?"

"Yeah, it looks like a big Alka-Seltzer pill. It's probably fifty feet tall and a half mile across, pure sulfur," he said. "Somebody, probably the bad guys, blew it up, and it caught on fire. Now it's burning, and they can't put it out. It melts and runs like lava."

"Really?" I said.

"They said the smoke is noxious. Maybe even poisonous. If the wind's right, we could all die."

"Oh, Doug. I might try and get up there and take a look at it on my next flight," I said, standing to go put my flight gear away. As I walked to my room, it occurred to me that I was already forming good relationships with several of the warrant officers. An open doorway separated Doug's room from mine, so I spent a lot of time with him. Little did we know at that time that a mission lay in my and Doug's future that we would carry with us for the rest of our lives.

When I returned to the TOC, Doug was gone. He'd been replaced by the SCO, who sat in my chair talking to Ken.

"What's on the agenda today?" Schiller said, appearing to be in a playful mood.

"I'm going to church this afternoon," I said. "The chaplains have turned one of the buildings into a chapel, so I'm going to go over and check it out."

"What faith are you, again?" he asked. The question somewhat surprised me. I thought he knew what I was. Then I realized that he was about to give me a ration of crap.

"LDS," I said. "I'm Mormon."

"Mormon!" he said. "Dan Laguna is a Mormon. You know Dan Laguna?"

"I know who he is, but I don't know him well," I said. Dan Laguna was a warrant officer in the 160th SOAR. He was a Little Bird flight lead in B Company, 1-160, which Schiller had commanded.

"Oh well, you're all quitters anyway," he said, and there it was. He was referring to the Protestant Reformation, of course. Everyone was Catholic before that in Schiller's mind. "Being from Georgia, I figured you for a Baptist."

"I was. I grew up Baptist. My family still is, and I love the Baptist people," I said.

"Why did you switch then?" he asked.

"Well, it's complicated," I said. "I guess you could just say, I found what I was looking for. Religion in my childhood was a complicated matter. There were a lot of contradictions."

"What do you mean by that?" he asked, genuinely interested.

"Well, I grew up around old men that were as likely to go to a beer joint as they were a church. They were all God-fearing men, diehard Christians, but they lived in a gray zone when it came to the application of religious principles. Not my father, though. Once he committed to religion, it was black and white. If it says 'thou shalt' in the Bible, that's the end of it. Throughout my childhood, he was rather militant when it came to the application of religion. We never missed a Wednesday night or a Sunday service. If we were not at least ten minutes early for meetings, we were late, and there was not a sickness on earth that justified being absent from the Lord's house when the doors were open. In fact, there was never an ailment that a good sermon would not make better," I said.

Schiller listened intently with a thin smile on his face. He was in a mood to give me a hard time, but now he was interested in my story.

"But the old men that I grew up around, they were different. They enjoyed a good preaching, but they were more likely to take a pull on a bottle just before they went into a service than they were to put on a tie. Some of them had a suit, just one, but they never wore it to church unless someone had died or was getting hitched. They called it their marryin' and buryin' suit, and that's the only time they wore it. The good Lord did get their best pair of overalls, though, clean ones anyway. *The Lord don't care what I'm wearing when I go to church,* they'd say. *'He just cares where my heart is,'* and that's what I had questions about.

"I've seen them, cross-eyed drunk and dog-cussing one another, talk about how the world was going to hell in a handbasket, and how men better get their lives straightened out, repent, and be saved, because the second coming is nigh at hand. Then they'd pass a bottle or throw a punch.

"Don't get me wrong. I loved those old men. I surely did, but when it came to religion, I had lots of questions that I had to work through on my own. As I say, I found what I was looking for, and I'm happy," I said.

"Well, I've known a lot of Mormons, and they're good people." Then he paused. "Still quitters though," he said and laughed.

I laughed with him.

"I don't blame their religion for the way those men behaved. Far from it. I've often said, just think how great the world would be if everyone lived the principles of their religion, whatever religion that happens to be, with exactness. But churches weren't made for perfect people. They were built for sinners, like us."

"You've got that right," Schiller said.

"I saw that talisman hanging around your neck. You're Catholic," I said, knowing he could take as much as he dished out.

"Yeah. The other cult," he said tongue in cheek, then threw his head back and laughed out loud.

Schiller's dog tag chain was filled with trinkets. Every soldier is required to wear two dog tags around their neck, which are imprinted with their name, faith, and blood type, to be used in the most morbid of situations. Schiller had added to the dog tags. It was the perfect moment to ask him to explain. "What is all that stuff on your chain?"

He reached down and took the chain in his hand, then removed it from his neck, and began, "This one is St. Christopher—the patron saint of travelers—which my mother gave me. This is St. Stephen for my namesake. Rhonda gave it to me. He was the first martyr, stoned to death for his belief in Jesus. This one is a St. Michael I was given by the Fort Rucker Catholic Church after receiving my flight wings, and this is another St. Michael I got at Fort Benning after airborne school. This is a lucky penny with a star cut out. I don't remember who gave that to me, but it's cool. A friend of mine gave me this crucifix, and here is one more cross," he said.

"That's a lot of *stuff* around your neck," I said.

He was in the midst of sipping his coffee. He stopped short and raised his eyebrows. "I'm not superstitious, nor do I believe these things are some sort of armor of protection. I just think I should be gracious enough to wear them since they were gifts. When I receive a trinket from a family member or a friend, this is where it ends up," he said, then took a sip of hot coffee. "On this chain."

"Whatever makes you feel good, boss," I said. "My best friend in high school was Catholic, but there weren't many Catholics in Calhoun, Georgia, in the seventies and eighties."

"I bet there weren't many Mormons in Calhoun, Georgia, either," he countered.

"You know," I said. "I can only recall one. He was a veterinarian. The only thing I ever heard about Mormons growing up was when Ms. Georgia Hardwick taught about the Mormon migration to Salt Lake City in her government class. That's it. Since we didn't know of any, I was left to assume that they all walked to Salt Lake and that's where they stayed."

It was a time before officers were scared to admit that they were religious, before they were afraid to admit they went to church and celebrated Christmas. It was before we believed that by letting others in on our dirty little secret—that we were Christian, regardless of denomination—we would inevitably offend those not of our faith. Nothing could be further from the truth. We did not care which church a soldier attended, or if they did not believe in God at all. We believed, as I still do, that a soldier has the right to his or her free agency. It is their personal choice to decide what they do and do not believe. I had always assumed that the freedom to choose one's religion was one of those rights to which we thought everyone was entitled, a right for which we were willing to fight. In our unit, all we truly cared about is that he or she was a good soldier.

Steve Schiller was not shy about his religion. Despite being far from both, he was a self-proclaimed cradle-to-grave Catholic. Our doctrines differed, yet we respected one another. I appreciated the fact that he had convictions. His beliefs differed somewhat from mine, but he knew what he believed and stood firmly. I appreciated that fact. Better yet, he respected me and my beliefs, and I never felt that he judged me in any way. That Sunday morning in the TOC at Q-West, he took another sip of coffee and asked, "Will you be back in time for euchre?"

"Yes, sir. I wouldn't miss it."

"Good, because God has no problem with a friendly game of cards."

We had developed somewhat of a ritual. On Sunday afternoons, we played euchre. I had never played euchre until Schiller introduced me to the game. Unless one of us was flying, Ken Hawley and I formed a team, and Schiller played with Doug Ford; however, when Doug was flying, we invited a guest partner for Schiller. We often asked Boomer Arnold to take Doug's spot since he loved the game and could be counted on for laughs. Schiller could be rough on his partners. He didn't take what he considered to be "dumb play" very well at all. He was prone to being rough on troop commanders in general, so it was always entertaining when Boomer was Schiller's guest partner.

Doug took Schiller's harassment quietly. He would scrunch his mustache up and sit back shaking his head when Schiller questioned a play. Boomer, on the other hand, would try to defend himself, which never worked out well for him but also never deterred him.

Card night was the night we chose to eat from our care packages. Our favorite snack was summer sausage, spicy mustard, cheese, and crackers. Care packages were rolling in from home on a frequent basis by that point in the deployment, so we had begun sending lists back to our families. Summer sausage and crackers were our number one request.

My wife, Lisa, gave me a knife the day I pinned on second lieutenant, a commissioning gift. It was a Parker with a straight four-inch blade and bone handles. Having been carried on my belt throughout my career, the old leather scabbard had worn considerably by that point. As a boy, every knife in our home was handmade and razor sharp. Once chainsaws came along, the old men who defined my childhood had no use for cross-cut saws. Not knowing exactly what to do with them, the Depression-era men who did not throw anything away decided to hang them on the walls of their barns, like pictures that froze their memories in time.

Eventually, they realized that the steel in the saw blades would rust away if they didn't put it to use. Like anything else in life, good steel lasts longer if it's used. They decided to make butcher knives. They cut the knife blades out of the saws and began sharpening them, and they would not rest until a knife would shave a grown man's arm. The old men sat on benches and stumps outside my grandfather's barbershop, spitting

Beech-Nut like a sniper rifle at leaves and insects, while they methodically dragged steel blades across whetstones. To the rhythm of scraping steel on stone, they'd tell stories and lies or a combination of the two for hours on end. Sharpening a knife became somewhat of a ritual. It was not uncommon to see a concave blade, the result of sharpening day after day, even when the blade did not need it.

Having grown up in that environment, I kept my Parker so sharp it would shave a man's arm. It was shameful to loan a man a dull knife. Unfortunately, today few men take the time to perfect the art of sharpening a pocketknife. Heck, few men carry a knife today, but that was not the case at Q-West in 2003; some soldiers carried two. I used my Parker to slice off pieces of sausage with ease. Despite the grease associated with a log of summer sausage, that Parker slid through it like a hot knife through butter. Thus, my duty during the card game was to slice off a chunk of sausage, a hunk of cheese, place them on a cracker, and hand it to whoever was empty-handed at the time.

"How many Mormons are there on Q-West?" Schiller asked me over cards that evening.

"There were about ten there today," I said.

"I've known a lot of good Mormons," he said, continuing the conversation where we left off that morning. "You'd like Dan Laguna."

"I'm sure I would," I replied. "We're all good people."

Schiller laughed.

That night, I lay on my cot and thought of home. A shaft of moonlight entered the room between a poncho and the wall, cutting across the room. Its presence reminded me of my wife, Lisa. She could not sleep if so much as a speck of light was visible in our bedroom. Many was the night that I pulled and tugged at curtains in a hotel room trying to block out all the light for her. I missed her and wondered what she might be doing at that moment.

A PAIR OF ACES

Having grown up in northern Georgia with no air conditioning, I was used to sweating. Other than the occasional spend-the-night party at a friend's house, the first air conditioner I slept under was at North Georgia College. I suppose I grew soft over the years because, on July 22nd, I woke up soaked in sweat and angry.

I rolled out of the cot and threw my sheet over a bungee cord to dry. The sweat would quickly turn to salt in the arid climate, making the sheet brittle and stiff for the next night's struggle for sleep. I grabbed a bottle of water on my way to the TOC. It was impossible to remain hydrated. Despite drinking liter upon liter of water each morning, I almost never had to pee before lunch.

Annihilator Troop had scheduled Doug and me to fly a route reconnaissance mission along Main Supply Route (MSR) Taurus. Having been in Iraq for just over a month at that point, I was finally starting to feel somewhat comfortable flying missions. It took time to memorize prominent landmarks used to navigate while flying in a new place, but with each flight, my confidence had increased. By late July, I knew the lay of the land pretty well, and I was getting comfortable making the multitude of radio calls that were required to operate within Mosul's airspace.

Route Taurus paralleled the Tigris River from Q-West to Mosul. Doug and I would fly trail with a crew from the Mississippi National Guard flying as our lead that day. When 2-17 Cavalry deployed to Iraq, they were short Kiowa pilots, so the army augmented them with National Guard crews. The National Guard crews quickly integrated into the squadron, becoming integral members of the team.

After three flights, Curtis Phipps designated me a readiness level two pilot, which meant that I was supposed to continue practicing mission tasks until he progressed me to the final level, readiness level one. I was using the flight with Doug to practice mission planning and reconnaissance as part of my continuing progression.

Being the new guy in the unit, I wanted to try and impress Doug, so I got up early and began planning the mission. Around 7:00 a.m., Ken walked into the TOC. "You got up early, roommate," he said. "Go for a run?"

"No. I wanted to plan my and Doug's mission, make sure I had everything ready to go," I said.

"Oh, I see," he said, while sitting down at his desk.

Around 8:00 a.m., Doug walked through the door. He was wearing his physical training uniform, and I could see beads of sweat on his forehead. "What's up, Doug? Did you have to run to the outhouse?"

"What's that supposed to mean?" he asked.

"Well, you're sweating," I said and waited for a reaction.

"Very funny, sir. I went for a run," he said, very matter-of-fact.

"Ohhh myyy goooosh," Ken said, throwing his head back and rolling it in a circle, reminding me of Archie Bunker.

Curious, I asked with complete sincerity, "Did you actually go for a run?"

"Of course, I did," Doug said, frowning, as if it were absurd to ask such a question.

"How far did you go?" I asked.

With an air of pride, Doug lifted his chin slightly and said, "'Bout a mile."

"A mile!" I said. "That's not worth getting dressed for, Doug."

Now, going on the defense, Doug said, "Hey, you guys are always talking about how everyone needs to do more *physical training*," using both hands to making the quote sign. "I go and run, which I hate, and this is what I get." Doug turned and started for the door.

"I hope you didn't shoot your wad," I said. "We've got to fly today."

"Smart asses," he said over his shoulder and shaking his head. "If smart asses were worth anything, we'd be rich around here," he added as he opened the door.

125

"I love you, Doug!" I yelled as the door slammed behind him.

"A mile," Ken said, shaking his head and turning back to his computer.

"You know he runs farther, right?" I said.

"What do you mean?" Ken asked.

"He actually runs about four miles, but he knows how I feel about running, so he says he only runs a mile just to try and piss me off. I play along because it's Doug, and he loves the drama," I said.

An hour later, I briefed our team on the mission, and then Doug and I drove the half mile to the flight line, where we conducted a preflight inspection of the helicopter. More serious now, Doug carefully walked me through a very thorough preflight. He quizzed me to make sure I knew everything I was required to know.

We cranked the helicopter and conducted radio checks.

"Doug?" I said as we prepared to take flight.

"Yes sir," he answered.

"I'm glad you recovered so well," I said.

He seemed confused at my statement. "What do you mean?" he asked.

"Well, you really exerted yourself this morning with that long run and all, so…"

"Screw you, SIR!" he cut me off.

I laughed aloud. "You're all right, Doug Ford. I don't care what everyone else says about you. I think you're all right."

Doug shook his head.

We departed Q-West as a team of two Kiowas. We began conducting reconnaissance of route Taurus at approximately 10:30 a.m. Our lead aircraft flew no more than fifty feet above the ground. They searched the road and surrounding terrain for anything that appeared to be out of place: roadside bombs disguised as trash, disturbed dirt that could possibly cover a planted bomb, and likely ambush sites along the road. Doug and I flew slightly higher and behind lead, so that we could cover them if the enemy suddenly attacked them.

It was a quiet morning. As we flew along behind our lead aircraft, Doug reviewed Standard Operating Procedures with me. Having been an AH-1 Cobra Instructor Pilot, Doug knew the questions I would likely be asked on a check ride with Curtis Phipps, so he drilled me on aircraft systems, emergency procedures, and aircraft limitations. We fully expected the mission to be uneventful, a great training opportunity, but that idea was tossed out the window at 10:50 a.m.

That morning, as Doug and I prepared for a routine reconnaissance mission, as average Americans lay in their beds sleeping, unbeknownst to all of us, a small team of special operations forces departed their compounds in Mosul and Baghdad and were on the move. Their objective: a house in northern Mosul where an informant, later alleged to be Saddam Hussein's cousin,[1] had told them they would find Saddam's sons, Qusay and Uday Hussein. Qusay was the ace of clubs and Uday the ace of hearts on the infamous most-wanted deck of cards.

Not much was known about Qusay, other than that he was Saddam's second son, who became the anointed heir after his older brother self-destructed and fell from grace. Uday Hussein, on the other hand, was a well-known figure. To say that Uday Hussein was an evil man is an understatement. He tortured Olympic athletes for poor performances, raped women, and murdered those who crossed him. He stabbed his father's personal valet to death with an electric carving knife at a party. For that, Saddam punished Uday by putting him in prison for a short stint. Once he released Uday from prison, Saddam banished him to Switzerland, but in 1990 the Swiss government expelled him from their country for repeatedly instigating fights.

"Saber TOC, this is Strike Six, over." It was unusual for Colonel Joe Anderson to call our TOC directly.

"Were those machine guns I heard in the background?" Doug asked, as we listened to the radio from our helicopter. Anderson was calling on our squadron command net.

"That's what it sounded like to me," I said.

"Strike Six, Saber TOC," came the reply.

"I need a team of Kiowas in Mosul now," Anderson said.

"Strike Six, this is Saber Three, over," I broke in on the radio using my call sign. I knew we were the only team out flying at the moment. If he needed Kiowas, we were that team.

"Saber Three, Strike Six. I need you in Mosul. Contact me when you get here," he said.

"Roger, over," I replied.

As Colonel Anderson had continued to speak, Doug and I clearly heard the distinct *cack, cack, cack* of machine guns in the background.

"That doesn't sound good," Doug said, his brow furrowed.

"No kidding. Sounds like they are in a serious firefight," I said.

"Lead, this is trail. Did you monitor that conversation with Strike Six?" Doug asked our lead Kiowa.

"Roger. We're heading that way," Lead responded.

I could feel my heart rate begin to increase, and an anxious feeling came over me. I had been the air mission commander on hundreds of training missions, but this was not the National Training Center. This was going to be my first firefight, a two-way range. Doug closed the distance between us and our lead helicopter as we followed them to Mosul. We flew north, directly over the Tigris River. As we passed Mosul airfield, I called Colonel Anderson.

"Strike Six, this is Saber Three, over."

"Saber Three, stand by for grid coordinates," Anderson said.

He passed the grid coordinates to his location, and I wrote them down. "Saber Three, I need you to shoot the second-story window on the south side of the house. You will see us outside the courtyard when you arrive. You are cleared hot when you get here," he said, meaning to come in shooting.

Second-story window! I thought to myself. Since joining 2-17 CAV, I had come to realize that the Kiowa's weapons could be fired with tremendous precision, but a window in the middle of the city?

When I was a student in the Kiowa Warrior aircraft qualification course at Fort Rucker, Alabama, an instructor pilot flew me out to the range to demonstrate the Kiowa's weapon systems in action. He came to a hover in front of an old Soviet tank. The instructor pilot said he was going to shoot the tank with the .50-caliber machine gun. He then depressed the trigger, and the aircraft yawed left as the gun sprayed rounds down-range, mowing down a small tree just off the nose of the helicopter. After about fifty rounds, he finally managed to get a few on the tank.

While I was thrilled to have a weapon on my helicopter—previous OH-58 models were not armed—I was amazed at its inaccuracy.

Having grown up in the 160th SOAR flying AH-6 Little Birds, Schiller brought their gunnery tactics to 2-17. I had heard the other pilots tell stories about Schiller shooting through doorways during the first month of the war, but Schiller had shot thousands of rockets in the 160th. I recalled what Curtis Phipps had told me.

"When Lieutenant Colonel Schiller first took command of 2-17, I flew him out to the range to demonstrate how we shot," Curtis said. "I shot a few, and he watched me. Then he asked me if I would like to 'see how it's done across the street,' meaning 160th. I told him that I would, so he commenced to shoot. He got a direct hit on everything he shot. The Kiowa no longer had 'area' weapon systems."[2]

As we flew over Mosul, I prayed that our National Guard crew was half as proficient as Schiller. Doug had flown with Schiller throughout the war, so he had not shot very many rockets himself. Schiller only flew in the right seat, so Doug didn't get any trigger time. Helicopter gunnery is a perishable skill. That concerned me.

We flew to the north side of the city, and I quickly located the target house. Soldiers were hunkered down behind a rock wall for protection, but I saw men randomly popping up to shoot at the window that Anderson had described to me. Bullets sparked as they hit the window frame and mortar wall. Other soldiers walked around between vehicles parked in the street. A thin layer of smoke and dust hung in the air around the house.

"There they are," I told Doug. "Lead, do you see them?" I asked over the radio.

"Roger, we see them. We're going to set up a pattern. We'll attack from the south, right turns," lead responded, meaning they would attack the target from the south and turn right when they finished shooting.

There was a mosque that sat a block southeast of the house and another building adjacent to the mosque with a tall spire extending up into the air about one hundred feet. Lead initially set us up on the north side of the mosque, which created an odd angle to attack the window. I could clearly see where the men on the ground were shooting. The second-story window was on the south side, as Anderson had described. I was not sure how lead was going to attack the target from the east, but I naively trusted what they were doing. In addition, I was concerned with how close the men on the ground were to the house. They were no more than fifty yards from the house, and having witnessed many rockets impact short and long of the intended target, I was not comfortable with them being that close to the house.

"Strike Six, this is Saber Three. Can you move everyone back a little? They are too close to the house, over."

"Roger, stand by," he said and began telling the men to move back behind their trucks, which were parked in the road.

In reality, Colonel Joe Anderson expected us to shoot through the window. Having served in the 75th Ranger Regiment, where he worked frequently with the 160th SOAR, and having witnessed Schiller's marksmanship during the initial stages of the war, he was confident that we'd hit the window.

Suddenly, I was nervous, not *scared* nervous, but rather *don't screw it up* nervous. The way a quarterback feels on the first play of a championship game. Here I was, the air mission commander of a team of Kiowas in combat going after two of the three most wanted human beings on the planet. It was my first combat shooting ordeal, and I had an audience giving me their undivided attention. It did not matter who else was in the flight; it was my call sign being used over the radio. I felt like a second-string quarterback bumped up to varsity because the starting quarterback tore his ACL and the coach said, *"Here's your big chance son, don't screw it up—we'll all be standing here on the sideline watching and rooting for you."* Only I had very little control. I was sitting in the left seat, along for the ride, as if flying and shooting would have mattered.

Once the soldiers on the ground moved back, lead called, "We're inbound hot, right breaks," to let Doug and me know they were going in on the attack.

"Roger, we're right behind you," Doug replied.

My mouth was dry. I could taste my own breath. A thousand thoughts raced through my mind. We were about to attempt a very tough shot in the middle of the city, and there were at least a hundred soldiers on the ground watching by that point. I was extremely concerned that we might hit the soldiers in front of the house. A short shot would spell disaster, so I made a radio transmission that, in hindsight, I probably should not have made, "Whatever you do," I said, "do not shoot short!"

They didn't.

As we waited for Strike Six to move everyone back from the house, lead shifted our flight pattern. The new pattern gave us a better approach to the window. *Please hit the window*, I thought to myself. Lead bumped and climbed higher into the air. Then as their airspeed dissipated, they nosed the Kiowa over and began to dive at the house but did not shoot.

"Misfire!" lead called and broke to the right.

As lead dove, Doug had pulled the cyclic to the rear, causing us to climb. Once lead broke right, Doug nosed our Kiowa over and began the dive. I switched the master switch to fire, Doug confirmed that the rockets were ready to fire, and he squeezed the trigger. Nothing! Again, he depressed the fire switch, but no rocket fired. 2-17 CAV had experienced trouble in Iraq with the electrical contacts on the rocket tubes getting dusty and sandy. Despite cleaning the contacts and brushing the rocket tubes with a bore brush, we still had many misfires.

"Dammit!" Doug said.

"Misfire," I transmitted to Strike Six. "We're coming back around."

"Trail, this is lead. We're heading back in with rockets again."

"Roger. We're going to try again as well," Doug said.

Preparing to shoot, lead climbed and nosed it over again. This time, a pair of rockets left the tube and sailed right over the top of the house, impacting a three-story building behind the target house. Doug climbed right behind lead. As we dove toward the house, I could see where literally thousands of bullets had chipped away at the house around the window on the side of the house.

Doug lined the helicopter up for the shot and depressed the fire switch, but nothing happened. "Shit!" he yelled, pressing it again and again, and then—*whoosh*—a rocket fired. I knew as soon as the rocket left the tube that it was going long. It was as though time slowed to a crawl. The rocket was lined up well, but we had continued to close the distance to the target as Doug repeatedly pressed the fire button. The trajectory had changed as we closed the distance to the target. The rocked sailed across the roof of the house and struck near where lead's two rockets had hit.

Doug quickly pushed the cyclic control forward, steepening our dive angle, and depressed the fire switch again. Another rocket launched, striking the target house on the roof. The rocket exploded but only made a slight divot in the roof. We broke right, and Strike Six called us on the radio.

"Cease fire, cease fire!" he said.

Instantly, I was sick to my stomach. I cringed in my seat, hoping that we had not hurt anyone with the errant rockets.

"I need you to hit the window on the second story," Anderson said. "They are holed up in that room. Shoot the window."

"Lead, this is trail. Do you see the window he is talking about?" I asked.

"Roger," Lead replied.

"Strike Six this is Saber Three. Request permission to reattack, over," I said.

"Roger. You're cleared," he replied.

Lead bumped and dove toward the target, this time intending to shoot the .50 caliber. I sent up a double prayer this time. *Please God, let them hit the window, and please let the gun fire.*

Despite being one of the most innovative and industrious leaders I had ever met, Steve Schiller had not been able to get us a new machine gun. The M296 .50 caliber was not very reliable. From the first day Schiller flew the Kiowa, he began lobbying for a better gun. In the 160th, they shot the GAU-19 .50 caliber. It is a three-barrel Gatling gun, with a proven record of accomplishment. Nevertheless, there we were, having experienced misfires with rockets and then having missed the target with an audience of fellow soldiers watching. If our guns jammed, I feared that we would have completely compromised our unit's reputation. *That's one heck of a way to be remembered*, I thought to myself.

Lead flew inbound to the target and began shooting. Thank goodness their gun worked. Their rounds initially struck the base of the house. I could see tracers striking the doorway and a first-floor room. A small fire had begun to burn inside the house. They did not shoot the window, but I was happy that the rounds had hit the house. Doug followed. His initial bullets struck the base of the house as well; then he adjusted them to the window, filling the room with .50-caliber rounds.

"Saber Three, Strike Six. Hold to the west, over," Anderson said, wanting us to fly to the west and wait.

I could only assume that it was over for us. I knew what Colonel Anderson had wanted. He wanted us to fill that second-story window full of .50-caliber rounds and rockets, but we had failed to meet his intent, so he was ready to move on to the next option. I heard Major Brian Pearl, the brigade operations officer, talking on the radio. In an attempt to figure out what was going on, I called him. He told me that there were four special operators wounded, and he thought the men in the house were number two and number three, meaning Uday and Qusay Hussein.

The operators had taken three casualties when they initially entered the house. Uday, Qusay and his fourteen-year-old son, and another adult male thought to be an aide or bodyguard had barricaded themselves in an upstairs room. The special ops soldiers had entered the house through a central room. As they entered, they were fired upon from the balcony above, wounding three men. They backed out of the house, but another soldier was shot in the courtyard before he could get to cover. At that point, they called the 101st for support, and Strike responded.

The SCO had monitored the radio calls from our TOC at Q-West. Routinely, I called him with updates to keep him informed as to what was happening. I assumed that he was crawling out of his skin to come take control of the situation. We were not the right crews for this mission. Still, I was relieved that he allowed me to remain in charge.

After Colonel Anderson told us to hold off the objective, he decided to shoot TOW missiles into the house. Like most things military, TOW is an acronym. It stands for tubular-launched, optically tracked, wire-guided missile, and they shot thirteen of them into the house that day. The next Kiowa team up for a mission was led by Curtis Phipps. Curtis's team arrived as the TOW missiles were being shot, but they never got an opportunity themselves to shoot. The operators went back into the house two more times before they finally brought the bodies out. Rather quickly, word spread that Uday and Qusay Hussein had been killed.

Doug and I flew back to Q-West in silence. The drive from the flight line to the TOC was painful for me. I had no idea how Schiller would respond. Would he be angry? Disappointed? Worse yet, would he be embarrassed at how we represented 2-17 CAV? Had he lost faith in me?

The idea tortured me, but torture soon gave way to anger. I was furious that the army had not prepared us for such precision engagements. Mad that we had to scratch and fight for every single bullet to shoot a gunnery range. *Ammunition costs nothing in the big scheme of things*, I reasoned.

How could they not fill our coffers with .50-caliber rounds and rockets? We're at war, for crying out loud.

The SCO was waiting on me when I entered the TOC. I walked into my and Ken's office to find him standing in the doorway. He made eye contact, and immediately his face relaxed and a gentle smile spread across his mouth. "Tell me how it went," he said.

I knew that he had followed everything over the radios, yet he seemed to act as if he knew nothing. Over the next half hour, I recounted every detail. He listened intently, rarely asking a question or breaking in. When I was finished, he patted me on the back. "Good job today," he said. "I'm proud of you."

And with that, he lightened my load. Schiller had not been embarrassed. I was embarrassed. My pride was hurt. I vowed that I would do everything in my power to never experience those feelings, for that reason, ever again, nor would I allow my pilots to be placed in a situation in which they were ill-prepared. I'd find a way to ensure that every one of them was as trained as possible.

Later, I was told that someone in Mosul had complained to Schiller about our errant rockets. He was furious. "Coordinate your missions ahead of time and you will get the right support for the right mission," he said. "Don't tell anyone you are going out and you'll get what you get! But don't come back and complain to me when you don't get exactly what you wanted."

News spread quickly that Uday and Qusay Hussein had been killed, but the search for Saddam continued.

RISKY BUSINESS

A few days after the excitement died down with the Uday and Qusay mission, Colonel Anderson called a meeting of all the battalion and squadron commanders in Mosul. A native of New York and 1981 graduate of West Point, Joe Anderson was a rare breed. Having deployed to Panama for Operation Just Cause as a Ranger Regiment company commander and Operation Joint Guardian in Kosovo as a battalion commander, Anderson possessed a wealth of experience. He had also deployed in support of Task Force Hawk in Albania before leading the first ground forces into Kosovo for Operation Joint Guardian, but it was not his operational experience that set Anderson apart. I had met him for the first time soon after arriving at Q-West.

The SCO introduced me to Colonel Anderson when he traveled to Q-West to thank our soldiers for their performance thus far in the war. Joe Anderson was lean and thin, a striking-looking man with intense blue eyes, and a slick bald head. That first morning at Q-West, I extended my hand to shake. He took my hand in his and did not let go. Then he stepped in close, only inches from my face, piercing me with those crystal blue eyes, and with a serious expression of intensity, he began shooting questions at me like a machine gun. He asked where I was from, if I had a family, if I was excited to be in the CAV, and then he made a joke and, while holding my hand, jabbed me in the ribs several times. As he spoke, everyone else around me disappeared into a blur. I felt like I was at the center of the universe, the only person in existence other than the man who addressed me and only me. I had his full attention. He never lost eye contact as he spoke. I don't think he even blinked.

Eventually, he turned to ask Schiller a question, at which time he moved his hand to my shoulder and squeezed slightly, maintaining contact. It was the most engaging encounter with a senior officer I'd had in my career. By the time he finished speaking, I was the self-appointed president of the Joe Anderson fan club. "I'd march to hell with a five-gallon can of gasoline and a box of matches in my hand if I was following that guy," I later told Ken Hawley.

Since I needed to meet with Major Brian Pearl, Anderson's operations officer, and visit my soldiers in Mosul, I asked Schiller if I could fly with him to his meeting in Mosul. He agreed.

When we conducted missions, we flew as a team of two helicopters, but for administrative flights, simply moving around Iraq from one place to another, we often flew single ship. Since the Kiowa is a single-pilot aircraft (capable of being flown by only one pilot), we often flew single pilot and even single pilot single ship, which in hindsight was not the smartest thing we did in combat. Later in the year, I would fly from Q-West to Tal Afar to pick up our newly assigned intelligence officer, Lieutenant Lauren Makowsky. I was all alone in a Kiowa with no wingman for over an hour in the Iraqi desert. Anything could have happened, and I would have been in a difficult situation. In hindsight, it was a dumb decision, one that I would not repeat on future deployments.

Nevertheless, Schiller and I planned to fly up to Mosul alone to meet with Colonel Anderson and Major Brian Pearl. Of course, he flew in the right seat. Only the pilot in the right seat can shoot the weapons systems in a Kiowa, and he was without question the best shot. He knew that not everyone could shoot equally well. Some pilots, regardless of rank and experience, have a natural talent for aerial gunnery. It made sense to put the best shooter behind the gun, because once the shooting started, it was too late to change your mind. That was another lesson I would not forget.

Schiller and I departed Q-West flying due north. We planned to fly "up the gut" as we called it. When we flew from Q-West to Mosul, we used one of three routes. We either paralleled MSR Tampa (Highway 1), which was the westernmost route, or we followed ASR Taurus, which paralleled the Tigris River and was the easternmost route. The third option was to fly directly north, between the two routes, over desert and fields.

After departing Q-West that morning, Schiller transferred the controls to me. "You can fly," he said.

Happy to do so, I took the controls and immediately noticed a local Iraqi man in a field waving his arms at us. The man was clearly trying to get our attention.

"What's that guy doing?" I asked Schiller.

"Not sure," he replied, shifting in his seat and leaning forward to get a better look.

"You ever been flagged down by an Iraqi in a field?" I asked.

"Nope."

Curious as to why the man was trying to get our attention, I flew farther west and descended slightly to get a better look. Little did I know, that's exactly what the man wanted. As we neared him and the man was certain that he had our full attention, he reached down and grasped his dishdasha with both hands. Then he quickly pulled it up to his eyes, revealing himself in all his glory, and began pumping and thrusting his hips, so that his genitals flopped in the breeze.

"Aww, I think he likes you, sir," I told Schiller.

"Asshole," he said, shaking his head.

As we passed over him, the man dropped his dishdasha, pointed at us, and bent over, laughing at himself.

"Morale must be pretty high around Q-West," I said.

"Must be."

The SCO and I proceeded north with me flying the helicopter. We made small talk as we flew. It was a bluebird day, not a cloud in the sky. Having only been in Iraq a few months, I was still fascinated with seeing the country. I was amazed at how much Iraq resembled the mental image I had formed in my mind of the Middle East in biblical times.

Fifteen miles or so north, I noticed five men sitting in a circle in a field. It was not uncommon to see men out in the desert, but usually they were shepherds with flocks. We trained our scouts to notice things that appeared to be out of place. A good scout is attentive to detail; he notices subtle cues that lead to more profound discoveries.

"Look at those guys," I said.

"Yeah," the SCO answered and began observing them more closely.

There were no sheep around them, no vehicles, just five men sitting in a circle in a field. I flew just west of the men so that when we passed over them, they would be right outside the SCO's door. A good scout pilot maneuvers the helicopter so that the pilot not on the controls is in the best position to observe. Seeing that the helicopter was approaching them, the men stared up at us but did not get up. I flew right by them at about two hundred feet above the ground. Just as we passed them, the cyclic control was suddenly snatched out of my hand. The helicopter banked radically right. Thinking that if I didn't recover the helicopter quickly, we'd crash, I instinctively reached for the cyclic, but that's when I realized that the SCO had taken the controls from me.

"What's up?" I asked, unsure what was going on.

"That son-of-a-bitch tried to shoot us!" he said.

As we had flown past, one of the men had jumped to his feet with an AK-47 rifle and aimed it at us. Having kept an eye on them as we passed overhead, the SCO saw the man when he rose. He then snatched the cyclic away from me and put us in a tight right-hand turn. He continued the turn and applied aft cyclic, causing the Kiowa to climb steeply. I realized that he was turning back toward the men. I assumed that since he was climbing, he was going to dive and shoot them. I glanced at his multifunctional display (MFD) and saw that the .50-caliber gun page was displayed. That page had to be up to shoot the gun. I quickly checked to ensure that the master switch was armed, which it was, and then I looked to see that the MFD read "Armed," which it did.

"You are armed," I said and prepared for him to shoot, but he didn't squeeze the trigger.

He dove the aircraft directly at the men. I looked over and saw the rage in his face. "Mother fucker," he said through clenched teeth. He was furious, but I was not sure why he was not yet shooting. By all rights, he was responding appropriately to the men who tried to shoot us. I looked back at the men and saw that all five were now on their feet dancing in place with their hands held out in front of them, as if begging us not to shoot them.

As we continued the steep dive toward the ground, I began to grow concerned. He was closing on them quickly. I was afraid that if he did not shoot or pull up soon, we would crash into the ground. We were diving directly toward one man in particular; I assumed he was the one who pointed the rifle at us. The AK-47 was gone. I expected to see it lying on the ground, but I could not see it. Trusting that the SCO knew what he was doing, I grasped my seat and prayed we would not crash. At the very last second, he leveled the Kiowa, but inertia carried us farther down toward the earth. He pulled in power, and I heard the audible *bong bong bong* audio sound in my helmet. I knew he had just over-torqued the helicopter.

The Kiowa had a very small power margin in high, hot environments. We had to finesse the helicopter to keep from using more power than we had available within constraints. One of the Iraqi men was right in front of us. He saw that we were going to hit him, literally fly right into him, so he dove to the ground. How we did not skewer the man with the lower WSPS (wire strike protection system), I do not know. He sprawled out on the ground as flat as he could, and we passed just over his back.

The SCO quickly came back around and was right back on the men. They were clearly panicking at that point, but I assumed they were too scared to run for fear of being shot.

"What do you want to do?" I asked.

"We ought to shoot these assholes," he said.

We made three passes over them. Not exactly sure what Schiller wanted to do, or what we should do, I began to explore options in my mind. Suddenly, I had an idea. It was a bad one; still, I blurted it out. "Do you want to land and get the gun?"

He hesitated. "What do you mean?"

"You keep the helicopter oriented on them so you can shoot if they do something crazy, but land, and I'll get out and grab the AK-47."

Because we were going to an administrative meeting, I did not bring my M4 rifle with me, another dumb mistake. All I had was my Beretta pistol. It was a really stupid idea, but it seemed like a good one at the time. I took my pistol out of the holster and prepared to exit the helicopter. Schiller slowly shot an approach toward the men, keeping the .50 caliber oriented on them.

"Where was the AK?" I asked Schiller as we neared the ground.

"They were sitting right over there," he said, nodding with his head.

I saw the general location. Realizing that we were landing, the men seemed to grow more concerned. We had not shot them, but they had to recognize that there was no way we could apprehend one of them and take him with us, so I'm sure they were nervous at what we might have in mind.

As soon as the skids touched the ground, I was out of the Kiowa. Fortunately, the men were all standing close together. I cocked the hammer on my pistol and kept it aimed at the chest of the man in the center. I figured I could quickly adjust left or right if one of them tried something. I walked toward them, but I could not find the rifle.

I wasn't scared at all. In fact, I didn't even have that heart-racing, adrenaline-surge feeling I suppose I expected.

When the SCO took the flight controls and banked right, the men must have realized they were busted. The man with the rifle must have hastily buried the rifle. As I searched for it, the men continued holding their hands up and shaking their heads no, clearly begging me not to shoot them. As I moved closer to them, they slowly began to back away from me, still pleading. I quickly stole a glance back at the SCO. He was pointing to my front. With my eyes darting between the men and the ground, I began to kick the loose sand. Finally, I felt the rifle with my foot. Keeping the pistol and my eyes on the men, I squatted down and retrieved the AK-47. Once I had it in hand, I walked backwards to the Kiowa, keeping my pistol on the men. After putting the AK in a back compartment of the helicopter, I climbed back into my seat, and the SCO immediately took off.

Schiller flew for quite some time without saying a word. I wasn't sure what he was thinking. I tried to think of a way to discuss what had just happened, but I wasn't sure what to say, so I just stared out the door. We flew over several herds of sheep, and I noticed that, as we passed them, the sheep huddled tightly together in a circle with their heads pointing inward. Having nothing but desert sand and a few weeds to eat in summer, I suppose I expected the sheep to be skinny as a rail and wild as deer, but I was mistaken. They were healthy and fat, and as docile as a house dog.

"Why do you reckon they do that?" I asked Schiller, relieved to have something to talk about.

"Do what?" he asked.

"Huddle up tight like that and point all of their heads toward the center."

"Protection," he said. "They are scared, so they huddle up as tightly as they can. If danger comes, a wolf or something, it only gets the one on the outside of the circle."

"Wow," I said. "Most animals scatter and make a run for it when they're in danger."

"Yeah, but they aren't fast, and there's really nowhere to go in the desert," he said.

"I guess they know they can't outrun much of anything, so the last guy to join the circle is out of luck. He gets sacrificed. Kind of like the old expression: 'I don't have to outrun the bear. I just have to outrun you.'"

Laughing, Schiller said, "I suppose so."

It would be years later before I finally asked Schiller what he thought about our little foray with the five Iraqi men. "In retrospect, it wasn't really a smart idea," he said. "First off, you and I were single ship, and it probably was not a good idea to have the squadron commander and the operations officer flying together in the same helicopter. Second, flying with no wingman made it twice as risky."

"I thought you were going to shoot them at first," I said.

"I never had any intention of shooting those guys," he said. "As a former gun pilot in 160th, I understand that what makes a great gun pilot is knowing when *not* to pull the trigger. Kind of goes back to an experience I had in Desert Storm."[1]

I knew Schiller had been in the unit that experienced a horrific engagement in Desert Storm that killed US servicemen, but I would not get his take on that situation until later in the deployment.

We landed at Strike Main, and I began shutting the helicopter down. Due to our little ordeal with the men in the field, Schiller was running late for his meeting. As the rotors coasted to a stop, he quickly exited the aircraft and strode across the landing pad for the headquarters building. Once the rotors completely stopped turning, I got out and retrieved the AK-47 to inspect it.

The rifle was old and rusty. There was a magazine in the well, but to my surprise, there wasn't a single bullet in it. I cocked the weapon and discovered the chamber empty as well. The man had pointed an empty gun at us, trying to impress his friends, I suppose. *What a stupid thing to do,* I thought to myself. It could have cost them all their lives.

When Strike occupied positions throughout Mosul, Schiller and Hawley decided to co-locate a TAC (Tactical Command Post) with Strike's headquarters. The men in the TAC were there to remain abreast of everything Strike was doing operationally and provide that information to each Kiowa team as they arrived in town for missions. They were also the subject matter experts when it came to planning aviation operations with Strike. Ken Hawley assigned two captains and a junior enlisted soldier to the TAC and rotated them between Q-West and Strike Main about once a month. Rowely and Captains Michael Osmon and Marek Wiernusz, whom the other officers called "Beer Nuts," rotated the duty.

They worked out of a small building that Strike had given us on the western bank of the Tigris River. We had numbered the bridges that crossed the Tigris from south to north. Five bridges crossed the Tigris in Mosul proper. Strike Main sat between bridges two and three.

Having heard us land, Mike Osman had begun making his way to the helipad to meet me. Mike was a quiet, reserved man who was never the center of attention in a group; however, he quickly took charge with authority and decisiveness when the situation required it. Wiernusz, on the other hand, was a stocky extrovert who didn't mind sharing what was on his mind. They were a very effective team in the TAC. Mike approached just as I was putting the AK-47 back in the helicopter. "Hey, sir," he said. "How was your flight up?"

"Well, Mike, it was a bit unusual."

"How so?"

I proceeded to tell Mike about the man with a crush on the SCO, which garnered a good laugh, and then I told him what happened with the men in the field. He shook his head and smiled in disbelief as I described landing and taking the AK from the men. "That's crazy, sir," he said.

"Yeah, now that I think about it, it was," I said, realizing that the story was going to spread throughout the squadron quickly. Secretly, I hoped we had not set a new precedent. "But enough about that. How are you guys doing?" I asked.

"Oh, we're good. Strike takes good care of us," he said, as we turned and walked toward the TAC.

Mike pushed the door open to reveal a dark, cavernous room. Rowely lay sprawled out on a cot sleeping. "He was on shift last night," Osman said, pointing at Rowely. "But it's time for him to get up, so don't bother being quiet."

"Oh, let him sleep," I said.

Mike then proceeded to walk me through a typical day for the men in the TAC, from the time they woke and assumed duty until they went to bed. We spoke for quite some time before Rowely and a young African American private, their Radio Telephone Operator (RTO), woke up. I will call him Private Snuffy and note that he was a great young soldier with a wonderful attitude—always positive and upbeat. He was raised by his grandmother in New York City, and I concluded rather quickly that he had grown up in a sheltered environment. He did not have a driver's license until he reported to 2-17 CAV, where the NCOs taught him to drive. It seemed strange to me that he had never learned to drive, but I had driven in NYC traffic, so I could understand the concern of a protective guardian. A very bright young man, Snuffy was eager to impress his superiors, sergeants, and officers alike.

Once Private Snuffy and Rowely were up and moving about, they turned the lights on, revealing the dark lair in which the men lived and worked. I looked around to make sure they were not living like pigs, but to my surprise, it didn't look too bad for three guys pulling twenty-four-hour shifts. In fact, it looked pretty good, but as I surveyed the room, I noticed a stack of books lying beside Snuffy's cot. I walked over to see what he was reading and, to my surprise, I found about five books on lovemaking. The top book was titled *Kamasutra*, which gave instruction on sex positions.

"What is this?" I asked, picking the book up.

"That's mine, sir," the private shyly said.

"You looking at porn, Snuffy?" I asked. "Don't you know this is against general order number one?"

"Sir, it's not porn," he contested.

"What do you mean it's not porn?" I opened the book and turned it toward him. "Naked people lovin' on one another equals porn," I said.

"Sir, those books are instructional," he said.

"Ooh. Okay," I said sarcastically. Then I turned on him, accusatory. "You expect me to believe that? You're trying to skirt around the letter of the law, aren't you?" I asked before he had time to answer the first question.

"No sir," he replied. Then, with clear embarrassment, he continued. "Sir, I've got a girlfriend. My first girlfriend," he quickly added.

"Okay."

"Well, I've never done any of that," he said, pointing at the book. "So, I ordered these books. I want to get it right."

I started to laugh, but I realized that he was as serious as a heart attack on Sunday morning. "Why don't you just ask these guys?" I said, pointing to Osman and Rowely. "That would be better than getting busted with porn."

"We talk about it," he said. "But I want to make an impression on her."

"Well, seeking professional advice is probably well advised. I'm sure these guys haven't figured it out yet either," I said, to which Osmon smiled and shook his head.

"You'd better not get caught doing the deed up here," I said. "You represent our unit, and I don't want some sergeant major kicking you off his outpost because you're having sex with his soldier. Besides, that's sinful. You go to church, Snuffy?"

"I'm religious," he said.

"You believe fornication is okay? Or was God just kidding with that one?" I asked.

"We haven't done anything, sir. I'm just reading about it," he said.

I raised my eyebrows and pointed to the stack of books. "Don't let anyone see those books!" I told him.

"No sir. I won't," he assured me.

Mike Osmon and I walked outside and sat down by the Tigris River. We spoke for an hour or so as I tried to get to know Mike better. He'd spent most of his time in Mosul at the TAC since I had arrived in country, so I had not had an opportunity to sit down and talk with him one-on-one. Developing personal relationships with my guys was important to me, one of my favorite aspects of being a leader. Every soldier has a story, and I found that it was hard not to like someone once you heard their story. I'd usually ask them simply why they joined the army. I've heard everything from "My father and grandfather retired from the service, so I felt obligated to join myself" to "It was the only way to keep from going to jail." The most important part about them telling me their story was the simple fact that the process built a rapport between us, planted the seed of trust. It was a very easy way to begin a very positive professional relationship. By simply asking the question and listening intently to their story—not listening to hear, but listening to understand—a bond began to form between leader and led.

After getting dressed, Rowely stumbled outside, hair unkempt, and sat down on the riverbank beside me. "Morning, sunshine," I said.

"Morning, sir," he said and began tapping a pack of cigarettes against the heel of his hand.

"Rowely, tell me about your family," I said. "You've never really mentioned them."

"What do you want to know, sir?"

"Everything," I said, and slapped him on the shoulder. "How did your family get to Australia? I assume you're not Aborigines."

He let out a short, high-pitched laugh.

"I always hoped that I was a descendant from the convicts that were sent over from England in the 1800s," he said.

"What?" I said, surprised at the answer. "Why's that?" I asked, assuming he was kidding.

"In Australia, that is like being a descendant from someone on your *Mayflower*," he said. "I appreciate the fact that there is a great deal of irony there. The *Mayflower* was comprised of willing and adventurous separatists destined for the land of the free and the convict ships were filled with captives destined for prisons, but in Australia it is a mark of honor."

"You're serious?"

"Yes sir," he said, then lit a cigarette, tucked the lighter between the plastic wrapper and the box, and set them on the riverbank beside him. "So, given my friendly disdain for the British, I was horrified to find out that my great-grandparents were English farmhands that sailed to Australia for their honeymoon just prior to World War I. They docked in Brisbane, WWI kicked off, and their ship was seconded to the war effort," he said. "So, they just stayed."

"Wow. That's a pretty cool story," I said. "They were lucky, actually."

145

"Yes, they were," he said.

Rowely, Mike, and I sat in silence for a while, looking out across the Tigris. Every few seconds, Rowely would take a draw on the cigarette, then tilt his head back, turn it slightly away from me, and blow smoke out the corner of his mouth.

I couldn't help but think about the significance of where we sat. It seemed surreal to be in such an historic place, war or no war. Nineveh, or modern-day Mosul, was one of the oldest cities in antiquity. It was settled as early as 6000 BCE. Nineveh had been an important religious center of worship for Ishtar, the goddess of love, procreation, and war. *Maybe that's why Snuffy is reading love books,* I thought. It must still linger in the air.

Nineveh had been the capital of the Assyrian Empire at one time. King Sennacherib reigned in Nineveh from 704 to 681 BCE. He built great walls around the city, and created parks and gardens, aqueducts, irrigation ditches, and canals. Later, the city would be home to the greatest library of its era. Under the reign of King Ashurbanipal, over thirty thousand clay tablets were collected, all the writings of Mesopotamia, but the Bible would not highlight the beautiful gardens or intellect of Nineveh's residents. In fact, Biblical writers focused on God, the Hebrews, and Nineveh's fall. "And it shall come to pass, that all they that look upon thee shall flee from thee, and say, Nineveh is laid waste: who will bemoan her? Whence shall I seek comforters for thee?" the prophet and poet Nahum wrote.

Who else has sat on this bank? I wondered.

Mike broke the silence. "Do you want to go see Major Pearl before you leave?"

I hoped I had not seemed aloof, distant, as my thoughts wandered. It was peaceful sitting there in silence.

"Yeah, I do need to go see him," I said as Mike stood.

"I'll see you later, Rowely," I said, shaking his hand.

"Later, boss," Rowely said. "Drop in more often."

"I plan to," I said and began toward the headquarters building. "Keep those love books hidden."

Again, Rowely chirped a short, high-pitched laugh.

Mike walked me over to Strike Main, and I caught up with Brian Pearl and Pierre Gervais, Strike's Intelligence Officer. They raved about the support we were providing them, and Brian told me that they planned to conduct door-to-door searches in several areas of town. "It will be slow going," Pearl said. "You may be flying small circles above us for hours on end, but we need you guys to cover us."

"We're here to support you," I said. "Whatever you need. Just let me know."

As we spoke, I learned that Schiller would be in his meeting for at least another hour. "Do you guys have a barber up here?" I asked Pearl.

"Yeah, we let a couple of Iraqi guys set up a barbershop. They do a pretty good job," he said.

"Where is their shop?" I asked.

"Go out of the TOC and walk past the little store, toward the gate. It's on the south side of the base along that wall, about halfway between the river and the gate," he said.

"Okay, I'll find it," I said, and left.

The barbershop was easy to find. I walked in the door and found both barbers sitting in their chairs listening to Arabic music over a small television set. One of the barbers hopped up when I walked in. "Please sir," he said, pointing to his chair. I sat down; he draped me in an apron and asked, "Are you married?"

That seemed a rather odd question to me. *Maybe the goddess of love does have a spell on Mosul,* I thought. He caught me completely off guard. He was also a very effeminate man, so I was unsure what he might have in mind. I wasn't sure if the conversation was headed toward a haircut or a date. "Yes, I'm married," I assured him.

"I will make you beautiful for your woman," he said.

"Handsome," I said. "I prefer to be handsome," I repeated, hoping he would understand my humor. "But I don't think I'm going to see my wife for quite some time, so let's just get a good fresh haircut."

"Yesss, of courssse," he said, airing out the "s" with a lisp and smiling broadly at me. "How you like it cut?"

"I just want some off the top and taper the sides and back," I said. He nodded and commenced snapping a pair of scissors like Edward Scissorhands. With a comb in one hand and the scissors snapping nonstop in the other hand, he went around and around my head, his pinkies stuck out like ballasts on both hands. I prayed that he wouldn't cut off my ears.

147

Every few seconds he'd grab a bottle and spray me down with water. He would cut and spray and cut and spray; then suddenly he'd stop cutting, jump back away from me with his hands on his hips, and inspect his work. Then he'd take a deep breath and say, "Hmm," as if my hair was perplexing. After the second time, I grew concerned. I was facing away from the mirror, so I had no idea what I looked like.

When he finished, he spun me around to face myself in the mirror. "It looks good," I said, relieved to be done.

"Okay, very good," he said, then spun the chair back around, but he did not remove the apron.

Instead, he took out a straight razor, which I love. A clean shave feels good after a haircut, but naturally, I was a bit concerned to have an Iraqi man holding a straight razor to my neck. I had no way of knowing his true allegiance. Was he on our side? Like a scene out of an old Western movie, I placed my hand on my pistol underneath the apron—as if I could react in time should he decide to bleed me out in his chair. I knew I would be finished if he wanted to cut me, but I figured I could empty that fifteen-round clip before I bled out. *What a way to go that would be,* I thought, realizing how silly the thought actually was.

The neck shave was nice. My neck tingled as he dabbed aftershave on me, but it wasn't over. He moved to my eyebrows, which suited me fine. They needed trimming. I've never been one for a unibrow or big, furry caterpillar eyebrows either. He trimmed them, and then he took something from a drawer. His back was turned, so I could not see what he was doing. He had something wrapped around his fingers, which he was twisting and turning. Not being able to see, I wasn't sure what he planned to do next.

Suddenly, he placed both hands on my face, and with a quick movement, he rolled something up my cheek. I flinched as I felt a slight pinch but didn't have time to move, and it would not have mattered if I did. He snatched his hands back, one, then the other, in a quick tearing motion like he was ripping athletic tape off a hairy-legged football player, and I squealed.

"Ow! What the heck did you do to me?" I asked, in a pained falsetto, squinting through tears.

148

He had two pieces of thread in his hands. He had rolled them up my cheek, twisting the peach fuzz in them as he rolled. Then he ripped them away, taking all the hair with it.

"I make you pretty for your woman," he said.

"I told you I wasn't going to see my woman any time soon, and all I asked for was a haircut," I said.

"Okay," he said, clearly disapproving, "but I must finish."

Fearing that I'd look like a guy with one sideburn, I let him torture me one more time.

I tried to hold still as he repeated the process. "Now. You look so nissse," he said, doing that lispy thing again.

I rubbed both cheeks. "Thank you," I said, paid him, and moved out smartly.

Schiller, having finished his meeting, was waiting for me at the helicopter when I arrived. I dared not tell him that a gay Iraqi man just made me cry using a piece of thread. We buckled in, cranked, and headed for Q-West.

"Good meeting?" I asked, once we were airborne.

"Yeah. You've gotta love Colonel Anderson. He's a good man," Schiller said.

"No doubt," I replied. "What was on the agenda today?"

"We spoke mostly about their troop to task issues," he said.

Troop to task is the army's way of identifying all the tasks that must be completed and assigning specific soldiers and units against those tasks. It's a very simple way of comparing work to manpower.

"Do they have issues with it?" I asked.

"Yeah. Colonel Anderson said it's his greatest challenge,"[2] Schiller said. "Strike soldiers are partnering with all the security forces in Mosul," he said. "I mean all of them, to include the city officials. They are also handling the monetary exchange. They've got guys all over the city collecting the old currency with Saddam's face on it and issuing the new money. They are assisting with all the city infrastructure projects and services too. Colonel Anderson said that he went out to a monetary exchange point the other day and there was a staff sergeant and his squad of nine men running the entire operation. It's crazy how many people it takes to do all the things that need doing to get this city moving forward."

149

"That sounds like counterinsurgency and nation building combined," I said.

"Yep."

"General Shinseki doesn't sound so stupid now, does he? I said, recalling that Shinseki had estimated the need for four hundred thousand troops and Donald Rumsfeld publicly disagreeing with him.

"You think?"

"The plywood came in for the MMS boxes," I said, changing the subject to our own initiatives.

"Yeah, I saw them unloading the truck when we left," he said.

"Do you think we'll catch a lot of grief for removing the sights?" I asked.

"No doubt there will be some pissed-off folks. Once the pictures start making their way back to the States of Kiowas with no MMSs on them, I'm sure I'll get some hate mail. This war is an opportunity for all the defense contractors to prove their equipment. At the end of the day, it's all about money," he said. "The reality is, we don't need the sights for the environment we're in and the fight we are fighting right now."

Since Schiller had made the decision for us to only use rockets and .50 caliber, we did not need the sight. In the city, it was hard to use the sight anyway. You had to almost hover the helicopter or fly very slowly to use it, and Schiller didn't want us doing that because we would become easy targets. He preferred that we benefit from the increased power margin gained by removing the weight.

"I'm not opposed to technology, but I believe in investing in warriors first. It's the swordsman, not the sword, Jimmy," he said, seizing an opportunity to mentor me. "We need to train our people and then give them the tool they need for the mission they face. Unfortunately, we're subjected to a military-industrial complex that pushes us to do things we don't always want or need to do; fielding technology and then forcing soldiers to adapt to that widget is not always the best thing to do. It's not *always* bad, but I think both of us can cite cases where it's been less than helpful or downright regressive," he said.

"I have always said, we only use the tools we have at about fifty percent of their capability. Our computers, our cell phones, you name it. Think about it, we don't maximize their capacity. Excel is a great program. It's powerful, but very few people know how to get the most out of it. I'd say ninety-five percent of the people using Excel only use five percent of its capability. Our helicopters and the various systems within them are not a damn bit different."

"What do you mean?" I asked.

"I'll give you an example. When I was the operations officer in B Company, 1-160th, early in 1996, all the Fully Mission Qualified (FMQ) pilots were out on missions all over the world. We were tasked to support the Association of the United States Army (AUSA) conference at Pinehurst, NC. Being the only FMQ pilot who could support the mission, I flew an AH-6 Little Bird to Pinehurst single pilot. As I got close, the weather deteriorated. I decided to land at Moore County airport, a few miles from the golf course. I phoned Captain John Evans, who was new to the unit. He was the action officer assigned as the liaison for the conference. I asked John to meet me at the airport and fly left seat with me to assist in navigating just above the trees, following the roads to the conference center. He did so, and we landed in the parking lot successfully. We folded the blades, pushed the aircraft onto a flatbed truck, and then pushed it into the conference center floor, unfolded the blades, and prepared the helicopter for the static display. Mission accomplished.

"Another unit in 160th was also tasked to fly helicopters to the convention. They were flying the newly fielded MH-60K Black Hawk and the MH-47E Chinook. Unbeknownst to me, they also took off from Fort Campbell flying to Fayetteville, NC, airport. The weather they received from flight service while at Fayetteville was legal to fly in, but they were uncomfortable continuing. They decided to wait the weather out for another day, so I made it in to Pinehurst and they did not.

"After I checked into my room, John Evans called me and told me that I needed to report to the regimental commander, who was there at the conference. The commander chewed my ass for 'pushing the limits of weather.' His underlying message was that by finding a way to accomplish the mission—safely, I might add—I made the all-weather, terrain-following, weather RADAR-equipped MH-60K and MH-47E model aircraft look bad. I had negotiated the weather in a Little Bird with none of the new technology, and they had not."

"Really?" I asked.

"I'm not kidding you. It's a true story, and I'm sure you understand the message. I did what I thought I could do to accomplish the mission within my capability and the capability of the aircraft. I didn't have any of the advanced technology or tools available to me, but I got the job done by maximizing the potential of what I did have available. I knew my capability, and I knew what the aircraft could do.

"Now, let me be fair," he said. "Fast-forward five years. The MH-60K Black Hawk and the MH-47E Chinook were used to invade Afghanistan after 9/11, and their performance was amazing. I was the Task Force 1-160 operations officer then, and no conventional army aviation organization could have done what we did then: thousand-mile infiltrations from a ship in the Arabian Sea at night, in bad weather, with aerial refueling three, sometimes four, times to assault a target in the hinterlands of Afghanistan. Our aviators learned to use those tools and technology to their maximum capacity. It was an awesome thing to see.

"Jimmy, I have done everything I can to bring that mentality to the CAV. Take the tool you're given and use it to the best of your ability to accomplish the mission; maximize the capacity of the tools you have. Man must master his machine, not be subject to it. I am not against technology. I am a proponent of superb leadership. We cannot get away from great leaders with the discipline, will, and capacity to *think,* and use the tools available to accomplish the tasks asked of them," he said.

"You want to land?" he asked, pointing at the airfield.

We were nearing the Q-West. "Sure," I said, having lost track of time.

"You have the controls," he said, relinquishing the flight controls.

"I have the controls," I repeated.

"You have the controls," and he took his hands off the flight controls. It was a three-way, positive transfer of controls, a technique that was instituted many years prior due to accidents. In the absence of a positive transfer of the flight controls, helicopters had crashed with both pilots assuming the other pilot was flying the airplane.

"What a day," I said, as I began the approach into Q-West.

"Yeah, no kidding," he said.

We had been flashed by a sheepherder, almost skewered a guy who decided to point an empty gun at us, landed and taken an AK-47 from five men while holding them at gun point with a pistol, and found out that one of my soldiers was studying *Kamasutra*. Plus, I had been brought to tears with a piece of thread. But Schiller didn't know that last part, and I had no intention of telling him.

CAT AND MOUSE

The next morning, I watched the sun climb above the horizon as I stretched for a morning run. It was hot. *I should have already finished my run, should have beat the heat,* I thought to myself. A pack of dogs had started hanging out at the southwest corner of the perimeter. They had not seemed overly aggressive the last time I ran that direction. Still, several of them barked, and I saw the hair stand up on their backs. That was enough to make me think twice about running around that corner of the airfield without a pistol.

Annihilator Troop had allowed a female dog to hang around their troop area. They had fed her, so she chose to have a litter of puppies in an old shed adjacent to their troop building. I figured she'd be back in heat soon and the males from every village surrounding Q-West would drop by for a visit. With all the stray dogs showing up, I figured it was only a matter of time before someone got bit, and I preferred that it wasn't me.

I decided to go north on the perimeter road to avoid the chance of an encounter with the dogs. There was more vehicle traffic on the north end of the airfield, which irritated me, but it was better than risking an encounter with the dogs. I preferred not seeing anyone when I ran. Chewing dust was not particularly fun. It was so dry that the dust boiled up behind convoys and stuck like glue to my sweaty skin.

I covered the first mile in just over six minutes. Despite not being able to train as regularly as I did before having deployed, my fitness held. My legs felt good that morning, but something wasn't right. I sensed a burning sensation in my throat that I'd never noticed before. The wind was out of the north, but there wasn't any visible dust or smoke in the air. For a minute, I thought, *Maybe soldiers are burning trash at the trash pile*

154

and I am downwind. I'm probably inhaling something nasty that's being incinerated.

I made it to the two-mile mark before I decided that I'd better head back to the house. Suddenly, my throat was on fire. Speeding up would get me back quicker, but the faster I ran, the more air I breathed in, and with each breath came a searing pain. It literally felt like flames were going down my throat with each breath. I tried to hold my breath, but I could only hold it for a few seconds at the pace I was running, and then when I finally exhaled, I had to breathe deeply for several seconds, which was tortuous.

There never has been a problem that panicking would not make worse, but I was extremely concerned at that point—on the verge of panic. I was all alone, and breathing became more and more difficult with each step I took. I stopped for a second to try and slow my breathing, but I soon realized that my eyes were now burning as well. If I lost my ability to see and breathe, I was going to be in real trouble.

Something was in the air, but I didn't know what. Then it dawned on me. Saddam had used chemicals on the Iranians and the Kurds. In fact, he had done so very close to where we were. What if the bad guys had gotten their hands on a chemical weapon and they were using it? Perhaps they had detonated one upwind from us. Suddenly, panic didn't seem like such a bad idea. I was all alone a mile and a half from our TOC, and my throat and eyes were burning. I took a deep breath and lit out for the TOC at full speed. This time, the more it burned, the harder I ran.

No one was outside when I sprinted up the front steps of the TOC. I went straight to my room. Making the turn into our doorway, I found Ken sitting on his cot wearing shorts, a T-shirt, and his gas mask. Sounding like Darth Vader, he said, "You better put your mask on."

"My throat and eyes are on fire!" I said. "What's going on?"

His breathing was audible in the mask. "It's the sulfur fire," he said. "We're downwind today. We've been told to keep the mask on until the wind changes."

"That could be days," I said, strapping my mask to my head. "Is it dangerous? Heck, I've already sucked down enough to kill a horse if it is."

"Well, they said it's not healthy. I don't think they know what it will do to us," he said. "They already told us not to breathe the smoke from the trash pit fire, and that's upwind as well. Now this."

"Great!" I said and coughed a dry hacking cough.

"That's what I've been doing," Ken said.

"What's that?"

"Constantly coughing."

I tightened the straps of my mask, sealing it to my face, and my eyepieces instantly fogged up due to the heat from my sweaty face. "Now I'm blind too," I said.

"They need to do something about this shit," Doug said, as he walked into our room and sat down. "This is some bullshit. We might not get shot while we're here, but this is sure to leave a mark."

"Worries me!" I said. "Who knows what sulfur fumes will do to our lungs? Is it toxic?"

"Oh, I've already looked it up," Doug said. "It can kill your ass, but since we're not dead yet, we can expect it to jack our lungs up for life."

"Thanks for the optimistic outlook, Doomsday," I said.

"Doomsday Doug," Ken repeated aloud.

"I'd be happy if it killed these damn mice," Doug said.

"Quit eating in your room and they might go elsewhere," I said as I stood. "I'm going to the TOC to see when the wind is expected to shift. This sucks."

I began for the door—then it dawned on me. "Hey, why didn't you guys come get me? You knew I was out running. What if I was lying in a ditch out there?"

"We were just about to do that, right, Doug?" Ken said.

"Hell, no," Doug said. "I told you all that running was not good for you. Darwinism at its best."

"It's survival of the fittest, Doug. I get fit running," I said.

"In this case it's intelligence, not physical fitness. I was smart enough to put my mask on and stay inside. You, on the other hand, were out getting exposed. If you die, it was meant to be."

"Oh, Doug."

I walked into the TOC to find everyone sitting still in their chairs as if paralyzed. It was deathly quiet. "What are they saying?" I asked the battle captain.

"I think they are about to give the all clear call," he said. All clear is the terminology we use when training for chemical or biological weapons use. When it is deemed safe to remove your mask, they call "all clear" over the radio, and everyone pulls their mask off. In training, soldiers instantly snatch the mask off their heads, but I suspect that if we were ever confronted with real chemicals it would take a while for the first person to actually pull their mask off. I'm confident that everyone would hope to observe the first soldier breathing normally without choking to death before they were willing to join in.

"Is the wind changing?" I asked Staff Sergeant Boucher, who was responsible for monitoring the weather on the staff.

"Yes sir. It has shifted to the west. We should be good to go," he said.

"All clear!" a soldier sitting by the radio yelled out. "All clear!"

Suddenly, everyone moved again, instantly pulling their masks off and letting out an audible sigh of relief as if they had been zapped back to life. I walked back to my room to put my mask away and get dressed. When I made the turn into the doorway that separated my room from Doug's, I saw Doug's butt sticking up in the air. He was down on his knees with his nose almost touching the ground, his head under his cot.

"What are you doing?" I asked.

"Setting rat traps," he said.

"You'd better be careful not to get your moustache caught up in that trap," I said.

"Ha. Ha. Very funny. I know what I'm doing," he said.

"It looks like it."

"Right after you left, Tim Merrell was sitting over there on his cot leaning back against the wall. He saw something move out of the corner of his eye. It was a mouse coming around the ledge. It wasn't even scared of us. It walked right up to Tim's head, on that ledge," he said pointing. "Tim decided to put a cracker down on the end of his cot to see if the mouse would go for it. I told him to try and kill it when it jumped down to eat the cracker."

"Did it go for it?" I asked.

"Hell yeah, it did. He put a little piece on the end of his cot, and that mouse hopped down on his cot to eat lunch. He swung at it with his boot but missed, and then we tore the room apart chasing it, trying to kill it."

"I take it you didn't kill it."

"No, but I will," he said.

"Well, I'm glad you have found new purpose in life, Doug."

"You'll be thanking me soon," he said. "If we don't kill these damn mice, we'll have snakes before long."

"We need a cat," I said. "That's what we need. I've known people to keep a cat in their barn to kill rats, so they don't get snakes."

"Hell no, we don't. They've got a cat down in one of the troop areas. It looks like it has the mange or maybe something worse. If we had a cat, the best we could hope for would be that it gave us all fleas," he said. "I'll take care of the mice!"

"You're more fun to watch than a cat anyway, Doug," I said.

"Very funny," he said. "If it were not for me, life would be pretty damn miserable around here."

"I'm not arguing with you, Doug." Then I thought for a minute.

"You know, our situation here in Iraq is kind of like the rat, snake, and cat dilemma," I said.

"How's that?" Doug asked.

"Well, there were rats in Iraq, so they sent us over to clean them out," I said.

"So, are we the cat or the snake?" Doug interrupted.

"Well, I guess that depends on your perspective," I said. "The way I see it, we are the cat that came to clean the rats out. We never expected the snakes to show up, though. But they did, and now they seem to be multiplying all around us."

"You got that right," Doug said. "Either way, I'm here to save the day."

"Yes you are, Doug. I'm just thankful that you have the mission and clearly the passion to go with it."

SULFUR, SANDSTORMS, AND RAT TURDS

The space between night and day was filled with fog and air as gray as smoke. Day fought hard to reveal itself as I ran the perimeter road. There seemed to be something strange in the air. I couldn't put my finger on it, but I could feel it hanging there like the calm before a storm. After my run, I walked into the TOC and found several warrant officers huddled around Staff Sergeant Boucher discussing the weather. "What's up?" I asked.

"Sandstorm," one of the warrants answered without looking up.

Instantly, visions of the story about the sandstorm early in the war flashed into my mind. It somewhat excited me. I wanted to be able to tell my grandkids someday that I weathered a shamal in the deserts of Iraq during the war. Still, it was a bit unnerving.

"I wish the damn things would come at night so we could just sleep through them," the warrant said.

His attitude was contemptuous, befitting a seasoned warrant officer who had already weathered a shamal of epic proportions. Something inside me wanted to imitate his manner, but I knew I couldn't pull it off. It would have been fake anyway. "When's it supposed to be here?" I asked.

"Another hour or so," he said. "That's what we're trying to nail down now. The crews are out on the flight line buttoning up the helicopters. We'll try and keep the sand out if we can."

"Looks like it'll be a big one," the other soldier said, and with that they left.

I walked into the office, where Ken sat reading an intelligence summary. "Do we need to do anything to get ready for this storm?" I asked.

"Go find your goggles and a bandana," he said. "I've already told the troops to prepare. Now it's just a matter of riding it out."

"Good idea," I said. "I'll go get my stuff ready."

A group of soldiers stood on the roof looking to the west. They had climbed up on the building for a better vantage point. I went to my room and fished a bandana and goggles out of my bags. Tim Slifko had called them his earth, wind, and fire goggles when he told the story about the storm. We'll see how well they work now, I suppose, I thought to myself. Once I tied the bandana around my neck, I climbed up on the roof to join the others.

"First the sulfur, now this. Who needs an enemy? It's like this whole damn country is trying to kill our asses," a young soldier said.

"Yeah, you can't even breathe the air over here," his buddy remarked.

The sun had already turned orange and was blotted out enough that you could look directly at it. Within minutes, a wall of moving sand appeared on the horizon. It boiled like tumbling clouds as it approached. Suddenly, the wind began to increase, at first in gusts, then steady and strong. As it neared, I pulled the bandana up over my nose and mouth and lowered my goggles from my forehead to my eyes. We lasted a few more minutes on the rooftop, but soon the blowing sand began to sting our skin, so we climbed down and returned to our rooms.

Ken was already sitting on his cot when I walked into the room. "Here we go again," he said sarcastically and shook his head.

"Wonder how long it will last?" I asked.

"No telling," he answered, required to speak much louder now. "The weather guessers said twenty-four hours."

The plastic over our window snapped and popped with the gusts. Because the wind could not blow directly into our room, a fine powdery dust hung in the air inside our room. Gradually, the light dimmed, and more sand filled the room. Within thirty minutes, I could barely see Ken sitting five feet from me. It was only noon, and yet it was almost as dark as night.

After sitting there for what seemed like several hours, I decided to go check on the guys in the TOC. I stood and started for the door. "I'll be back in a minute," I yelled. "I'm going to check on the guys in the TOC."

"Don't get lost," he shouted back.

When I opened the door to the TOC, wind disturbed the dust that hung in the room. It swirled in the air like a tornado. No one even looked up. All the soldiers sat in their chairs, bandanas covering their faces and goggles protecting their eyes. They sat motionless, staring straight ahead as if in a trance.

"You guys okay?" I asked.

The battle captain turned and looked at me. "We're good, sir. Just waiting it out," he said, then turned his head back to the front and resumed staring at the wall.

"Okay, if you need me, I'll be in my room," I said and departed.

As I entered the doorway, I peeked into Doug's room. He was sitting in a red plastic chair. His hand was under his bandana putting something in his mouth. "What are you doing, Doug?"

"What does it look like?" he said. "I'm eating."

"How can you eat in this storm?"

"I eat when I'm hungry. Don't matter where or when."

By eight o'clock, we were happy to go to bed. We'd been sitting motionless for almost eight hours. The storm had lost its appeal. I couldn't imagine a three-day storm. I prayed that I'd be able to sleep through the night.

The next morning, I woke to a high-pitched squeal. Other than the God-awful screech, there wasn't a sound to be heard. The storm was gone. The sun was already up, and the air was perfectly still. I opened my eyes and could feel the dust and sand. Instantly, I dug in the corner of my eyes with my finger, but it felt like sandpaper on my eyelid, so I quickly retracted my hand. Everything was covered in a layer of brown dust and sand at least an eighth of an inch thick. "What's that sound?" I yelled out.

No one answered. "Doug! Is that sound coming from your room?"

Nothing.

"Doug!" I yelled louder. "What's that squealing?"

I heard his cot squeak as he rolled over, and then he mumbled something. He had buttoned himself up in his mummy bag to try to escape the sand. Then, suddenly, I heard him explode from his cot. "I got you, you little bastard. I got your ass!"

"Doug, what are you doing?" I yelled out.

"I got him! I got him!" he said.

"You got what?"

"That damn mouse. He must have come out after the storm. I got him," he said and came running into my room to show me.

I looked up to see Doug standing there in his underwear and flip-flops. The entire top of his head was light brown, as if he had frosted the top of his jet-black hair. He held a square of sticky paper in his hand. The mouse, which was still squalling relentlessly, was plastered to the sticky paper.

"I'm surprised that sticky paper worked after the sand settled on it," I said.

"Oh, it worked. He's not going anywhere," Doug said.

"You'd better whack him in the head and kill him," I said. "With that distress call, there's probably a snake already on the way."

Doug turned to go back to his room. He looked down at the mouse as he walked and spoke to him. "I told you I'd get you, you little bastard. It was only a matter of time."

Ken had listened to the whole ordeal from deep within his sleeping bag. Ken rarely said a word before a cup of coffee. Nevertheless, with the mouse screaming and me yelling at Doug, he was well awake.

"Morning, roommate," I said as he sat up and slid his feet into a pair of shower shoes.

"Morning," he said in a gravelly voice, rubbing his head with both hands, then rising to his feet and heading for the door.

"Going to try out the new porta potty?" I asked.

He just grunted.

Our brigade had somehow figured out how to contract porta potties with a local Iraqi guy. No longer having to burn our own crap was a huge morale booster. Our porta potty was blue, which we aptly named the Blue Canoe.

After Ken left the room, I laced up my running shoes, dusted off my shorts and T-shirt, and then headed out for a run. Ken was always better after a cup of coffee, so I made every attempt to give him space until he woke up. He and Schiller liked their designer coffee and exotic cigars. Their favorite coffee came in an ornate bag, 100 percent Kona coffee. "Smooth to the taste with just a touch of cream and sugar to sweeten slightly," Ken would proclaim. "That's how you begin a day right." The SCO, on the other hand, preferred his coffee black.

The following morning, an Iraqi contractor delivered three more porta potties. Ken sat at his computer sipping a cup of coffee when I walked in from my run. "Life is improving around here," I said.

"How's that?" Ken asked without looking up.

"Porta potty man is out there. He's giving us three more johns. We've got four now," I said.

"Living like kings," Ken replied.

I went back to my room to towel off and get dressed, but as I was preparing to pull my pants on, I noticed a small rip in the leg of my britches. I fished through my rucksack to find a sewing kit and a patch. A sewing kit had been a staple on the army's field packing list my entire career, but I'd rarely, if ever, seen a soldier use one. Unlike a whetstone, which every soldier attempted to use—most of them unsuccessfully, I might add—no one seemed to want to take a crack at sewing. I suppose dragging a blade across a stone felt manlier than sticking a thimble over one's finger. My grandmother had taught me to sew when I was just a young boy, so I didn't hesitate to put it to use.

Having heard me return to my room, Doug walked in. "What are you doing?" he asked.

"Patching up my trousers," I said. "I ripped them somehow."

"Oh, that's special," he said sarcastically and moved in close to inspect my work. "I didn't know you knew how to sew."

"I can do lots of things you don't know about, Doug," I said.

"Oh, yeah, like what?"

"Well, I can sew, and I can stick this needle through your leg for patronizing me," I said and stabbed at him with the needle.

He squealed and jumped back, almost falling over my cot. "Knock it off," he said. "You poke me with that thing and I might get infected with some weird-ass disease."

He then turned and disappeared into his room.

BROTHERHOOD

Summer days in Iraq were a blur of heat. The sun rose early and stole what little shade could be provided by the walls of buildings. There were only a few scraggly trees scattered around Q-West, none of which had leaves enough to provide ample shade for even Doug's mice. Any time we spent outside a building was miserable, the sun bearing down on us. The troops tried to do as much maintenance on the helicopters as they could at night. They improvised during the day by pulling trucks up beside the helicopters and draping camo netting or ponchos over the spot where they needed to work. They'd shift the shade as the sun crawled across the sky. Sometimes a crew chief would lay a wrench down on the ground, in direct sunlight. That mistake caused many a blister. It only took three or four minutes in the sun before a wrench would be too hot to touch with the bare hand.

We drank as much water as possible, but kidney stones still spread like the plague. Soldiers blamed the bottled water. "It's all that sodium in the water," they would say, but I don't know if that was true. Besides, there were no good alternatives. One of the support units had a water-purification system, which enabled them to pump water out of the Tigris River and purify it in massive quantities, but it still tasted like swamp water. I shivered every time I turned up a canteen, praying I would not swallow some strange bacteria and die a slow and painful death in a cold sweat. I decided to take my chances with kidney stones, and the gamble paid off.

I often fetched my camera and climbed up on top of the roof just before sundown to try to freeze those incredible sunsets in time. They were splendid. I am sure there is a scientific explanation for why the sun appears so much larger in Iraq. I often wondered why but was never motivated enough to research the answer. Instead, I simply took pictures and enjoyed the moment.

I was born busy, always in a hurry when there was something to be done, but I could lie still and listen to the world around me when that's what needed to be done.

Self-diagnosed, I have had attention-deficit/hyperactivity disorder (ADHD) all my life. As a little boy, I rocked so hard in the bench seat of my daddy's Chevrolet pickup that the bolts worked loose. "You tryin' ta make us go faster?" Daddy would smile and ask.

But I was also touched with obsessive-compulsive disorder (OCD), which allowed me to focus all that excess energy, a blessing, I suppose. It made me incredibly efficient at getting things done. Daddy would leave a list of chores to be accomplished while he was at work. My heart being set on hunting or fishing, I would view the chores as a distraction. Most kids my age would drag their feet, end up *halfway* doing the chores and never getting to go hunting at all, but not me. I would complete the chores in half the time a normal kid could do it, and the work would be above average. That's what the OCD did for me. Everything had to be done right. That's why I was so good at watching the sun set and the moon and stars take over the night sky in Iraq. I had decided that's what needed to be done, and I was driven by some inner force that I could not explain to do it well.

The sun was an enormous orange ball that looked like another planet slipping past the earth just over the horizon. As it neared the skyline, heatwaves became visible around its edges. The closer it got, the more noticeable the heatwaves—dancing, transparent, yet visible to the eye.

The sun's descent was imperceptible until it finally touched the horizon, and then it fell with increased speed, providing a few fleeting moments in which to snap pictures. Ironically, in a land that was brown, desolate, in many ways ugly, sunsets were breathtaking. But the night was not to be outdone. The number of visible stars in the night sky was stunning, a tapestry of brilliant white dots that my grandmother once told me were holes in the floor of Heaven. Every constellation was on display—an astronomer's outdoor planetarium.

"Ranger B, what are you doing up there?" John Rowell asked with a thick Australian accent from the courtyard below. Rowely had recently rotated back from Strike Main so he could fly a few missions and work in the TOC.

"Taking pictures," I said.

"Come on, sir. Let's go play *Halo*," he said with clear excitement in his voice.

My Ranger School buddy John Uharriet often called me Ranger B. When we first began playing *Halo*, I named my avatar Ranger B, so Rowely, Tim Slifko, and Doug Ford began calling me by that name.

"I'll be down in just a minute," I said. "Just a few more pictures."

"Yeah, yeah, love your work," he said, using one of many phrases I didn't completely understand.

As the sun disappeared below the horizon, I climbed down from the roof using the ladder that Schiller had propped up against the wall, so that he had access to his starlit bedroom on the roof.

Australia always sent their very best captains to serve in 2-17 Cavalry. Rowely was no exception. When he arrived at 2-17 CAV, he had no idea that the US was planning to invade Iraq. Upon realizing we were going to war, he immediately reached out to his leadership in Australia and requested to accompany the unit to war. As our close ally, the Australian army readily consented.

Rowely wore a one-piece coverall flight suit unzipped to the waist that evening. He had pulled it down off his shoulders. The arms were tied around his waist in a knot. His brown T-shirt had large patches of white salt on the front and back. As I stepped off the ladder, he took a final draw from a cigarette, flicked the butt away, and turned to walk with me to Tim Slifko's room. We played *Halo* in Tim's room because he was the keeper of the overhead projector. He and Doug had figured out a way to connect the Xbox to the projector so that we could cast the image on the wall above Tim's cot.

Ordinarily, we played after late-night missions. We would land back at Q-West, debrief the mission, put our gear away, and play for an hour or so before going to bed. Growing up, I had never played many video games. It showed in my lack of skills. To say that I was an average player would have been an extreme compliment. It was not even considered good sport to shoot me with a rifle or shotgun, so they stuck me with sticky grenades or made it a rule that you could only kill Ranger B by

166

butt-stroking him. I would have been humiliated and simply given up the game had I not enjoyed the camaraderie so much. Trash talk prevailed among all players, but particularly so between Tim and Doug Ford. Doug would kill Tim and then scream out, "Sit down!" or "Suck it!" to which Tim would smile and gently say, "Shut up, Doug."

Passing insults back and forth is a natural part of growing up as a boy, especially for those who participate in team sports and are forced into close fraternal relationships with other adolescents. One might naturally assume that those tendencies fade as a boy grows into a man. As Paul the Apostle wrote, "When I was a child, I spake as a child, I understood as a child, I thought as a child: but when I became a man, I put away childish things," but I think even Paul would have made an allowance for soldiers. Soldiers don't put away childish insults. If anything, they get better at it. And so, Tim, Doug, and Rowely passed insults like a plate of hot biscuits.

Slifko was already setting up the Xbox when Rowely and I walked into the room. Doug sat on a cot, supervising, as Tim struggled to untangle a wad of wires. A forthright man who was known to salt his speech with a liberal amount of both criticism and sarcasm, Doug looked up as we entered the room. "How's Double Stack?" he asked Rowely with a cheesy grin on his face.

"Good, I suppose, mate," he said. "I haven't spoken with her in quite some time."

While being assigned to the TAC in Mosul, Rowely had gotten to know a female captain who commanded a military police company out of Fort Bragg, and whose call sign was Double Stack Six. Apparently, she had been seduced by Rowely's charm, good looks, and the irresistible accent. The other guys in the TAC told us that she often brought Rowely breakfast in bed, so they constantly ribbed him about Double Stack Six.

But I suppose Rowely was just as stricken with Double Stack. Over a decade later, he would tell me, "I was attracted to a gun-toting, incredibly powerful woman and officer that was kicking dudes' asses by night. She was a bloody good officer."[1]

"How did your PT test go?" Rowely sarcastically asked Doug in an attempt to deflect his chiding.

Rowely was referring to the physical fitness test we had recently taken. Doug hated running. He hated working out, for that matter.

"No problem. I passed," Doug said with an air of confidence.

"How about you?" Doug fired back. "Cigarettes kill your run?"

"No. No problem at all, mate. In fact, I carried Ranger B to the finish line," he said.

"Yeah, right," Doug said, rolling his eyes.

"No, really," Rowely said. "He only ran that fast because I carried him."

The PT test consisted of two minutes of push-ups, two minutes of sit-ups, and a two-mile run, which I ran in ten minutes. I was standing at the finish line when Rowely crossed it. He finished the run, then quickly spun around and picked me up in a fireman's carry and began running back down the road with me over his shoulder.

"Take a picture," he told Ken Hawley. "Everyone needs to know that the only way he ran that fast was because I carried him."

Doug turned his attention back to Tim Slifko. "Hurry up!" he said. "Stop dicking around. I have to fly in the morning."

"I'm trying to get these cords untangled," Tim said. "You ass clowns just wadded everything up and threw it under my cot that last time you played."

"I didn't touch it. You're just stalling because you don't want me to kick your ass," Doug said.

It was a true locker room atmosphere, irreverent but collegial. Doug named his *Halo* character Fat Bastard, the morbidly obese Mike Myers character in *Austin Powers*.

Tim and Doug were somewhat evenly matched. Rowely was better than I was, and Captain Brian Woody, our squadron logistics officer, was better than all of us.

Woody did not play that often, but when he did, he always won. Despite being the best among us, each time Woody played, he mentioned a young soldier who worked for him who was much better than he was. I suppose curiosity got the best of us, because eventually one of the guys sought this young man out and invited him to join us for the evening.

He was a tall, thin African American kid. I had seen him working in the S4 shop. By all accounts, he was a quiet, young soldier, but when that Xbox controller touched his hands, a transformation took place that I haven't the words to explain. He became possessed. We were taken aback by the stark contrast in personalities. He was not simply "good," as Woody had said. He was ridiculous. He just looked at me, and my character fell dead. I would respawn and he seemed to always be running by, so he would kill me again before I could run away and hide. My goal for the game quickly became trying to die fewer times than everyone else versus killing other players. And if we thought Doug Ford talked trash, we had no idea what trash talking was. He ran through the board killing us and screaming out insults as he went. He did not shut up from the time we began playing until we finally told him it was time to call it a night, prematurely, I might add. I don't think we played *Halo* for weeks after that first night playing with him. We each seemed to have a bad taste in our mouths, no desire to play at all. Sadly, I began to think that, perhaps, he had spoiled the game for us, but we soon returned to our old ways, and morale was restored.

Two nights later, Tim Slifko and I flew a reconnaissance and security mission over Mosul. He and I had grown close rather quickly. Tim grew up in northeastern Pennsylvania, where his grandfather had bought a large plot of land near the Pocono Mountains. When I looked at Tim, I saw a wrestler. Short, stocky, square jawed, athletic, complete with a dimpled chin, yet Tim's passion was soccer until snow stole his heart. By the time he was in high school, Tim was already a professional ski instructor. He spent every available hour on the mountain, but eventually the army caught his attention.

"I was the only one of my tight group of high school friends that didn't go straight to college,"[2] Tim told me. "The army really appealed to me, so I set my sights on becoming a soldier. My friends thought I was crazy. They couldn't believe I didn't want to go to Penn State and join a fraternity like them. For some reason, I just really wanted to be in the army."[3]

Following his own heart, Tim went to the local recruiting office and took the army's entrance exam. "I scored well enough to pursue any field I wanted. So, in 1988, when all my friends were applying for colleges, I enlisted in the army as a medical specialist,"[4] he said. Then he laughed and added, "Read the small print: combat medic, humping a rucksack. But I loved it."[5]

Tim took to the army like a duck to water. He was promotable to sergeant first class in just eight years; a "fast tracker" as we call them. At that point, he decided that he was going to make the army a career. After a stint in the 10th Mountain Division, where he deployed to both Somalia and Haiti, he tried out for the 160th SOAR. He w   ccepted into the unit and quickly earned a superb reputation as a flight medic. Tim Slifko might have become the sergeant major of the army one day, and Lord knows I would have endorsed him, but a desire to fly, and a touch of luck, sent him walking down another path.

Having ridden for over a thousand hours in the back of a CH-47 Chinook, Tim decided he wanted to sit in the front seat and become a pilot. So, he applied for warrant officer candidate school. Being in the top percentage of one's flight school class had its perks; you got to choose which helicopter you wanted to fly. That seemed fair enough for Tim, so, as was the norm for him, he scratched his way to the top of his class. He chose the OH-58D Kiowa Warrior, and his first duty assignment was 2-17 CAV. "I'm damn glad I did it,"[6] he told me years later.

Slifko was a gear geek, which appealed to me for some reason. He wore a Suunto watch that was so large Rowely claimed that, in the early days of the war, Slifko, being out of ammunition and desperate yet ever resourceful, threw the watch at an enemy combatant and killed him instantly. Slifko packed knives like a chubby Boy Scout packs pogey bait. (The term *pogey bait* entered the army lexicon sometime during World War I; it simply means sweets and candies, luxuries not normally afforded soldiers in combat.) He wore what we called a "cool guy" black baseball hat with an olive drab American flag on the front, and his neatly organized gear reflected his obsessive-compulsive personality. Tim and I hit it off from the start, but there was more to our friendship than enjoying each other's company. I trusted Tim Slifko and admired him as a warrior.

Every time I flew with someone new, I sized them up. I asked myself, if we get shot down and our whole world goes to hell, if I'm injured, can this guy drag me out of the helicopter? Can he carry me to safety if my legs are broken? Can he shoot well enough to keep the bad guys off us until help arrives? If we are forced to escape and evade, can he keep up, or will he slow us down? With Slifko, the answer was yes, yes, yes, and yes! He was as good of a battle buddy as I'd ever flown with.

I am not sure why, but that night as Tim and I flew toward Mosul I had fried potatoes on my mind. My mother cooked the best fried potatoes I'd ever eaten. She was a master of the cast iron skillet. She would cut potatoes up, slice an onion in with them, and fry them crispy brown in Crisco. The more I thought about it, the hungrier I got.

It was harvest season in Iraq. On each daytime mission, I saw Iraqis out in their fields digging up what appeared to be potatoes. Large burlap bags filled with potatoes lay along the sides of several fields on the north side of Mosul. "You know that big field on the west side of the river?" I asked Tim. "The one just past bridge five."

"Yes sir," he said, as we flew up Highway 1 under night vision goggles.

"Last time I was up there they had burlap bags, full of something, lying all down the side of the field. You reckon those are potatoes?" I asked.

"That's what I assume they are," he said.

We flew in silence for a few minutes as I considered how we might obtain some potatoes. "You know that Iraqi guy that runs the little restaurant on Q-West?" I asked.

"Yes sir."

"He's got oil, and we've got a skillet," I said. "If we had some potatoes, I could fry them. I've been wanting fried potatoes for a while now."

"Well, what are you thinking?" he asked.

"The way I see it, we are protecting the Iraqi people. We're spending a lot of money in this country to help them out, so I don't think it's too much to ask for them to give us a few potatoes," I said.

"That seems reasonable to me," Tim said. "How do you plan to get them?"

"Well, I thought we'd land in that field and you can run out and get us a few from those bags," I proposed. "They won't even realize they are missing."

I could see Tim's eyes under the green glow of the night vision goggles. He was thinking it over, and I knew by his hesitation that he would do it. "You just want to land in that field, right by their houses, and go get potatoes?"

"Well, I'll land as close as I can to the bags and as far away from the houses as I can. You unbuckle as we get close, then jump out and run grab a few. You can put them in your helmet bag. Get about eight or ten good-size potatoes," I said.

After a silent pause, I said, "Man, I'm getting hungry just thinking about it. We'll need to get an onion, ketchup, and some salt and pepper, too."

"Okay, I'm in," he said.

It was a quiet evening. We flew the standard reconnaissance and security mission over Mosul, checking in with each battalion as we flew. As the time neared for the next team to come replace us on the mission, I told Tim that it was time to go.

"What are you going to tell the other aircraft?" he asked.

"I'll just tell them we are landing, so cover us for a minute," I said. "They will probably assume that one of us has to pee."

"Okay."

"Trail, this is lead. We're going to land in this field for a minute. Just circle above and cover us," I said.

"Roger that," came the reply.

I began the approach to the field, and Tim unbuckled his seatbelt. As soon as our skids hit the ground, he was out. He rushed back to the aft avionics compartment and retrieved his helmet bag. Then he ran off across the field. He had to run about one hundred yards to get to the bags. I could see him clearly through my night vision goggles.

Once he got to the potato bags, he seemed to be struggling to open them. I could not tell what he was doing, but the bags appeared to be tied up with cord. I had hoped that the entire operation would only take about a minute, but it was taking much longer than expected. I saw his head-lamp turn on. A single white light in the field frantically flashing around. Suddenly, I saw a flash in my goggles. A porch light at one of the houses had been turned on. As I looked, another light came on, then another and another. My heart began to race. The whole village was waking up. *Come on, Tim*, I thought. *It's time to go.*

"Lead, this is trail," our teammate called to me.

"Yeah, send it," I replied.

"Hey, there are lights coming on. I see some guys standing outside their houses now," he said. "You might want to get out of there."

"Are they walking out toward us?" I asked.

"No." Then a pause. "Not yet!"

I had to signal Tim. I needed him to abort the mission and return to the helicopter immediately. I decided to turn the anticollision light on for just a minute in hopes that he would see it. The anticollision light is a red flashing light on the top and bottom of the aircraft. I knew the local men could hear me, but if I turned the light on, they would know exactly where I was located. Nevertheless, I flipped the light on for a second and then turned it off. Tim was already up and jogging back across the field. He threw his helmet bag back into the aft avionics compartment, then jumped into the helicopter. As soon as his butt hit the seat, I took off.

As we flew away, I could see that a large group of men had gathered outside their houses. Tim plugged his helmet back into the aircraft, and I instantly heard his heavy breathing over the mic. "Did you get them?" I asked excitedly.

He shook his head no and between breaths said, "Ginger!"

Our dreams were dashed. It had been a ginger field. No potatoes.

We flew to Mosul airfield and fueled up for the flight back to Q-West. Flying has a way of opening people up. It's amazing what pilots will tell each other in the cockpit. It's as if the helmet blocks all inhibition. As we flew over the open desert back to Q-West that night, I broke the silence.

"What did you fear most as you got ready to deploy, Tim? Did you ever think about dying?"

"My wife asked me that same question," he said. "Before we left, she asked how I felt about going to war with the unit.

"I'm wrapped pretty tight when it comes to things like that. I don't like sharing my feelings in that way, so it's hard to get much of anything out of me, but she pressed for me to open up. What concerned me most was how the rest of the troop—the leaders, warrant officers, crew chiefs— were going to react in combat. Since I would be flying with them, I guess I worried most about the aviators. I wondered how each person would respond once they were being shot at. It is hard to know how you will respond until it happens, and then it's too late to do anything about it. While I was a new pilot-in-command on my first assignment as an aviator, I was raised in the infantry, where I understood exactly what was expected of me and what I expected of the men I would fight alongside. I had been tested in real firefights already in my career. In Somalia, my convoy had been ambushed twice. And we were attacked at the embassy complex while I was there. Shortly after that, running with foot patrols in the unstable streets of Port-au-Prince, Haiti, I was attacked again. I had also been through intense training, high-risk exercises, and worldwide contingency missions while assigned as a special operations flight medic in 160th.

"I wasn't egotistical about it, but I knew that I would could and would perform well in the heat of battle. What I was unsure of was how my fellow troopers would handle it. Some of them, I thought, would do just fine, but again, you never know until you're there and in a firefight. Some of them, having not been tested in combat, concerned me.

"In the end, sir, after our first day fighting in An Najaf and witnessing what each person did under the most extreme fighting conditions, I knew I could sleep easily. From that day forward, I knew what they were capable of, which was much more than we would expect from most men. Al Hillah, Karbala, and south Bagdad solidified it even more. I admit, I feel embarrassed now that I ever doubted them,"[7] he said.

"How tough was the fighting?" I asked.

"The enemy shot at us constantly. Since we were out front of the division, they hit us hard," he said. "They shot at us with small arms weapons, RPGs, and antiaircraft guns. Everyone did great, though. Since we fought in the daytime, you could see everyone clearly. I remember seeing a Kiowa on a gun run and RPGs being fired up at them. The pilots dodged and kept hammering them. It gave everyone great confidence to see their brothers taking it to the enemy."

"What concerned you most about the enemy?" I asked.

"Honestly, I never feared getting shot. Maybe I was conditioned from past experiences, or perhaps just a bit off my rocker. My greatest fear, the thing I dwelt most on throughout the invasion, was air defense artillery and chemicals. Specifically, I worried about persistent liquid nerve agents, 'VX' as the extreme. The chemical threat was real. It made me feel somewhat hopeless. You know what I mean, sir?" he asked.

"Yeah. I know what you mean. I remember at basic training, they showed us all those nasty pictures of people who had been exposed to chemical weapons. It scared the piss out of me," I said.

"You're not kidding, and we knew that Saddam had used chemicals on the Iranians and the Kurds," he said. "So, we flew in MOPP Two, with our protective suits on and our mask ready. I prayed that we wouldn't be slimed. I remembered in medic school they showed us the secondary effects of that stuff. Those images haunted me. It is a helpless feeling, not knowing if or when you might be attacked and that you can't do a dang thing about it."[8]

"How did that affect how you flew?" I asked, eager to pull every detail out of him.

"Well, the chemical threat didn't affect us, really. Like I said, there was nothing you could do about that, but the air defense systems were a different story," he said.

"Well, tell me about it," I said, urging him to continue.

"Right after we crossed the berm, I remember our long open-desert flight to FARP Shell. The fear of surface-to-air missiles and big air defense guns forced us to fly low. We flew at about ten feet off the deck, but we wished we could fly even lower—maybe tunnel our way across the battle-field,"[9] he said, laughing.

"I remember seeing dark objects on the horizon way out in front of us. As we neared them, they began to take shape. They looked boxy; they were square shapes. We got nervous. It felt like I was trying to crouch down in the cockpit to try and get a little more protection or something. We started flying offset from the objects, just in case they were enemy vehicles. When we were finally able to see clearly, we realized that it was the most perfectly square wild shrub bushes we'd ever seen. There was actually a line of them that looked just like a formation of some sort. After that, we loosened up a bit, laughed a nervous laugh, and trekked on.

"We were flying and fighting off old maps with alcohol pen graphics marked on them. The intelligence reports were vague, guesswork at best. Big red circles on a 1:100,000 map marking where the enemy was supposed to be. There was no precision at all, and our maps were horrible. The map would show open desert, yet there was a city there.

"I remember when we departed for the first day of fighting in An Najaf. There were reports of possible air defense systems. We thought we might be shot down at any moment, so we flew the skin off those Kiowas. We flew every second like it was life or death. One wrong decision with our airspeed or a miscalculated turn and bump would be the end for you. Flying took every bit of focus and concentration we had. We flew to survive.

"We flew low and fast to limit our exposure time to any threat, and, yes, flying under electrical wires was safer than hanging our butts out on the skyline crossing a large set of wires, a tower, or crossing buildings at the highest points. I cringed every time we had to climb to get over an obstacle that we could not go under. It was essential to remain ahead of the machine. You had to scan the battlefield out in front of you as far as you could and anticipate wires, buildings, towers, and the terrain," he said.

"We're still flying like that," I said.

"I know, but that's what started it all. That's how it began just a few months back," he said, then hesitated. "Wow. Now that I think about it, it seems like forever ago now, but it really was just a few months back. Anyway, we didn't have a baseline, no reference to say what was safe and what was not. None of us had been to combat in an aviation unit before. We could not look to see what the last unit did when they were here the previous year. We were the first. There was no time to worry about anything other than shooting the enemy before they shot you and maneuvering the helicopter to make that happen.

"Another key point is how we maintained crew and team integrity. Combat crews. Prior to the deployment, and through the invasion up until we got to Q-West, we kept our crews and teams the same. Every cockpit crew remained together from our train-up through the ground invasion. The teams became cohesive. They got so used to flying as lead and wing that they could anticipate each other's moves. It made a huge difference when flying that low and fast and fighting so hard. It reduced how much we needed to talk on the radios.

"Matt Harris was my wingman. It was comforting to have him read every move I made as lead, and always, no matter what position I was in, know that he had me covered. It was the same with right-seaters and left-seaters in a single cockpit. We knew each other's techniques, strengths, and weaknesses. We could execute a lead change on a single turn and do it without a thirty-second discussion over the radio. We could intercept radio calls and not miss a beat between transmissions. It doesn't always fit the long-term sustained or steady-state operations paradigm, but it is critical if you are going into the unknown, invading fast and furious or fighting street to street,"[10] he said.

"How did your wife, Carey, handle the first few months of the war?" I asked him.

"How's your wife handling it?" he shot back in return.

"Well, she just informed me that she is pregnant," I said.

"You're kidding!" he said. "Why didn't you tell us?"

"I just found out. She sent me an email yesterday. She is happy to be pregnant, with our fourth child I might add, but she isn't keen on doing it all alone," I said.

"How is she with you being in a combat zone?" he asked.

"Well, she would certainly like to talk to me more often. I get to call her about every two weeks. Now that we have internet, even though it sucks, I try to send an email every other day," I told him. "She said she hangs on every word of the news."

"Carey does too," he said. "Not knowing when we will come home, when it will be over, is tough. Carey says that the war is on every channel, and she almost always sees a Kiowa buzzing over the city in the background when they show Iraq."

"Yeah, I get it. It's hard, but it's better that it's on every channel than on no channels," I said. "I could see a time when people would no longer be interested in the war. How long will they stay so engaged, I wonder?"

"Good question," Tim said.

"I mean they are still fired up about 9/11, but the retaliation for that is in Afghanistan. This is Iraq, and a whole other ball of wax. If we don't find some weapons of mass destruction, this could become an ugly issue for the American people," I said.

"Yep."

We flew in silence for quite some time. While nothing was said, I knew both of us were thinking about the same thing—our families.

When we returned to the headquarters that night, Doug was sitting in the courtyard with his feet kicked up on a chair. "How was the hunting?" he asked as we walked up and dropped our gear on the ground.

Tim snickered, "Ranger B had potatoes on his mind tonight," he said.

"How's that?" Doug asked.

"He landed and kicked me out in the middle of Mosul to abscond with some potatoes, but it turned out to be a ginger field, not a potato field," he said.

"Geesh, you, a country boy redneck, and you don't know potatoes from ginger?" Doug said, shaking his head.

"It looked like bags of potatoes," I said, defending myself.

"Next time you two are feeling adventurous, y'all ought to rustle up a sheep," he said. "Lamb would be pretty tasty right about now, but be sure and get two of them," he added, then waited for the obvious question.

"Why's that, Doug? Why two?" I had to ask.

"Well, Tim will need one to catch up on all the lovemaking he's missed since he's been over here," he said.

Tim just shook his head. "I won't even honor that with a response, Doug," he said.

"That's because you know it's true," Doug said.

"Whatever. I'm going to debrief this mission and go to bed," Tim said and took his gear to his room.

That night, I dreamt I was home with Lisa and the kids. I wrestled in the living room floor with my kids; everyone laughed and smiled. I woke as Ken sat down on his cot to untie his boots. Like when I was a child, I tried to rush back to sleep and pick the dream up where I had left off.

It was gone.

The author and Chief Warrant Officer Four Bob Keiffer

The 101st Airborne Division Headquarters (Saddam Hussein's Palace in Mosul)

Saddam as the 2-17 CAV Guidon Bearer

General David Petraeus at a memorial

Chief Warrant Officer Four Doug Ford with his lizard

The author at Q-West

The author delivering candy from his daughter, Kasey, to the children of Stayla

The author with the villagers at Stayla

Chief Warrant Officer "JC" Carter attending Air Assault school at Q-West

The graveyard at Najef

(Top) The author with Captain
John Rowell; (Right) Captain
John Rowell carrying the author
across the finish line after a
physical training test

The fleet of helicopters from the 101st Airborne Division at Udairi Airfield, Kuwait

Lieutenant Colonel Stephen M. Schiller with the Mukhtar of Stayla and other village men

The SCO, Lieutenant Colonel Stephen M. Schiller

Command Sergeant Major Mark Herndon in front of the 2-17 CAV Headquarters at Q-West

The author with Todd Royar in Anbar Province

(Left to right) Colonel Joe Anderson, Major General Petraeus, Lieutenant Colonel Schiller, Lieutenant General Wallace, and Colonel Bill Greer

DARWIN

The following morning, I awoke to the sound of terse, unrecognizable voices. They were Arabic and they were close, so I quickly dressed, holstered my pistol, and walked outside my room into the hallway to investigate. There were two men at the end of the hall speaking rather tersely to one another beside a rusty circuit breaker box. A wad of bare wires hung from the wall in front of the two men.

One man held two wires in his hands. As they spoke, the man switched wires, letting one go and grabbing another, then shook his head and jabbered to the other Iraqi. His brow was furrowed, revealing his frustration and apparent confusion as to which wire he should be holding. Eventually, he settled on one. Then he yelled something to a man at the other end of the hall who I had not realized was standing just around the corner. The man yelled back, apparently confirming whatever the first man had said. Then the man holding the wire at the breaker box screwed the wire into the box, attaching it to a circuit.

Curious at what the man behind me was doing, I walked down the hallway to have a look. He was just around the corner, which prevented him from being able to see the other two men at the breaker box.

The man around the corner was also staring at a bundle of wires—the opposite end of the wires that originated at the breaker box. In unison, the two men at the breaker box yelled to him once again. The man yelled back in Arabic. Then he began some sort of obvious and dramatic preparation. He shook his arms and hands as if to loosen them up. He licked his lips and pursed them like he was about to attempt some death-defying feat. Slowly, he brought both hands up, shook them out one final time, gritted his teeth, and grabbed a bare wire. Nothing happened. He first

189

opened one eye and then the other. Still, nothing happened, so the man bent the end of the wire ninety degrees to separate it from the others.

The man then went through the preparatory routine once again and grasped another wire. This time his jaw seized, causing his teeth to smash together so loudly I could hear the snap, like an alligator slamming his mouth shut. His arms flexed as the live surge of electricity seized his body. How he kept from peeing himself, I do not know. I considered tackling him to free him from the electrical grip. Fortunately, after a two- or three-second convulsion, to my astonishment, he managed to let go of the wire.

A bead of sweat ran down his face as he yelled something to the two men at the breaker box. I assume he told them to kill the circuit. Then he took out a screwdriver, attached the wire to an outlet in front of him, and readied himself for the next iteration. In the absence of a voltmeter, I suppose one must improvise. I shook my head in amazement and walked to the TOC.

Ken Hawley was sitting at his desk when I walked into the office. "You're not going to believe what I just saw."

"What's that?" he asked.

I described what I had witnessed, and he shook his head and laughed. "Well, you should have seen what I saw at Strike a few days ago," he said.

"Have you noticed that they are painting the buildings at Strike Main?" he asked.

"Yeah. I've seen them."

"Well, the other day I flew up there, and they were painting the top of one of the buildings, not the roof, but the top portion of the side, above the second-story balcony. Two Iraqi workers were painting. They were up on the second-story balcony.

"They had made a ladder by nailing two-by-fours together. They wedged the base of the ladder on the balcony, and the top of the ladder was outside the building against the side of the wall above. The ladder was actually leaning out away from the building. The only way it remained against the building above was because one of the Iraqi guys was pulling it back against the building. He held the ladder with both hands and had his feet jammed against the railing of the balcony, so he could pull the ladder back into the side of the building above."

"You're kidding?" I said.

"No! He was straining like crazy, holding that ladder against the wall, while his buddy was on the top of the ladder painting the building," he said. "If he slipped or let go, the guy on the ladder would have died. All the boys at Strike were out there taking pictures. They said they were going to submit it for the Darwin awards," he said. "Have you ever heard of the Darwin awards?"

"I don't think so."

"The Darwin award is this tongue-in-cheek award given to those who have contributed to human evolution by taking themselves out of the gene pool."

"Oh, I get it!" I said.

"You two working today or telling stories all day?" Schiller asked as he walked the ten feet from his office to ours. He had been listening to our conversation.

"Storytelling today," Ken said. "No work, just stories."

"That's what I figured," he said as he poured a cup of coffee.

"I was up at brigade last night," Ken said, meaning the aviation brigade at Q-West. "They were talking about some things 'Big Army' is working on."

"Oh yeah," Schiller said.

"They plan to get us some precision rockets."

"What?" Schiller said, sitting down in a chair.

"Laser-guided rockets. They say that because they are laser guided, it will reduce collateral damage."

"I don't want our guys inside the cockpit punching a bunch of buttons to fire a laser-guided rocket," Schiller said. "That's just one more thing that will bring our focus inside the cockpit."

"Well, there's more. They also have a prototype of a digital knee-board," Ken said. "It has a moving map display on it. As you fly across the earth, it moves with you."

"So now a pilot is staring at his knee while he's flying. That's even worse than looking ahead at a screen in front of you. At least you are glancing outside when you look at the screen. If you're working on your leg, you can't see anything."

Both the precision rockets and the digital kneeboards were developed with good intent. At that time, Black Hawks and Chinooks did not have digital maps, maps that move on a screen in the cockpit as the helicopter moves. Schiller did not oppose the technology nor the premise. What he recognized was that our survivability relied on the pilot's close attention to the terrain and enemy outside the airplane. Wires and unlit towers were perhaps our biggest threat at that time. It took complete vigilance to avoid flying into them. Even kites were a threat in Iraq. We encountered kites daily at three to four hundred feet above the ground. While laser-guided rockets would certainly reduce collateral damage, it would require the use of the MMS, something Schiller was already in the process of removing. The same idea applied to the digital kneeboard.

"We're talking about digital kneeboards with moving maps and laser-guided rockets. Meanwhile, there are two Iraqi dudes standing outside my room sticking their finger in a light socket," I said.

"Is that some crazy shit or what," Schiller laughed.

THE CHANGING
OF THE WINDS

Flies swarmed as I opened the porta potty door to find the disaster that had been deposited. *You have to be kidding me,* I thought. The entire back of the seat was covered in poop—an explosion of human feces. It was not only a serious health hazard, but it obviously stank to high heaven. *Who could have done this?* I wondered, then I saw the evidence. There were two footprints, one on either side of the toilet seat, in the shape of sandals.

Iraqis do not use Western toilets. They squat to do their business. The Iraqi workers we hired to work on Q-West were clearly enjoying the privacy of our porta potties, but they refused to sit on the seat. Instead, they climbed up on the shelf and squatted over it. But clearly, they could not squat and hit the hole. Disgusted, I went to the next toilet.

Schiller was thumbing through a Cabela's catalog when I returned from the porta potty with a scowl on my face. "You're not going to believe what I just found," I said, as I straddled the picnic bench and sat down.

Schiller laid the catalog down on the table and turned his attention to me. "What's that?"

I explained what I'd discovered. "That's nasty," he said. "I know it stank."

"It'd gag a maggot on a gut wagon," I said, a pained expression on my face.

Schiller shook his head. "Wait until it cooks in the sun for a couple of hours. I wouldn't go out there until the shit sucker truck comes by."

"And that's the thing," I said. "They'll spray it down, but how do we know that it's disinfected? Who knows what's in that spray they use?"

"No idea," Schiller answered. "Tell Omar to talk to those dudes. Tell them to knock it off."

"I am, and I'm going to tell them that they will not be able to use our toilets if they don't stop," I said. The Iraqi workers did not speak a lick of English, so I'd have to get Omar to explain the newly established, hard-and-fast rules for the use of a porta potty to them.

Ken Hawley suddenly stuck his head out of the TOC door. "Boss, Colonel Gass needs you to give him a call."

"All right. Be right there," Schiller said, laying the Cabela's catalog on the table and standing. I picked the catalog up and began thumbing through it. Within minutes, Schiller returned.

"What's up?" I asked.

"We're having a commander's huddle up at brigade," he said.

"Now?" I asked.

"Yeah," he said as he buckled his Western holster around his waist.

"That's short notice. Anything big going on?" I asked.

"Not sure. I didn't ask, and he didn't say. I'll know in a few minutes, I guess."

"What do you have going today?" he asked as he adjusted his hat.

"Today is SOP day. I am going to read the SOP again."

"Cool. See you in a bit," he said and headed for his vehicle.

As the operations officer, I was responsible for planning all our squadron missions. It was critical that I fully understand how the unit conducted business, our Standard Operating Procedures. Having previously served as the operations officer and now the executive officer, Ken was a priceless resource. Besides, he was a complete team player. In the short time I had been there, Ken had already gone out of his way to help me get up to speed on how the unit operated. Very quickly, we had become close friends.

I spent the rest of the morning pouring through the SOPs with Ken. Just before lunch, Schiller returned.

"At ease," the battle captain shouted as Schiller walked into the TOC.

"Carry on," Schiller said. "You don't have to do that every time I walk in," he told the battle captain. "Just the first time of the morning. After that, just assume I'm around the area."

"Yes sir," the captain said.

"What's kickin'?" I said.

"Oh, just the warrant officer mafia," he said, hanging his holster and hat on the rack.

"And what exactly does that mean?" Ken asked.

"They want to make Q-West, Campbell Army Airfield."

"How so?" I asked.

"They want full lighting on the helicopters at night. They want square traffic patterns. Stuff like that. Shit that will increase our predictability and risk," he said.

"Well? What's the verdict?" I asked.

"I disagreed. No hard decision today, but I think Colonel Gass will side with the warrants. We'll see," he said.

Later that evening, I climbed up on the roof to watch the sunset and write in my journal. In a very short period, I had accumulated countless experiences, all of which I felt obligated to record. Writing it all down would preserve those events for me and my posterity, but it also seemed to help me process it.

I wrote for a while, then stopped to watch the transition from day to night. I had always been fascinated with that sliver of time between sunset and night. It reminded me of home when I was just a small boy and the world around me was quiet. That is the way it was in the rural North Georgia mountains.

I often fished until dark and then sat down on the bank of the lake to enjoy the utter silence in the brief space between day and night. It only lasted for a moment. The sun would set, and the world was suddenly silent, almost eerie at times. Then it would begin. A lone bullfrog, the impatient one who could not stand it any longer, I suppose, would sound off with a deep baritone *ribbit*, and suddenly the silence would be replaced with a cacophony of sound. Frogs, cicadas, and katydids joined in a symphonic night chorus, a comforting sound that would forever transport me back in time to my childhood.

But there was no symphony of sound in Iraq, only the steady drum of generators. Once it was completely dark, I switched my headlamp on and climbed back down to the courtyard. When I entered our room, Ken was sitting on his cot reading a book. "Where you been?" he asked.

"I was up on the roof. So much has happened since I got here, and I haven't written in my journal like I should. I wanted to catch up," I said.

"Ooohhh, you keep a diary, do you?" he said sarcastically.

"No. Men keep journals. Women keep diaries," I said.

"Isn't that sexist?"

"Give me a break. Anyway, I was also thinking about how involved you guys were in every battle during the early days of the invasion. It's interesting to me that the squadron seemed to be in the middle of every fight. I mean, it makes sense. 2-17 CAV is the divisional cavalry squadron, but it seems to me that it could not have been scripted any better than it went for the squadron."

"Well, that's primarily due to the SCO," Ken said, dog-earing a page and laying his book down on the cot beside him. "I know he told you about flying Petraeus for the first time, but has he told you how he planted the seed in General Petraeus's mind while we were out at Fort Leavenworth?"

"No. I don't think so."

"He hasn't told you about the planning conference at Fort Leavenworth?" Ken asked.

"No."

"Well," Ken said. "When we met you at Fort Leavenworth, we were there to plan the invasion. Near the end of the planning conference, General Petraeus held one final meeting with all his senior leaders. At that meeting, he gave them an opportunity to raise any final concerns they had with the plan. Most of the leaders recognized that the Iraqis were not likely going to meet us head-to-head in the open desert like they did during the first Gulf War. Everyone pretty much assumed that the Iraqis would force us to fight them in the cities—urban fighting," he said.

The complexity of fighting in an urban environment cannot be overstated. Clearing large built-up areas is a slow, methodical, and dangerous business. "Eventually, aviation came up as a point of discussion," Ken said. "There were some present in the room who felt that it was too dangerous to fly helicopters over the cities. Mogadishu was still fresh in their minds."

In 1993, Task Force Ranger, a special operations task force, deployed to Mogadishu to capture Mohamed Farrah Aidid. During the operation, two Black Hawk helicopters from the 160th Special Operations Aviation Regiment (SOAR) were shot down. Stephen Schiller was in green platoon

(160th SOAR's training course) when the Battle of Mogadishu took place. Task Force Ranger provided many lessons learned, particularly regarding the use of aviation in an urban environment. Schiller had already implemented many of the flight techniques learned as a result of the 160th's involvement in Mogadishu.

"I sat in the cheap seats off to the SCO's side that day," Ken said. "We just sat there and listened as the infantry brigade commanders said a few words. They went in order, Colonel Ben Hodges, then Colonel Anderson, and finally Colonel Mike Linnington. They presented a few logical concerns, but they were all very positive and encouraging about the mission we had planned. But there were a couple of senior leaders who were very concerned about the aviation brigade's lack of training in urban terrain. They were reluctant to support us fighting over the cities.

"The SCO sat there and listened for a while. I knew he didn't like what he was hearing. He kept rolling his eyes at me and fidgeting, but I never dreamed he would actually speak up. Not in that meeting. It was primarily for the generals and the colonels. He was there because he was the cavalry commander. Not necessarily to speak."

Ken shook his head and smiled. "I should have known better."

"He's not one to hold his tongue, is he?" I said.

"He was respectful, but he was also very candid," Ken said.

"What did he say?" I asked.

"He directed his comments to General Petraeus, who was really the only one he needed to convince. He said that the darkness of night was our friend and our best use of concealment. He suggested that we conduct most of our operations at night. He said that Iraqis didn't have a lot of night vision equipment and that what they did have was no better than first-generation stuff; therefore, the night was our best bet for being effective," Ken said.

"Well, all of that makes sense," I said.

"He went on," Ken said. "He said that if we *must* conduct daytime operations, then we had to do so using airspeed and minimal altitude. He said that speed would be our friend during the daytime."[1]

"Bucket speed, right?" I said.

"Yes. You can't fly slow, or you'll be shot down. Then he said that we needed to fly at sixty knots airspeed in unpredictable flight patterns: high enough above the ground to avoid obstacles yet at an altitude low enough to conduct reconnaissance, where we could see. He said that low altitudes would keep us from being seen by most of the enemy."

"So, he told them that the darkness of night, airspeed, and altitude combination would minimize our exposure and reduce the risk," I said.

"That's right. Then he said that the disadvantage to this technique was that flying that low for hours on end would be extremely fatiguing to the pilots. Nevertheless, he said that he believed we could do it. He said that the 160th learned a lot of lessons in Mogadishu, but they had trained for this type of environment for quite a few years since. He said that he brought those techniques to the CAV and that he felt that our unit was as ready as any unit to meet the challenge. Also, he said that we fly a small, maneuverable helicopter that presents a small target."

"What were you thinking?" I asked Ken.

"I thought my boss was about to get crushed. I remember giving him a slashing sign across my throat, telling him to stop. I was not sure how the other senior aviators would take him contradicting them publicly, especially in front of General Petraeus. The SCO was professional, but it was a risky move."

"How did they react?" I asked.

"They just listened. Other than a few of us backseaters in the room, the SCO was the junior commander there. I don't think anyone expected him to speak up," Ken said.

"What did General Petraeus say?" I asked.

"Before anyone could even counter what the SCO had to say, General Petraeus thanked him for the input, then closed the conference.[2] It was hard to tell what he thought."

"Well, it looks like Schiller was right in the end," I said.

"Absolutely."

"Say, what are you planning to do tomorrow?" Ken asked.

"I am going to get up and run in the morning. Then I plan to get around and talk with all the troop commanders. I want to try and start establishing good relationships with them, so that will require some time," I said.

"Yep, but well worth the time," Ken said, spinning around on the cot to lie down.

"Night," I said, as I clicked my headlamp off.

"Goodnight," Ken said.

Silently, we both lay on our cots thinking to ourselves. Ken broke the silence. "Have you started planning for the mission down south yet?"

"Yeah, I've got Matt Wolfe taking a look at the FARP requirements. Reggie Harper is planning the ground convoy routes. Candy Smith is working with brigade on the intelligence piece, and Tim Merrell and I are working on the flight routes," I said, excited to have a very different mission for which to plan. Days had become repetitive, so a little foray to Anbar Province sounded exciting to all of us.

"Well, have fun," he said. I could sense a smile on his face. Then, very sarcastically, he said, "You go play, while the ole XO keeps everyone happy back here."

Todd Royar had called down just two days prior to instruct us to begin planning an operation well to the south in Anbar Province. We were to assemble a rather large package of helicopters and support equipment to go after a terrorist cell in Anbar. Ken would remain at Q-West to lead the squadron while the SCO and I flew to Al Asad airfield to lead the missions.

"How long do you think you'll be gone?" Ken asked.

"Todd didn't say. Supposedly, this is a group that moves weapons and trains fighters before sending them to Baghdad. I suppose if we get lucky and find them quick, we'll be a week or so. If not, I'm not sure how long they'll want us to keep looking for them," I said.

"A boondoggle," Ken said, kidding.

"An adventure," I replied.

ANBAR

On August 19, 2003, a truck bomb exploded outside the Canal Hotel in Baghdad, Iraq, killing twenty-two people and wounding over one hundred more. The United Nations had used the Canal Hotel as its headquarters since the early 1990s. Among the dead was the United Nations' Special Representative to Iraq, Sergio Vieira de Mello. Months later, Abu Musab al-Zarqawi's Jama'at al-Tawhid wal-Jihad claimed responsibility for the deadly attack.

A mere week after the Canal Hotel bombing, the 101st Airborne Division received the mission to kill or capture men associated with the UN attack. Intelligence sources revealed that those same men were smuggling weapons into Iraq and training terrorist recruits in Anbar Province. General Petraeus instructed his staff to write the order sending a large task force primarily made up of 1st Brigade Combat Team (Bastogne) and the 101st Aviation Brigade (Destiny), both of which operated out of Q-West.

While our squadron was still under the operational control of 2nd Brigade Combat Team (Strike) in Mosul, we were tasked to send a troop of Kiowas and our tactical command post to participate in the missions. In total, ninety-three helicopters from both the 101st and 159th Aviation Brigades moved several hundred Bastogne troopers and equipment to Al Asad Air Base, northwest of Ramadi, to stage for operations.

Ken waved goodbye and made a few disparaging remarks in jest as the SCO and I departed on the mission. The flight from Q-West to Al Asad was one of the most stressful flights of my career. 2-17 CAV always flew in echelon formation. The lead aircraft would depart, and each subsequent aircraft would position itself behind and to the right (right echelon), or

200

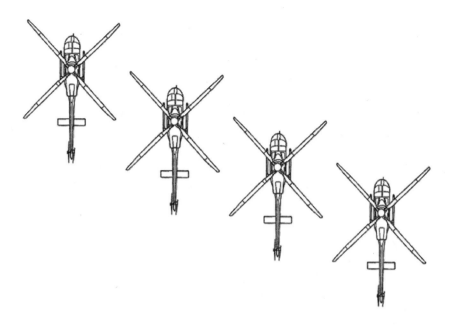

behind and to the left (left echelon), of the helicopter ahead. The flight would form a diagonal line from the lead to the trail aircraft. We flew echelon right to Al Asad, and Chief Warrant Officer Four Bob Keiffer and I drew position three of seven aircraft—square in the middle.

The pilots were ruthless in enforcing the unit's exacting standards. Everyone cranked their engine at exactly the same time. Run-up procedures and radio checks were executed to a precise standard, and formation flight was impeccable. If the aircraft spacing and alignment was not perfect throughout the flight, those who screwed it up heard about it later. Of course, younger aviators suffered the wrath of the senior pilots much more so than if a senior pilot made a mistake.

The morning we were set to depart, I walked outside to load my gear into the Humvee. Boomer Arnold's smile arrived before he did. I saw him coming up the road to the TOC. He wanted to check in with me one last time before we headed to the flight line. He was excited to get to take his troop on the mission. "Saber three," he said, grabbing my ruck and throwing it into the truck for me.

"Boomer," I nodded. "How are you this morning?"

"Couldn't be better," he said. "Ready to do this!"

"Well, let's just hope none of your birds break on crank," I said and winked at him. "That would be pretty embarrassing."

"Sir, come on. Don't go busting my balls. You're talking about Condor Troop. We've got the best maintenance in the Squadron. Our birds don't break."

"Yeah, okay. We'll find out in a few minutes."

"Besides, I have some guys cranking spare helicopters. If anything breaks on crank, we've got a bump plan."

Helicopters are finicky. It was not uncommon to have a maintenance issue when cranking and running the systems up for a mission. For that reason, we often have pilots not flying the mission crank other helicopters. If a mission bird breaks, the pilots can simply transfer their gear to the other bird that is already running and ready for the mission.

"Smart move," I said.

"Any last-minute instructions?" Boomer asked. "Any changes to the plan?"

"Nope. I think we're all set."

I saw Omar's pickup truck make the turn onto the road in front of our headquarters. He was stopping by to see us off, and I was glad to see him.

"Boomer, I need to talk to Omar before we leave. I'll see you at the flight line," I said, already turning to walk to Omar's truck.

"Roger that, sir," he said and headed back to his own truck.

"Omar, I'm glad to see you," I said.

"It's good to see you, my friend," he said, extending his hand.

I shook it, then said, "I need you to do us a favor."

"Anything for you, Jimmy," he said, always courteous.

"The Iraqi workers are not sitting down on the toilets. You know the porta potties?"

"Yes, I understand."

"They are squatting over them and making a mess. Their poop gets all over the seat, and we can't use them until the cleaning crew comes to wash them."

He began gently shaking his head. He seemed to understand my concern, but I wasn't sure he understood how dire the situation was, how unsanitary.

"I need you to talk to them," I urged him. "Tell them they need to sit down on the toilet seat or we will not let them use the toilets anymore. Can you do that?"

"Yes, of course. I will talk with them, but this may be very difficult, my friend."

"Why's that?" I asked, instantly irritated at the thought of them refusing to comply.

"Well, they have never sat down to do *their business*, as you say. It will be difficult to get them to start now."

"Then they are going to have to go out in the field to *do their business*," I said bluntly. "Talk to them. Convince them. I'm sure you can reason with them."

"I will try, Jimmy."

I patted him on the shoulder. "Thanks, Omar. I appreciate it," I said, then walked to my helicopter satisfied that he would find a way to reason with them.

We departed Q-West with Bob Keiffer on the controls, flying the helicopter. Once we were established in formation flight, Bob transferred the controls to me. "This is good training, sir," he said gently.

I took the controls and fought to keep the helicopter perfectly in position. It was my first time flying in a larger formation with the squadron. I did not want to screw it up.

At first, the flight went smooth. In fact, after half an hour of complete focus, I found myself relaxing a bit, but the farther south we flew, the stronger the winds began to blow. I saw the wind before I felt it. As I looked to the east, I saw a dust devil spiraling several hundred feet into the sky. It reminded me of El Paso, where I'd seen the first one and felt the effects of the wind that produced it. Soon our formation of Kiowas looked like Santa's sleigh flying through the air, climbing and descending, up and down, riding invisible hills of air. The cockpit workload quickly increased.

"Don't fight it," Bob said, meaning the wind. "Just ride it."

Each helicopter encountered the same updrafts and downdrafts, just at different times. The lead helicopter would hit an updraft and begin to climb. A second later, the second and then the third helicopters, and so on. Each would hit the same updraft and climb until each helicopter was clear of the current. If the fifth helicopter in the flight saw lead ascending and reacted to it, when they themselves hit the current, they would not encounter it in the same way that the other helicopters had, and thus they would lose their position in the formation. The trick, as Bob was coaching me to do, was to ride the wind as a flight.

The flight to Al Asad took us almost two hours. By the time we finally landed, I was exhausted. I had fought to keep the helicopter perfectly in position the entire time, but I slipped out of place a few times along the way.

After we landed, we collected our gear and met to quickly debrief the flight. Good units always conduct after action reviews to identify what went well, what went wrong, and what required immediate correction. While I prayed that it would not be brought up, I was sure someone would mention that I had botched the formation a couple of times.

Sure enough, when we got to the en route portion of our flight, someone said, "Who was chalk three? They got out of formation a couple of times."

With a desire to just own it, I spoke up. "That was me," I said, and before I could begin an excuse, Bob Keiffer jumped in.

"I'm sure that's when I was on the controls," he said. "I probably messed it up. Won't happen again," he added, knowing that was enough to put it to bed.

I was floored and humbled. Bob was a master aviator, a chief warrant officer four with over five thousand hours of flight time. He was a standardization instructor pilot, and everyone knew he could have easily kept the aircraft precisely in formation. We moved on to the next subject, but I will never forget Bob's kindness for shielding me from embarrassment. He was a wonderful example.

Our first mission was to fly from Al Asad airfield to three target houses where the terrorists were operating and observe as five-hundred-pound bombs were dropped on each of them. After the bombs destroyed the targets, we would then isolate the objective areas to prevent anyone from escaping or counterattacking as ground assault forces cleared each of the houses. Ideally, the terrorists would be killed as a result of the explosions, and the mission on the ground would consist of nothing more than exploitation of the houses to gather potential intelligence and confirm the success of the attacks.

As the squadron operations officer, I had the job of leading the planning for our portion of the overall mission. I was also to serve as a flight team lead for a scout weapons team assigned to one of the objectives. Due to the distance to the targets, we were required to plan the missions in excruciating detail. We had to limit what each aviator could carry in their helicopter because a heavier helicopter burns more fuel in flight. We planned exactly how many gallons of fuel we would need at the time we started our engines so that we would have enough fuel to execute the mission and then fly to the FARP for refueling.

The FARP consisted of five-hundred-gallon fuel blivets, pumps, hoses, and palletized ammunition. We planned to transport the FARP to a predesignated site in the middle of the desert using Chinook helicopters. As we flew to observe the bombs, the Chinooks would fly First Lieutenant Matthew Wolfe and his team to the designated FARP location. Ideally, they would have time to set up the FARP before we ran low on fuel and began cycling in for gas.

The FARP was critical for helo operations, but no one doubted that they would be ready when we needed fuel because Matt Wolfe was one of the best in the business. A Chalmette, Louisiana, native, Matt had served as a platoon leader in A Troop before Schiller tapped him to lead the FARP platoon. He had a reputation as a gritty, hard-working lieutenant who could fly and shoot with the best. He etched his name in 2-17 CAV history when he shot a duck in flight with his 9mm Beretta pistol one evening. He and Tim Slifko were flying over the Tigris River on the way to Mosul when ducks rose off the water below them. Matt pulled his pistol in flight, took aim out the door, squeezed the trigger, and poof— nothing but feathers. Everyone trusted Matt Wolfe to get to the right location, set the FARP up, and be ready to pump gas and load bullets when the shooting started.

Captain Candy Smith, our intelligence officer, helped me plan the mission by laying out the enemy situation. She explained who and what we thought we were up against in great detail. Furthermore, she wrote out and later briefed how she thought the enemy would react as we entered their territory.

Candy was a small, black-haired, brown-eyed intelligence officer from Michigan, where she had thrived as a competitive runner in high school and college. As is the case with so many soldiers, Candy's army story began out of economic necessity. Trying to figure out how she'd pay for college, Candy discovered the Reserve Officer Training Program and decided to capitalize on an ROTC scholarship.

"I took the scholarship," Candy told me, "but what hooked me on the army was the rappel tower," she said, laughing. "I was, and still am, terrified of heights, but when I got to the top of the rappel tower, I was more afraid of the cadre yelling at me to *get off their tower* than I was of the height itself, so I rappelled. That experience made me realize that I could be a part of something that could and would force me to face my fears."[1]

Like many other intelligence officers I'd encountered, Candy was an introvert, a stark contrast to the loud, boisterous cavalrymen with whom she served. Having been with the unit since the start of the war, she knew them well. She often sat on the sidelines, smiling quietly as they put their antics on display, acting out their life adventures for anyone who was willing to watch and those who weren't. She was a super teammate.

In the days leading up to the mission, I studied everything about my team's target. I planned our flight route to the objective, trying to use what little terrain there was available to conceal our helicopters in flight. I selected the location from which we would observe the bomb drop and studied every detail of the surrounding terrain, anticipating the routes any survivors might use to try to escape. It was critical that we learn as much about the target house, the enemy, and the surrounding terrain as possible, but there was more to the equation than terrorists. Unquestionably, the men whom we planned to eliminate trained terrorists to shoot mortars, rockets, and surface-to-air missiles to kill American soldiers and Iraqi security forces. They were certainly our enemies, but they did not live alone. Numerous women and children inhabited those houses as well. Though the men came and went, their families were always present.

On August 28, 2003, I recorded the following in my journal: *It is sad to think that two mornings from now this family will be going about their daily routine as usual when a bomb will end their lives. Killing the terrorists does not bother me; it is the women and children who I regret must die.*

We had determined their fate two days prior. They were walking dead, and I could not get that idea out of my head. I saw the children playing in the yard over and over in my mind's eye. I then saw them lying dead in the rubble. The images haunted my thoughts.

The flight from Al Asad to the house would take approximately one hour. Once again, I was crewed with Bob Keiffer. Respected by everyone in the unit, Bob was a quiet man, a Christian who treated everyone he met with tremendous respect. Bob was past forty, but you could not tell it. Tall and lean, he was a natural athlete, an integral part of our softball and volleyball teams. As an instructor pilot, Bob routinely asked me questions about the helicopter's systems, aerodynamics, and ballistics. Unlike some instructor pilots, Bob never showed frustration when I did not know the answer to a question. With Bob, my lack of knowledge simply provided an opportunity for him to teach, and with his experience, it was impossible not to learn a great deal. Needless to say, I enjoyed flying with Bob.

The mission called for numerous helicopters, which were to be broken up in multiple flights. Our Kiowas would depart as a flight of six at 3:00 a.m. Each team of two had its own target house. We would move as a flight of six to a predetermined release point. Once at the release point, the teams would break up and fly directly to their respective target areas.

At Al Asad airfield, we operated out of a cement hangar that was open on both ends. Saddam had built the hangars out of cement to try and protect his jets. By the time we occupied them in August 2003, they were littered with bird feces and trash left behind by looters. We set up a small command post at the entrance of the hangar, a table filled with radios, a map, butcher board, and several folding chairs. We slept on army cots inside the hangar.

The days were miserably hot, well over one hundred degrees. Big, black, biting flies swarmed us as we grazed on army rations. During the day, soldiers slaved in the heat, and at night they huddled around cots slamming dominoes, or bones as they called them, on makeshift tables made from plywood they'd scavenged. Those who didn't play bones sat in groups of four playing spades or reading books.

I packed light for the trip. Since it was so hot, I decided that I would only take my thin, lightweight sleeping bag with me. It was a terrible mistake. The temperature dropped to around seventy degrees at night, which seems relatively warm, but the thirty-five degree drop in temperature shocked my body. I lay on my cot in the fetal position shivering throughout the night. I recall peeking out of my mummy bag, looking to the east, praying for the sun to hurry up and rise.

On the morning of the mission, Bob and I woke around 2:00 a.m., gathered our flight gear, and made our way to the helicopter. We charged our M4 rifles, loading a bullet into the chamber, and snapped them into the dash of the Kiowa.

Bob and I emptied our bladders, then reviewed the mission details one final time before cranking. It was deathly quiet at that time of morning. There was no visible moon. The only light came from the headlamps each of us wore. In preparation for flight, Bob and I buckled our seatbelts and turned on our night vision goggles to focus them. Bob checked his watch to see how long we had until it was time to crank.

Priding ourselves on meticulous discipline, all six aircraft would crank at the exact same time. Cranking simultaneously prevented anyone from knowing how many helicopters were participating in the mission. Starting the turbine engines at different times made it easy to count how many would be in the flight. Crank one second early and you would suffer the wrath of the other pilots in the unit.

"We've got about four minutes, sir," Bob said, then paused. "Hey, sir."

"Yes, Bob," I answered, sensing something was on his mind.

"Would you mind praying with me?"

I looked over at Bob, his eyes glowing green from the light of the NVGs. He stared straight ahead, out across the airfield. "I'd love to, Bob," I replied.

We bowed our heads, and Bob offered a very humble and sincere prayer. He prayed that the women and children would not suffer, that they would not know what hit them. He prayed that they might be taken from this world without pain and that we would kill the men we were targeting. Instantly, I knew that Bob was struggling with the same issue as me: the women and children. It had been eating at me for days, yet I knew it had to be done.

We launched into utter darkness as a flight of six. The barren desert of Anbar Province, with no artificial light, reminded me of flying over water. The surface of the earth was black as oil, preventing us from sensing how high we were off the ground. We were forced to trust our radar altimeters, which provided a digital reading of our height above the ground, measured in feet. We flew in a very tight echelon formation at approximately fifty feet above the ground. Only a single rotor disk separated each helicopter in the flight. Bob and I did not speak. The only radio calls were those marking our progress as we made our way toward the target houses. As we crossed certain landmarks, the SCO called out code words, so that those following our mission could track our progress on a map. Men and women in tactical command posts scattered all over Iraq monitored the mission. With an execution checklist and a map, they followed our mission from start to finish.

Bob flew in the right seat. He divided his attention between the helicopter that flew mere feet in front of us; the radar altimeter, which told him our altitude above the earth; and our front, searching for wires that may not have been on the map. Mess any of those three things up and we'd meet certain death. Glowing under the monochromatic green light of the night vision goggles, Bob's eyes quickly darted, scanning from the helicopter to the altimeter to the front. An endless cycle of vigilance.

I sat in the left seat, following our progress across the earth with my finger on a map that I'd meticulously prepared for the mission. We call the process of preparing the map *chumming*, which meant that I had marked all the known wires and towers in red, drawn the graphic control measures that divided our teams in black marker, and circled every checkpoint at which point we changed our course heading. I also followed the execution checklist, backing up the SCO as he called out the code words over the radio to mark our progress. Like every other pilot, I feared wires the most, so my eyes darted from our front, searching for high-tension wires, back to the map.

Approximately forty-five minutes into the flight, a crystal-clear voice transmitted over the UHF radio, causing me to jump in my seat. The sound was so crisp and clear that it had startled me. It was the jet pilot checking in with the bombs. Everything was a "Go" for the mission. We were mere minutes from the target area, and my anxiety continued to build. I pictured the children in my mind. I'd see them outside playing, running around the house. Then I'd see them lined up on a mattress in the house fast asleep. The bomb would penetrate the house, rocking it with a massive explosion. I shuddered at the thought of wounded children wandering around, crying and bleeding, screaming for their mother after the bomb exploded.

Silently, I reiterated the prayer that Bob had already so beautifully offered. *Please Lord, if this must be done, don't let the women and children suffer; but if there's another way, please let it be known.*

Schiller called out the code word, noting that we were at the release point. Under the night vision goggles, I could see Schiller's team begin a turn to the west. The second team flew straight. Bob and I turned west. We flew on, into a dark abyss, for several minutes. The next radio call I would make would be to Schiller, telling him we were in position and set to observe the bomb, but before we reached our observation point, another voice pierced the silence on the FM radio.

"Saber Six, this is Eagle Six, over." It was Major General Petraeus. Petraeus was flying in a UH-60 Black Hawk command and control bird. "The bombs are a 'No-Go.' I say again: the bombs are a 'No-Go.' We are going to take the targets with the assault force, over."

"Roger. Understand all. The bombs are a 'No-Go.' Take the target with the assault force, over," Schiller repeated.

I could almost hear the relief over the sound of the turbine engine as Bob and I both audibly exhaled, relieved. Assaulting the target from the ground certainly meant more risk to our forces, more risk to our helicopters as well, but it just felt right.

Bob and I flew in ahead of the assault force and took our position to the southwest of the objective. Since we were no longer going to observe a bomb drop, we focused on the routes that Candy had indicated the enemy might try and use to escape. We were also tasked to ensure that no reinforcements show up unannounced to surprise our infantry brothers on the ground.

I saw the Chinooks and Black Hawks on the horizon, black shapes moving quickly across the desert floor. They reached their release point and began to slow their airspeed. The entire house disappeared in a cloud of dust the size of two football fields as the helicopters sat down in the front yard of the target house. "I don't know how they keep it right side up," I told Bob.

"Me neither," he said.

"They can't see anything when they land, can they?"

210

"Nope."

As the wheels touched the ground, air assault troopers from Bastogne exploded from the helicopters like angry bees from a shaken nest. With purpose and precision, squads of men moved quickly to predetermined positions to isolate the objective. Others moved to the front and back doors. Once everyone was set, they planned to enter the house, but before that could occur, women began pouring out of the house, clearly upset and agitated—frightened.

Bob and I split our attention between the target house and the surrounding terrain. I expected to see Bastogne soldiers dragging men out of the house any second, but instead women and scared children continued to flow out of the house. As they ran into the front yard, soldiers collected them and ordered them to sit and wait in a specific area.

Within minutes, the call came over the radio, "The house is clear. No military age males," he said. "I say again, no military age males are present—only women and children. The objective is secure. We are going to begin sensitive site exploitation, over," which was the army's way of saying we are going to search the house.

Not a single man present, I thought to myself. "I'm glad we didn't drop that bomb," I said to Bob softly.

"Me too," he said. "Me too."

Later, we learned that Lieutenant General Ricardo Sanchez, the V Corps Commander in Baghdad, had called off the bombs. I don't know if those women and children were simply supposed to live or if General Sanchez had information that we never received, but I do know that my prayer was answered that dark morning in Iraq and, for that, I was grateful. I remain grateful. Those hypothetical mental images were tough enough to process, much less a lifetime of real ones.

With the houses clear, Bob and I relaxed a bit. We still kept a keen eye focused on reconnaissance, but we began to talk more.

"You think they were tipped off?" I asked Bob.

"Hard to say, but maybe," he said.

"With cell phones, they can keep up with our movement pretty easy," I said. "In this desert, they hear us and just call each other."

"Yeah. Those cell phones are a game changer," he said.

Bob and I spent the rest of the day rotating between the target house and the FARP. "I just love snooping and pooping around like this," I told Bob.

He smiled and listened.

"That's what drew me to the cavalry," I said. "You know, I planned to branch infantry right up until I had to put my choices down on paper. I regretted not going infantry throughout flight school."

"Why's that?" he asked, clearly curious.

"Flight school was miserable. All those crusty, old, retired instructor pilots whose aim in life was to make you feel like an idiot, was not for me."

Bob laughed. "You must have had a bad instructor pilot."

"I assumed they were all angry," I said. "Every one of them I flew with barked at me nonstop. It was a sport to them. I remember the day I tried to hover for the first time. The instructor brought the Huey to a hover in a field. It was perfectly still. You could have set a glass of water on your knee and it would not have spilt. He turned the controls over to me, and within two seconds we were almost upside down. It was like the helicopter was suddenly possessed. When I was sure that a crash was imminent, he just touched the controls and we were back at a rock-solid hover."

I wrinkled up my nose and pretended to be the old Vietnam-era instructor pilot. "'Just hold the damn controls still, like I told you to do, and it will hover, Lieutenant,'" I said, mocking him.

Bob chuckled out loud.

"That old buzzard called me LT a lot. He could make LT sound like a curse word. Seriously, when he said LT, he may as well have been calling me an SOB," I said. "He gave me the controls again, and once again I almost wrecked us."

Bob shook his head slowly and continued wearing a smile.

"Again, he started barking at me, so I told him to take the controls, which he did, but he was clearly confused." Bob raised his eyebrows, surprised that I was so bold as a student. "He couldn't figure out why I would tell him to take the controls. He was used to taking the controls from a student when he was good and ready to do so. I could see by his expression that I suddenly had him in an uncomfortable position, which is exactly what I wanted. Then I asked him calmly, 'Do you think I'm trying to kill us?'

"He didn't answer. I could tell that he didn't know what to say, so before he could say anything, I continued. 'Do you think I want to crash us?' Still, he wasn't sure how to respond," I told Bob. "'I came to flight school to learn to fly helicopters. I'm trying my best, but you yelling at me isn't going to help.'"

"What did he say to that?" Bob asked.

"He was quiet for a few seconds. He just stared out in front of the helicopter, and then, after maybe a solid minute, he said sarcastically, 'Well, keep trying, LT. You'll probably get the hang of it in a year or two!'"

Again, Bob laughed out loud.

"Another one of my instructor pilots at flight school used to complain about Fort Rucker and his bosses every day," I said, then snarled my nose to mimic him.

"'I don't need this job, you know. I'm a chicken farmer. I got four chicken houses. I don't *have* to do this,' he'd say.

"Every day it was the same old crap, so one day I told him, then why don't you go be a chicken farmer, because I'm tired of listening to you complain every day."

"What did he say to that?" Bob asked.

"Like the other guy, he didn't seem to know what to say. I think they had behaved that way to students for so many years that it had just become their routine. Students probably feared that they would get an unsatisfactory flight if they said anything that might piss them off, so they just kept quiet and listened to it, day after day."

"Probably so," Bob said.

"But once I got to my first CAV unit, I fell in love with the cavalry mission. This," I said, indicating what we were doing at that very moment, "is fun."

"Yes sir, it is," Bob said. "It certainly is."

Bob and I listened to the radio as soldiers rounded up men and women at other target houses in the distance. They were detaining quite a few people and loading them on Chinooks to take them back to Al Asad for questioning.

We left our objective area and went to the FARP for fuel several times throughout the morning. After each FARP turn, we'd go back to the target house, check in with the Bastogne soldiers, and continue searching the surrounding terrain for anything out of place, anything that didn't look right.

Once the Bastogne soldiers were satisfied that they had thoroughly searched each objective and found everything that might be of use for the intelligence guys, we flew back to Al Asad. That evening, I went to the bunker where the 101st Aviation Brigade had set up their command post. I needed to discuss our follow-on operations with Todd Royar, my counterpart at brigade. On the way there, I saw the Chinook guys spraying the back of their helicopter out with a pressure washer. Curious as to why they were washing the aircraft, I walked over to say hello.

"What's kickin'?" I asked as I approached the back ramp of the Chinook.

"Iraqis puked in the back of the aircraft," one of the crew chiefs said.

It was the crew that had flown all the detainees from one of the objective houses back for questioning. "Damn near every one of 'em got sick," he said. "Stinks like shit."

"Well they've certainly never flown before, so I guess that makes sense," I said.

"It'd be okay with me if they never flew again," he said.

"Where did they take them?" I asked.

"They're all over there," he said pointing to one of the bunkers.

"All right, take it easy, guys," I said and decided to go take a look at the detainees.

When I visualize "bad guys," I get this mental image of an evil person. I figure, anyone who can kill other human beings should look the part. I remember the first time I saw a picture of Jeffrey Dahmer. He didn't look like a serial killer. Charles Manson looked the part; Jeffrey Dahmer did not. The detainees were certainly not serial killers, but somehow, I expected them to look like hardened fighters—lean, bearded men with hatred in their eyes. That's the mental image I had as I approached the holding area.

They were being held behind a simple makeshift fence, fashioned to create large pens. It looked more like a chicken coop than a prisoner holding cell. I was surprised, caught completely off guard, when I looked inside the fence. Men and women alike sat on the floor staring into space. None of them spoke, not even to one another. I saw fear in the women's faces. The men appeared defiant. One elderly man with a lengthy gray beard and leathery brown skin thumbed through prayer beads, his fingers long and thin, knotted like bamboo. In a motionless, full squat, he stared into the distance.

Having not bathed in perhaps a week or more, sweating profusely, having been wrestled from their homes and forced into a helicopter, and then caged like animals, they were filthy. The stench of body odor and vomit, and I'm sure urine, turned my stomach. Not one of them looked at me or even indicated that they saw me standing there looking at them. If they could have seen inside my mind, they would have felt the turmoil.

Compassion and justice wrestled with one another inside my heart. Perhaps that was the mistake. They wrestled in my heart and not in my head. The soldier in me tried to balance the scale with logic and reasoning. They were involved in arming and training terrorist fighters. Those fighters would attack American soldiers, as well as Iraqi security forces. In some cases, these men may have directly fought against us. I hated how I felt. It was disturbing, yet on some level, I recognized that it reminded me of my humanity. I turned and walked to the brigade command post.

TENDER MERCIES

Early September found us back at Al Asad chasing the same group of terrorists. On the second trip, we established our command post near 4th Squadron, 3d Armored Cavalry Regiment, which was based out of Al Asad airfield. In the early 1990s, 4th Squadron had been my first unit of assignment in the army. I was excited to visit them, to go back in time and somehow relive memories, if only for a brief moment. It had not occurred to me that the things I was remembering were gone from everywhere except my own mind. The unit in which I had served remained in name only. The flags were the same, but the soldiers with whom I had served were gone. Then I saw with clarity. It is not the flags or the names of organizations that make them what they are—it is the people that define them.

The whole idea was bittersweet. Understanding that the most important thing in any organization is its human capital forced me to recognize the importance of people and relationships; yet it saddened me to know that once we returned from Iraq, our soldiers would begin to move on to their next assignment and that would slowly transform 2-17 CAV. The Greek philosopher Heraclitus said, "No man steps in the same river twice, for it's not the same river and he's not the same man." And so it is with organizations. It does not mean that the organization will not be as good as it once was. It might be even better. But it will never be the same.

Our plan was for our soldiers traveling in vehicles to drive to Al Asad the same day we flew there, but they were delayed a day, so the first night, we did not have anything other than what we could carry in our Kiowas, which was not much. After setting up our radios, maps, and butcher boards, I turned to Doug Ford and said, "Doug, make it better."

216

Doug knew exactly what I meant. Without saying a word, he departed on foot.

"Where's he going?" the SCO asked me.

"To make it better," I said.

The SCO rolled his eyes and continued unpacking his rucksack.

About two hours later, Doug returned in a truck with two coolers filled with ice and soda. He hoisted a huge garbage bag, filled with chips, out of the back of the truck. Several guys patted him on the back as they reached in for a bag of Funyuns. "You're the best morale officer I've ever met, Doug Ford," I told him.

Doug didn't answer. He just scrunched up his moustache and walked over to the area he'd selected to pitch his bedroll. The truth is, Doug had a knack for making any situation better. I suppose it was partly because he liked creature comforts himself, but also because that's just the way he was wired. *Don't embrace the suck, make it better* was his mantra.

What surprised me most about Doug's little adventure was the fact that the truck he had borrowed from another unit had a .50-caliber machine gun mounted on top of it. "Doug, did they let you take that weapon?" I asked.

Again, Doug scrunched his upper lip, causing his thick black mustache to narrow, and squinted his eyes as he thoroughly considered the situation. "I just asked them if I could borrow a truck for a few days, and they said yes," he said. "I went out and looked at one of their Humvees, but there were wallets and stuff lying in it. I went back in and told the captain that there was a lot of personal stuff in the Humvee, so he said to take the big truck." Then Doug raised his brow and looked me in the eye, "He didn't seem to be too concerned about the machine gun."

"Don't you think that's a little strange? I mean, I think they are going to miss that .50 caliber. Don't you?"

"I don't know. If they do, they'll come get it," he said and continued unpacking his gear.

I heard the truck as it roared down the road in front of our building at a high rate of speed. A first sergeant was speaking in his falsetto when he exited his truck and rushed into our command post. "Damn, chief, we didn't say you could take a machine gun," he said, looking directly at

Doug, who now sat with his legs crossed in a folding chair, eating Funyuns and sipping an ice-cold Coke.

"Oh," Doug said, nonchalantly. "Well, I took care of it. You can have it back," he added, shrugging his shoulders.

"Come on, chief," the first sergeant said. "Jeez."

"The captain knew it was on the truck," Doug protested.

The first sergeant rolled his eyes, then took the weapon off the truck, and walked back to his vehicle, shaking his head.

As the sergeant drove away, I looked at Doug and shook my head. "Doug, if we had three of you, we could open a circus. People would pay good money to watch you in action."

"Sir, if we had three of you, we could declare this outfit handicapped and get a tax break," Doug shot back, to which the room erupted in laughter.

"Well played, Doug," I said, shaking my head and smiling. "Well played."

"Now, eat your Funyuns and thank me later," he said.

"Thank you, Doug," I said with as much sarcasm as I could muster. "You're the best."

"Hey, you asked, and Doug made it better," he said, then began digging in his rucksack for something. "Made it all better," he muttered under his breath.

Because our trucks had not yet arrived, we had to sleep on the floor that night. I inflated my thin, army-issue sleeping pad and threw my sleeping bag down on top of it. By midnight, everyone began retiring for the night. It quickly grew quiet. Several headlamps flickered as men dug into their rucksacks or read books. I saw Schiller wrapping a T-shirt around his head. "What are you doing, boss?" I asked.

"Getting ready for bed," he said.

"What's up with the T-shirt?"

"I've never been able to sleep with light in the room," he said. "Gotta cover my eyes."

After completely wrapping his head up like a mummy, Schiller lay down, and the room grew quiet. "Good night, Dougie-Boy," I said, smiling in the dark.

"Good night, Mary Ellen," Doug answered, to which Tim Slifko snickered.

The floor of the room was filled with men lying on their backs staring at shadows on the ceiling.

Doug broke the silence. "I can handle cots, but after sleeping on this concrete floor, my back is going to kill me in the morning."

"I'll crack it for you when you wake," Slifko said. "Straighten your back out."

"Yeah, that's what you'd like to do, hug up to your daddy," Doug said.

"I once used the ole *I'll pop your back* to get close to a girl," I said.

"Here we go. It's story time with Ranger B," Doug said.

"When I was in fifth grade, all of us boys liked to pop backs. We did it all the time. Well, there was this girl that I really liked, but she didn't even seem to know I existed. She never paid me any attention. Fifth grade in my school was in trailers, and sometimes the teacher had to go to the office in the main building. She would threaten us with a paddling if we got out of line; then she'd leave for five or ten minutes.

"One day she left the classroom and, as soon as she shut the door, this girl I liked asked me to pop her back. I broke out in a cold sweat the second she asked. She walked straight to the front of the class, so I'd have room to do it and stood waiting on me.

"I was suddenly terrified. The girl of my dreams just asked me to pop her back, which meant that I was about to hug her in a full embrace from behind."

"That's what Slifko wants," Doug interrupted.

"Shut up and listen to the story," Slifko said.

"It would be the closest I'd ever been to a girl," I continued. "I slowly made my way to the front of the class. Every student in the room watched in silence as I wrapped my arms around her chest. She relaxed, and I paused just a second, took a deep breath, enjoyed the smell of her hair. Then, gently, I lifted her off the ground and bounced her, and when she bounced, I farted. Loud."

"Nooooo!" at least five soldiers shouted in the dark.

"Yes. As I bounced her, I farted, and it was loud. But I didn't have sense enough to let her go. I bounced her about three more times, and every time she bounced, I farted again."

219

"Noooo!" again they shouted.

"She started twisting and turning, trying to fight free. Finally, I had the sense to let go. The entire class was laughing at me. I turned beet red, ran to my desk, and put my head down."

"You made that up, right?" Slifko asked.

"No. I am dead serious. I remember it like it was yesterday. The most embarrassing day of my life."

Slowly, the laughter quieted, and another day in Iraq faded to darkness and a memory.

We divided the desert up into square grids or zones. "I wanted to use our forces like a special operations force on that mission,"[1] General Petraeus later told me. "My intent was to use the Kiowas like 160th 'Little Bird gunships' and our Pathfinders as the assault force. That gave us great flexibility and speed."

The purpose of our reconnaissance mission was to locate weapons caches, and man, did we hit the jackpot. "This is about as fun as it gets," I said to Bob Keiffer on our first day out.

"Yes sir, it is," he agreed.

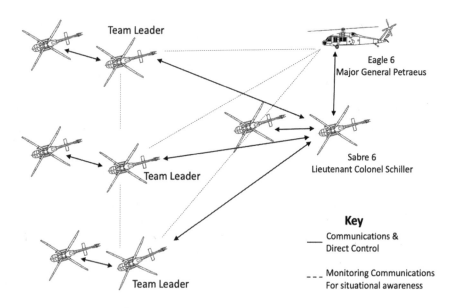

We found stack after stack of weapons. Some were carefully hidden in the rocks, while others were so large that brown blankets had to be thrown over them to try and conceal them. All the weapons were being transported through Anbar Province. Their intended destination: Ramadi, Falluja, and ultimately Baghdad.

Bob and I flew in a scout weapons team with Chief Warrant Officer Three Tim Merrell and Chief Warrant Officer Two Mike Blaise. We combed the desert floor with Tim and Mike in lead, scanning and searching for anything that seemed out of place or unnatural. We landed several times at caches where Mike and I got out and took pictures before we shot and destroyed the stockpiles with rockets and .50-caliber machine gun.

For over a decade, I had trained to conduct real-world reconnaissance missions. It was incredibly rewarding to be in combat actually executing the missions we had trained on for so long in peacetime. At one particularly large cache, we landed, and Mike Blaise and I got out to take pictures. Both of us were flying in the left seat, so our primary task was to scout, search for caches, and report to Schiller. Bob and Tim served as our chauffeurs.

We bent at the waist to exit the rotor system and then walked away from the helicopters to take a closer look at the cache. As soon as Mike peeled his flight helmet off, I saw a big smile plastered across his face. Like me, he was excited to be having such success.

Mike Blaise was a small-town boy from Missouri, who had been an outstanding defensive tackle on his high school football team. Standing six feet tall and weighing just over two hundred pounds, he was solid as an oak. His tree trunk thighs made for a tight fit in the less-than-roomy Kiowa. Mike's wife, Kate, was also deployed. She was a logistician who served as a battle captain in Lieutenant Colonel Jeff Kelley's unit, the 426th Brigade Support Battalion, also stationed at Q-West. Mike was fortunate to be able to see his wife on a routine basis but cursed in that they were both constantly in harm's way. Mike had been a ground scout before going to warrant officer candidate and flight school, so he made the transition to aerial scout with ease.[2] At that time, I had no idea what an impact Mike would have on me, on everyone in 2-17 CAV. If I had known what fate lay ahead, I'd have savored those missions even more.

Mike and I inspected the carefully stacked cache of RPGs, SA-7 surface-to-air missiles, mortar rounds, weapons cleaning kits, and mortar tubes. There were several crates with labels that read "The Republic of Yemen."

"I bet the intel guys will want to see that," I said and snapped a picture.

Mike and I were both silently eyeing the pile for a souvenir, something we could take back with us.

"Do you think it's booby trapped?" Mike finally asked, nodding at the pile.

"I don't know," I said. "I doubt it. I'd imagine they're planning to move this stuff soon. They wouldn't bother with a trap, would they?"

"I don't know, but I'd like to take one of those weapons cleaning kits with me," he said, pointing.

Stories my father told me as a boy suddenly flashed into my mind. I vividly recalled him telling me that the Germans wired Luger pistols to grenades and mines because trophy-seeking GIs liked to collect them as souvenirs. I was nervous about touching anything, yet it seemed natural to want something to show your grandchildren one day. Then I saw it. There was one kit, a small green metal box with a cleaning rod and a brush, on the edge of the mound of weapons.

"How about that one?" I said, pointing to the box. "I think you can get to that one without moving anything else."

"Yep. I'm taking it," Mike said and carefully removed the box from the stack.

We snapped several more pictures and then returned to our helicopters, where Tim and Bob sat idling. I called the SCO and reported what we had found. Because our helicopters were running low on fuel and we needed to immediately fly to the FARP, I sent Schiller the grid coordinates so that his team could destroy it.

As we flew away, Schiller said he was already on his way to blow the cache up. It took Bob and me about ten minutes to fly to the FARP. Once there, we sat at idle, listening to the radios as Schiller's team searched for the cache.

Due to its size, it wasn't overly difficult to find.

"Holy shit," Schiller said over the radio. "This fucker's huge."

"Yes, it is," I said.

Their intent was to shoot the stack of weapons with rockets first. If they were lucky, there would be a secondary explosion and a subsequent fire that would render all the weapons inoperable.

Chief Warrant Officer Four Curtis Phipps flew lead for Schiller's team that day. He would take the first shot at the weapons cache. As Curtis circled and lined up for the shot, Schiller spoke. "Don't miss, now. If you can't hit it, then move over, and I'll take care of it for you."

Curtis Phipps keyed the mic and laughed with him. Bob and I had just finished refueling when Curtis initiated his bump and subsequent dive at the cache. We were over ten kilometers away when Curtis depressed the trigger and sent the 2.75-inch rocket into the air. At just over six miles away, the Kiowas looked like tiny specs on the horizon, mosquitos in the distance, yet when the explosion occurred, it appeared as though the mosquitos had triggered a nuclear bomb.

"Holy crap," I said as an enormous mushroom cloud climbed into the sky. Then I heard Schiller's worried voice over the radio.

"Are you okay?"

"I think so," Curtis replied, then paused. "But we don't have a chin bubble anymore."

Curtis had shot the cache at close range. He did not anticipate the magnitude of the secondary explosion.

"I saw the shock wave go through your aircraft," Schiller said.

"I saw it coming at me and felt it go through us," Curtis answered.

"Fly to the FARP and land," Schiller instructed. "You need to see how bad the damage is."

"Roger that," Curtis said, turning toward the FARP. Seconds later, he keyed the mic. "That was like flying the Millennium Falcon out of the Death Star as it's blowing up behind you. That's what it felt like, anyway."

Schiller laughed again over the radio.

"I shot, then broke, but the concussion and shockwave caught us," Curtis said.[3]

The explosion blew the chin Plexiglas at the pilots' feet completely out of the helicopter, but neither pilot was injured. After a thorough inspection of the aircraft, Curtis limped the Kiowa back to Al Asad airfield. Schiller joined other teams for the remainder of the day.

By midafternoon, our team had found and destroyed numerous caches. It had been an incredibly exciting day, searching for weapons cleverly hidden throughout the wadi systems. Other Kiowa teams had experienced similar success in their areas. We had found the artery through which weapons flowed into Iraq. Our ground forces had also gone into several target houses and found money, computers, and weapons. They detained several men whom they planned to take back to Al Asad on the Black Hawks for interrogation.

The day was quickly coming to an end, the mission almost over, when Bob and I rounded a curve in a large wadi and saw two men sitting on a bank with a large brown blanket stretched out beside them. The blanket was pinned down by rocks carefully placed in each corner. The men were miles from any house. There were no sheep in the area, so we quickly concluded that they were not shepherds. The men were out of place and, in our opinion, up to no good. We made several passes over them to get a closer look. With each pass, they sat calmly and stared up at us.

"You'd think they would have run off when they heard us shooting," I said.

"Not if they are here to watch something, or if they have some other purpose," Bob said. "They are still here for a reason."

"What do you think's under that blanket?" I said.

"Not sure, but I know they are hiding something," he answered.

"We might be able to blow that blanket up off the ground with the wind from the rotor system," said Tim Merrell, who piloted our lead aircraft.

"I agree," Bob replied over our team internal radio. "That might work."

"I'm going to fly in steep right over the blanket, then pull up and break hard right. You cover me and watch the blanket," Tim said.

"Roger, we've got you covered," Bob replied.

"Let me get my M4 out first, Bob. Keep them on my side," I said, as I took my rifle out and prepared to shoot if the men tried to go for a weapon or shoot at us. The weapons on a Kiowa are fixed forward. The M4 would give me the latitude to keep a weapon oriented on the men even when we broke away from them. I feared that they would wait until we turned to try and shoot us.

Tim Merrell climbed a couple of hundred feet, then dove in toward the men. The two men were clearly getting a bit nervous. They rose to their knees. At less than one hundred feet above the ground, Tim flared his Kiowa and broke hard right. We were right behind him, observing the blanket. Just as he broke, his rotor wash sent a wall of wind straight toward the ground. The wind hit the blanket perfectly and the right corner of the blanket blew up. Bob and I immediately saw weapons stacked under the blanket.

"They've got weapons," I told Bob.

"Yep. I see them under the blanket," he replied.

Realizing they were busted, the two men jumped to their feet and held their hands out as if to say, "Don't shoot. We're innocent."

Tim and Mike Blaise had continued their turn and were right back in on the men very quickly. On the second pass, we confirmed what we had seen as I reported to the SCO.

"We've got two males with a cache of weapons," I said. "They were hiding the rifles under a blanket, but we blew it up with rotor wash."

"Maintain contact with them while I call it in," he said.

The SCO reported what we had found to Colonel Greg Gass, who was monitoring the mission from a Black Hawk. Gass then reported to Petraeus, who was also airborne in a Black Hawk. Meanwhile, we made pass after pass over the men. By that time, the two men were begging us not to shoot them. They shifted their feet, almost dancing in place. They held their hands out, palms upward, and shook their heads no.

"Destiny Six, Eagle Six, over."

"Destiny Six, over," answered Gass.

"Do we have room in the Black Hawks to go pick those two up?" he asked.

"Negative. The Black Hawks are full," Gass replied.

"Roger, stand by," Petraeus said.

Suddenly, I realized that General Petraeus was about to tell us to kill the men. They were clearly weapons facilitators—men with bad intent. They were certainly planning to use the weapons to attack American soldiers, but I didn't want to do it this way. Somewhat unconsciously, I began studying everything about the two men in great detail. They wore dishdashas. One man wore blue, and the other was dressed in white. Both

225

had thick beards, although the man in blue's beard was wider and hung to his Adam's apple. The man in white had a thin, light brown beard that narrowed until it came to a point eight to ten inches below his chin. We overflew them so closely that I could see the detail of their faces. I realized that we were about to shoot them down and that I'd see those faces for the rest of my life. I began to wish that they would go for a weapon to try and shoot at us. I began to pray that they would do something. *Please Lord, don't make me shoot them like this. Not with them begging me not to do it.* Images of the men wounded and bleeding out suddenly flashed into my mind. I pointed my rifle right at them on each pass, secretly hoping that I would provoke them, force them to panic and sprint for a weapon under the blanket. I hated that feeling.

The longer we waited for Petraeus to give us guidance, the more detail I recorded in my mind. I have been blessed, or cursed, with an almost photographic memory of events. I can see images with great clarity decades after I experience them. I recalled a wreck I once saw. When I arrived, a woman's broken leg was swinging outside the window of her wrecked car. The image was so clear that, when I recalled it later, it was as if it had just happened.

I knew I'd live with the images of that moment, so I began to consider in my mind what the best image could be. The best case would be instant death. I did not want to see them writhing on the ground wounded. *Make a clean shot and kill them instantly*, I thought.

"Destiny Six, Eagle Six, over," we heard over the radio.

My heart raced. "Can you destroy the weapons with rockets?" he asked.

"Stand by, over," Gass replied.

"Saber Six, Destiny Six. Can you destroy the weapons, over," Gass asked Schiller.

"Roger that."

"Eagle Six, Destiny Six. We can destroy the weapons, over," Gass reported to Petraeus.

"Okay, destroy them, over."

"Roger," Gass replied. "Break. Saber Six, did you monitor that call?" Gass asked Schiller.

"Roger," he replied.

Bob and I breathed a huge sigh of relief. On the next pass, we opened fire. Once again, my prayer was answered; *a tender mercy*, I thought. Still, the graphic image of those men was burned into my mind. The texture of that moment would always be a part of me.

The next day, we set up a FARP in the middle of the desert. There was nothing but flat, brown desert for as far as the eye could see. Todd Royar and I flew together in a Kiowa. We followed the Chinooks to the site and set the FARP up before daylight. Todd and I then set our radios up and swatted flies as helicopters rotated in and out of the FARP throughout the day. It was unbearably hot, and we had no shelter at all. Our ground forces cleared village after village, finding weapons, money, and random laptop computers that were as out of place as the Coke bottle that fell from the sky in the film *The Gods Must Be Crazy*. That night, Todd and I flew back to Al Asad and immediately began planning for the next day's mission.

Bob Keiffer and I were back up together the following day. Our plan was to fly to a bombed-out airstrip and set up a FARP. We'd land there and wait for intel on a few key individuals we'd been tracking. Once their location was pinpointed, we'd fly in and capture them.

Eventually, the call came. One of the men we hoped to capture was suspected to be in a village about thirty kilometers from our location. With a grid location in hand, everyone raced to their helicopter, cranked, and departed. We swarmed the village quickly with Kiowas leading the charge. As Bob and I swooped in, I noticed old men squatting in a circle drinking chai and smoking cigarettes. Once they realized that Black Hawks with soldiers were about to land in their front yard, they stood and stared. No one tried to escape the village. The attempt would have been futile. The Kiowas were tasked to ensure the village was isolated, preventing anyone from leaving or entering.

Two Black Hawks landed directly in front of the house where we suspected the wanted man was staying. As soon as wheels touched the ground, Pathfinders exploded from the helicopters. One enormous sergeant moved forward with a shotgun in his hands. Two Iraqi men began walking toward him. They appeared very animated, gesturing with their hands as they spoke. The sergeant pointed to the ground, urging them to lie down. All the Iraqis understood and complied, except for one man. He kept walking toward the sergeant, hands flailing. As he closed the distance to the sergeant, he began pointing and screaming at him.

"That guy won't lie down on the ground," I pointed out to Bob.

"I see him," Bob said. "He'd be wise to listen and comply."

Suddenly, the sergeant dropped the shotgun, which was slung around his body. He grasped the man by the dishdasha, one hand at his neck and the other at his belly. He then lifted the man off the ground, over his head, and slammed him to the ground on his back. The man bounced off the ground and did not move.

"Did you see that?" I asked Bob.

"No, what did he do?"

"That huge sergeant just body-slammed him. He wouldn't get down, so he threw him down," I said. "He's not moving. I think he knocked him unconscious. Heck, he may have broken his back."

"Hey, there's a truck trying to leave," Bob said.

"I see it," I said.

I called the SCO on the radio and told him we were moving to stop the truck. "Roger that," he said.

Bob and I quickly flew over the top of the small pickup. From my vantage point, I could see inside the truck. "It looks like a man and a boy," I said.

Bob didn't respond. "They look harmless," I added.

"We need to stop them," he said.

"Oh, I agree, but I don't think they are trying to escape. They are just going somewhere."

Bob flew past the truck, then turned left, but kicked the Kiowa out of trim so that we slid through the air sideways in front of them and squarely in the middle of the road. The man stopped about fifty yards from us. I had already taken my M4 from the dash, so I was prepared to shoot if he tried anything.

The man and the boy, his son I assumed, immediately jumped out of his truck, ran to the front, and then lay down in the road. The man was wearing sandals, and the air from our rotors blew one of them off his foot. It flew down the road, flipping with the wind, about twenty meters. "He's scared," I said.

"Yeah," Bob said in a hushed voice.

I began trying to gesture to him to get up. At first, he didn't see me. "Bob, hover lower to the ground. Maybe he'll look at me," I said.

I began to feel sorry for the man, a sense of remorse. He was clearly frightened. His son lay still beside him. "Look at me!" I said over the intercom system to Bob. Bob didn't comment. I hated the way I felt.

Finally, the man looked up and saw that I was gesturing for him to get up. Suddenly, he grabbed his son by the arm and jerked him up. "He has his son with him, and he's scared we'll hurt them," I said.

I could not imagine what it might feel like from his perspective, but being a father, I knew it must be horrible to fear that something terrible could happen to your son. He and the boy now stood in front of the truck. I began motioning for him to return to the village. At first, he did not understand what I was trying to tell him. I pointed to the village, then shooed them away with my hand. Suddenly, he realized what I wanted him to do. With one sandal on and the other lying in the road about twenty meters away, he took his boy by the arm and escorted him to the truck. It was clear that he wanted to do exactly what he thought he was being instructed to do.

I tried to motion for him to get his sandal. The man got back out of the truck, eager to do whatever I asked him to do yet confused. We could not hover closer because we would blow the sandal away, so I pointed to it and then at him. After a few futile minutes of pointing and motioning, I simply shooed him away again. He jumped back into the truck and tried to start it, but it would not start. For whatever reason, it had stalled. The man and his boy quickly jumped out of the truck and, with both doors open, began pushing it backwards down the road toward the village.

They were at least a mile from the village, and with the man and the boy both pushing as hard as they could, they were barely moving the truck. I felt conflicted. I pitied the man. With one sandal on and the other lying in the road, he and his young son pushed for all they were worth. I was completely satisfied that they were not trying to flee the village. I just wanted it to end. Once again, I tried to get his attention, but he did not look back up at me. I wanted him to retrieve his shoe and stay there until our operation was complete; then he could go on about his business.

"Let's just fly away. Maybe they will leave," I told Bob.

We flew to the other side of the village, and within minutes the ground forces were calling the Chinooks to come get them. They had detained several men whom they wanted to transport to the holding facility at Baghdad International Airport.

It only took a few minutes for the Chinooks to arrive. As we departed, I flew over the village one last time. A part of me didn't want to look and see if the man and his son were still there. I wanted to forget the whole ordeal, shake it out of my head. I glanced over at the truck and found the man and his son still doing their best to push the truck back to the village. My heart ached.

The sun was setting as we flew back north. I began to feel the fatigue of the day set in. We'd begun the day before first light, flying night vision goggles, and we'd ended the day flying goggles. "How you feeling, Bob?" I asked.

"I'm okay, sir," Bob said gently.

"I'm tired," I said.

"It's been a long day."

"Honestly, Bob, I'm struggling to stay awake. You might want to keep talking to me," I said.

"I'm good," he said, not offering that I sleep but assuring me that he was feeling okay.

I fought sleep all the way back. All I could think of between the nods was the range of emotions that I had experienced. One minute I was angry; the next minute I was scared. One minute, rage burned within me; the next minute, compassion seared my heart. I had felt these emotions before but never with such intensity. They were feelings I would experience repeatedly over the coming decade-plus of war. I would get much better at compartmentalizing while deployed, but back home the feelings would frequently return with color and texture that never seemed to fade.

Little did we know at that time that we had begun a high stakes game of cat and mouse with Abu Musab al-Zarqawi's men that would quickly transform into a major campaign. Zarqawi would go on to lead Al Qaeda in Iraq (AQI), becoming the central target and focus of General Stanley McChrystal's Joint Special Operations Command.

THE HEAT IS ON

The next morning, Candy Smith approached me. "Sir, I've been looking at the attacks in Mosul. IEDs, roadside ambushes, rockets, and mortars have really picked up. We're seeing them almost daily now and sometimes multiple attacks in a single day. This thing is escalating, and we'd better figure it out."

"Yeah, I know. It's seems like Kiowas are responding to attacks all day. Let's sit down and try to find a way to anticipate rather than respond to attacks," I said. "There has to be a method to their madness, some sort of pattern."

"I agree. They're predictable. I'm sure of that. If we can figure it out, I think we can start catching these guys," she said.

"Or at least disrupt them. Force them to constantly move," I added.

"Right!"

"Okay, when we get back let's get together and work it," I said.

"Sounds good."

I had been a hunter my entire life. Hunters, particularly those who pursue their quarry with bow and arrow, understand the importance of patterns. Archery hunters require close-range shots, so it's essential that they study the habits of their prey. Deer, antelope, elk, rabbits, all animals establish patterns, including humans—especially humans. Candy and I knew that the enemy fighters, who were hunting us, were inevitably setting predictable patterns. We simply needed to figure it out, decipher those patterns, and exploit them.

I thought back to June, just a few months prior, when I had first arrived. We had felt relatively secure as we drove around Iraq. Sure, there

231

were random attacks, but the attacks were sporadic, and they were not overly complex. But suddenly, enemy activity had drastically increased.

Two days later, we flew back to Q-West.

"Well hellooo," Ken said as I walked into the headquarters with my gear draped over my shoulder.

"Roommate," I said with excitement. "Miss me?"

He threw his head back with his mouth open and held out, "Ummmmm. No."

"Oh, come on," I said, sticking out my bottom lip.

"While you and the SCO were out gallivanting, I was patrolling the skies over Mosul keeping Strike soldiers safe."

"I'm sure you were, roommate. The fine citizens of Mosul are safe with my brother, the legendary cavalryman Kenneth Hawley, on patrol," I said and left the TOC to put my gear away.

When I returned, Ken and the SCO were standing in the breezeway talking to a very large soldier who stood with his back to me. "Jimmy, meet our new sergeant major," the SCO said. "Sergeant Major, this is our operations officer, Major Blackmon."

Command Sergeant Major Mark Herndon turned and extended his hand with a pleasant smile. "Sir, good to meet you."

"Good to meet you, Sergeant Major," I said. "And that Southern drawl is music to my ears, sergeant major. Music to my ears."

He laughed, "I know what chu mean," he said.

Mark Herndon stood six feet, five inches tall and weighed two hundred pounds. He had a thin halo of tightly trimmed, blond hair around the back of his head; otherwise, he was bald on top. Command Sergeant Major Herndon was no stranger to the cavalry. 2-17 CAV was his fourth cavalry assignment, and he was thrilled to be back in the CAV.

"Where you from, sergeant major?" I asked.

"Murray, Kentucky," he said.

"Heck, you're just up the road from Fort Campbell."

"Yep, just on the west side of Land Between the Lakes," he said. "How about you?"

"Ranger, Georgia, just south of Chattanooga, Tennessee."

"Hmm. Where's that?"

"Do you know Dalton? The carpet capital of the world?"

"Oh yeah, I know where Dalton is."

"Well, we're right by it."

"Know exactly where you're talkin' about."

"Well, welcome to the CAV," I said.

"It's good to be here," he replied.

"Well hell, let's have a hoedown," Schiller said, to which we all laughed.

The following morning, Candy and I sat down to brainstorm our problem. We began with what we knew. First, we knew that we did not have control over the enemy or the environment; therefore, we could not control its complexity. The best strategy for coping with external complexity is to develop a greater capacity for adaptability—a hallmark trait of the cavalry. In our case, we had smart, adaptable cavalrymen, but we lacked systems and processes to set them up for success. We knew that in order to achieve our organizational goals, we had to reschedule our resources to reduce and ideally eliminate disruptive events before they occurred.

"Let's begin by looking at our own patterns," I said.

We laid a map out on the table and began reviewing the routine places we flew and the times of day we flew there. Then we marked the routes the ground forces routinely drove in their vehicles.

"We have Kiowas up in the air around the clock," Candy said. "We're covering ground patrols while they are out on the roads."

"We're providing aerial security for all of the major meetings in Mosul, and we're conducting reconnaissance all around our bases and outposts," I added. "But we never catch anyone in the act of emplacing IEDs or rockets. We keep showing up right after an attack has occurred."

Candy leaned back in her chair, closed her eyes, rubbed her hands over her face, and then took in a breath. "So how do we get ahead of the attacks?" she asked, audibly exhaling.

At that time, other than an army field manual, we had no tools to help us with trend or pattern analysis. We were certain that the enemy was setting patterns, but we had no tool to help us track it.

"If we could somehow plot the time and location of enemy attacks, along with what type of attack it is, we might be able to piece this together," I said.

"Exactly," she agreed.

Staff Sergeant Eric Bucher spoke up. "But we do know where they will attack," he said. "We don't know when or precisely where, but we do know that they will attack where we are. They are attackin , so wherever we go, they will be there. We need to know our own patterns, where we are most vulnerable. That's where they will be."

"You're spot on, Sergeant Bucher," I said. "It's like the field of dreams. Build it and they will come, right?"

"Yes sir. I think if we look where we drive and then narrow it down to the places from which they are likely to attack, it will help us focus our efforts more quickly," he said.

As we brainstormed the problem, Candy's assistant, Lieutenant Shaleen Stevens, who had been intently listening to our conversation, spoke up. "I think I can write a program or build a database that will enable us to record all of the attacks and overlay them onto a map," she said. "Sergeant Bucher and I have already been talking about it. We think we can do it."

"Seriously?" I asked.

"I think so," she answered.

"If you can write a program that will enable us to track attacks and we can decipher patterns, I'll put helicopters on it. Hopefully, that will get us in the right place at the right time."

"Anticipating the enemy versus chasing them," Sergeant Bucher added.

"Right," I said.

"With a database, we should be able to plot attacks by type, time, and size, and color-code them," Lieutenant Stevens said.

"How long will it take you to write the program?" Candy asked.

"Give me a few days," she said. "It's not that complicated. I'll figure it out."

"Okay, meanwhile, can you have your guys start calling the infantry units and manually recording attacks?" I asked Candy.

"I've got that," Sergeant Bucher said. "I'll have my soldiers start calling tonight."

"Once she writes the program, we can begin inputting the data we've collected from the units," Candy said.

"Sounds good. Let's get started," I said and departed the TOC for the porta potty.

I opened the door and was instantly angry by what I saw. Once again, an Iraqi worker had squatted over the toilet and done his business all over the seat. I couldn't believe it. I slammed the door and moved to the next one, only to find the exact same thing. They had ruined two of the four porta potties. It had to stop!

Not wanting to be anywhere near the latrines, I went to the piss tube. Then I found Omar. "Omar, they've done it again," I said, scowling.

He smiled gently, as he always did, which made it particularly difficult to vent on him.

"Done what, my friend?"

"They've crapped all over the porta potties," I said.

"I told you it would be difficult," he said.

"Omar, this has got to stop. Did you talk to them?"

"Of course, I did, Jimmy," he said.

"What did they say?"

"They listened."

"And?"

"They just listened to me," he said, smiling.

"Dude, I don't get it. I've also noticed that they take a pitcher of water in there with them. They crap on the seat and then they spill water all over the rest of the toilet. What the heck are they doing in there?" I asked.

"The water is to clean their hands," he said.

"What do you mean?" I asked.

"After they finish."

"We have a five-gallon water can set up outside the porta potty for washing your hands afterwards. We have soap and water out there, as well," I said.

"No. You don't understand, Jimmy," he said. "They have to clean their hands after they wipe."

"I get it," I said, confused and irritated. "We wash our hands after we finish our business as well."

"No, Jimmy. They wipe *with* their hand and then have to clean up."

"What?" I said, snarling my lip. "They are wiping with their hand?"

"Yes, of course," he said.

"But, Omar, there is toilet paper in the porta potty. We are giving them toilet paper," I said. "It's free."

He smiled and shook his head. "Jimmy, the toilet paper is too rough on the backside. The hand is soft."

"Omar, I know it's not two-ply Charmin, but for crying out loud, it's toilet paper. We get baby wipes in care packages. I can give them baby wipes," I said. "Those are soft."

"They will not use this," he said. "This is our custom. It's how we have always done it. I do not think you will change them."

"This just blows my mind," I said, shaking my head. "Taking a crap does not have to be so difficult. You go into the porta potty. You sit down on the seat. If it's nasty, you can clean it off with wipes before you sit down, but you sit down. You do your business inside the hole. Then you wipe your butt with toilet paper or baby wipes. You pull your drawers back up, go outside, and wash your hands. It's that simple. Seriously, every time one of them takes a crap, the porta potty is ruined for all five hundred of the rest of us until the little Iraqi man comes around to wash it down with a firehose, but it's still disgusting to go in there after you've seen one of them set off a bomb on the toilet seat."

I had worked myself up. Recognizing that I was angry, Omar had calmly listened to my rant, shaking his head as if he completely understood, smiling the entire time, but he did not respond. He simply smiled and listened.

"Okay, Omar. I'll tell you what I want you to do," I said. "Make a sign in Arabic. I want the sign to say that they must sit on the seat and use toilet paper, or they will lose the right to use the porta potty. Can you do that?"

"Yes, of course, Jimmy. I will make the sign, but I do not think it will change them," he said.

"This is their last chance, Omar. Tell them this is it," and I returned to the TOC.

The following week, Candy asked me to come look at their work. "We've figured it out," she said.

"What do you mean?" I asked.

"The program works great. We input the data we've been collecting on attacks, and you can clearly see the patterns. I think this will make a huge difference," she said, clearly excited with the breakthrough.

Armed with this information, we sat down with our mission schedule and began tasking Kiowa teams to be at specific locations at specific times based on the trend analysis. We were also able to tell the pilots exactly which indicators they should be looking for. They might not see guys lying in an ambush, but they could see if the enemy had begun preparing fighting positions.

As Candy explained the success of their new program, Slifko walked in. As the Tactical Operations officer (TACOPS), he had a keen interest in enemy tactics. The TACOPS officer is critical to all aviation mission planning because his job is to understand enemy capabilities and ensure that the unit employs the right tactics and technological solutions in order to reduce the risk.[1] Tim was an expert on enemy technology and weapons systems, and he constantly studied their tactics.

"When do you want to get together to plan our mission for tomorrow?" Tim asked.

"I can plan it, Tim," I said, wanting to pull my fair share of the load.

"I'm happy to help," he said. "Let's do it after dinner."

"You sure?" I asked. "Seriously, I can plan it when I get done here."

"Let's do it together."

"Okay, how about we plan on hooking up at 7:00 p.m.?" I suggested.

"Sounds good. I'll see you then," he said, and he turned and walked away.

Candy and I continued laying out the initial schedule. We wanted to make sure that our first stab was as accurate as possible, but just as importantly, we wanted to make sure we monitored enemy activity in those locations to know if our presence had an impact on the enemy.

As expected, Tim walked into the TOC at 7:00 sharp that evening. He sat down beside me and placed a couple of zippered pouches on my desk. "Is this still a good time?" he asked and began opening the pouches.

"Yep. I'm ready," I said.

Tim pulled out a set of Sharpie colored markers and an alcohol pen. Everything was meticulously organized. He laid his map out on my desk.

"I've already written out most of the mission instructions," I said, reaching for a clipboard on my desk. "Candy, Sergeant Boucher, and I went over all the attacks in Mosul by type and time today, so we need to check out a couple of spots at a specific time, otherwise we just need to decide how we want to skin the cat," I added, meaning how we would move around Mosul to conduct reconnaissance and security.

"Well, let's begin right here at Q-West," Tim said. "I suggest we reverse the order of what we normally do. We usually check the villages and hotspots around Q-West when we return from Mosul. Let's do it before we leave and after we get back this time."

"Okay, sounds good to me, but we'll need to start our mission earlier so we're in Mosul on time," I said.

"No sweat. We have been trying to figure out enemy patterns, but we set our own patterns, you know," he said. "If the enemy is paying attention, and I suspect they are, they can predict us just as easily as we can predict them, perhaps better since we're flying around in big green helicopters and driving the roads in easily identifiable vehicles. So, we don't just have to figure out the enemy's patterns, we also need to stop setting patterns ourselves," he said and retrieved a can of Copenhagen from his pocket.

"I agree, Tim. That is the argument the SCO has been making about the airfields ever since we got here. The safety guys want to make these airfields into airports that mirror how we do business back in the States. Yes, it is safer for us to fly with the predictable rectangular traffic patterns. It's safer to fly with our lights on so that everyone sees us too. All these things reduce the accidental risk, but they increase tactical risk. We become more predictable and easier to target. We're in a combat zone," I said.

"Exactly!" he agreed, then began popping the can of Copenhagen with his finger to pack it. "We should depart the airfield and return using a different route, speed, and altitude every time. We like to set up reporting points, so we can call the tower and tell them where we are as we approach the airfield, but that means every helicopter flies across that same point every time they approach the airfield. The enemy is watching us. It's just a matter of time until they set up an air ambush."

"Yep. So, right now the air traffic control guys are still allowing us to depart and approach in any cardinal direction we choose, but several of the safety officers are pushing to change that. We need to get Doug to plead our case with the folks at brigade. Meanwhile, we'll continue varying our approaches and departures," I said. "There is a balance between accidental and tactical risk."

Tim and I spent the next hour planning our mission. Once we were satisfied, I looked at him and raised my eyebrows. "*Halo?*" I whispered.

"*Halo!*" he repeated, nodding his head.

We didn't even get through the door before it began. "Where have you been, Tim?" Doug asked. "Kissing Ranger B's ass?"

"No. Preparing to kick your ass," Tim said. "Actually, we've been planning our mission. Some people have to actually work around here."

"It's overrated. I didn't even have to set up the entertainment for the evening. I had Rowely do that for me," Doug said, without cracking a smile.

"Bloody hell," Rowely protested through a high-pitched chuckle. "You never let up do you, mate?"

"I can't play for very long," Tim said. "I've still got work to do in the TOC."

"That's fine. I'll get tired of spanking your ass after a few games anyway," Doug said.

Tim finished packing a fresh dip into his lip, then reached for an empty water bottle to spit in. "Well, bring it on, then," he said, looking at Doug.

"I'm glad you guys showed up. Rowely was trying to tell his sniper story again, for the one hundredth time," Doug said, rolling his eyes.

"What sniper story?" I asked.

Rowely visibly lit up, his eyes wide open. "That's right. I've never told you, have I, sir?"

"Oh hell," Doug said.

"You'll love this story, mate. Seriously," Rowely said, then turned in his chair to face me and laid his controller on the cot.

"We'll never play now," Doug complained.

"You see, it was when I moved out with Strike toward Baghdad," Rowely began, ignoring Doug. "We were driving up Highway 8. I was traveling with Strike's lead vehicles. Strike Six himself, Smokin' Joe Anderson, was leading the charge.

"We drove through several small towns on the way north. There were children out playing and waving at us as we drove by. I saw women walking around as well. Most of them covered their faces, but they didn't run away. The older men stared at us expressionless. You could see something strong in their faces. To this day, I don't know if that look, that presence, was strength, fear, trepidation, a lifetime of conflict, or all of the above, but it struck me as strange. Still, the atmosphere seemed somewhat normal for Iraq. Nothing too alarming, until we got to Mahmudiyah."

Doug sat his *Halo* controller down on the cot, resigned to listening to Rowely's story. Slifko, ever respectful of anyone telling a good story, gave his full attention to Rowely as well.

"As we moved through Mahmudiyah, we had to slow down because there was a lot of debris in the streets. Hanging out of the Hummer with an M4 rifle at the ready, I got a good look around," Rowely said.

Slifko smiled and Doug shook his head at the idea of Rowely scanning the streets with his rifle at the ready.

"Things were different in Mahmudiyah. I didn't see a single female. Open doors were slammed shut as we drove by. There were only a few kids outside playing, but they stopped playing immediately as we approached. They were not smiling," he said.

"He's going to tell the whole story," Doug said. "We'll be here all night."

"Mate, give me a break. Ranger B hasn't heard this story, and it's one of my best."

Rowely turned his attention back to me, shaped his face back to a serious one, the brow slightly lifted, and proceeded. "Anyway," he said, "curtains moved and doors slammed in the houses along the road, but there were no women to be seen. Most alarming was the complete lack of young men. We didn't see any military-aged males at all, and that was not normal. It gave all of us a bad feeling.

"No one said anything, but the Humvee went completely silent at that point. Everyone just stopped talking. It's like…you know how a helicopter cockpit goes silent when bad weather closes in on you, fuel is low, or it is as dark as the inside of a cow and you are flying night vision goggles? You know what I mean?" he asked. "Everyone just stops talking."

"Yeah, sure I do. I get it," I said. "Everyone stops talking and focuses intently on the task at hand in anticipation of something bad. High stress."

"Exactly! It's not a good feeling. It was like that all the way through Mahmudiyah. We were ready for a fight at any second, but nothing happened. Widowmaker Six assigned an infantry company to remain in Mahmudiyah for security as we passed through it and continued on to

Baghdad. I moved on to the north with Strike Six to link up with 3rd Infantry Division," he said.

"So they just left a company there?" I asked.

"Well, it was more than a company. Quite a few soldiers remained there. They didn't want to get surprised from the rear after we moved farther north. That's why they left them. Mahmudiyah had a bad feel to it. We knew there was a fight to be had there. We linked up with 3rd Infantry under an overpass along Highway 8," he said.

Then, turning to Doug, he asked, "What's the name of that overpass? Is it the Dora Expressway?"

"Hell, I don't know. I was flying," Doug said.

Rowely turned back to me. "I think it was Highway 8 and the Dora Expressway. Anyway, there were a lot of burning vehicles, the smell of battle, and the sounds of small arms fire not too far away," he said. Rowely always seemed to cover all the senses when he told a story. He seemed to always note the smell.

"You could hear them still shooting?" I asked.

"Sure. It was sporadic, but they were still fighting. It's funny how you react when you drive up to a gunfight—strange, actually. There is this idea of battlefield credibility that must be balanced with your own safety—your survival. In reality, it's somewhat comical. As an officer, turning up to a gunfight, you don't want to look like a douche and run to take cover behind the nearest object. Me personally, I would always look around and take my cues from the *Infanteers*," he said, referring to the Infantry soldiers.

"But having a unique understanding of American soldiers at that point, I didn't want to take unnecessary risk to my life either, so I always took their lead and then pulled back a touch on the bravado."

"What do you mean by that?" I asked, finding his observation interesting.

"There is something in the American blood that I don't quite under-stand. You guys have either a lack of fear, an overwhelming sense of self, or some sort of national pride in battle, or maybe it's a combination of all that. Hell, I don't rightly know."

His perception intrigued me. I completely understood what he meant, but it was interesting to hear a foreign officer explain his own perception of our bravado in combat. It certainly wasn't universal. There were some that would cower in a fight, but for the most part, our soldiers simply put fear aside. I assumed it was our sense of duty. To execute the mission, you could not let fear rule the day. That did not mean one should be reckless, but it did mean that you would assume a certain degree of risk that the average person might consider lunacy.

"By the time I was at Mahmudiyah, I was well aware of this American phenomenon. So, the bottom line was, if an American infantryman was walking around ten feet tall and bulletproof, but taking a keen eye on the surrounding approaches, building tops, side alleys, and so forth, I would make damn sure I sighted the nearest solid cover to hide behind if the situation suddenly required it. If a *grunter*[2] was already behind cover, there was no question what I would do: get behind cover as quickly as possible. That day, when we got out of our vehicles, most of the grunters were taking cover and looking north along the highway. So, I immediately sought protection.

"Strike Six, ole Colonel Anderson, he walked around like he was shopping in a Macy's store. This would be a recurring pattern. As I took cover behind a highway berm, I saw something I could not believe—a burning M1 Abrams tank!" he said with his brow elevated in total awe and surprise.

"This is the part where he gets excited," Tim said.

"Mate! Can you believe that?" Rowely said, still amazed. "An M1 Abrams tank burning! I didn't know whether to laugh or cry. Here was the world's most superior tank, between me and God-knows-what and how many bad dudes, and it was burning!

"*This was not in the brochure,* I thought to myself. I am a helo driver, a Cavalry scout driver to be sure, and we do have a preeminent reputation to uphold, but pride be damned. I did not sign up to walking around in a tank fight with an M4 carbine rifle. Particularly, not a fight in which the result is the world's most badass tank burning," he said. "So I couldn't help but ask the nearest *Infanteer*, 'Mate, what the fuck happened to that M1?'"

Tim, Doug, and I burst out laughing in unison. Rowely was all worked up as he relived the story. "I think he's beginning to break a sweat," I said.

"Hell, he may piss himself when the sniper starts shooting at him," Doug said.

"That's later," Rowely said. "Don't get ahead of me."

"So, this *Infanteer* understood my concern and smiled at me. He said, 'Hey, sir, don't worry about it. It took a lucky hit in the left rear bay and caught fire. Ammunition started to cook off, so the crew got out. They [the tankers] thought it might get overrun, so they shot it from behind with another M1.'"

"So, they blew it up with another M1 to ensure the enemy couldn't do anything with it?" I asked.

"Roger that," Rowely said. Then he continued.

"'Fuck!' I said, in bewilderment, staring at the burning M1. But suddenly I was calm again, which was a strange feeling when you think about it. How could I be calm standing next to a burning M1 tank with gunfights ongoing all around me?" he said. "Strike Six did his business with 3rd Infantry, and then we moved off to our new headquarters location, which was at a water treatment plant just south of Baghdad.

"Two days later, I receive a call from Widowmaker Six on the brigade secret phone," Rowely said. "I knew *of* him. I had met him, but I didn't know him personally. His name was Lieutenant Colonel Chris Holden, and he appeared to be a calm, strong, and capable leader. As time went on, that proved to be true. When I picked up the call that day, it was just beginning to get dark out. The locals were finishing up evening prayers, and the gunfire had started back up. Widowmaker Six told me about his problems down in Mahmudiyah. He said that they were being attacked at his company command post at an increasing rate. The previous day, they had found a huge cache of weapons in a building. As the soldiers were carrying them outside, a bad guy threw a grenade over the wall right on top of them. It wounded eighteen Widowmaker soldiers and one lad lost his eye."[3]

"Oh, seriously?" I asked with a pained expression. "But none were killed?"

"Not that I'm aware of," Rowely said. "But that was a shithole area. Widowmaker Six said he wanted to clear the city the following morning. I never even thought about it. I told him we would be there with a troop of Kiowa Warriors to join in the fight the next morning," Rowely said, proud of himself.

"So you committed a troop of Kiowas just like that?" I asked.

"Yep. That's the important part," he said. "And when I told him that, Widowmaker Six paused on the phone. I suspect he was taken aback by the fact that we were ready to support him immediately, without question, and with no other bullshit or administrative minutia. Perhaps he was most surprised by the fact that an officer at the rank of captain could commit one-third or his boss's combat power on his own judgement—an Aussie at that. It's one of the greatest aspects of working for Schiller, and it is why we are so damn effective in battle, I might add. Schiller taught us how he thinks. He made sure that we understood his priorities, how we should think and make decisions, and he gave us the unfettered authority to act! Armed with that knowledge, and his assured backing, we knew that supporting the ground force was the only thing that mattered. After all, that's why we exist.

"I told Widowmaker Six that he would get a troop of Kiowas for his fight. That was a big deal for him. Ten scout/attack helos at his beck and call. He would probably get more, but I committed a full troop. He was grateful. He asked when we could link up and coordinate for the fight. I told him I could drive down right then," Rowely said.

"You told him you'd hit the road then and drive back down there alone and at night?" I asked.

"Yes," Rowely said and let out another high-pitched chuckle. "I think he was actually more impressed by my willingness to drive there immediately than he was at getting ten Kiowas. The fact that I would move at that moment, in a soft-skinned vehicle, alone at night, in Baghdad, after prayer time with the usual gunfights going on, impressed the hell out of him. I had figured out a while ago that a bold approach would get me through the war and the cotton wool approach would probably get me killed, so I was ready to get in a Hummer and go. I am not sure at what point in the war I had earned my US Cavalry combat spurs, but in hindsight, I feel I could have proudly worn them from that point forward," he said.

"Widowmaker Six said that if I could meet up with him the following morning, that would achieve his aim. So, I agreed to meet him the next morning in Mahmudiyah," Rowely said.

"That's probably the only reason you are still alive," Doug said. "Going that night would have been stupid."

"Were you nervous?" I asked.

"Well, no man likes to say he was scared, but hell yeah, I was nervous," Rowely said. "Widowmaker Six was impressed."

"I'm sure he was," I said.

"I called Major Hawley and gave him the news. He said that was awesome and told me to call him when I had the plan all worked out. Then he told me, 'Don't fuck it up!'" Rowely said and giggled. "That was my guidance. Don't fuck it up. I love the CAV! He called back later and said that Schiller would have another troop available if it was needed. They also knew that it was going to be a solid gunfight.

"Next morning, I got on the road early. It was still dark when I left. Sometimes being left-handed has its advantages. Our Humvee had no doors, so I was able to lean out of the front right passenger seat with my right foot in the doorframe and my left-handed M4 naturally at the ready. For some reason, I always enjoy chambering a round as I leave out on a mission. Not in a macabre sense, but the action and sound really focus one's mind to the severity of what may be about to occur. The decisions that I would make, in the vehicle and on the radio, coordinating scout/attack operations, would have a tremendous impact on a lot of people. That responsibility was never lost on me and was always driven home with the same clarity as the sound of the 5.56mm round taking up its position in the chamber. It was a shot of reality," he said. "Does that make sense?"

"Actually, that's pretty profound. And yes, it makes complete sense. I get it," I said.

"It's serious business, what we do," Rowely said. "As much jackassery as goes on, what we do has high stakes, and it's nice that we can do something so high risk, so dangerous, yet have so much fun doing it," he said.

"You're not kidding," Slifko said and spit snuff juice into the water bottle.

"I agree. I've had nothing but fun since I've been here," I said. Then I paused. "Well, except when I was peeing out of my rear end with the crud."

"Weak system," Doug piped in.

"Anyway," Rowely jumped back in to ensure he did not lose us. "We got on Highway 8 and headed toward Widowmaker's location. A single vehicle is an easy target, but my driver kept his speed up. I trusted his driving after having previously given him a heated in-vehicle dressing down about how his 'Stateside' driving was going to get us both killed. I told him to forget peacetime driving. I told him to drive over curbs, through crowds, the wrong way, whatever was needed to keep the speed up, avoid the potholes, the roadside cars, dead animals, and discolored patches in the road—all of which could carry a mine or IED. He got it. We made such good time we actually passed Widowmaker Six on the way to the linkup point. I saw his call sign written on the window of his Humvee as we passed him," Rowely said. "I figured it would be good to get into position early."

Slifko spit Copenhagen again but never took his eyes off Rowely, who was leaning forward with his elbows on his thighs at this point. Doug sat back in a chair beside the cot with his legs crossed. I sat on a stool directly in front of Rowely. The only light in the room was the *Halo* image being cast onto the wall above Tim's cot. The significance of the bonds we'd forged in that environment was not lost on me.

"We pulled up next to two Bradley fighting vehicles just outside the Widowmaker command post," Rowely said. "It's always a wise move to pull up on the good side of some armor—keep them between you and the enemy. We got out in the courtyard, and I met Major Brian Pearl. I had spoken to him on the radio, but it was the first time I'd actually met him. He seemed like a calm and unassuming guy, which I liked. I've never liked a hothead. He was calm but seemed very focused that day. But there certainly wasn't time for pleasantries that morning. He thanked me for our support and then told me that Widowmaker Six would be along shortly."

"You didn't tell him that you'd just passed Widowmaker Six?" I asked.

"No. I just let him talk. He told me a little bit about the hard time they were having in Mahmudiyah. I could sense the genuine concern for his men. He gestured for me to move to the hood of his Humvee, where he had a map of the city displayed. I used the time to consume as much information as I could about the city, his plan, and his expectation for the pending fight prior to Widowmaker Six's arrival.

"Once Widowmaker Six arrived, him, myself, Pearl, and a few others viewed the map together. Pearl briefed us on the pending battle. He made sure I was clear on the key areas of his concern where he wanted helicopters, where he thought his guys would be vulnerable, and where he expected to be engaged by the enemy. We discussed some informal control measures—lines on the map that we could quickly refer to in the heat of battle to coordinate on the fly.

"This is where, as a planner, you make your money. People often think that the tactical genius of a battle plan itself wins a battle, but it doesn't. You can never plan everything out and expect it to go as planned. Once the fight starts, it takes on a life of its own. The enemy always gets a vote. You never know what you are going to get, so what matters most is a flexible plan that enables good leadership to make decisions and audible from a standard set of graphics on a map. Simple, flexible graphics enable a unit to fight the battle, not the plan itself. After the first round is fired in battle, the plan is a sunk cost. The art of planning is to weave the secret sauce into the plan: flexibility of maneuver and fires," he said.

"Do we have to pay for this lecture?" Doug asked.

"No mate, it's free. You can't understand it anyway, so it would be a waste of your money," Rowely said.

Tim and I burst out laughing. Doug smiled, "Not bad," he said. "Your comebacks are improving, grasshopper."

"As we discussed the finer points of the graphic control measures, we heard a bullet zing by overhead," Rowely said. "It was not surprising. Single rounds often cracked or zipped by overhead. Often it was a stray round or a ricochet from a nearby gunfight, but the first round was followed by a second one. What I noticed was that it was timed. It almost seemed metered, meaning that those rounds could have been a coincidence, or they could have been carefully aimed shots.

"I looked around at the group to judge their reaction as I anticipated the third round. No one moved. Now, I had seen this before, and as an Australian, I had the suspicion that it might be an American thing. It seemed to me that to startle in a gunfight was not proper. I grew up watching American war movies. I thought it was bullshit that the sergeant in *Black Hawk Down* stood in the open as bullets hit the vehicle beside him. Nevertheless, Americans seem to like to appear invincible. The third round cracked, and I could tell that it was closer to us. I was certain that a sniper was shooting at us."

Rowely was more concerned with his life than his reputation, but pride is a terrible thing. He continued.

"Rounds passing close by always sound impressive with their violent crack," Rowely said. "You can feel their energy. I can't always tell how close they are when they crack, but I can tell when they are getting closer, and after three rounds, it was clear to me that they were getting very close."

We were all glued to Rowely at that point, intently listening to his story, even Doug, who claimed to have heard the same story many times over.

"Still, no one moved! I thought, *This is bullshit!* There was no doubt in my mind, if I was an American officer, I would have run into the building behind us at that very moment, but Widowmaker Six didn't move. He continued giving guidance as if he had not even heard the crack of the bullets. I was an Australian, so I was stuck in a tough spot. I wanted to seek cover, but I couldn't let the first person to run and duck be from my country. I wouldn't have it.

"The fourth round cracked! It was well into the emotive range where you could hear and feel the limb-ripping energy in the crack. It was a sniper, damn it!" Rowely said. "He was probably not very good or at least one of us would have been bleeding by that point, but my money was on the fifth bullet. He would not continue to miss. Finally, at an opportune pause, Major Pearl calmly suggested that we move inside. Perhaps he was saving face for all of us with that suggestion. I really didn't care. I jogged over to the vehicle and told the guys to move out. I had the guidance I needed to pass to Major Hawley and Saber Six.

"The next day the CAV kicked ass," he said, smiling broadly.

"Well told, Rowely," I said. "As a connoisseur of fine storytelling, I have to say that was a good one."

"I don't know what we would have done without him," Doug said with as much sarcasm as possible. "Now, speaking of snipers, let's play some *Halo*. I'm looking forward to giving you some sniping lessons."

THE GRANARY 500

Tim and I departed Q-West an hour and a half before sunset the following afternoon. As planned, we conducted reconnaissance of all the traditional firing points from where the enemy had previously shot rockets at us. Then we headed north along Route Tampa. We didn't say much at first. Sometimes it feels nice to break contact with the earth. From the air, the troubles of the surface sometimes seem miles away.

"Sir, have you done the granary 500 yet?" Tim asked, breaking the silence.

"Granary 500? I know where the granary is in Mosul, but I'm not sure about the granary 500."

There were several large grain silos on the west side of the city. The infantry battalion responsible for that area, 1-502nd Infantry, had asked us to see if we could help them keep the looters shooed away from the silos.

"You'll see, sir. It's a lot of fun," Tim said. He then proceeded to fly us to the northwest side of Mosul.

"See those silos there to our front?" he asked as we approached.

"Yeah. I see them. Like I said, I'm familiar with the silos and the looting that's been going on. It's been in all the situational reports from 1-502nd."

"But if you haven't participated in the granary 500 yet, you're in for a treat," he said. "Okay, sir, look to the east. You'll see a dirt road right along that line of houses over there." He switched hands, putting his left hand on the cyclic control and pointing across the cockpit with his right. "It parallels the wall where the houses stop and the field begins."

"I see the road," I replied.

249

"Do you see people gathered along the road? They should have donkeys and hand carts or sacks in their hands. You can't miss them if they are there."

"I don't see anyone," I said. "There are a couple of kids playing in the road."

Tim's head kept darting back and forth from watching where he was flying to trying to stealing a glance at the road. A set of high-tension powerlines, over two-hundred-feet tall, passed just by the silos.

"They're not out yet then," he said. "It's not dark enough. Once it's dark they will line up along that road, and when they are ready, they'll make a run for the silos to steal grain. That's when we'll swoop in to run them off. It's funny to watch. We'll come back right at dark and see if they are here."

"Okay," I replied.

We worked our way north, throughout Talon's area of responsibility and then checked in with Top Gun, Strike's artillery battalion. All was quiet in their area. From Top Gun area, we flew east to the river, then began working our way back to the south. By the time we reached bridge three across the Tigris River, we were running low on fuel. "It's about time to go get some fuel," I said. "We'd better head to the FARP."

"What do you say we stop and get an ice cream on the way?" Tim said. Before I could answer, he pushed the point. "We've got plenty of time. We can grab an ice cream quick and then go. After we get gas, it will be time to go back to the granary," he added.

It didn't take much convincing. "Okay, tell trail we're stopping at Strike Main," I said, which he did.

Strike had allowed a local Iraqi man to set up a shop on their outpost. The man sold Magnum bars, which were the only ice cream available to us at that time. They were incredible!

We landed the two helipads at Strike Main, and one pilot from each cockpit jumped out. Tim made the run for us. The shop was only about 150 meters from the helipads, but it was hot out that evening. Tim bought the Magnum bars and hustled back to the aircraft as fast as he could. Still, by the time he reached the helicopter, the ice cream was already melting. He reached inside the door and handed me one. I carefully opened the top of the package, making sure I did not spill it on my flight suit. Then, with the top open, I drank it like a milk shake. At that moment in time, it was the best ice cream I had ever tasted. You could not have convinced me otherwise.

The area where we landed at Strike Main was very small. Due to the tall trees and several two-story buildings, we had to fly steep approaches to land, and we had to maximize every inch of available space for takeoff. We did not have the power to depart vertically. One at a time, we backed into a corner of the outpost, turned into the wind, and nosed the Kiowa over to try to get through effective translational lift as quickly as possible. Once the aircraft gets above about fifteen knots airspeed, the flow of air going across the rotor system becomes cleaner. At a hover, the blades are fighting their own downwash (wind), but in forward flight, the air flows horizontally across the rotor system; thus, the aircraft is more efficient in flight. Once this occurs, the pilot can maneuver the helicopter using less power. We used every inch of space available to pull in all the power the Kiowa would give us to quickly get through effective translational lift and then climb out of the outpost.

That night, Tim and I backed our helicopter into a corner and departed Strike Main first. Trail followed us out, then we headed to the FARP at Mosul airfield. The fuelers at the FARP handed us two bottles of frozen water, which would be thawed enough to drink in less than ten minutes.

After fueling the aircraft, we put on our night vision goggles. At that point, it was just dark enough to use them. We departed the FARP and flew back to the grain silos. This time, I clearly saw people gathering on the dirt road. There were at least one hundred men and boys all lined up like they were about to begin a 5K road race. Just as Tim had said, they had sacks in their hands or pushed wooden two-wheeled carts. Some rode their donkeys, while others pulled the donkey by a lead line.

We flew in high over them at first. As we circled in the dark sky, five hundred feet above them, they did not pay us any attention. We were completely blacked out, so they could not see us, but they certainly heard the helicopters. I wondered why they didn't realize that we were watching them. Within a minute of our arrival, apparently, someone fired the starting gun because they all lit off across the field toward the grain silos. It reminded me of movies I had watched about the 1889 Oklahoma

Land Rush. Carts flipped and donkeys fought back against their owners as everyone raced to get to the silo first. Young boys led the race, all with bags in their hands.

"Man, look at that!" I said in amazement.

Tim chuckled over the intercom system. "I told you."

"I guess those young boys are trying to get there first to get what they can before the older men show up and run them off," I said.

"Probably so. I'm sure their parents sent them to get a bag full of grain," he said.

As the boys neared the silo, they began pushing and shoving one another. One boy, near the front of the pack, hung his sandal on something. That sent him flying head over heels, tripping at least three more boys in the process of falling. The pileup gave others, not so quick of foot, a chance to gain the lead.

Soon the lead runners arrived at the silo. From the sky, they looked like bees pulsating on a nest, but they were not producing honey. They were throwing elbows, pulling hair, gouging eyes, scratching, clawing, all in an attempt to get their bag under the spout that now flowed with grain.

"Okay. Let's go," Tim said and dove the Kiowa in over the top of them.

Suddenly, those caught in the field, not quite to the silo yet, detected our presence, and I was left to assume that they thought we might shoot at them for stealing because complete chaos ensued. Donkeys threw their riders, boys lay down in ditches to try and hide, and sandals flew into the air as old men dashed for the road. "Watch this," Tim said, eyeing one man who was somewhat separated from the others.

The old man was shuffling across the open stretch of dirt between the road and silo as Tim descended and came to a hover about one hundred feet above him. The man scrambled over to a power pole and stood beside it. "He's trying to hide," Tim said.

"What do you mean?" I asked. "He can't hide from us."

"That's the funny thing. They don't seem to realize that we can actually see them," he said. "Despite the fact that we were flying circles above them, they didn't seem to be alarmed until we were right over them. I don't know if they understood that we were watching them."

As I observed their behavior, I could see that Tim was right. Some of them tried to hide in plain sight. They held very still in the open, hoping we would not notice them in the dark. One man stood completely still out in the open field. "Look at that guy," Tim said. "Let's see how long he can stand it."

Tim moved the helicopter right over the man. The rotor wash was rushing down on him. He stood perfectly still, the hot, sandy wind visibly whipping his clothes around like a giant hair dryer. Then Tim began to slowly descend, right on top of him. At fifty feet, he remained motionless, eyes closed and mouth tightly shut against the wind and dirt. The rotor wash picked up sand from the desert floor and blasted him. It had to feel like sandpaper against his coarse skin. At twenty-five feet, he was in the midst of a tornado, yet he fought to stand perfectly still.

"He must think that if he runs, we'll see him," I told Tim.

"I don't know, but I'm positive he thinks we can't see him right now. Otherwise, he'd make a run for it," Tim said, shaking his head.

At about fifteen feet, the man could no longer stand being pelted by the sand and wind. He bolted. We took off and flew a small circle. By that time, many of the would-be looters were back on the road, deterred for the moment. Once they reached the dirt road, they no longer tried to run away. It was as if they were in a safe zone, like a kid touching home base in a game of tag. They simply dusted themselves off and walked back toward their homes, almost like they had been playing a game. Eventually, all the Iraqis faded into the city. At that point, we decided to call it a night as well. Mission accomplished.

We flew back to the FARP at Mosul airfield, filled up with fuel, and then followed the Tigris River south, back to Q-West, in the darkest of darks. Where there were no houses, it was as if we flew over an ocean of oil. It was impossible to see the surface, much less judge how high you were above it. Were it not for the radar altimeter, I'd have climbed several hundred feet into the air. But we had grown accustomed to flying on the edge of discomfort. Work together as a crew. Scan the instruments. Take pride in just how disciplined we are. Discipline, precision, high standards. Those things seemed to fuel our squadron.

After the mission, Tim and I put our gear away, conducted a debrief of the mission, and gave our intel guys all the notes we took during the mission. I took a few minutes to catch up on emails, and then I made eye contact with Slifko and raised both brows. Knowing exactly what I meant, he just smiled and shook his head no.

"Why not?" I asked.

"I've got to get some things done here," he said.

"Me too," I said. "Just a couple of games and then we'll come back to the TOC."

"Okay, just a couple," he said and headed for the door.

I slapped Tim on the shoulder as we walked out of the TOC. "It didn't take much to change your mind," I said.

"Actually, I think I am just going to go to bed after we play. I'll grab a few hours of sleep, then get back up and finish what I need to get done before first light," he said. "It can wait, and I don't feel like doing it now."

"You think they are playing?" I asked.

"Probably so."

Sure enough, we turned the corner into Slifko's room, and there sat Doug and Rowely, their faces lit up by the glow of the *Halo* image cast on the wall. "What are you peckerheads doing?" I asked as we walked in.

"What does it look like, sirrr?" Doug said, exaggerating the "sir" as much as he possibly could.

"Why didn't you come get us?" Tim asked.

"You guys were out flying your mission," Doug said.

"We've been back for an hour, but I get it. After that ass whipping I gave you last night, you needed the extra practice, didn't you?" Tim said.

Without taking his eyes off the screen, Rowely spoke, "Yeah, yeah. How was your mission, mate?"

"Good," I said. "We flew the granary 500 tonight."

"Oh yeah?" Rowely said. "Fucking awesome."

The *Halo* game abruptly restarted.

"Bloody hell, what are you doing?" Rowely chirped in a high-pitched voice, looking at Doug with a scowl.

"I'm restarting the game," Doug answered. "They want to play now."

"But I was winning," Rowely replied.

"Whatever," Doug said, rolling his eyes.

"If you were winning, you would not have restarted the game. You'd have told them to wait," Rowely argued. Then he set his controller on the cot and looked at Tim and me. "Anything else exciting tonight?"

"There was a report of a sniper shooting at guys right as we left, but the team that relieved us will deal with that," Tim said.

"I got into a bit with a sniper in Baghdad once," Rowely said.

"Oh yeah? You'll have to tell me about it sometime," I said.

"Good grief! You told that story two nights ago, dumbass. And two nights before that. Do you even know what day it is?" Doug said.

Rowely laughed at himself.

"What about you, Tim? Any good war stories to tell tonight?" I asked.

Tim had already taken control of the situation with the Xbox. Doug was taking too long. "Tell him about your lieutenant making water in the cockpit, mate," Rowely said.

"Making water?" I said, confused. "Your lieutenant pissed himself in the cockpit?" I asked.

"No, no, mate," Rowely said, laughing. "He puked. You know, got sick."

"Making water is pissing yourself," I said.

"Not in Australia, mate."

"I had a captain puke on me once," I said.

"Oh yeah?" Rowely answered, clearly interested in hearing the story.

"Yeah. We were in Louisiana at the Joint Readiness Training Center. The captain was my left seater. He was new to the unit, but it was his second assignment in the army. I think he'd been stationed at Fort Stewart before he came to us. He'd been talking big about his experience for several days," I said.

"Experience. The only experience you officers have as lieutenants and captains is kissing ass. They must teach that at the basic course," Doug interrupted.

"Oh, that's a side-slapper, Doug," I said. "Anyway, before we took off, I asked him if he ever got sick in flight. He looked at me as if I had lost my mind, clearly offended that I would ask such a thing."

"Typical," Doug broke in again. "Weak-ass officers. Don't have the stomach for it."

Having relinquished the task of setting up the game to Tim, Doug was now sitting back in his folding chair supervising. "Are you going to let me tell my story or not?" I asked Doug.

"Oh, pardon me," Doug said. "Go ahead, sir. I'll try not to interrupt... except when I need to throw the bullshit flag."

"Anyway, this captain assured me that he never got sick, so I took him at his word. We took off and flew a route reconnaissance mission along one of those hardball roads in the Box." [We called the Fort Polk training area "the Box."] "I was in the right seat flying, and he was darting his eyes in and out of the cockpit. He was trying to work the sight as we flew," I said.

"That's a mistake," Doug noted.

"Yeah, he'd look at the road below us, then back inside, staring at the screen in the cockpit. I was flying aggressively because we expected to make enemy contact. He seemed to be doing fine for a while, so I flew it hard. We'd be zipping down the road at about eighty knots and he'd see something on the side of the road that looked suspicious, so he'd tell me to come back around. Instead of turning around in a circle, I'd pull the cyclic control back fast and climb, trading airspeed for altitude. The helicopter would suddenly climb and slow; then, right as we peaked in the climb, I'd cram pedal in and, in one quick movement, turn the helicopter 180 degrees and begin diving back toward the road to regain our airspeed," I said.

"That will get your gut," Rowely said.

"Yeah, but he seemed to be doing fine, and he'd been so offended when I questioned him about getting sick. I assumed he was okay."

"But, of course, he got sick, right?" Tim asked, still struggling with a wad of wires.

"Yep!" I said. "Suddenly, he said, 'Sir, I think I'm going to be sick.'"

"No other warning?" Tim asked.

"Nope. I saw an opening in the trees. It was a small area in the middle of those big one hundred and fifty feet Louisiana pine trees, so I immediately committed to landing. I was slow and steep on the approach to the ground. We got just below the tops of the trees. We were committed to the approach. It was too late to go around or climb back out of the trees. We were descending through the trees, when I heard this cough over the intercom system. He didn't say a word—just popped. I realized what it was, so as quickly as I heard the sound, I jammed in the pedal to kick the helicopter sideways in flight, hoping that the wind would carry his vomit away from us, but I was too late. The puke went out the door, hit the wind, and came right back in, past him, and hit me in the side of the helmet and face.

256

"Oooh, damn, that is disgusting," Rowely said, scrunching his face up and closing his eyes.

"He had eaten two Slim Jims before we took off," I said. "But he clearly didn't chew it up before swallowing. A big chunk of Slim Jim hit me on the bottom lip and stuck."

"Noooooo," all three of them squealed in unison.

"Here we are vertically descending into a tiny landing area, and now I am about to blow grits. I thought to myself, *If I puke, we will die*. It was all I could do to hold it in. As soon as we hit the ground, I got out and told him to clean it up. The observer controllers [cadre] landed beside us and gave him two big bottles of water and some shop towels to help with the clean-up. It was nasty," I said.

"Did you call it a day after that?" Rowely asked.

"Yes. Once he cleaned the bird up, I took off and flew us straight back to the airfield," I said. "It stunk so bad. I flew nice and easy all the way back, but as soon as we landed, he puked out the door again. This time it landed on the .50 caliber. The crew chiefs were pissed. They brought him a pressure washer and made him clean it up."

"That is nasty," Tim said.

"You think?" I replied, and we sat silently grinning for a few seconds. It was late, and we were yet to even play the first game.

"I think it's about bedtime," Tim said suddenly, knowing he could not sleep until we left his room.

"*Un juego mas*," I said loudly.

"What the hell is that supposed to mean?" Doug asked.

"One more game in Spanish," I said proudly.

"What do you know about Spanish?" he said. "You're from Georgia. You barely speak English."

"I studied Español," I said.

"In Georgia?" he asked, exploding in laughter.

"I went to Guatemala and did that total immersion deal," I said. "Lived with a Guatemalan family and everything."

"Really?" Tim said.

"Yes," I confirmed with pride.

"Okay, enough of that. Let's play some *Halo*," Doug said, shaking his head. "How do you say, 'Doug is going to kick some ass in Spanish, sir'?"

"It's too late now," Tim maintained, before I could begin working it out. "I need to get up in a couple of hours."

"Go to bed," Doug said. "You won't bother us."

"Okay, genius. The game screen is over *my* cot. I can't sleep while you play *Halo* over my head."

"Why not?" Doug genuinely asked. "We'll be quiet."

"No, you won't!" Tim said.

"Sure we will. Just lie down and close your eyes. Do you want Ranger B to tuck you in?" Doug asked.

"Whatever," Tim said, then stripped down to his skivvies, crawled into his sleeping bag, and faced the wall.

Suddenly, we heard a crashing explosion outside that vibrated the walls. The whole building shook with the shockwave, and the room was at once filled with dust. "Incoming!" someone yelled from the center of the courtyard. "Incoming."

Each of us flinched, but no one ran for the bunker.

Ka-thunk. Ka-thunk. Two more rockets impacted somewhere close.

"I hate this fucking place," Doug said.

"I'm accounted for," Tim said, from his sleeping bag. "Tell them I'm still alive, but I'm not getting up, and I'm sure as hell not going to a bunker to sit until someone says it's all clear."

"Yeah, I'm not going to that nasty-ass bunker either," Rowely said.

"It's filled with condoms," Doug said. "Someone, or several someones, has been going in there to get some."

"So, isn't that a safety violation?" I asked. "Shouldn't you put a stop to it because someone could get pregnant or a sexually transmitted disease since we're all so dirty over here."

"Not my lane," Doug said. "That's a leadership problem. Besides, they are being safe. They are using condoms. That's *safe* sex," he proclaimed, proud of himself.

"I need accountability!" the sergeant in the TOC yelled into the courtyard. "Let's go, get your headcounts in."

I stood. "I'll go to the TOC and make sure everyone is okay."

"You know what we should be doing?" Doug said before I could leave. "We ought to be shooting back. We know where it's coming from. If we returned fire a few times, I bet they'd quit shooting at us. The locals would put a stop to it."

"You know we can't do that, Doug. We'd kill a bunch of women and children, and then we'd really have a mess on our hands," I said. "That would turn more of them against us."

"So, we just sit here and take it? What kind of a plan is that? If they kill me, I'll haunt your ass forever, Ranger B."

"Bastogne is working with the local village elders," I said. "They are trying to find these guys and roll them up."

Doug just shook his head. "I'm telling you—we've been lucky. We've had aircraft damaged, but no one has been killed or maimed, yet. It's only a matter of time. They are shooting more and more. They are going to hit us eventually. Saddam controlled them with fear and violence. That's all they know. They understand power and pain," he said.

"Night, gents," I said and headed to the TOC to ensure we had accountability of our soldiers and that no one was hurt.

Bridge Five
to the Palace

A few days later, Slifko and I strapped a Kiowa on and headed back out into the skies over Mosul. For quite some time, Tim and I had been flying evening flights together. We would depart Q-West about an hour before dark and return later that evening under goggles, like we did the night of the granary. Most days we flew for about six hours, but Condor Troop had asked us to fly a daytime mission. Even though day missions could be slow and often uneventful, particularly when it was hot, we were excited to get to see the sun rise versus set for a change.

Candy Smith and her intelligence team had been hard at work trying to narrow down enemy trends. It had become clear that the enemy conducted the majority of their attacks in the early morning and early evening hours. They rarely attacked in the middle of the day. In response to their activity, we adjusted our team cycles. Often, we'd put two teams of Kiowas up during the periods that we were most likely to encounter an attack, but during the slow periods—middle of the day and middle of the night—we'd land at Strike Main or Widowmaker and remain on standby. There were two helipads at Widowmaker's outpost on the east side of the Tigris, and they were kind enough to give us a room with a couple of cots, plastic chairs, and a folding table to use. Pilots took naps, read books, or played cards but remained ready to launch at a moment's notice.

It was early and we had shifted schedules, so Tim and I were still adjusting to the new circadian rhythm. Before we strapped in, Tim stuffed his lip full of Copenhagen. Pilots have two spitting options when flying a Kiowa and dipping. They can either spit into a bottle and cap it, or they can spit out the door hole of the helicopter. Since we do not fly with doors on the aircraft, the spitting part is easy. Keeping the spit off the side of the helicopter is a different matter altogether. The only way to prevent the tobacco spit from slathering the side of the helicopter is to apply pedal, which turns the helicopter sideways in flight, causing wind to assist, by blowing through the helicopter and out the spitter's door, the same trick I had attempted when the lieutenant puked on me. However, the other pilot does not always appreciate being blasted with a gust of wind every time his copilot must spit, particularly in winter when it's cold out. If both pilots dip and apply this technique, it looks like two drunks flying along, yawing left then right as they take turns spitting. Fortunately, very few pilots chewed tobacco. Most of them dipped snuff, which did not require as much spitting.

Pilots are seldom as good as they think they are, or claim to be, so try as they may, spit always ends up on the side of the helicopter, which naturally pisses off the crew chiefs. Seasoned crew chiefs demand that the pilots clean the aircraft after they return from a flight. Having been an enlisted man on the back end of a Chinook for many years, Slifko was respectful of the crew chiefs. He chose to spit into a bottle.

We flew up the Tigris River to Mosul airfield and topped off on gas. Then we began checking in with the battalions one at a time. All indications were that it was going to be an uneventful morning. The sun was rapidly climbing into a deep blue sky. The market on the west side of the river, just west of bridge three, was active with pedestrians. Iraqis crowded the streets buying and selling produce, which was a good sign. Clearly, they felt safe enough to get out and shop.

After checking in with Talon, Falcon, and Top Gun on the west side of the river, we flew to the FARP and filled up with fuel again. It was already getting hot, so I grabbed each of us a bottle of frozen water from the soldiers at the FARP. Then we transitioned over to the east side of the river.

We decided to start in the far north, on the outskirts of town in Battle Force's area. We flew direct from the FARP to Battle Force's far northern positions, then slowly, we began working our way down to the palace where the division headquarters resided. It was a massive brown building surrounded by a perimeter wall and fence.

From the sky, we could see soldiers scurrying about everywhere. They seemed especially busy. "Must be trying to beat the heat," I told Slifko, breaking the silence.

"What's that?" he asked.

"They look like ants running around this morning. I assume they want to get as much done as possible before it gets too hot," I explained.

"Yeah, but then again, we do more before 9:00 a.m. than most people do all day," he announced, mocking the old army commercial. "You remember that one?"

"Certainly, I do. Some of the army's claims may be suspect, but that one is true," I said, laughing.

"It's actually not that hot today," he said, then kicked the helicopter out of trim so that wind blew through the cockpit, allowing us to test the temperature.

"No, it's much cooler than it was a month ago," I said.

"Fall will be here before we know it," he said. "Football season."

"Deer season," I retorted, to which he chuckled and spit into the bottle.

Looking down on the division main, we could see soldiers performing maintenance and inspections on vehicles. Others loaded trailers with supplies that they planned to transport back to their unit outposts. Some walked to and from breakfast while others stood in groups of two or three smoking and talking.

"What do you reckon General Petraeus is doing in there this morning?" I asked, pointing at the palace as we circled it.

"I don't know, but he should come out and at least wave at us," Tim said.

"He's probably picked a few leaders to punish on a run, then with push-ups and pull-ups," I said.

David Petraeus was an avid runner. If he set patterns, it was that every day when the sun came up, he'd be running circles around the Division Headquarters perimeter. He could also do chin-ups like a piston. So, his methodology for motivating officers, or leading by example, or sadistically enjoying pain and suffering, was to take them on long runs. There were only a few soldiers who could handle his six-minute pace for very long, but if they did survive, they knew that they would get the privilege of being crushed on the pull-up bar after the run ended. One way or another, he'd find a way to win. Being an out-of-shape, or portly, lieutenant colonel in Dave Petraeus's division would be a very uncomfortable experience.

"Looks like they are getting ready," Tim said, nodding at the front gate.

Several convoys were lined up on the street near the gate.

"Yep," I said. "Looks like they are about to pull out."

"Let's fly down to bridge five and work our way back up the road in front of them," Tim said as he flew the helicopter in a big looping circle. "Just to have a look at the road before they pull out."

"Sounds good," I said.

The main highway that led to bridge five was a four-lane road with a small grassy divider between the lanes. It was a busy highway, crowded with Iraqi traffic as well as military vehicles that moved back and forth to and from the 101st Airborne Division headquarters.

"I tell you what. They look like they are about ready to roll. Instead of going to the bridge, let's start at the gate and work to the south in front of them," Tim said. "If we go to the bridge and work back this way, we won't cover much ground in front of them."

"I agree. It looks like they are already opening the gate."

Tim circled around and brought us down lower to the ground. I straightened up in my seat so that I could get a good view out the door. "Now, if I were going to set up an IED this morning, this would be a good place to put one. There are plenty of potential targets going to and from the division headquarters," I said.

"Yeah. They could set IEDs up at night and wait for our morning convoys to depart the compound," he said.

"Yep. And they'd be out here somewhere, watching the device now. If it is command-wire detonated, they will be somewhere nearby, so be on the lookout for someone watching the road," I said. "Hey, they're opening the gate now."

Four Humvees slowly made their way through the gate on the south end of the compound. Two of the Humvees pulled trailers behind them. A guard post soldier held the massive gate open until the convoy was on its way; then he closed the gate behind them.

"Let's get ahead of them," Tim said. "That's surely the first convoy to depart this morning, so we need to take a close look at the road."

Tim swooped down even lower over the road and paralleled it. I suppose we flew at seventy-five to one hundred feet above the ground, just high enough to avoid the trees and powerlines but close enough for me to observe the road with the naked eye. Tim flew in the right seat that day, so he put the road out my door. We moved rather slowly, so that I could scan the road closely. Not wanting to fly slow and straight for a prolonged period, every minute or so Tim would nose it over, speed up, and make a quick circle. We didn't want to become an easy target for anyone who decided that they would rather try and shoot a Kiowa down versus detonate their IED.

I noticed a white car sitting on the right shoulder of the road. It didn't seem all that odd, since cars commonly pulled over on the side of the road in Iraq. Still, I noted that it was sitting there, and the passengers were not out filling it with a gas can, changing a flat, or trying to cool down an overheated radiator.

"There's a car with dudes in it," I said. "They could be watching something."

"Watch them," Tim said.

Each time we flew a circle, we could see the convoy on the highway. Flying circles or loops enabled us to keep an eye on the convoy as well as remain in front of them. My eyes scanned the sides of the road looking for anything that didn't seem right. I concentrated hard, trying to make darn sure I didn't miss anything. *It has to be somewhat comforting seeing us up in front of them, checking everything out,* I thought.

"Let me call that convoy just to let them know that there's a car sitting on the side of the road up ahead," I told Tim. "I don't see anything in the road that looks unusual or out of place, but I'll let them know we're up here keeping watch, at least."

"Roger," Tim replied.

"Convoy departing DMAIN, this is Stetson 2-1, over," I called into the mic on my helmet.

The call sign *Stetson* was a point of contention for us. Despite the fact that army helicopters operated below the coordinating altitude (three thousand feet) and the Combined Air Operations Center (CAOC) did not have the authority to task us to do anything, they wanted all airplanes—helicopters and fixed-wing alike—on the Air Tasking Order (ATO). Navy and Air Force aviators ran the CAOC, and they managed all the air space over Iraq. Each day they published an order that listed all the airplanes that would be flying missions that day. Most of the army pilots felt that it was senseless to list our helicopters on the order, because they did not have control of army helicopters flying below three thousand feet above the ground. "If they can't task us to do a mission, why put us on there?" they'd argue.

The truth was that many of us feared that if we were listed on the ATO, eventually they might try to task us, and we did not work for them. We worked for the 101st Airborne Division. Nevertheless, we were listed on the ATO, which meant that each helicopter was assigned a specific call sign. Traditionally, we used our *Hollywood* call signs, which were assigned to the person in a given position. For example, the SCO was Saber Six, because we were Saber squadron and he was the commander. All commanders have the number six as a part of their call sign. Colonel Greg Gass was Destiny Six, and Major General Petraeus was Eagle Six. The command sergeant major was seven, the operations officer was three, the executive officer was five, and so forth.

When we were forced to put our helicopters on the ATO, the CAOC gave us a list of available call signs from which to choose. Saber was already taken, which naturally irked us. We were proud of that call sign and wanted to leave a legacy in Iraq that was remembered as Saber squadron. No one knows who submitted our preferences, but the first name that came back was *Kelp*. "Who the fuck picked that?" Doug exclaimed upon seeing it. "Probably some ass clown above us. He thought that would be funny, and he's laughing his ass off now," he said, snarling his lips and scrunching his moustache.

We kicked it back and were reassigned *Stetson Hat*, which at least was a cavalry term. "A different ass clown came up with that one," Doug pronounced.

"Just shorten it," Schiller said. "Use Stetson and be done with it." And that settled it. Each helicopter had a number individually assigned to it, but all were known as Stetson.

The second or third time Tim and I circled, I saw a car pull in behind the convoy. It was the white car that had been sitting on the side of the road. "Hey," I slapped Tim on the shoulder and pointed. "That car pulled in behind the convoy."

"Convoy departing DMAIN, this is Stetson 2-1, over." No answer.

The car only trailed the convoy for a second, and then the driver stomped the gas and flew past the Humvees. "Tim, we'd better follow that car," I said.

"Convoy departing DMAIN, this is Stetson 2-1, over."

Still, nothing.

Without speaking, Tim followed the car, remaining about one hundred meters behind it. The driver raced up ahead of the convoy. He appeared simply to be driving away but at an unusually high rate of speed.

"Convoy departing DMAIN, this is Stetson 2-1."

Silence.

"Are you up on the right frequency?" Tim asked.

"Yes. I made sure."

We were calling the convoy on the Sheriff's Net. Because all units have different radio frequencies assigned for their internal use, the Sheriff's Net was established as a 911 emergency net. Every convoy and helicopter in Iraq were supposed to have one radio monitoring the net at all times. That way, if you were in trouble, you could call for help, and if someone else was calling for help, you'd hear them and be able to go help them.

We were nearing the overpass at bridge five, but suddenly, about 150 meters short of the overpass, the car abruptly stopped in the passing lane. "He's stopping!" I said.

"Yep," Tim replied. "I've got to come back around."

The car had been moving so fast that we had to fly quickly to keep up. When he suddenly stopped, we flew right past him, so Tim had to circle around. Tim banked hard left to remain between the car and the convoy that was still making its way slowly to the south. It happened so fast we could not react. The brake lights had illuminated, and the car stopped on a dime. A man opened the right-side passenger door and ran around the back of the car. He set something out on the side of the road and dove back into the car before it sped away.

A thousand thoughts filled my mind at once. *He just planted a bomb! Tell Tim to follow him! Go back and stop the convoy! Call the convoy again! Shoot the car and kill the bombers!*

"Tim, he just set something out on the side of the road. Keep an eye on the car. I'm going to try and get the convoy again," I said.

"Convoy departing DMAIN, this is Stetson 2-1. I say again this is Stetson 2-1." Nothing.

The convoy was headed straight for the roadside bomb. We had to stop them. "They pulled in under the overpass and stopped," Tim said.

They were about 150 yards from where the potential bomb now sat. "They are going to detonate it on the convoy. We've got to stop them," I said.

"I'm going back to try and get their attention," Tim said, turning back toward the convoy.

"Convoy departing DMAIN, this is Stetson 2-1, over. Answer the friggin' radio, dang-it!"

Tim flew as low as he could right at the convoy. As we passed them, head on, I waved out the door, attempting to get their attention. They waved back at me and continued down the road.

"I'm going to try and stop them," Tim said, as he quickly maneuvered the helicopter back around in front of the convoy. I could see the bomb just past us. This was our last opportunity. If it was a bomb and we got too close, they might try and bring us down.

"Don't hover over that bomb," I said.

Tim didn't answer. He brought the helicopter to a hover over the road in front of the vehicles. "I hope they don't have AK-47s in the car with them," I said. "If they do, we're a sitting duck."

"They must know we see the bomb by now," he said.

We could only descend to about fifty feet due to wires over the road. I frantically waved out the door, but the convoy still did not stop. They continued right under us. Tim had to transition back to forward flight. He pulled in power and began a right-hand turn. The convoy was right outside my door as they approached the box, which we were convinced was a bomb at that point.

I watched as the first vehicle passed. Nothing happened. Then the second and third vehicle drove by, and nothing happened. I was beginning to have hope, to think we had simply been overly cautious. Either it was not a bomb or it wasn't working. Finally, the last vehicle approached. Seemingly in slow motion, I watched as the vehicle passed the box, but just as the trailer was abeam the box, it exploded, lifting the trailer high into the air.

They timed it poorly. The explosion seemed to happen in slow motion. We felt the concussion of the blast, smoke and debris shot into the sky, and the trailer lifted off the ground almost perpendicular to the Humvee, then fell back to the ground and bounced. Both back tires were destroyed in the explosion. The driver quickly pulled over on the side of the road as soldiers bailed out of the vehicle, machine guns at the ready. They must have called the other vehicles in the convoy because they stopped as well. "Go get the car!" I screamed to Tim while pointing at the overpass.

He immediately pulled in all the power we had in an attempt to get to the overpass before the bad guys could get away, but it was too late. The car was gone. We searched the entire area. No white car.

Fortunately, no one was hurt in the attack. Eventually, we were able to get them up on the Sheriff's Net. We provided security for them while they changed the trailer tires. At one point, we had to leave them and go get gas at the FARP, but we returned and continued providing security until they could drive again. They thanked us for our help, and I urged them to always keep a radio up on the Sheriff's Net.

We got lucky that day. When Tim and I returned to Q-West, we were able to add one more data point to Candy Smith's tracker. "Attacks are increasing," she said grimly, staring at the location of the IED on the map. "We're having an effect on their timing and locations, but the sheer number of attacks continue to increase."

Two days later, Tim and I were up again. "When we get to the east side, I want to take a look at the area where the IED was placed in the road the other day," Tim said.

"I was thinking the same thing," I said. "That area gets a lot of US traffic. I'm sure the enemy is watching and timing our convoys."

"Yep, no doubt."

Once again, Tim flew in the right seat, and I was in the left. "I am going to start with the road," Tim said. "Let's fly from the bridge to the palace on the east side and then back to the bridge on the west side. We'll look for bombs or anything that might be prep work, like aiming or timing stakes. Then we'll conduct a very deliberate reconnaissance of the surrounding area," he said.

"Yep. Perfect," I said.

As we started up the east side of the road, my focus was on the road, but I happened to look to the right, at a building. Because we were about fifty feet above the ground, I had a good view of the buildings and their rooftops.

"There's a sniper team on top of that building," I told Tim, surprised.

"Did anyone mention a sniper team when we checked in?" he asked.

I had checked in with Battle Force when we arrived. "No."

"It looks like they are set up to watch this area where the bomb went off," I said.

"They sure are. That has to be soldiers from Battle Force," he said. "But they should have told us they were going to be out here."

"Yeah, this is their area of operations, so I guess it's them. Let's call their TOC," I said.

I called the Battle Force TOC and asked about the team. They confirmed that they had forces out there watching the road for IED emplacers. Wanting to talk to the sniper team, I asked for their frequency, which the TOC passed to me.

"Why didn't they tell us that when we checked in?" Tim said.

"They probably assumed we'd never see them hiding on the roof," I said.

"They have no idea who they are dealing with," Tim said, trying not to laugh. "You can't hide from us."

I called the TOC back and told them we would be flying up and down the road looking for IEDs from the division main to the overpass. We wanted them to know exactly what we were doing. They acknowledged, and Tim and I continued our reconnaissance along the road to the DMAIN.

When we got about halfway between the division main and the overpass, Tim flew a small circle, and I saw a convoy driving out of the gate. "Here comes a convoy," I said.

"Yep, let's stay ahead of them," he said.

"Hopefully, they are up on the Sheriff's Net this time," I said.

"No kidding."

So, just like before, we searched the road for IEDs in front of the convoy, but this time, I was paying particularly close attention to all the civilian vehicles on the roads. We didn't see any pulled over along the road. We made it to the overpass well ahead of the convoy and didn't see anything out of the ordinary. Tim made a lazy turn at the overpass and, as I looked out my door back at the convoy, I suddenly saw puffs of smoke coming from their machine guns. "They are shooting at something in that wood line," I said.

"What?"

"They are shooting into the palm grove by the river."

"Are they taking fire?" Tim asked.

"Heck if I know. I am calling them now."

"Convoy that just left the DMAIN, this is Stetson 2-1, over."

I could hear the rat-a-tat-tat of machine guns in the background when the convoy commander answered. "We're taking fire from the wood line to the west," he said.

"Okay, we're moving in to observe," I told him.

Tim began flying erratically just in case the enemy decided that they preferred to test their luck with a Kiowa. He flew us closer, and I saw something moving in the thick green bushes.

"What is that?" I asked Tim.

"What?" he said.

"That!" I said, pointing to the edge of the woods. "It's moving back and forth. Is that a flag or a signal?"

"I think it is." He paused. "Are those friendlies?"

"I think so," I said, straining to see better. "Move in closer."

As we flew in for a closer look, I could clearly see that they were extending a stick into the air with an American military uniform jacket tied to it. The soldier was waving it back and forth attempting to show whoever was shooting at them that he was American. "Cease fire, cease fire!" I called over the radio.

Tim immediately descended to try to put us between the halted convoy and the friendlies in the woods. He hoped that they would stop shooting for fear of hitting us, but they didn't stop. He turned and began flying straight toward them.

At that moment, time seemed to slow down for me. I saw a man on a bicycle peddling toward the convoy. He was traveling from the overpass toward the DMAIN, and he had almost reached the trucks. The man was going to pass the vehicles on the western side, where they were shooting. *Surely, he sees them shooting. Certainly, he hears the machine guns,* I thought. Nevertheless, he continued.

The snipers on the east side of the road watched the event through their scopes. The US soldiers in the palm grove waved an army jacket in the air while hugging the ground as closely as possible. The men in the convoy, apparently convinced that they were in a firefight with the enemy, continued to shoot, and we flew directly toward them to try to stop them.

I see memories in vivid pictures. The man on the bicycle had jet-black hair and a mustache, and wore a bright yellow, button-up shirt. We were close enough that I could see the sandals he wore, angling off the pedals. His seat was too low, so his knees lifted high as he pedaled. Perhaps it was his child's bike. Maybe he rode it to the store to get something for breakfast. That meant he had a family. They were waiting for him to return home from the market. My mind raced in slow motion.

Horrified, I watched as he rode the bicycle straight into the middle of the shooting. The bullet struck him in the neck, on his right side. I was staring at him when it pierced his neck, tore the skin. He dropped instantly, and the bicycle slid away. "Cease fire!" I screamed over the net. "Damn it, cease fire!"

"Stetson 2-1, understand, cease fire," finally came a reply, but it was too late.

"Roger. Blue-on-blue," I said, indicating that they were shooting at other American forces. "Those are friendlies you are shooting at."

"Roger. Understand. Cease fire."

The shooting stopped, and a soldier ran to aid the wounded Iraqi man. I watched as the man's shirt turned from yellow to red, neck to waist, like a sheet slowly dipped in red dye. He was lying on his side, grasping his neck when they reached him. Fortunately, there was a medic in the convoy, who was able to tend to him quickly.

Slowly, cautiously, a soldier from the woods emerged and walked forward to the road. Once he reached the vehicles, he began speaking with the convoy commander. He pointed to buildings across the street and then back to the wood line.

As it turns out, after the IED attack, Battle Force decided to put out sniper teams on both sides of the road, but they failed to inform other units. Apparently, the convoy saw armed men in the woods as they drove past. The convoy commander said they took fire, but the soldiers on the ground said they did not shoot. They only took cover.

Either Battle Force did not tell anyone that they were putting sniper teams along the road, or the information was not properly disseminated to the convoys. Either way, it was a failure in coordination and communication.

Miraculously, no Americans were injured that day. While I've often wondered, I do not know if the Iraqi man survived or not. Once they put him in their vehicle, I could no longer see him. It was time for fuel, so we departed the area and flew to the FARP.

MISCREANTS

It was as though a year's worth of rain had been held in reserve for late fall. Blue skies and dry heat gave way to gray clouds and relentless rain. The wood in our buildings was so dry that once it was given a drink, it swelled up like a tick, making it all but impossible to close most of the doors.

"Is that rain?" Doug yelled from inside his sleeping bag the day the faucet was turned on.

"Yeah," I shouted back from my room.

Soon several of us stood under the awning at the front of the TOC in flip-flops, shorts, and our Stetson hats. We stared out into white sheets of rain that came in waves with the wind that accompanied it. No one said a word. We just stood there staring at all the water, as if we were seeing a unicorn. "Holy shit, is it raining," Rowely said, joining us.

"Like a cow pissing on a flat rock," I said, which was a bit salty for my language, but I liked using that expression because my grandfather said it when I was a boy, back before he pickled his liver with likker. A man can live without a lot of things in this world, but a liver ain't one of 'em. Saying it seemed apropos at that very moment.

"It pissed on us for two days straight in the spring, back when we were camped out on the hill above Mosul," Doug said. "But this is gonna leave a mark. I bet Stayla floods."

"No kidding," I said, "that little village may be washed away." Then I shivered hard. Suddenly it was cold. We had put a kerosene heater in the TOC for warmth, which quickly became the central gathering spot. That also reminded me of my childhood.

I was in high school before I knew what a thermostat actually did. We didn't have enough money to risk not being able to pay an outrageous electric bill, so we never touched the thermostat. My father knew how many sticks of firewood he had piled up behind the house, and besides, if we ran low on wood, we could always take the chainsaw and go cut more. We also used a kerosene heater, because like logs, my father knew exactly how much kerosene he possessed. The furnace was an unknown. He could have turned it on and warmed the house, but he had no idea how much it would cost until the bill came in the mail at the end of the month. It was not worth the risk of being unable to pay the bill. Therefore, we huddled around a kerosene stove or the fireplace for warmth.

Once I was older, we began to sparingly use the furnace, but when we did turn it on, Momma closed every room and vent off except the living room. To ensure that no warm air escaped and that we maximized its use, Momma placed towels under every door in the house.

"You don't need heat in your bedroom," my father would say. "You can get under the blankets when you're in your bed."

It wasn't much different in Iraq. Some guys ordered space heaters from Walmart and Amazon, but our generators could not handle the load, so we had to ban them. We told the men to bundle up in their rooms and warm themselves in the TOC.

"I'm freezing my ass off," Doug said and headed back to his room.

I walked into the TOC to warm by the kerosene heater. Soon the SCO entered the TOC.

"At ease!" a soldier yelled.

"Carry on," Schiller replied in a raspy morning voice.

He shook to get the water off him, unzipped his physical training jacket, and hung it on a nail to dry. He held a package of baby wipes in his hand. I laughed and pointed at the wipes. "You had to go, huh?"

"Yeah, and your boys are back at it," he said.

"What do you mean?"

"One of the Iraqis squatted on the toilet and shit all over it again," he said.

"You have got to be kidding me," I said.

"Nope. Now don't go shooting one of them," he said, knowing how badly it irritated me.

"I'm done. That's it!" I said. "They are no longer allowed to use the toilets. When Omar gets here, we'll go tell them. They can find another place to go."

"So, we're going to have Iraqis squatting behind the buildings now?" Schiller asked.

"I might really shoot them if they did that," I said. "They'll figure it out, but they have lost their privilege of using the Blue Canoe."

"Okay," Schiller said, shaking his head. "I don't want to see you chasing half-naked Iraqis all over Q-West with a broom because they don't understand Western defecation etiquette."

"No promises. Hey, speaking of dirty, Doc was in here last night," I said, changing the subject.

"Oh yeah, what's up?"

"Said some of the guys have worms," I said, then turned around to face the heater and warm my front side.

"Worms!" Schiller repeated, suddenly wide-eyed.

"Yes sir, from living in this dirt and filth. Doc said we need to make sure we emphasize hygiene. The soldiers need to wash their hands more, especially before they eat. He said this change in weather is making matters worse."

"How so?"

"It's getting colder, so they don't want to take showers," I said.

"Worms," he repeated, shaking his head and turning toward the coffee pot.

"I'll put the word out to all the troop commanders and first sergeants," I said, washing my hands in the barely visible, wavy heat emanating from the kerosene heater.

Schiller poured a cup of coffee and walked into his office. He put on his black fleece jacket and a Dillon hat, which had an M134 Gatling gun stitched on the front of it. The black fleece jackets had been issued just prior to the deployment. They were warm and comfortable. Soldiers loved them, but initially we were forbidden to wear them. It made no sense to any of us. The army issued the jackets, but the jackets did not have a spot on them to place a name tag or rank, so we were told that we could not wear them as an outer garment—that is, until we saw the commanding general wear one.

We had attended a memorial ceremony at Top Gun, Strike's artillery battalion. Major General Petraeus had worn his black fleece to the ceremony, which we had seen and taken, perhaps erroneously, as implicit permission to wear the jackets from that point forward. We never looked back.

The baseball hats were a point of contention as well. They were unauthorized, but special operations soldiers commonly wore baseball hats. Being *special operators*, they also wore civilian clothes or fatigues from a different era, which was out of the question for conventional soldiers, but the hats found their way into almost every company and troop area. The most common hat was brown or black with an American flag on the front, and like rosin on a baseball player's batting helmet, the dirtier the hat, the better. I suppose the hats made soldiers feel like a "cool guy," a term we often used when referring to operators.

"Are we flying tonight or not?" Schiller shouted from his desk.

I walked to the doorway. "Looks like the weather is clearing. We may have a low ceiling of clouds, but I think we can fly."

"Good. I might need to shoot something tonight."

As the squadron commander, Schiller had a professional obligation, as well as a strong desire, to mentor his junior officers. He decided that one of the best ways to do that was to fly missions with each of his lieutenants. Flying with them allowed him to get to know them on a much more personal level. It would also afford him an opportunity to see firsthand how their flight skills were progressing. I published a schedule, and on most of the flights, I flew as his lead aircraft. As each lieutenant's turn came, they were responsible for planning and briefing the mission that evening.

First Lieutenant Ian Anderson was scheduled to fly with the SCO that night. "I was a little nervous for a couple of reasons," Ian later recalled. "First, I looked up to him. He was a 160th SOAR guy and the SCO. Someday, later in my career, I hoped to try out for the 160th. It was important to me that he knew that I could plan, brief, and lead the flight. Second, I had a need to impress the father figures in my life. My father ran away from my family when I was twelve years old. So, I've always had this need to substitute the father I never had with father figures in my life."[1]

276

I flew with Chief Warrant Officer Four Tim Merrell, the squadron standardization instructor pilot and Doug Ford's roommate. That evening, Tim, the SCO, and I gathered around my desk as Ian began briefing the mission. His delivery was good, but soon Tim Merrell grimaced.

"Hey, LT," Tim interrupted. "Are you sure you're using the right briefing format?"

Ian hesitated, then timidly answered, "This is the format we use in the troop."

Prior to moving up to the squadron headquarters to serve as the senior instructor pilot, Tim had been the Ban'shee Troop senior instructor pilot where Ian served as a platoon leader. "Have you read the new Squadron Standard Operating Procedure (SOP)?"

"I've seen it," Anderson said.

Neither Schiller nor I weighed in on the matter. Tim calling Ian out in front of us was enough. Ian would carry the message back to the troop, and both Schiller and I knew that Tim would go pay the troop instructor pilots a visit the next day. It wasn't that we cared that much which briefing format was used. We only cared that there was one standard in the squadron. We'd discovered that each troop had their favorite format, but that created a bit of confusion when we mixed pilots from troop to troop on missions. It was not uncommon for the pilots to cling to the format they preferred and resist change. It would take our leadership to force standardization across the squadron. It was refreshing to see Tim Merrell take ownership of the SOP and gently correct Ian.

Once the correction was made, Tim allowed Ian to continue with the briefing, which Ian did very well. Following the briefing, we loaded our gear into Schiller's truck and headed to the airfield.

It was cold, wet, and muddy—another dreary day in northern Iraq. By late fall, we'd been robbed of the splendid Iraqi sunsets. Instead, gray days only grew darker until the light was eventually extinguished. Every walk outside meant sticky mud clinging to our boots. I often carried a stick so I could pry the mud off my boots once I reached a building or the helicopter. We walked around like we had crotch rot, feet spread wide apart to keep the mud from rubbing off on the inside of our pants legs.

After thoroughly inspecting our helicopters, we departed Q-West to the north. Darkness had just fallen. It was a night vision goggle mission from the start. Our mission was to fly to Mosul and conduct a standard reconnaissance and security mission within each of the battalion areas. "The intel guys said to be on the lookout for three to five men setting up a mortar system near the division rear, at Mosul airfield," Ian had told us during the briefing.

Reflecting back across the years, Ian recalled, "With the thick cloud cover, it was dark, very dark. Everyone knew that the SCO flew close to his lead aircraft, but on dark nights he flew even closer."

It's much easier to see the lead aircraft and maintain proper spacing by flying close on dark nights. "We tucked in really tight; so tight in fact, I was nervous," he told me. "I had flown almost five hundred hours in combat by that point in the deployment. I'd flown a lot of formation flight, but that was the closest I had ever flown before and probably have ever since. Our rotor blades were almost overlapping yours," he said, referring to me as flight lead. "I kept pushing back into my seat as if that might move us back a little bit."

Schiller did fly close, and he did it effortlessly. When I first reported to 2-17 CAV, the senior instructor pilot at that time was Chief Warrant Officer Four Tracy Owens. Tracy asked me, "Sir, have you flown a lot of formation flight in your career?"

"I suppose I have, Tracy," I said, not wanting to sound overly confident, yet not inexperienced either. "I've flown a lot of AH-1 Cobra and OH-58 mixed formation flights, as well as a Kiowa formation flight," I said.

Continuing to probe, he asked, "Have you flown close?"

I sensed there was some point to the questioning. "Well, we flew relatively close, Tracy. Why do you ask?"

"Well, you've never flown as close as we fly," he said matter-of-factly.

Most pilots, even the most seasoned aviators, appear more alert and stressed when they fly tight formation flight under night vision goggles, but Stephen Schiller was the coolest customer I'd ever seen. He would fly the helicopter with his left hand on the cyclic control while tossing chips into his mouth with his right, his rotor disk mere feet from his lead aircraft the entire time. He took to it naturally, "like a duck to water," as my father was fond of saying. Schiller knew that it was stressful to fly close and maintain one's spacing, but that was his intent. He wanted his pilots to work hard at precision flight. It would have been easy to fly loose and relaxed, but Schiller knew that a unit that strove for perfection on the simple things would be able to perform the difficult tasks when required.

That evening, we flew to Mosul and checked in with the first battalion. Since Tim and I were flying lead, it was our responsibility to contact the ground unit. I called their command post on the radio and told them we were on station. They had small outposts scattered throughout their area of responsibility. We knew where each of them was located, as well as the key Iraqi locations, such as police stations and government buildings. Our plan was to conduct reconnaissance of those locations to make sure no enemy forces were snooping around them or trying to maneuver to attack them. Next, we would conduct a thorough reconnaissance of their entire area, from one end to the other.

When we checked in with the command post, they usually told us if there were any patrols out on the roads. When they did not offer that information, we asked for it. When they had patrols out on the roads, we'd go check in with them to provide security as they drove through the streets of Mosul. If the unit had received mortars or if any of their forces had been ambushed that day, they'd ask us to conduct reconnaissance of those locations.

The only excitement we encountered that evening was at a gas station on the north side of Mosul. Iraqis had been protesting the price of fuel throughout the day. Tempers flared as security forces had clashed with the protestors several times. When we arrived, angry men remained in front of the gas station, chanting. We tried to disperse them by diving our helicopters at them, then pulling up and turning sharply to pop our rotor blades. The maneuver was aggressive, and the blades popping in the wind sounded somewhat like we were shooting. It always got their attention.

On the first pass, they quickly scattered, moving back from the US ground forces, but they soon realized we were not actually shooting at them, so they returned. After about ten minutes of flying circles over the crowd, the ground forces reported that someone was shooting at us as we flew over. The sounds echoed between buildings in the city, so they were not sure where the shooter was located. We could not hear the bullets over the turbine engines, nor could we see tracers, so we weren't sure where the shooter was hiding either. Nevertheless, within a few minutes of receiving that report, the crowd began to slowly disperse. Detecting no real threat and running low on fuel, we headed to the FARP.

After refueling, we returned to the gas station, but the crowd had dispersed and our soldiers were heading back to their outpost. We escorted them back and then continued to the next battalion area. When we were in the FARP, I had felt like I needed to pee but not badly. I made the mistake of thinking that I could hold it until the next stop. The constant bouncing and vibrating in the cockpit was too much. I had to pee.

"Saber Six, Saber Three, over," I called to Schiller.

"Yo," he answered.

"I have a yellow duck, over."

"Do you want to go back to the FARP?" he asked.

"I don't think I can make it. Let's just land outside the city," I said.

"Rog-o," he answered.

We were already out near the eastern edge of the city, so we only had to fly a short distance to get away from any houses and land. We found a spot and set the helicopter down. I got out and moved away from the helicopter, outside the rotor disk, so that the wind wouldn't cause me to pee on myself. Many rookie pilots have soaked themselves trying to negotiate the wind under a rotor system. It can be done, but you have to relieve yourself very close to the helicopter, just where the fuselage and tail boom join. I always found it much easier to simply move away from the helicopter.

While I was relieving myself, Schiller and Anderson were supposed to be keeping an eye out for any Iraqis who might be in the area. They flew a large circle around me and then lined up on me. Flying directly at me, I heard the distinct sound that the Kiowa rotors make when you execute a cyclic climb. I realized that they were about to do a gun run on me. I looked up through my goggles, and sure enough, there they came, diving at me. *Little boys never grow up,* I thought to myself. Then I looked back down to finish my business, and to my surprise, my privates were glowing red. It took a second for my mind to work out what I was seeing—then it all computed. They were lasing me. Lasing my pecker!

I turned and ran for the helicopter. As I started climbing back into the cockpit, I could see Tim laughing. It was clear that they had been discussing it over the radio. When I plugged my helmet into the radios, I could hear them all laughing.

"That's not funny! You could have damaged the goods," I said.

"It was just a laser pointer," Schiller said. "No damage done."

"You don't know that," I said.

"You'll be all right," he said. "But you must admit, that was a good shot. To hit a target that small, you have to be an excellent shot."

With that, Tim and Lieutenant Anderson once again bellowed out in laughter. "Very funny," I said. "Very funny."

The remainder of the evening was uneventful. By 10:00 p.m., our mission was complete. Another scout weapons team from Annihilator Troop called us on the radio as they approached from the south. We conducted a battle handover with them, filling them in on everything that had happened throughout the night, and departed to the FARP to fill up with fuel before heading back to Q-West. Refuel complete, we called the control tower and received permission to depart the airfield to the north, quickly turned east, and then flew south to parallel the Tigris River.

The Division Rear Command Post (DREAR), located on the southern end of the airfield, had been receiving a lot of mortar attacks over the previous weeks. Despite our best efforts, we had been unable to catch the mortar team. We were told that sometimes they stopped their car on the side of the road, quickly set up a mortar tube, shot three to four mortar rounds, and then jumped back in their car and fled. They were very good and extremely accurate. Other intel analysts said that they had a mortar tube hidden by the riverbank. They suggested that the mortar man might be shooting a few rounds, then throwing the tube into the river after he shot. "He might have a rope tied to the tube," an analyst told me. "After he shoots, he can throw it in the water to cool it, then act like he's fishing in the river when you guys show up," he added.

The water would quickly cool the mortar tube, preventing us from seeing it clearly under thermals. The latter report was what we were told to be on the lookout for as we flew over Mosul on the night of December 6th.

As we turned south to parallel the river, we descended so that Tim and I could look closely at the field adjacent to the runway. Just as we departed the airfield, we saw what appeared to be a flashlight in the middle of the field.

"We're going to check that light out on the way by," I reported to Schiller.

"Roger," he replied.

As we passed midfield, the light suddenly disappeared. I struggled to locate the exact spot from where the light had emanated. Tim flew while I scanned the field.

"Hey, there they are," Anderson said. Schiller made a quick 360-degree turn.

Having not seen them, I had already passed the men when Schiller and Anderson saw them, so they turned back quickly and assumed duties as the lead aircraft in the team. Tim Merrell and I made a lazy, slower turn and took up outer security.

Upon hearing rotors and realizing we were flying very low to the ground, the men had turned the light off and immediately dove into a ditch. Clearly, they did not want us to see them.

"We've got two guys in this field by the trail that leads to the river," Anderson reported.

A dirt trail paralleled the fields. There was a small ditch adjacent to the trail.

"Hey, there's another man lying flat on the ground farther out in the field," Anderson said, with clear excitement in his voice.

"Roger. Looks like there are three of them," I replied.

"Yep. Two men are lying on the west side of that little ditch that parallels the dirt trail, and another man is in the field. I also see what appears to be a shovel," Anderson reported. "That guy in the field is hard to see. He blends in with the terrain."

Schiller broke into the conversation. "You call the tower and tell them we'll be working here, inside the traffic pattern, for a few minutes. I'll report it to the division rear," he said.

"Roger," I replied.

I called the air traffic controller in the tower and told him what we were doing. Meanwhile, Merrell had found some other interesting stuff to report. "They have several bags in that ditch with them. They were carrying those bags. See them?" he asked, as he maneuvered the Kiowa to put them right out my door.

"Yeah. I see them. What do you think it is? Could it be mortar rounds in the bags?" I asked.

"I bet it is. I think we've caught these guys," Merrell said.

"I agree."

Once Schiller had finished speaking with the division rear command post, I called him. "We've found a couple of bags that these guys were carrying. We think they might contain mortar rounds. They look like burlap bags. Whatever they are, the bags appear to be full," I reported.

"Okay. We need to get a ground force out here to get these guys," he said. "Call the quick reaction force (QRF). Do you have their frequency?" he asked.

"Roger. It's on my communications card. We'll give them a call."

While I called the QRF, Schiller and Anderson watched the three men and continued to search the trail for anything else that looked out of place. The QRF consisted of a fifteen- to twenty-man patrol from a coalition partner nation, which I will not name, partnered with a few American soldiers. The American soldiers helped our coalition partners negotiate US Army systems, which were often confusing to them. They also bridged the English barrier. Some of them spoke broken English; others spoke no English at all. Either way, it was difficult to understand them on the radio, so the American made radio calls for them.

After a couple of attempts, I reached an American sergeant on the radio. I reported what we had observed and urged him to come out and detain the men. He agreed, so while he prepared the QRF to move out, we continued to search the area.

We flew down the trail the men had been walking on but didn't see anything out of the ordinary until we reached the river. As we searched the riverbank, we found a small flat-bottom boat with more burlap bags hidden under willow trees. The small boat had been dragged up on the bank and carefully hidden. This further confirmed our certainty of their guilt.

"Saber Six, Saber Three, over," I called Schiller.

"Go," he answered.

"We've found a jon boat down by the river. It's hidden under some willow trees, and there are several more bags beside it," I said.

"Groovy. Keep looking," he said.

By this time, the three men had been lying in the ditch for about fifteen minutes. Despite us flying right over the top of them, we were sure that they did not realize that we could see them. Two of the men decided that they would get up and sneak off down the trail.

"Two of them are up and moving," Tim reported and quickly maneuvered our helicopter around to get behind them.

"Yep. I see them," I said. They took high deliberate steps, reminding me of Elmer Fudd sneaking up on Bugs Bunny. "They are trying to sneak off. They really don't think we can see them."

"I'm going to white-light them," Merrell said and flipped our searchlight on them. They immediately dove back into the ditch and lay flat on the ground.

"That got their attention," I said.

"Yes, it did."

Finally, the sergeant with the quick reaction force called us on the radio. He said they were on their way. We saw them as they exited the airfield perimeter gate, so Merrell and I flew over to link up with them.

"X-Ray 19, this is Saber Three, over," I called to the sergeant.

"X-Ray 19, over," he replied.

"X-Ray 19, just follow us. We are going to fly over the dirt road that leads to the location of the three men," I told him.

"Roger that, over."

Meanwhile, Schiller and Ian Anderson kept a watch on the three men. The QRF began slowly following us as we hovered down the road in front of their vehicles. After about five hundred meters, they stopped and began dismounting their trucks.

"What are they doing?" I asked Merrell.

"It looks like they are stopping there," he said.

Rather quickly, the QRF got out of their trucks and lined up in single file. Merrell and I watched in amazement as they went to port arms (rifles in both hands held diagonally across their torso about six inches in front of their chest) and began high-stepping down the dirt road. Now, when I say "high-stepping," I mean they were jogging but their knees were lifting up waist high, so that their thighs were parallel to the ground. The American sergeant jogged along at the back of their file to keep up with them. I called him on the radio. "X-Ray 19, this is Saber Three, over."

Already out of breath, he responded, "This is X-Ray 19, over."

"You're over a click [one thousand meters] from the bad guys. Get back in your trucks, and we can lead you to them. They are flat on their bellies. You can drive right to them, over," I told him.

"Roger. I'm trying to stop these guys now," he said.

Tim Merrell and I watched as he ran up and down the line trying to get them to understand that it would be a much easier task if they would listen and follow his instructions. They high-stepped down the road a bit farther before he finally convinced them to stop. Some of them were already bending over at the waist, hands on their knees, most certainly out of breath.

Meanwhile, the three men tried to get up and sneak off again. "Shoot your rifle in front of them," Schiller told Anderson.

"Shoot the ground?" Anderson asked.

"Yeah. Just shoot into the ground in front of them. They'll stop," he said.

Anderson, who already had his M4 in his lap, stuck the barrel out the door. Schiller put the helicopter in a position just over and in front of the three men. Anderson switched his rifle from safe to fire and pulled the trigger. Tracer rounds spit from his rifle like hot sparks and impacted the soft ground about twenty yards in front of the men. The three men simultaneously dove to the ground and lay still.

"Told you they'd get down," Schiller said.

Anderson giggled. It was the first time he'd fired his personal weapon while on a mission.

By that time, the QRF had gotten back into their trucks and were following us once again, but after about five to six hundred more meters they stopped and dismounted their trucks once again. I called the sergeant. "X-Ray 19, just keep following us, over," I urged him.

"I am trying to get them to follow you, but they will not listen. They think they need to get out," said the clearly frustrated sergeant.

"Roger that," I replied.

I could see the sergeant running truck to truck trying to convince them to get back in and continue following us, but they refused to listen. Once again, they formed up in a file, came to port arms, and began high-stepping down the road. Every now and then, we lit up the road in front of them with the white searchlight to keep them going in the right direction. After about one hundred yards of high-stepping in a tight formation, the line of QRF soldiers began to stretch out. They were quickly tiring, yet they still had a long way to go. Over the next fifteen minutes, we watched them reach complete exhaustion as they slowly made their way to our three suspects.

The sergeant was at the front of their file when they finally made it to the three men lying on the ground, but he too was having difficulty talking on the radio by that point.

"Say...Saber Three...X...Ray here. Where are they?" he asked between deep gasps of breath.

Merrell used our searchlight to point them out. The sergeant shined a flashlight in the ditch and saw the three men lying on their bellies. Suddenly, our coalition partners took off in a sprint indicative of renewed energy. They pounced on the men, dragged them up to the road, and put them face down with their hands behind their backs. They then flex-cuffed the men. I thought for a minute that our friends might give the three evildoers a little roughing up simply for causing their exhaustion, but they maintained their professionalism. I did see several of them light up cigarettes, but otherwise, those who were not handling the detainees simply sat down in the road trying to recover.

"X-Ray 19, they were carrying two bags when we found them. The bags are farther down that trail," I said.

"Can you show me where they are?" he asked, still out of breath.

"Roger that," I said. "We'll hover back down the trail and spot them with the light."

"Okay," he answered.

The sergeant briefly spoke with two other men, and then all three began walking down the trail together. We hovered about fifty meters down the trail and spotted the bags. "They are right there," I called, as Merrell kept the light on the bags.

The sergeant shined his flashlight into the ditch. He and the other men slowly approached the bags, inspecting them carefully before opening them to see what was inside. Then, completely out of breath and exhausted, he keyed the radio and in a disappointed voice said, "PO-TA-TOES!"

Without missing a beat, I keyed the radio and came right back with, "Tater rustlers! We've caught ourselves a bunch of tater rustlers."

Tim Merrell threw his head back and burst out in laughter. I called Schiller and Anderson. "Looks like we caught these guys in the middle of a potato heist, over."

"What?" he asked.

"They just opened the bags. They are full of potatoes," I said.

"Have them come take a look at the jon boat," he said.

I called the sergeant on the radio and asked him to look at the john-boat, which he did. The bags at the boat were also filled with potatoes. In the end, it was determined that the men floated the Tigris River each night raiding potato farms. They filled their bags by night and sold the potatoes at market by day.

"What a story for my grandchildren," Anderson said. "The only shots I fired in combat were to stop a bunch of potato rustlers."[2]

"Well, they were smarter than I was," I said.

"Why's that?" he asked.

"Well, they knew where to look for the potatoes. I sent Slifko off across a field in the middle of the night to abscond a few potatoes so we could cook them, and he came back empty-handed. At least these guys knew where to find what they were looking for," I said, laughing.

I made the call to air traffic control as we neared Q-West, telling them we were inbound for the Cavalry pads. "Hurry up and get in there," Schiller said over our internal radio. "I have to get to the shitter."

"What?"

"Hurry up and land. I have to use the latrine," he said.

"Oh. Okay."

We'd built a wooden outhouse on the flight line, so the crew chiefs didn't have to go all the way back to the squadron area to use the latrine. We shot our approach to the east, then did a pedal turn on the pad and landed facing west. While Anderson shut their helicopter down, Schiller got out and rushed to the outhouse. Tim and I shut down our bird and began walking over to the outhouse where Schiller's truck was parked.

We were no more than ten yards from the outhouse when we heard, *whoosh, whoosh, whoosh,* in the distance.

"What was that?" I asked.

"Sounded like a launch," Tim said, and then it continued.

Whoosh, whoosh, whoosh.

By then, we were looking at the origin of the sound, so we saw what appeared to be roman candles firing into the sky about five miles away. Suddenly, it clicked. *"Rockets!"* Tim and I shouted.

"I see them," I yelled and began running back to the helicopter. "I've got you now."

As I ran toward the helicopter, the first rocket exploded on the north end of the runway. *The SCO is in the outhouse. Man, that would be a horrible way to go. Killed while sitting on the pot!* I thought to myself.

I didn't even bother with my helmet or the seatbelts. Catching the guys shooting rockets at us was the only thing on my mind, and I felt like I had them. Time was of the essence. I had to get there before they had a chance to escape.

"What are you doing?" Tim asked as I began cranking the helicopter.

"I'm going to kill those guys shooting at us," I said.

He began strapping in and putting his helmet on. Meanwhile, I cranked the helicopter and took off. I was halfway there before Tim motioned to me that he had the flight controls. Relinquishing the controls to him, I buckled my seatbelt and put my flight helmet on. "Man, my ears are ringing," I said once I was plugged into the radio system.

"I bet," he said.

The rockets had continued to launch as we approached. "How many do you think there were?" I asked.

"At least fifteen or so," he said. "I bet they were daisy-chained together."

"Probably so," I said. "And they were most likely on a delayed fuse so they could get away."

"Yep."

Smoke billowed into the air, and the ground glowed with heat under the night vision goggles when we arrived. "I don't see anyone. Do you?" I asked Tim.

"Nope," he said.

"There's a car pulling onto Route Remington," I said. "It looks like they are on the dirt road that came down here by the launch point."

I took the controls back from Tim and flew us over to the car. It appeared that there were four men in the car. They pulled onto Route Remington, which ran east to west about five miles north of Q-West.

Meanwhile, Schiller had finished his business and called Bastogne. They were launching their ground quick reaction force to investigate. "Bastogne is on the way. We are coming up on your six," he said over our internal radio.

"Roger," I said. "I have you in sight. We've got a car that appears to have been close to the launch point."

"Stop them and we'll let Bastogne check them out," he said.

"Okay. We're on it."

I flew us about one hundred yards in front of the car and came to a hover in the road. "They should see us and stop," I said to Tim.

"Hopefully," he replied, but the car didn't stop. They drove directly toward us and once they were within about twenty meters, I took off. "I don't want to let them get close enough to see us and get a shot. Maybe they didn't see us," I said.

"Use the searchlight," Tim said.

"Okay."

I flew us back out in front of them again, and this time I turned our white spotlight on and shined it in the road in front of the car. Suddenly, the car stopped. "They have stopped," I told Schiller over the radio.

"Roger, I see them. I'm talking with Bastogne on their internal radio. They are about a mile out."

"Okay. The driver is out of the car. They don't know what to do," I said.

"Don't let them move. If they take off, shoot your .50 caliber in the road in front of them," he said.

"Roger that."

Within a few minutes, Bastogne's quick reaction force pulled up and took control of the situation. We remained overhead for another hour, but there was no proof that the men had any knowledge of the rockets. Bastogne then investigated the launch point. Nineteen rockets had been fired. Another five had failed to launch. As we suspected, they used a delayed fuse.

"We've got to figure out how to catch these guys," I told Schiller.

"Yeah, I agree," he said.

"It's only a matter of time until they figure out how to aim them good enough to put a few right into our headquarters," I said.

"Yep. That was a lot of rockets. Hopefully no one is hurt," he said.

"No kidding," I said. "Hey, we're getting low on fuel. I think these guys are okay on their own now. We need to get some gas."

"Roger that," Schiller said. "I'll tell them we're heading back, but if they need more coverage, they can call the TOC."

As it turned out, no one was injured in the attack. Several helicopters were damaged on the north end of the airfield and shrapnel stuck in the sides of buildings, but not one soldier was hurt. We were lucky, but that luck would soon run out.

Once we had accountability of all our soldiers and determined that none of our equipment had been damaged, I went to the porta potty. Once again, my Iraqi friends had left me a present.

I give up, I thought to myself. *I give up!*

After finding Omar and telling him to make a new sign that read "Iraqi Toilet Only" and hanging it on one of the porta potties, I went to my room to change into my shorts and a T-shirt. As soon as I rounded the corner into the hall, I heard a banging sound coming from Doug and Tim Merrell's room. "What are you doing?" I asked as I walked into the doorway.

Doug looked up at me. "It's called progress," he said. "Rome wasn't built in a day, you know." Then he turned his attention back to his project. "We're not burning our shit anymore, because we made progress, sir. And now, I'm not going to have to take cold showers anymore. I'm sick of freezing my ass off in the shower."

"How do you plan to make it hot?" I asked.

"The Iraqi gravel guy, you know the one that delivered the gravel to the flight line?"

"Yeah, I know who you're talking about," I said.

"He gave me some copper tubing and braided hoses. I hooked the braided hose to the water barrel on the roof. Then I ran it into the shower and clamped it to the copper tubing. I've coiled the copper tubing up like a snake. I clamped more braided hose to the end of the copper tubing, which will run to the showerhead. I've got my propane stove sitting here on this ledge, so when we take a shower, we'll turn the propane stove on. Put that blue flame right on this copper tubing. The water will flow through the coiled-up tubing, which is hot as hell. It will warm the water," he said, satisfied with himself.

"When you're done, let me know. I'll give it a try," I said.

"My ass! You're not using my hot shower before I do," he said.

"But you *are* going to share, right?"

"Of course," he said. "But my room is not going to become a damn locker room."

"Doug, you're not near as dumb as Slifko and Rowely say you are," I said.

"Whatever." Doug rolled his eyes and returned to his project.

Then, under his breath, I heard him mumble, "I hate this fucking place."

RAMADAN

Ramadan began on October 26th. We had been warned to expect an increase in attacks. I wasn't sure what to make of that. The enemy would fast throughout the day, and at night they would celebrate with a feast. It was unclear if they would attack us during the day, while they were pissed off and hungry, or if they would forego the one meal of the day after dark and attack us then. Logic led me to believe that they would engorge themselves right after dark, attack us throughout the night, then sleep all day. I was wrong.

On November 2nd, we received word that a Chinook helicopter, flying soldiers from Habbaniyah Air Base to Baghdad Airport, was shot down near Fallujah. The soldiers were on their way home for mid-tour leave when the Chinook was hit with a surface-to-air missile. The crash killed sixteen soldiers, and twenty-one others were wounded. Later, we discovered that local Iraqis were chanting and waving pieces of the wreckage in the air in celebration at the crash site, a far cry from their liberation celebration just seven months earlier.

During the week prior to the Chinook shootdown, several convoys had been attacked, including a Strike convoy near bridge number two in Mosul. Three died in that IED attack, bringing the number of US soldier deaths to twenty-seven over an eight-day period.

Using the light of my headlamp, I recorded the events in my journal. "I dread driving out of here when we head back south to Kuwait," I wrote. "We have to drive through the Sunni Triangle, right by Fallujah. We will be the last convoys in our division to drive the same route, so the enemy will know our path well."

It was a tough week to celebrate a birthday, so I chose to quietly tick off another year in private. I turned thirty-five on the fourth. On November 7th, the attacks continued. A Black Hawk from 5th Battalion, 101st Aviation Regiment, stationed at Q-West with us, was shot down in Saddam Hussein's hometown of Tikrit. Six soldiers were killed, including the crew of four: Captain Joseph B. Smith, Chief Warrant Officer Three Kyran E. Kennedy, Staff Sergeant Paul Neff II, and Sergeant Scott C. Rose. Passengers Chief Warrant Officer Five Sharon T. Swartworth and Command Sergeant Major Cornell W. Gilmore I also died in the crash.

On November 11th, Veteran's Day, we attended a memorial ceremony held on the flight line at Q-West for the 5th Battalion crew killed in the shootdown. At that same time, in Mosul, a memorial service was held for Staff Sergeant Morgan D. Kennon of 3rd Battalion, 327th Infantry "Battle Force." 3-327 was assigned to 1st Brigade, but they served under Strike in Mosul. In that attack, insurgents had ambushed Staff Sergeant Kennon's convoy. Three other soldiers received horrible wounds. One soldier lost both legs, one lost his hand, and a third lost the use of his arm in the attack. Suddenly, it seemed that we were being ambushed at every street corner, and enemy attacks were becoming more and more effective.

That same week, we were informed that we would be returning to Iraq in 2005. We were not even home from the first deployment, and they told us when we would return. It was clear that Iraq was going to play a significant role in our lives. The 101st Airborne Division's next rendezvous with destiny would begin eighteen months after we redeployed to Fort Campbell. "I haven't told Lisa yet," I recorded in my journal on November 12th. "If I told her now, she would not handle it well." Lisa was pregnant with our fourth child. It was not lost on me that she would endure this pregnancy alone. Hopefully, I'd make it home for the birth and first year; then I'd leave again. She'd negotiate the terrible twos alone as well.

Three days later, November 15th, I flew to Mosul to conduct a day reconnaissance and security mission. It was a brisk, sunny morning. We flew sector to sector checking in on the radio with each battalion as we flew over their areas, searching for IEDs on the roads. As we flew north, on the east side of the river, we saw that traffic had stopped on the highway. A small crowd gathered around a vehicle. Quickly, we flew over to investigate the situation. We saw that a car had driven off the right side of the road. It appeared that the vehicle had simply veered off the road and come to a stop about twenty meters from the highway. We circled and came back in over the vehicle slow and low. From my vantage point, I could clearly see a man slumped over the steering wheel of the vehicle with blood covering his shirt. Bullet holes riddled the car. A young boy lay against the passenger door window, his shirt also blood-soaked.

We soon learned that a blue Opal had pulled up beside them on the highway and opened fire with machine guns. They swerved off the road, but not before the mayor of Mosul's interpreter and his young son were shot and killed. The men in the Opal also threw grenades at the car before speeding away. *Drive-by shootings and mobile ambushes! How do we stop this?* I silently wondered.

The sight of the man and his son killed together bothered me. We flew back to Q-West in silence, but the tragedy was not complete. Strike had decided to pair their ground quick reaction force with a Black Hawk from 9th Battalion, 101st Aviation, so that they could respond to attacks more quickly. Sending a team out to respond in vehicles took too much time, particularly in traffic. Putting them in a Black Hawk sped up their reaction time significantly. At 6:30 that very evening, the quick reaction force launched to investigate activity just north of Mosul airfield.

At the same time, a Black Hawk from 4th Battalion, 101st Aviation was flying from Tal Afar to Mosul airfield. The 9th Battalion helicopter was hovering when the team received small arms fire from the houses below. They were hovering on the approach path into Mosul airfield, blacked out (no lights), when they performed evasive maneuvers to avoid the gunfire. The 4th Battalion helicopter was on approach to the airfield, also blacked out. The two Black Hawks collided just north of the airfield and crashed onto Iraqi houses below.

Boomer Arnold was on a mission over Mosul when the crash occurred. He later filled us in on the details of the crash. Strike was notified immediately. Colonel Joe Anderson personally jumped in his Humvee and raced to the scene. He climbed onto houses and fought through the burning wreckage to rescue surviving troopers. "It was a horrible sight," he later told me. "One soldier was trapped in the Black Hawk, and it was burning. I thought we'd never get him out. We finally did, but he was badly burned. I'll never forget the horrific images of that night,"[1] Anderson said.

294

By the end of the evening, seventeen soldiers had perished in the crash. Six others were wounded. The night ended with a rocket attack on the oil refinery adjacent to Q-West.

On November 19th, the SCO and I flew to Mosul to attend two separate memorial services for the soldiers who died in the crash. The following day we flew to 1st Battalion, 320th Field Artillery Top Gun, to attend a memorial in honor of their fallen. It was Top Gun troopers who had served as the quick reaction force onboard the 9th Battalion Black Hawk. Tears ran down my face as I watched Major General Petraeus stand in front of the memorial and salute Sergeant Michael D. Acklin II of Louisville, Kentucky; Specialist Eugene A. Uhl III of Amherst, Wisconsin; Private First Class Damian L. Heidelberg of Batesville, Mississippi; Private First Class Richard W. Hafer of Cross Lanes, West Virginia; Private First Class Joey D. Whitener of Nebo, North Carolina; and Private First Class Sheldon R. Hawk Eagle, a twenty-one-year-old Sioux Indian from Eagle-Butte, South Dakota. Sergeant Acklin, just twenty-five years old, was the oldest of the six Top Gun men killed.

Six helmets rested on the butts of M4 rifles. Dog tags hung from the charging handle of the weapons, and a pair of brown combat boots sat in front of each rifle. A bouquet of yellow flowers bookended the memorial. A framed picture of each soldier hung behind the memorial. Most of the men smiled or posed for the picture, reminding us of the happiness they found in life and service. Petraeus approached the memorial alone. He stood rigidly at attention for a moment, then leaned over and placed a commander's coin by each pair of boots. He then returned to the position of attention and slowly brought his right hand up to the brim of his hat, rendering a salute to honor the fallen.

November brought more than a change in weather. A profoundly somber tone descended upon us. Suddenly, without consciously thinking about it, the idea of just getting out alive seemed to never stray far from my thoughts.

Four days later, two Kiowas from Annihilator Troop flew a route reconnaissance mission along highway two, which leads north from Mosul to Dahouk. It's a beautiful flight that passes by the Mosul Dam before continuing on to the far northern city of Dahouk, just south of the Turkish border.

Chief Warrant Officer Three Chris Lusker and Lieutenant Larry Marson flew lead in a team of two Kiowas that early morning. Their mission had begun under night vision goggles. They flew close to the ground to observe the road as carefully as possible. Multiple strands of high-tension wires crisscross the highway along their route. It was just beginning to grow pink on the eastern horizon, the time between night and day when the rods in the eyes are giving up the ghost and the cones are coming on shift for the day. Lusker told Marson, who was flying the aircraft at the time, that he was going to take his goggles off and see if it was bright enough to see with the naked eye. "I was sitting in the right seat, on the eastern side of the helicopter as we flew, so I figured it would be best if I checked the light,"[2] Lusker told me after the mission.

Marson continued flying north along the route as Lusker removed his goggles. "I looked to the east and saw that it was indeed getting light enough to take our goggles off. I only looked for a second, then turned back to tell Lieutenant Marson that it was time to take the goggles off, but I never got those words out of my mouth. Just as I turned my head back to the front, I saw a wire coming straight at us. The lieutenant seemed to see it at the same time as I did, but it was too late,"[3] Lusker said, shaking his head and looking at the ground, clearly still shaken from the event.

Fortunately, they were flying fast. That's the only thing that saved them. The wire struck just under the rotor system. The upper wire protection system caught the wire, but it was a multistrand cable, which is very difficult to cut with the protection system. As they flew forward, the wire began wrapping around the front of the helicopter. The wire protection system did not immediately cut the wire. It began cutting through the doorframe on Marson's side of the helicopter at a height almost even with his neck. Suddenly, the Plexiglas windscreen gave way, exploding on Marson's side of the cockpit. The only thing preventing the wire from continuing to cut through the helicopter was a sliver of doorframe that remained intact. If the wire cut through the doorframe, it would give way and instantly decapitate Marson. It lacked only a half inch before the protection system finally cut the wire.

Lusker, who had taken the flight controls as they struck the wire, was able to land the helicopter safely, but the aircraft was badly damaged.

Both men were visibly shaken up, but alive. It was the closest encounter with death we'd had thus far.

For the remainder of the morning, we coordinated with Battle Force, the northernmost battalion in Strike's area of operations. They assembled a recovery team, including a large flatbed truck with a crane and security team. Within only a few hours, they drove to the site, loaded the Kiowa onto the back of the truck, and hauled it back to Mosul. Thinking we had avoided disaster, we exhaled a deep breath in relief, but the day was only beginning.

Later that morning, Command Sergeant Major Jerry Wilson, the senior enlisted noncommissioned officer in Strike, and his driver, Specialist Rel A. Ravago IV, drove through the streets of Mosul. Enemy forces threw large rocks through the windshield, causing Ravago to wreck. The enemy then attacked Wilson and Ravago, killing them both.

Wilson was a towering, muscular African American man from Thomson, Georgia. Ravago was a tiny soldier from Glendale, California. I'd only met Wilson twice before he was killed, but both times I was struck by his presence and beaming personality. He was survived by two sons, a granddaughter, and his mother.

Specialist Rel Ravago also possessed a larger-'   -life personality, but he housed it in a small frame. Standing only five feet two inches tall, he looked out of place beside Command Sergeant Major Jerry Wilson—a somewhat comical contrast in soldiers—yet both were warriors in their own right. Their loss was felt throughout the 101st Airborne Division.

With Lusker and Marson safe, we felt relief, only to feel sick again when we received news of Wilson's and Ravago's deaths. No one in 2-17 CAV had much to say that evening. Attacks had increased tenfold, it seemed. I began to sense that everyone simply wanted to get home alive—to survive the deployment.

By late summer, Kellogg Brown & Root (KBR) had built a dining facility on Q-West. It was a welcome change from MREs and T-rations. They prepared a very nice Thanksgiving meal for our soldiers. November had been a challenging month. The weather had significantly increased the stress of flying. There were very few days with clear skies, but we felt obligated to continue our support over our brothers on the ground as long as weather permitted. They were constantly being attacked, and the casualty toll was quickly rising. There was much to be concerned about. It weighed heavily on us, but in the midst of darkness, I heard angels singing.

Fiji had provided a contingent of soldiers to guard a monetary facility across the airfield on Q-West. It was the heart of the money exchange program. In October, Iraqis began circulating the new Iraqi dinar. The old Iraqi currency was collected and subsequently destroyed as they put the new currency into circulation. Massive, muscular Fijian soldiers guarded the monetary exchange facility. The only time we saw them was at the dining facility. Otherwise, they quite convincingly stood guard across the runway. Their thin, dark skin covered muscle and sinew. Their appearance caused everyone to take notice. Each looked like he could be a starting back on the Fijian national rugby team.

On Thanksgiving Day, I walked into the large KBR festival tent that served as our dining facility, and I heard the most beautiful sound I can ever recall hearing in Iraq. About twenty Fijian men stood at the end of the tent singing Christmas carols a cappella. Their beautifully harmonic voices sent instant chills down my spine. I stood for several minutes enthralled. I rushed through the chow line and sat for an hour in front of them, listening intently and thinking of home. Christmas away from family made me homesick, but it seemed that Angels gave warmth to our souls at a very dark time in the deployment.

Ramadan ended on November 25, 2003, but the war had only just begun.

SHRAPNEL

By early December, my Atlanta Falcons had already lost ten out of their first twelve games, and it was clear that we would not make it home for Christmas. There were plenty of reasons for soldiers to hang their heads. We feared that our troopers' spirits might begin to plummet, but morale remained surprisingly high. In fact, we were extremely proud of our soldiers' attitudes, despite the open-ended deployment and challenging living conditions. Constant rainfall had turned Q-West into a pigsty. Mud persistently clung to our boots. We had no heat in our living areas because our generators could not handle the electricity load of space heaters, so at night we slept bundled up in our sleeping bags. Middle-of-the-night porta potty runs were torturous. When we woke, we quickly dressed and hustled to the command post, where we hugged the kerosene heater until we finally thawed out. Flying with our doors off was brutally painful. Since we deployed from the temperate state of Kentucky, we were not issued extreme cold weather flight gear, so pilots bought Smartwool long johns and layered up for missions.

On December 14, 2003, I was sitting at my desk reading and halfway listening to the television when the press conference began. Paul Bremer stepped to the microphone. Our corps commander, Lieutenant General Ricardo Sanchez, stood to his left in desert fatigues. Bremer placed his right hand on the front of the podium, licked his lips a couple of times, and then said, "Ladies and gentlemen, we got him."

The room exploded with cheers. "Boss!" I yelled. "You can finally get rid of PIR number one," I said.

Schiller's number one Priority Intelligence Requirement (PIR) had been *Where is Saddam Hussein?*

"How are we supposed to answer that PIR?" I had asked him on numerous occasions.

"I don't know but that's why we're here, so it will remain number one until it's answered," he'd replied.

Schiller walked into the room and stared at the television. "Where?" he asked.

"Just outside Tikrit. Fourth infantry division's area. Sounds like 1st Brigade, 4th Infantry Division and Task Force 121 got him. They rolled him up at about 8:00 last night."

"I'll be damned," he said and walked back to his desk.

Within forty-eight hours, a picture of Samir, an Iraqi interpreter working with Task Force 121, spread across Iraq. In the picture, he crouched over a handcuffed Saddam Hussein, who lay belly down on the wet, muddy ground. The man who had built elaborate palaces all over Iraq and ruled with an iron fist appeared feeble and unshaven. He'd been captured in a hole in the ground.

In the back of my mind, I kept wondering why we announced that *we* got him. Certainly, we did get him, but why not let our Iraqi partners own it from the start? An Iraqi should have made the announcement, not Paul Bremer.

On December 23rd, I woke around 6:00 a.m. to the sound of rustling in the room next door. "What are you doing, Doug?" I yelled.

Doug mumbled something back in a grunty voice. I could tell that he was bending over. "What are you doing?" I yelled again.

With that, I heard him drop what he was doing and walk to my door. He was almost out of breath. "I'm packing," he said.

"Why so early? And why so dern loud?" I asked with clear irritation.

"I'm getting ready to go on R&R," he said. "I leave in three days."

"Three days, Doug," I said, my face the only thing exposed out of the mummy bag. "That means you have the middle of today, tonight, tomorrow midday and afternoon to pack. But you choose now."

"I'm awake, and it's on my mind," he said. "That's when I do things. When they're on my mind."

"So, screw the rest of us?" I asked.

"It's time to get up anyway," he said, turning back toward his room.

Peeking out of my mummy bag, which was drawn tightly around my face, my frosty breath was visible in the dim gray light. Now fully awake, I quickly unzipped the bag, threw some pants on, laced up my boots, and pulled my black fleece jacket over my shoulders. Blinking like a man coming out of a cave into bright light, I rushed to the command post to warm up. Ken was already there.

As I walked through the door, he raised his cup of coffee and nodded. "Morning," he said.

"Morning, roommate," I replied. "Funny how you can get up, get dressed, and depart the room without waking me, but Doug will wake the whole dang building packing his underwear."

"Yep. That's Doug. Our Dougie," he said.

Ken was planning a mission that he and Schiller would fly later that morning.

The TOC was filled with pogey bait, as we called it. Christmas care packages had been arriving by the truckload. Churches, families, and friends demonstrated their support for the troops by sending boxes packed with baby wipes, candies, designer coffee, chips, beef jerky, and hot chocolate. They also sent touching letters, sincere messages of love and support. It was evident that while some Americans vocally opposed our presence in Iraq, their support for the soldiers was unwavering. Furthermore, I was convinced that the American people had not forgotten how we received Vietnam veterans home and vowed that our experience would not mirror theirs.

I poured cocoa powder into a cup of piping hot water and stood with my back to the kerosene heater while Captain Bob Jenkins gave me a quick rundown of the night's activities. All in all, it had been a quiet evening. When he finished, I went to my desk and read the intelligence reports, then thumbed through the daily Fragmentary Order (FRAGO) to see if we'd received any taskings from brigade headquarters. I wanted to go for a run, but I planned to wait for the sun to warm things up a bit first.

Running had become dirty business. Due to the mud and slop, I'd return from each run covered in a brown soupy mess. Nevertheless, I loved getting out and clearing my head on a run. By noon, it had warmed up significantly, so I dressed and departed the command post for a six miler. I ran the perimeter road, which was perfect since very few vehicles used it, but I often encountered a pack of dogs that gave me pause. On several occasions, we came under rocket attack while I was out running, which also concerned me. There really wasn't a place on the perimeter to seek cover during an attack. The terrain was flat and wide open. Once, when I was out running, I heard the distinct sound of rockets launching in the distance. It was a muffled explosion and a *whoosh*, somewhat like roman candles launching into the air—a sound I will never forget. Frantically, I searched for a place to seek cover, to no avail. It is a chilling feeling when you hear the launch and know that rockets are on their way but have no idea where they will land. The anticipation is nerve-racking. I thought, *What if I am hit out here? How long until they miss me? Will it blow me up or just wound me? Which would be worse? I guess that depends on if you live or die, stupid.*

Then I wondered what my death would mean for those still living. What would Lisa do when they pulled up at our home and knocked at the door in their dress uniforms? She knew the routine. What would life be like for them with me not in it? My thoughts began to hurt, so I focused on *not* thinking, only running.

I had been lucky that day. Five or six rockets had landed on the far end of the runway, well away from me; nevertheless, I had run a sub-five-minute mile on the way back to the TOC.

On December 23rd, I ran three miles out and back. When I returned, I saw that the SCO's vehicle, which he always combat-parked beside the building, was gone. (To "combat park" is to back in, so that you can quickly evacuate should the need arise.) Most commanders do not drive a vehicle. They are driven. Schiller had a driver, but his job was to service the vehicle and ensure that the radios worked properly. Schiller drove himself. "Never give up the keys to your escape pod," he would counsel. With this in mind, I assumed that he and Ken Hawley had already driven to the flight line to preflight their helicopters in preparation for their mission.

I stretched for a few minutes in front of our building, kicked the mud off my shoes, and then turned to walk into the TOC. I was reaching for the door when I heard the distinct sound of a rocket exploding. I had not heard the launch, so it caught me by surprise. It sounded like the rocket had hit near the flight line, on the south end of the runway, where Schiller always parked his helicopter.

I quickly stepped inside the command post. "Where did it land?" I asked the battle captain.

"Don't know yet, sir. No one has called on the radio. I think there were three or four rockets," he replied.

We all stood there waiting for someone to call in a report over the radio. Everyone took cover when rockets or mortars landed on the forward operating base (FOB). As soon as feasible, those who witnessed the impacts would call their higher headquarters with an initial damage report. They would report the location of the impacts and whether anyone or anything had been damaged. It was kind of like watching lightning strike. If it looked like it hit close to a highly populated area, you held your breath and prayed until someone confirmed that no one was hurt.

Finally, the radio cackled to life. "Saber TOC, the SCO has been hit! Send the doc to the flight line."

Death could not have been quieter than it was in the TOC for the next few seconds. It was as if God hit the pause button. We froze in place, trying to process what we'd just heard. I felt like lightning had struck my chest and was burning a hole through me.

"Go get the doc!" I ordered a soldier. "I'll pull my vehicle around front," and I ran out of the building.

The doc's makeshift clinic was right around the corner of the TOC. I pulled the Humvee up in front and sat anxiously idling. Doug Ford jumped in the truck with me and, within seconds, Captain Brian Meece, our "doc," burst through the doorway with his medical kit slung over his shoulder. He dove into the truck, and I stomped the gas.

No one said a word on the way to the flight line, yet each of us silently carried on an internal conversation.

It's probably just a flesh wound, I told myself. *It just scared everyone on the flight line who saw their commander bleeding a little bit.*

That rationalization worked for a minute; then the other, more pessimistic guy inside my head spoke. *What if he's fatally wounded? Do you really want to see this? What will happen if we lose the SCO?*

The pain of that thought was too much at the moment. I shook my head to try and rattle the image loose, like clearing an Etch A Sketch. *Stop thinking the worst,* I told myself.

As I turned the corner onto the flight line, I saw a small group of soldiers huddled around someone lying on the ground. He was on his back. I began carefully processing what I saw, praying it wasn't him—yet I recognized the boots, the one-piece brown flight suit, and the brown wool shirt, all of which confirmed that it was him. Yet, I still didn't want to believe it. All the way to the airfield, I had held on to the hope that the report was a mistake, that he really hadn't been hit.

I stopped the truck just behind the crowd, and we all jumped out. An ever-calm Ken Hawley was giving directions to everyone.

"It's just a slash wound," Hawley told Schiller. "You'll be fine."

"Bullshit," Schiller mumbled. "I feel like someone hit me with a base-ball bat."[1]

Those words sounded good—*slash wound*. That's just a cut. "Where did the rocket land?" I asked, not wanting to talk about his wound.

"We were preflighting the aircraft when it exploded," Ken said. "It hit just off the nose of the helicopter."

An excited crew chief, Sergeant Pletcher, broke in. "I was standing at the tail of the aircraft when it hit. The SCO was looking at the engine. He had the engine cowling in his hand when it landed. After the dust settled, he turned and looked directly at me, and said, 'I think I'm hit.' Then he turned and tried to take a step but fell down."

Finally, I forced myself to look at him, to see the wound for myself. Having sprinted to Schiller after I'd stopped the truck, Doc was now inspecting him from head to toe. Schiller was ghostly white, clearly fading into shock. "You okay, boss?" I asked.

"Hurts like hell," he said in a faint voice. If he was not in shock, he was knocking on the door.

A piece of shrapnel had hit him in the hip flexor, right where the heel of your right hand would rest if you put it in your pocket. I looked into the wound, and to my surprise there was very little blood. The shrapnel had torn into his flesh and cut a massive hole. I could see deep into his torso. It appeared that the hot metal had cauterized the flesh as it cut into him, leaving a gaping hole that was yet to start flowing blood.

I wasn't sure how worried I should be. It looked clean, but it was a gaping hole. Being able to see so deep into his body concerned me.

"I can't get the ambulance on the radio," one of the soldiers yelled out in frustration.

"Get a Hummer," Ken told a sergeant. "We'll drive him to the aid station."[2]

A sergeant jumped into a cargo Humvee and pulled it up beside Schiller. "Be easy, now. Let's keep him as straight as possible when we lift him," Doc directed.

I started to reach for him but was instantly crowded out. So many soldiers had reached for him that there was no room left. Everyone wanted to help as quickly as possible. The soldiers gently grasped him and prepared to lift. He was in a lot of pain, but he had been relatively quiet up to that point. He grunted from time to time, but never cried out in pain, until they picked him up.

As the men lifted him off the ground, he bent slightly at the waist.

"AAARGH!" he yelled.

It was tough to know just how deep the shrapnel had cut into him. I wasn't sure if it had cut clean through to his spine or it was lying deep inside his abdomen somewhere. Doc had asked him if he could feel his legs, and he could. He moved his feet, so that was a good sign. Still, he had a huge hole in his hip, and that did not look good to me.

With Doc holding pressure on the wound, the men drove him to the 426th Brigade Support Battalion's (BSB) medical aid station. I stood numb on the flight line staring at the Humvee as they drove away. The thought that I might never see him again entered my mind and, as I considered that possibility, it was as though a searing icepick stabbed me in the chest. I tried to clear the Etch A Sketch again, but I couldn't. My chest was on fire. Recognizing that I was needed in the TOC, I turned and headed for my own truck. Everyone who had not been on the flight line would want an update from someone who had actually seen him.

Lieutenant Colonel Jeff Kelley commanded the 426th BSB. A colorful character who was never at a loss for words, Jeff Kelley had become close friends with Schiller. Kelley could lighten almost any situation with humor, and that's just what he did when Schiller arrived.

Kelley later related the story from his perspective. "I was in my TOC when my folks told me that 2-17 CAV had a casualty. When the truck pulled up, I ran out to do what I could to help. I thought it was a joke at first. I saw him and thought, *That's the mighty gunslinger—no way in hell is Steve Schiller injured.* But sure as shit he was," Kelley said. "I feared the worst because he was bleeding badly when he arrived."[3]

While the scorching-hot metal had cauterized his flesh initially, once we moved him, the wound began to pour blood. He lost a lot of blood during the ride to the aid station.

"I didn't want my young medics to get nervous just because a squadron commander was on the table, so I tried to lighten the mood," Kelley said. "My wife had sent me a digital camera, so I started taking pictures of his wound. The gash was pretty close to his hip, so I told him he'd never live down getting hit in the ass. Steve had a Forrest Gump wound. It seemed to lighten the mood a little, but he was in a lot of pain."

As soon as Schiller had fallen to the ground beside the helicopter, he had told the crew chief to retrieve the first aid kit from the helicopter. Before everyone had gathered around Schiller, trying to help, the crew chief had caught a quick glimpse of the wound and realized it was bad. He had put bandages over the hole and applied pressure.[4]

Kelley's doc removed the dressing and cleaned the wound, and was considering sewing him up, but decided to take an X-ray just to make sure there were no metal fragments left in his body. It's a good thing he did because what he found was alarming. The X-ray revealed a large piece of shrapnel lying directly on Schiller's femoral artery.

"We need to get him to the hospital in Mosul quickly," the doc said.

"The medevac is ready to go," Kelley replied.

The medevac helicopters were assigned to the 426 BSB, so Jeff Kelley's battle captain had already told the medevac pilots to have the helicopter cranked and ready. Kelley remained at his side as they drove Schiller to the medevac bird and then helped load him into the Black Hawk. Jeff Kelley leaned in and shouted over the roar of the turbine engines, "Hell, Steve, if you wanted to ride in my helicopter, all you had to do was ask. You didn't have to go and get yourself injured just to ride."[5]

Though in pain, Schiller stopped grimacing long enough to smile, and the Black Hawk departed toward Mosul. Twenty-five minutes later, they landed at the south end of Mosul airfield, on the medevac pad. Like a scene from M*A*S*H, a team of medics rushed the helicopter to retrieve their patient. They carried him inside to prep for surgery. As Steve lay there on the table, someone handed him a satellite phone. It was two days until Christmas. Back home, Rhonda and the kids were preparing to drive to St. Joseph, Missouri, to spend the holidays with family. The phone rang and rang. Steve was about to hang up. *I'm about to go into surgery, and I'm not going to be able to tell Rhonda what happened*, he thought to himself.[6]

"Hello," Rhonda finally answered.

Relieved at the sound of her voice, Steve explained that a 107mm rocket had hit him. He told her that he was okay, but that he was about to undergo surgery. Steve had not received any medication until he arrived at the hospital, so he was coherent enough to explain. Once they rolled him into the operating room, they administered morphine. As he spoke to Rhonda, trying to assure her that he was going to be fine, the morphine made its way down the IV line and into his bloodstream. "I'll be fine," he assured her. "Don't worry." The pain was washed away. They took the phone and surgery began.[7]

Meanwhile, having been notified that his cavalry commander had been seriously wounded, General David Petraeus made his way to the hospital. Steve was groggy but awake when Petraeus entered the tent and made eye contact. "How's my Sam Damon?" Petraeus asked as he crossed the tent.

"It was all I could do to hold back the tears," Schiller later told me. "It was the greatest compliment I've ever received."

Since its writing in 1968, Anton Myrer's *Once an Eagle* has been a staple on almost every officer's bookshelf. The war novel follows the careers of two officers as they rise through the ranks. Courtney Massengale serves primarily in staff positions. Throughout his career, Massengale astutely plays politics and will do whatever to whomever to advance his own career. Sam Damon, on the other hand, is a field soldier, an honorable man who always puts his soldiers first.

To be referred to as a "Courtney Massengale" says volumes about an officer's self-centeredness and lack of character. To be called "Sam Damon" is the greatest of compliments.

Petraeus walked to Schiller's side, leaned down, and pinned a Purple Heart on his T-shirt. "Don't let them send me to Landstuhl, sir," Schiller pleaded with Petraeus.

Landstuhl Regional Medical Center was in Germany. Wounded soldiers unable to return to duty were evacuated there.

"We'll see, Steve. Let's let the doctors make the call," Petraeus said.

Schiller felt powerless with the doctors. He knew that if anyone had the power to keep him in Iraq with his troopers, it was Petraeus. If he was evacuated out of Iraq, most likely another lieutenant colonel would replace him as the 2-17 CAV commander. He didn't want to give up command like that.

Wisely, Petraeus did not commit either way. He decided to leave the decision in the hands of the medical professionals. That meant Schiller would have to find a way to convince the doctors that he could remain in Iraq and recover.

The mood was somber back at Q-West. There was so much uncertainty. Schiller's surgery was a success. We knew he would recover, but we did not want to lose him. He was our SCO.

Two days after the surgery, I planned to fly up to Mosul and visit Schiller. As I exited the TOC that morning, I saw a large formation of soldiers. A sergeant stood in front of them barking out instructions. It was a group going home for R&R, and among them were Slifko and Doug. Seeing me exit the TOC, Doug approached me and spoke in a low tone so as not to disturb the sergeant's briefing. "We're riding to Mosul in the back of a truck," he said. "Do you believe that shit?"

"You have to go to Mosul to catch the airplane to Kuwait, Doug," I said. "How did you expect to get there?"

"We're an aviation outfit, right?" he said. "Hell, I see a lot of Chinooks flying around. Why not one of them?"

"I suppose they are all tasked out for other missions, Doug."

Doug rolled his eyes. "I don't think half these soldiers understand how dangerous this trip is to Mosul."

"Yeah, a truck was hit a few weeks back going up there for R&R," I said. "I think a female took shrapnel to the butt."

"We might not be so lucky. The SCO was almost killed two days ago. If you lost me and Slifko, this unit would go to hell," he said, trying to lighten his genuinely grave demeanor.

"You guys will be fine, Doug," I said. "Have fun at home. I'm headed up to Mosul to see the boss."

"Be safe," he said and extended his hand.[8]

I grasped his hand, then pulled him in tight for a man hug. He slapped me on the back, and I departed for the flight line.

Visiting the sick has always been an uncomfortable experience for me. I feel awkward, never knowing quite what to say, but somehow this visit was different. The SCO wasn't sick per se. He was injured. Knowing Schiller, I figured he'd be mad, eager to know if we'd found and killed those who had tried to kill him.

The flight to Mosul took just over thirty minutes. We landed to the medical evacuation pads, then hovered over to a corner and shut down, being sure to leave room for a medevac bird to land.

The hospital was nothing more than several large army tents lashed together over a built-up wooden floor. I had to wade through ankle deep water and muck, a brown soup, just to get from the helicopter pad to the door. In that environment, the doctors feared infection more than anything else, but it was early in the war, so even the hospitals were primitive. I cleared my head and parted the tent flaps to enter.

Schiller was lying on his back with his eyes closed when I walked in, but he slowly opened them when he heard me approaching his bed. He was pale. "Hey, boss," I said. "How you doing?"

"Not bad, considering," he said.

He lay on a hospital cot with a green, wool army blanket draped over him. The cot was raised slightly at the head. A single Christmas stocking, a red boot with white fuzzy fur at the top, hung from the tent liner above his head. His bloodstained brown wool shirt lay across his waist. He had a typical hospital band on his right wrist and an IV in his left arm. His rings had been removed.

Seeing how groggy he was, I assumed he was doped up with narcotics, but he wasn't. He grimaced as he raised up on his left elbow. "Can you believe I'm in here with these assholes?" he said, and I instantly felt better. He was going to be okay.

Schiller was angrily referring to three Iraqi men who had been wounded as they were detained by US forces. A military policeman stood behind their beds watching them.

"These guys nearly kill me, and I have to recover in here with them. That's bullshit," he said.

They were not the men who had shot the rockets at him, of course, but they were Iraqis and they had guards watching over them—bad guys, in his mind. I thought Schiller had a valid complaint; nevertheless, there they lay.

"All they do is lie there whining and complaining, expecting to be waited on hand and foot by our folks," he said, genuinely pissed off.

Hating on lazy men, enemy or otherwise, did not bother Schiller's Catholic soul. After all, slothfulness was a sin.

"How are you feeling?" I asked.

"Sore as hell," he said.

"I bet you are."

"Plan on coming to get me in a few days," he said. "You need to get Doc up here, so they can show him how to keep the wound drained and dress it."

"You're kidding," I said, amazed. "They are going to let you stay in Iraq?"

"Hell no, I'm not kidding," he said. "I'm not going home. Just get Doc up here so they can train him up."

"Doug and Slifko left for R&R this morning," I said. "Why don't you just go on R&R? You could rest up and then come back."

"I am not going on R&R when not all of my soldiers have been able to go," he said stubbornly. "I'll leave this country when we redeploy."

I knew it was pointless to argue with him. If the docs did not medevac him, then he would not leave. "Okay, sir," I replied.

I had bought a small digital camera before deploying. As I prepared to leave, I remembered that it was in my cargo pocket. I pulled it out and took aim at Schiller.

"Smile for me, boss," I said.

He looked up at me, saw that I was pointing a camera at him, and shot me the bird.

"Got it," I said.

We tried to make Christmas as merry as possible, but I'll admit, it was difficult. Schiller was injured, the weather sucked, and the enemy situation was getting worse. Our living conditions were pitiful at best, and we were not with our families. There was plenty to complain about, but I was among some of the finest men and women with whom I'd ever served. In hindsight, I guess I should have been more thankful.

2-17 CAV was assigned the only Catholic chaplain in northern Iraq. Every Sunday, our staff aviators racked up flying hours by shuttling him from outpost to outpost, so that he could provide services for Catholics spread throughout northern Iraq. On Christmas Day, I flew the chaplain to the hospital to give Schiller communion. By then, Schiller was more than ready to return to Q-West, and I could sense that the doctors were about ready to release him. He was no trouble for them. In fact, he was quite helpful, but he wanted to return to his soldiers and he persistently reminded the doctors that he was fit to return to duty.

While the chaplain was at the hospital, spending time with the SCO, I flew to another base in Mosul and picked up Lieutenant Kate Johnson's husband. First Lieutenant Kate Johnson was our signal officer. A petite redhead, Kate led by example in literally everything. Her soldiers, the majority of whom were male, absolutely loved her. A soldier with her energy is rare, which could have had something to do with her caffeine and nicotine consumption, but regardless, she rarely stopped working. I seldom saw her without a cup of coffee and cigarette in her hand. Kate's fatigues were always oil and dirt stained; grease was lodged under her fingernails. If you could not find Kate, the best place to look for her was wherever work was being done. If her soldiers were changing the oil in one of their trucks, you'd see Kate's feet sticking out from under the vehicle. She shared in, or led, every task her soldiers were required to accomplish. When Kate did run low on energy, she would simply sit down, close her eyes, and instantly go to sleep. It was not uncommon to find her balled up in the corner of a room on top of some gear, taking a power nap.

Kate's husband was an infantry officer in Strike, so I picked him up in a Kiowa and flew him back to Q-West to spend Christmas with Kate, and apparently ruined him for the infantry in the process. In the years that followed, he resigned his commission and became a warrant officer and Kiowa pilot.

After dropping him off at Q-West, I flew single pilot back up to the hospital, retrieved the chaplain, and returned to Q-West. That evening, I called home for the first time in about a month. The phone died during the call, but not before I heard everyone's voice. As I was walking back to the TOC, enemy rockets began to rain down on Q-West. I counted twenty-nine impacts. *Merry Christmas to you as well*, I thought.

A few days later, we flew our physician's assistant, Captain Brian Meece, up to Mosul in a Kiowa. The doctors at the hospital instructed him on how to care for Schiller's wound. Because the spinning shrapnel had torn away so much flesh inside Schiller's hip, the surgeon had removed the steel, cleaned the wound, and sewn him up, but he had left a drain tube in place. It would take time for the wound to heal on the inside. In the meantime, the tube had to be cleaned and the bandages changed twice daily.

On December 31st, I flew a Kiowa to Mosul single pilot to bring the SCO home. He was stiff and sore, but I managed to fold him into the Kiowa and fly him back to Q-West. I landed right outside the TOC, where a large group of soldiers had gathered to welcome him home. Schiller gingerly exited the Kiowa, and the soldiers immediately gathered around him to shake his hand and welcome him home. He was a rock star.

I was particularly happy to have him back because it had grown quiet around the headquarters. With Doug and Slifko gone and the SCO in the hospital, the gray, dreary days had grown long and depressing. January crawled by at a snail's pace.

WEATHER

Because Ken Hawley had fought his way from Kuwait to Mosul in a truck during the invasion, it was only fair that he be allowed to fly back to Kuwait in a helicopter, so I planned to lead the ground convoys back south in my Humvee. Along the way, Ken and the SCO, who continued to slowly heal, would help protect our movement from the air. The drive from Q-West to Kuwait would take three days and would force us to drive through several areas that had become extremely dangerous. With the end in sight, reflection came naturally.

It had been an incredible year, during which I had learned more than I could have imagined. I had experienced many new things. The rollercoaster of emotions we experienced and the harsh combat environment in which we lived had caused us to grow exceedingly close to one another. A brotherhood had formed. The bonds we had forged were much stronger than those I had experienced in previous units. Living that close, suffering together, fighting together, sharing our deepest thoughts and feelings had built extraordinary friendships. Truth be known, I didn't want to give that up. I had begun to realize that once we returned to Fort Campbell, each of us would move on to our next job, our next chapter in life. Slowly, as each soldier departed the unit, the face of 2-17 CAV would transform. Even among those who remained, the conversations would change. Once again, the shields would go up to protect our sensitivities. Things previously shared with fellow soldiers would no longer crack the surface of conversation in the cockpit.

I was jealous of the relationships I had formed. I treasured them, yet those feelings seemed silly to me. I had a young family to return to. And so, I grew somewhat ashamed that a significant part of me did not want to leave Iraq. How was that possible? We were constantly in grave danger, with the risks to our lives increasing daily. Nevertheless, a part of me wanted to stay. Not knowing what to do with those emotions, I compartmentalized them for the time being and focused on the mission at hand, driving to Kuwait.

We had packed the vast majority of our gear into trucks and containers. 3-17 Cavalry had established their TOC in the building where our brigade headquarters had been set up. They did not plan to use our headquarters building, so we had reduced our footprint to the bare necessities required to command and control the aerial teams in the closing days of our deployment. 3-17 Cavalry was already conducting the majority of the missions independently by that point.

I was scheduled to fly my final flight in Iraq on January 23rd, with Chief Warrant Officer Four Joe Nestor. Joe was the 3-17 CAV Standardization Instructor Pilot, their senior flight instructor. He and I had flown several missions together since his arrival. Prior to that, I had known Joe by reputation only; nonetheless, I had gotten to know him quite well in the skies over northern Iraq. Pilots seem to learn more about one another while flying than at any other time. There is something about the cockpit, flying side-by-side and communicating through the intercom system, that causes us to open up to one another. We share a side of ourselves that would otherwise never see the light of day. I thoroughly enjoyed flying with and getting to know Joe. *3-17 Cavalry is blessed to have him*, I thought to myself.

The weather did not look favorable for my last flight. Thick, gray clouds blanketed the sky over northern Iraq. Nevertheless, Joe and I planned to give it a try. We departed Q-West at 5:30 p.m. Being winter, it was already dark when we took off. Slowly, we made our way north through the bitter-cold January air. After approximately ten kilometers, we turned slightly west to parallel Highway 1. Seeing car lights, strung out like a long strand of Christmas lights on the highway, made it much easier to navigate on dark, foggy nights. I was extremely careful to make sure that we did not push the weather beyond our ability to see. A few weeks prior, I had exceeded my comfort level, and I had no desire to repeat that experience.

On that night, I had flown with Warrant Officer One Rob Minton. Rob had reported to the squadron fresh out of flight school. Chief Warrant Officer Three Lou Papesca, the Condor Troop Instructor Pilot, had completed Rob's flight progression and subsequently turned him loose to fly missions with the other pilots. Rob and I were flying lead for the SCO. The weather had been horrible—low clouds, fog, and rain—for weeks. Bad weather had made it difficult for us to fly to Mosul, yet once there, the weather over Mosul was significantly better.

Rob and I departed Q-West just after dark that night. A few miles north of the airfield, a large tower stood over two hundred feet tall. Unlike in the US, where the Federal Aviation Administration (FAA) requires towers exceeding two hundred feet above the ground to be lit with a blinking red light, Iraqi towers were not lit. From the time we broke contact with the ground at Q-West, locating that tower was my number-one priority. The fog was thick, a layer of clouds blocked the moon, and a light mist filled the air. I flipped our infrared spotlight on to see if it would help. The light reflected off the moisture in the air, turning my night vision goggles bright white. Blinded with the sudden flash of light, I flinched and quickly turned the light off with a grimace.

"Use the Mast Mounted Sight [MMS]," I instructed Rob. "Find that dang tower. It should be to our front left."

"Roger, I'm searching," he said.

Several tense and stressful minutes passed. Since becoming an army aviator, I had noted that more helicopters had crashed due to pushing bad weather and flying into wires than anything else. I did not like the odds of having both of those factors stacked against me at once. Wire strikes are unforgiving, almost always resulting in fatalities.

"Got it!" Rob said, clearly relieved.

I glanced over at the multifunctional display in front of him. I could see the white-hot outline of the tower on the screen. "Okay, just stay on it. I am going to climb a little, and we'll pass to the right of the tower," I told him.

"The tower is to our ten o'clock position, five hundred meters," I told Schiller over our team internal radio.

"Tally," Schiller replied, indicating that he had the tower in sight as well.

I was completely focused on scanning to our front and cross-checking the instruments. As we passed the tower, the terrain began to gently rise. There were no houses for several miles after that, which meant no porch lights to assist our navigation. It's amazing how much comfort a single porch light provides a pilot flying in utter darkness. From the tower, north for about ten miles was the darkest stretch of terrain between Q-West and Mosul. We had memorized where the wires crossed our flight path, so we could anticipate them.

"Seven-six grid line," a pilot would call out as we flew north. "One kilometer until the wires."

"Roger. One kilometer until the wires. Searching," would come the reply. It was a routine we repeated every flight day and night, no matter how many times we'd flown it.

We also used the radar altimeter to monitor our height above the ground; still, it was stressful flying into utter darkness. As Rob and I passed the tower, the sight's picture, displayed on the screen in front of him, turned grainy and dark, somewhat like static on an old television set in the days before twenty-four-hour broadcasting. All I could see was grainy monochromatic green through my night vision goggles. I sped up my scan to ensure that I was flying the right azimuth and that I was not descending toward the earth. My eyes darted from the altitude indicator to the radar altimeter, then back out in front of the helicopter into the darkness. *This is crazy*, I thought to myself.

"I can't see crap," I told Rob.

"Me neither, sir," he responded.

I called Schiller on the radio. "Hey, sir, I've reached my comfort level here. I can't see."

"You want to go over to Highway 1 and follow it north?" he asked.

My gut told me *no*. I wanted to turn around. "Okay. We'll give it a try," I said.

"Okay," he replied.

"Keep the sight out in front of us," I told Rob. "Keep scanning."

I flew slightly west and headed directly toward Highway 1.

"I see the road," Rob said, after a minute or so.

I saw it for a second through my goggles, then it disappeared, then I saw it, and then it was gone again.

"This sucks!" I exclaimed to Rob. "We're going home."

"Saber Six, we're turning back. I can't see, and I'm uncomfortable," I transmitted.

"Roger that. No issue. We're right behind you," he said.

I began a slow left turn to the south.

"Okay, find that friggin' tower again. We'll keep it to our left as we pass this time," I told Rob.

He began searching for the tower again but could not find it. My heart was pounding at that point. The guy-wires attached to the tower extended over one hundred meters away from the tower itself. I did not want to hit a tower or the wires. *Please, Lord, let us find the tower. Help us get this thing back on the ground safely*, I prayed.

"It's out my door right now!" Rob said, as we passed the tower, having not seen it until we were abreast of it.

"Okay, the airfield should be at our ten o'clock," I said, but despite a multitude of lights on Q-West, we could not see it. *How can we not see the airfield?* I thought to myself. *There are lights all over Q-West.* We continued flying blindly in the direction of the airfield until, finally, out of nowhere, I saw the faint glow of light and a sweet feeling of relief came over me. It was the two silos that the Iraqis had erected on the northwest end of Q-West. We were well off course, but now at least we had a landmark and we could see well enough to find our way to the flight line. We slowly flew to our parking pad at no more than twenty-five feet above the ground. I landed and thanked God to be alive; then I vowed never to scare myself that badly again.

So, on the night of January 23rd, my final flight in Iraq, I was overly cautious. The visibility was decent—good enough to continue toward Mosul—until we reached the nine-six grid line. At that point, the terrain rose until it met a ceiling of clouds.

"That's it. Let's head back," I called to our lead aircraft.

"Roger that," he replied and began a slow turn back to the south.

Ten minutes later, we landed at Q-West and shut down the helicopters. Chief Warrant Officer Four Daniel Hauf had watched us land. Dan was a small man with a dark black mustache. He was the Ban'shee Troop instructor pilot, whom the guys jokingly called "Angry Dan" because he did not smile easily and had a keen eye for even the smallest of deficiencies.

Dan was the air mission commander of the team that was scheduled to replace us in Mosul at the end of our flight period. Since our flight had been delayed due to weather, Dan's team was already preparing for their mission window. Once our rotors stopped turning, Dan approached me.

"Weather turn to crap?" he asked.

"It wasn't bad until the nine-six grid line," I said. "There was a wall there; visibility went down quickly."

"Mosul is clear," he said. "We've been talking to the air force weatherman. He says the weather will continue to improve between here and Mosul. It should be good in a couple of hours. We'll give it a little while, then see what it looks like in a couple of hours. Worst case, we'll launch and turn around and come back if it gets bad."[1]

"Sounds good," I said and gathered my gear.

Dan was flying with Chief Warrant Officer Two Aaron Teichner from 3-17 Cavalry. Dan and Aaron were flying lead, and Chief Warrant Officer Two Mike Blaise was flying trail with Chief Warrant Officer Two Brian Hazelgrove, another 3-17 pilot.

Captain Adam Frederick, the Ban'shee Troop commander, was supposed to fly with Hazelgrove that evening, but Ken Hawley had scheduled a command and staff meeting, which he needed all troop commanders to attend. Adam asked Mike Blaise to take his place on the mission, which Mike was happy to do.[2]

Mike's wife, Captain Kate Blaise, was scheduled for her last duty shift as battle captain in the 426th BSB TOC that evening anyway, so they wouldn't be able to spend their last night on Q-West together. Kate was supposed to drive south to Kuwait with her unit the following morning.

That morning Major Kirk Whitson, the 426th BSB executive officer, had asked Kate and Mike to play cards with him, Lieutenant Colonel Jeff Kelley, and Command Sergeant Major Stokes that evening. He told Kate she could play cards and still be on duty in the TOC. If she was needed, someone would come and get her. Kate agreed, then drove over to our area to see Mike.

Mike was sleeping when she arrived, which surprised her since he was not scheduled to fly. He rolled over in his cot and told her he was going to fly in Captain Frederick's spot on a mission that night. He needed to get a few more hours of sleep. They agreed to meet later for lunch.[3]

Every time I saw Mike Blaise, I was fondly reminded of our missions running around in the wadis of Anbar Province in August, searching for caches. That was one of the more exciting and memorable missions of the deployment for me. Searching for and finding caches of weapons had reminded me of Easter egg hunts during my childhood.

Like Mike Blaise, Brian Hazelgrove was married to another soldier. Ironically, Brian had met his wife, Kimberly, at Fort Campbell, where they both served in the 311th Military Intelligence Battalion. In 1996, Kimberly had gone out with girlfriends for an evening of fun in Clarksville. They'd gone to the Blackhorse Pub & Brewery for drinks, then decided to go dancing at a local country club. "I was slow dancing with another guy when I noticed him,"[4] Kimberly later told me. "I saw a very heavy girl ask him to dance, and he said yes. Strangely, that attracted me to him. He was a good-looking guy. He could have probably danced with anyone he wanted to, but he did not hurt that lady's feelings by saying no just because she was overweight."

As soon as the first song ended and the next one began, Kimberly had asked if she could cut in. "We were inseparable from that moment on," she said.

Brian and Kimberly married in 1999. By that time, Brian was a staff sergeant and Kimberly was a sergeant. "He called me a cherry just to remind me that he outranked me," she told me, laughing.

They bought a home in Clarksville, Tennessee, and within a year, Kimberly was pregnant with their first child, Brandon. In 2000, Brian applied for and was accepted to attend Warrant Officer Candidate School and flight school. Brian was still learning to fly at Fort Rucker when the attacks of September 11, 2001, occurred. Kimberly had to deploy immediately, so her father kept Brandon until Brian finished his training. Upon returning from her deployment, Kimberly, Brian, and Brandon moved to Fort Drum, New York, to the 10th Mountain Division, for their next assignment. Brandon was two years old by then, and due to military schooling and Kimberly's deployment, it was the first time the three of them had all lived together since Brandon was four months old.

Kimberly's sister was also in the army. She had to deploy to Iraq, so her three-year-old son moved in with Brian and Kimberly. In June 2003, Kimberly gave birth to their second child, Katelyn. When Brian deployed to Iraq in November of that year with 3-17 CAV, Katelyn was seven months old and Brandon had just turned three. Kimberly was left at home with three children under the age of four, a dog, and her military duties, and she voluntarily served as the Family Support Group leader in Brian's unit. It was tough on a young mother. Kimberly certainly had a lot on her plate, but she loved her career and her family, and she was a strong woman.

After speaking with Dan Hauf about the weather that evening at my helicopter, I drove back to the headquarters building, put my gear in my room, and walked to the TOC.

"Weathered out?" Schiller asked as I walked through the door.

"Yes sir. Weather was okay until the nine-six. Then it went to crap," I said. "I spoke with Dan Hauf down on the flight line. He said Mosul is clear and it's supposed to continue improving between here and there. They should be able to get up there later on this evening."

I went back to my room and changed into my winter physical training uniform, then returned to the TOC. Schiller and Hawley were walking out as I approached the door.

"Heading to your briefing?" I asked.

"Yeah. See you in an hour or so," Schiller said, as he and Hawley walked down the steps in front of the TOC.

From my desk, I could hear the radios in the TOC, which was right around the corner. Aviators grow accustomed to listening to multiple radios simultaneously. A team of helicopters has an internal frequency to talk to one another. We flight follow and speak with air traffic control on another radio. We speak with ground forces on yet another radio. And we usually monitor the higher headquarters radio net on yet another frequency. Sometimes all four radios are filled with chatter, particularly during a firefight. Pilots learn to hear and understand all the radios at once. It becomes somewhat easier over time, because pilots learn that each radio—UHF, VHF, FM, and SATCOM—all sound slightly different. We know who should be speaking on a given net and the importance of what that person might be saying. Armed with that knowledge, we assign pilot responsibility to various nets, and adjust the volumes of each radio based on the priority of the nets. On the ground, the ability to hear multiple radios and various sidebar conversations in the headquarters is often referred to as having a TOC ear. Despite working on other projects in the TOC, the pilot's ear is always tuned to the sound of the radio.

That evening, as I worked at my computer, I had my TOC ear on. About an hour after settling into some work at my desk, I heard Dan Hauf, Aaron Teichner, Mike Blaise, and Brian Hazelgrove report their departure over the radio. They were on their way to Mosul. Without consciously thinking about it, I noted that data point mentally.

Not more than five minutes later, I heard Dan's voice on the radio calling for Mike, which struck me as strange. We had UHF, FM, and VHF radios set up in the TOC, each of which, as I said previously, has a slightly different sound. I first heard Dan on the FM radio. He called Mike a couple of times but did not receive an answer. Then he called Mike on the UHF radio. No reply. It occurred to me that he was unable to establish radio contact with his trail aircraft. That was unusual. Somewhat concerned, I got up, walked to the stack of radios in the TOC, sat down in a metal folding chair, and listened closely. Again, Dan called but didn't receive an answer. I began to sense the concern in his voice. Unable to stand it any longer, I decided to call Dan and ask what was going on.

"I'm not sure," he said. "Just past ACP 1 [Air Check Point 1], Mike said he was reaching his comfort level. I said okay and then asked if he wanted to fly over to Highway 1. I thought it would be easier to follow the roads back to Q-West, but he never answered me, and now I can't get him on the radio," he added.

I tried to call Mike myself. No one answered. The TOC had grown completely silent. Every soldier in the room stared at the radio, hoping to hear Mike's voice.

"We've circled back around," Dan said. "We don't see them out here anywhere. I am going to retrace our route."

Painfully, we waited for Dan's next report. About two minutes later, he called. In a very low and quiet tone he said, "We've found their aircraft." He paused. You could have heard a pin drop in the TOC. "They are down. I'm going to land."

Everyone in the TOC held their breath. I wasn't sure what "down" meant, but the icepick had already begun to penetrate my chest. Had they landed to work out a mechanical problem? Did they lose their radios and that's why we did not receive an answer? Or had they crashed?

"Go get the SCO," I told Staff Sergeant Eric Bucher, our intelligence NCO. He ran out the door and sprinted to the classroom.

"I composed myself before going in," Bucher told me. "I didn't want to alarm anyone."[5]

Sergeant Bucher opened the door and looked for SCO. He was sitting near the front of the room. Casually, Sergeant Bucher walked up behind Schiller's chair, knelt beside him, and leaned in to whisper in his ear. "Sir, we've had an aircraft go down. You need to come to the TOC now."

"Where?" Schiller asked calmly.

"North of Q-West," Bucher answered.

"I'll be right there," Schiller said.

"I had seen Lieutenant Colonel Schiller's serious demeanor many times, but his expression was different," Sergeant Bucher said later. "It was more determined and focused, yet calm. There was a different sense about him right then that gave me an immediate heightened sense of duty to do whatever I could to get us through the next few hours, days, weeks. I kept asking myself, *what can I do? What do I need to do to help us get through this?*"[6]

Meanwhile, I sat by the radio, giving Dan time to land his helicopter and sort through the situation. *They're okay*, I thought to myself. *They could have lost communications and had no other choice but to land and troubleshoot their radios.* Sergeant Bucher returned to the TOC with both the SCO and Ken Hawley.

"What's up?" the SCO asked, as he walked through the TOC door, not visibly stressed. He seemed alarmed but focused. From the second he walked through the door, everyone keyed on him. It was as if they were judging how to respond to the situation based on how they perceived the boss reacting. It was a lesson in and of itself; one I'd not forget.

"They called off when they departed the airfield and then, just a few minutes later, I heard Dan calling for Mike on the radio. I asked Dan what was going on, and he said that just after ACP 1 Mike called and said he had reached his comfort level. Dan asked him if he wanted to fly over to Highway 1 and parallel it back to Q-West, but Mike never answered him. Dan found the helicopter and he said, '*It's down.*' I don't know exactly what that means, but he's on the ground now."

Schiller, Hawley, Todd Royar, Doug Ford, Tim Slifko, and I all hovered by the radios waiting for Dan to report what he'd found. Seconds seemed like minutes. Finally, Dan spoke, "Left-seater is out."

Slifko suddenly ran out of the TOC. "Being a former medic, I was thinking that every minute was precious. We had to get moving. I ran out to start getting my gear ready, so I could go help recover them,"[7] Tim Slifko later told me.

Assuming the aircraft was damaged to some degree, we needed to know what to send with the recovery team. The anticipation was killing us all. I decided to call Dan on the radio and ask him for a situation report. "We've found them," he said and left it at that.

I did not want to ask the question, did not want to hear the answer I knew I was going to get. "Dan, I need to know the status of the crew," I said, then paused. "You have to tell me."

There was a long pause, and then I heard Dan's quivering voice, almost sobbing, "They're both gone. We lost them both," he said.

Everyone just stood there in silence in the TOC. We were two days from leaving and had not lost a soldier all year. It was as though everyone in the TOC began to grieve in silence at once. You could almost feel the pain in the air. Soldiers stared at the floor in silence; then suddenly, as if the lights were suddenly switched on, we snapped back to reality with the realization that we had work to do. We had to get out there and recover them, and we had to get to Kate Blaise quickly.

"Ken, get a recovery team together," the SCO directed. "Todd, go get Jeff Kelley. I don't want Kate finding this out the wrong way. I will tell her myself. I need to call Lieutenant Colonel Mason [3-17 Cavalry squadron commander] and let him know what's going on."

Our brigade headquarters had already departed Q-West for Kuwait, but Major Todd Royar, the brigade operations officer, remained at Q-West with us to close everything out. Since 3-17 Cavalry had taken over the brigade footprint, Todd had moved in with us. Todd knew the squadron very well because he had served as the 2-17 CAV operations officer and Schiller's executive officer before moving up to the brigade. Earlier that morning, Todd had spent an hour with Mike Blaise talking about adoption. Todd and his wife, Mary Lou, were well along in the adoption process, and Mike and Kate had seemed interested in learning more about the process.[8]

Soon Captain Adam Frederick and Mike's roommate, Chief Warrant Officer Two Scott White, walked into the TOC. The SCO filled them in on what had happened. "I sensed something was up when I saw Sergeant Boucher whispering in the SCO's ear and he got up and left the meeting. My guys were the only ones out flying,"[9] Frederick later told me.

Ken Hawley gave the battle captain instructions, "Get the doc, medics, a wrecker, and put an aircraft recovery team together. Have them start lining their vehicles up out in front of the TOC," he ordered.

"I'm going!" Doug said. It was a side of Doug I had not previously seen. For a guy who was always joking, sarcastic, and lighthearted, suddenly he was very serious. I saw grave concern in his face. "I'll get my gear and meet you out front," he told Ken and departed the TOC.

"I'm going with you too," Staff Sergeant Bucher said.

"Okay," Ken replied. "Meet me out front."

"Roger, sir," Bucher said and departed the TOC to retrieve his gear.

We were not sure if a medevac helicopter would be able to fly in the weather or not. While we didn't know for sure what had happened, we assumed Mike had inadvertently flown into the clouds and subsequently crashed, but Dan Hauf had not mentioned the weather being all that bad. Still, it was muddy and wet, and we had to go recover the aircraft via ground.

Dan passed us the grid coordinates to their location. Slifko drove Ken's Humvee with Sergeant Bucher and Doug in the backseat. We collected the best flashlights and headlamps we could find. I had just received a new high-beam Petzl headlamp in the mail. I handed it to Slifko.

"Here, this might be helpful," I told him.

Once the team assembled, they drove out the gate. Slifko later recalled every detail of their movement to the site.

"I hung on the last words I heard from Dan Hauf before I ran out of the TOC to get my gear, '*Left-seater is out.*' That gave me hope," Slifko said. "I thought maybe Dan meant that he could see Mike's left-seater outside checking the aircraft for damage.

"It began to rain steadily as we departed Q-West. We managed okay until we had to leave the paved road and drive across a field. The trucks spun, then lurched forward in the slick mud of the field. We couldn't see ten feet in front of the Humvee. As we drove, I heard the medevac fly over us. That was a good sign. We could see the faint lights of the Black Hawk as it landed in the field out in front of us. Assuming it was landing right beside Mike's Kiowa, we drove directly to where it landed, and we all jumped out of the truck. Doug and I still couldn't see the Kiowa. Expecting to see it sitting there, I was somewhat confused. We spread out and just started walking forward, looking for it.[10]

"It was like my head was a globe of misty light. There was a circle of light around my head, but the light could only penetrate the misty fog for about three feet. I could almost reach out with my hand and touch the wall where the light ended and the darkness began," Slifko recalled.

Stars were absent from a sky normally crowded with innumerable pinholes of light. There was no moon, or it was hidden behind a blanket of thick, black, soggy clouds.

"Tim!" Doug Ford yelled. "Tim! It's over here."

Slifko turned and rushed over to where Doug was standing, but walking was laborious in the soft, muddy field. His feet had picked up a pound or more of sludge in the first ten yards he walked after exiting the Humvee. Now he could feel caked mud rubbing against his calves as he walked in boots that were at least eight inches wide.

"It didn't make sense," Slifko recalled. "I had an image in my mind of what it would look like. Maybe the skids would be spread apart and it would be sitting low to the ground, but it should not look like what I was seeing. I could make out the loose shape of the helicopter, but it was crumpled up. The nose was buried, and it sort of folded over on its right side."

As I would later see for myself, the helicopter looked somewhat like an egg that had been dropped on the floor. It didn't come apart so much as it lost its shape when the structure gave way to the force of the impact.

"I rushed to the aircraft and began looking for them," Slifko said. "I saw one of them almost immediately. I remember seeing a name tape on his helmet—*Hazelgrove*."

Then Slifko hesitated, licked his lips, and took a few deep breaths. The detail of that night had lain dormant for over a dozen years, but it still hurt to tell it. I broke in.

"I never asked for the details back then, never felt comfortable asking," I said.

"I know, sir. I know. It's just, well, I don't know," he said, then shook his head, drew in a deep breath, and kept going. "I quickly checked Hazelgrove's carotid artery. It still didn't make sense to me. I can't explain it, but I could not process it. They were not supposed to be like that. Nothing looked like I had pictured it in my mind," he said, still seeming baffled by the entire ordeal as he told me years later.

"There was no pulse, so I went to his wrist. Nothing. Suddenly, I was aware of this pain in my chest. I guess I was slowly beginning to process it all, beginning to accept what I was seeing," Slifko said.

"But where was Mike? Dan said the left-seater was out, but Mike was in the right seat. *He must have gotten out*, I thought. He wasn't there. I got up and began looking for footprints in the mud. He must have walked out," Tim said.

Then Doug, who'd been looking over Tim's shoulder, looked closer. Mike was still in his seat. Mike was lying underneath Hazelgrove.

"No!" Slifko said. "I checked him for a pulse as well. By that time, one of the flight medics from the medevac bird was looking over my shoulder. Images of Mike; his wife, Kate; and his friends Scott White and Mike Young flashed into my mind. They were always together in Ban'shee Troop. I would often see the four of them hanging out together. It hurt to think about it, to see that picture in my mind, but I could not make it go away."[11]

Army doctrine did not allow us to fly the deceased in a medevac helicopter. The flight medic, who was the official medical officer on the scene, confirmed Tim's assessment: both men were deceased. "I remember trying to take comfort in knowing that they had died on impact. They were in a dive, and the right-side nose hit the ground first. The helicopter sort of darted into the ground on Mike's side, then folded over. That's why Hazelgrove, who was in the left seat, was on top of Mike. I then realized that when Dan said the left-seater was out, he meant that his own left-seater was out assessing the crash.

"The medevac bird departed, and we could see a string of lights approaching from the south. It was the Stryker vehicles from the unit that was replacing Bastogne at Q-West. The Stryker vehicles had big powerful spotlights on them, so they lit the area up rather well. We evacuated Mike Blaise and Brian Hazelgrove in the Strykers,"[12] Slifko said.

Meanwhile, Todd Royar drove to the 426th BSB TOC, where he found Lieutenant Colonel Jeff Kelley playing cards with Kate Blaise. "I was immediately uncomfortable," Royar would later recall.[13]

"Sir, Colonel Schiller sent me over to see if you could come by the CAV headquarters," he said, trying not to even look at Kate.

"Does he need something?" Kelley asked, confused at the late-night request.

"He just wanted to talk to you before everyone left," he said.

Kate Blaise's heart skipped a beat. She had just heard the medevac helicopter cranking, which alarmed her. She knew Mike's was the only team flying that night. Todd Royar showing up uncharacteristically to ask Lieutenant Colonel Kelley to stop what he was doing and go visit the CAV was more than strange. Sensing something was not quite right, Jeff Kelley rose and began moving toward his vehicle.

"You'd better go too," Whitson urged Kate.

She rose and followed Jeff Kelley to his vehicle. Once there, Kate got in the back seat. Todd Royar spun out fast and raced to the CAV headquarters. He had to beat Kelley there, so he could prepare Schiller. Kate was on the way with Kelley.

I stepped outside when I heard the vehicle pull up in front of the TOC. Schiller was already standing on the front stoop with Adam Frederick and Scott White. Royar ran up the steps to warn Schiller, but Kelley had already pulled in behind him. I saw Kate step out of the vehicle, and my chest began to ache. I knew that she didn't know for sure yet, but I could tell that she knew something was going on. None of us could help ourselves. We all looked directly at her. She saw Scott White and Adam Frederick, Mike's roommate and troop commander, standing on the steps, clearly shaken.

Steve Schiller wasted no time. He walked directly to her and looked her straight in the eyes, "Kate, we had a Kiowa go down tonight, and Mike was flying," he said. "I'm really sorry, but it looks like he didn't make it."

I thought my chest would explode as I watched her accept the full blow of those words. Every eye was on her, yet she stared straight ahead into the center courtyard of our headquarters. She appeared numb, unable to express any emotion at all.

Not feeling like it hurt enough, I internalized. I thought how it would feel if I'd just received that news. The pain increased, and I was oddly more content. It was supposed to hurt. I should hurt as much as possible, because I could not imagine how bad she was hurting.

Suddenly, I wished there was some way to undo it all, to make the day run backwards until Dan Hauf stood by my helicopter asking me about the weather. *At that moment,* I thought, *if I could do it all over, I would say that there was no use in trying to go out later, that the weather was too bad.* But I could not unwind time. Mike Blaise and Brian Hazelgrove were dead.

Not knowing exactly what to do, we all waited to see how Kate would react. Finally, Scott White walked up behind her and hugged her. His chest began to pump as he wept. Then I saw tears streaming down Adam Frederick's face. Now, I began to really hurt. I felt a searing pain in my chest that I had never felt with such intensity. I wanted to do something, somehow help her, but I didn't know Kate, and I knew that only time would heal the pain that had just entered her life. Silently, I prayed that she would have the strength to endure, that she would, in some way, be comforted.

With Scott White embracing her, Lieutenant Colonel Jeff Kelley asked her what he could do. She asked if he would send Major Kirk Whitson over.

The SCO told Scott White to take her to his room. Scott, with his arm around Kate's shoulder, walked her past me, down the hall to Schiller's room. Schiller went to his office and retrieved the satellite phone from his desk. He then went to his room. Kate and Scott stood when he walked in. He told Kate that she needed to make two decisions.

"Kate, do you want to notify Mike's family, or do you want the army to do it?"

"I will tell them," Kate said. And with that, Schiller handed her the satellite phone.

"Okay, what do *you* want to do?" he asked. "Do you want to travel back with your unit, or do you want to go back now?"

"I want to go back with Mike," she said.

"Okay, that's what I needed to know. What else can I do for you right now?" Schiller asked.

"Can Scott go with me?" she asked.

"Certainly," Schiller said.[14]

The SCO then left them alone to grieve and call Kate's family. He stepped back out into the courtyard, where Adam Frederick was still struggling to deal with the pain of losing one of his pilots. Schiller hugged him. "We'll get through this, Adam,"[15] Schiller said.

Adam composed himself and walked back to his troop area. Now it was his responsibility, a twenty-nine-year-old captain, to tell his men that one of their brothers had been killed and would not be coming back.

"I had lost friends prior to that night," Adam later told me. "But Mike was the first soldier, a man for whom I was directly responsible. The first sergeant brought everyone together. Most of them knew that something was going on but did not know exactly what had happened. I composed myself and informed Ban'shee Troop that we had lost Mike. I can still see the looks of sadness in each one of their eyes. January 23rd was one of the longest nights of my life."[16]

Everyone in 2-17 CAV wanted to say something, had a need to talk about it, but no one quite knew what the right thing was to say, so we just walked around, all of us, with an empty feeling inside that could not be filled.

The pain was not over yet.

The following day, as we prepared to move out, everyone worked in silence. A somber mood hung in the air like a cloud of depression. Soldiers only spoke to one another when necessary, and then they whispered. After losing Mike, everyone was ready to leave Iraq. Despite almost losing the SCO and many other close calls, we had been very fortunate. To lose one of our soldiers so close to the end was tough to swallow.

We spent the twenty-fifth of January lining our vehicles up in convoy order on a small road adjacent to our TOC and conducting our final equipment inspections. We planned to sleep on the hoods of our trucks or on cots beside them that night. The crews that would fly over our convoys had prepared their helicopters for takeoff at first light. 3-17 Cavalry had completely taken over the mission in Mosul. All that was left for us to do was drive to Kuwait.

I set up a tactical command post for the night, so that we could monitor 3-17 Cavalry's radio nets. That evening, a Zodiac boat capsized in the Tigris River between bridges two and three in Mosul. Due to the heavy February rains, the river flowed fast and cold. A team of 3-17 Cavalry Kiowas was called to help search for the missing soldiers. There was a small cable that stretched across the river between the two bridges. Being so thin, the cable was very difficult to see. Just like when we approached power lines, we alerted each other when we neared that cable across the river. The cable had become part of our crew coordination drill all year. As we approached the bridges in flight, the pilots would call out, "Bridge two coming, cable after that," and the other pilot would acknowledge the callout. It was our way of ensuring that we didn't forget about it and accidentally fly into it.

The 3-17 Cavalry crews searched for the missing soldiers for several minutes. They were focused on trying to find their missing brothers. Unfortunately, Chief Warrant Officer Three Patrick Dorff and First Lieutenant Adam Mooney drifted into the wire and crashed in the Tigris River. Colonel Joe Anderson raced to the site. The aircraft was totally submerged in the deep, frigid water. A call went out to find a diver, but none was found. Local Iraqis gathered at the river to investigate what had happened.

An Iraqi man stepped forward and said he could swim down to the helicopter. He stripped down to his skivvies and dove into the water. "It seemed like he was under forever," Colonel Anderson later told me.

When he reappeared, he exploded through the surface and gasped for air; then he said that he found the helicopter, but there were no pilots in it. The seatbelts had been released. They were simply gone. So, the search began for Dorff and Mooney.

We later learned that the men had drowned. In the investigation that followed, the army determined that the pilots' inability to extricate themselves from their body armor while underwater wa a contributing factor to their deaths. That crash served as the impetus for fielding body armor with quick release tabs that would enable soldiers to rapidly drop their body armor plates. It was a hell of a price to pay for such a small lesson.

THE LONG DRIVE

One thousand kilometers, or 621 miles of road, lay between Q-West and Udairi, Kuwait. We planned to cover it in three days at an average speed of forty-five miles per hour. The only thing positive about the entire situation was the fact that we were going home.

I woke up cold and sore to the sound of noncommissioned officers rousting their soldiers out of sleeping bags. The mourning was over. It was time for the next mission, and the noncommissioned officers took control. "Let's go. Get up! It's time to get moving," they said as they strode from truck to truck. "Put your shit away, and let's get moving."

Having slept on the hard steel hood of my Humvee, mostly on my side, my right hip ached. Eager to get on the road, I quickly laced up my boots and started walking down the long line of vehicles. I pulled my Gore-Tex jacket up around my neck to stave off the cold. It was thirty-five degrees, and a brisk wind blew from the northwest. Otherwise, it was a clear day, which I appreciated because our Kiowas planned to stay close as we moved south. Just in case we needed them.

Lieutenant Lauren Makowsky had recently replaced Candy Smith as our chief intelligence officer. Lauren was the all-American girl. An honor roll student who not only played sports but was also typically chosen by her peers to be team captain, she was a natural leader. Lauren was pretty, smart, confident, driven, and thick-skinned, and had a wonderful sense of humor—perfect attributes for the Cavalry, especially 2-17 CAV.

Lauren grew up in the suburbs of Northern Virginia. Born into a family of intelligence analysts, she intended to carry on the family tradition. It was in her blood, I suppose. As an ROTC student at the University of Virginia, she set her sights on commissioning into the military intelligence branch. Everything leading up to 2003 had prepared her to serve as the intelligence officer for a squadron in combat.

The evening prior, Lauren had clearly articulated the risk we'd assume the following day. She told us that if the wind did not blow, we would be driving through a heavy fog. The fog would prevent our Kiowas from supporting us from above, as well as enable the enemy to move undetected along the edges of the roads. Furthermore, the fog would make it more difficult for us to maintain the interval between vehicles. We would have to slow the rate of march, which would present the enemy with slow-moving targets. There was no question: fog would give the advantage to the enemy.

As she spoke, I saw images of enemy fighters digging in the roads, setting IEDs for the convoys they knew would arrive the next day. I could see them using the fog to hide close to the road—and to watch as they blew us up.

Fortunately, we woke to the bite of a steady breeze that morning. I tucked in my chin and thanked God.

We would travel in two march units or convoys separated by fifteen-minute intervals. The first march unit consisted of forty-nine vehicles, and the second fifty-four. We placed a vehicle with a .50-caliber machine gun at the front and rear of each march unit.

Concerned with our vehicles' lack of armor, we had filled sandbags full of dirt and placed them in the floorboards and beds of our trucks. Some of the vehicles were so heavy the axles sagged under the weight. We were destroying our equipment, but the alternative—no protection—was unthinkable.

"Morning, mate," Rowely said as he walked up. Slifko and Doug followed closely behind him.

"I'm surprised you guys are up," I said. "You're not taking off for a few hours."

Since we didn't expect the enemy to attack us along the first stretch of highway, we decided to delay the departure of the helicopters. They'd pick us up farther south, where the enemy historically attacked convoys.

"Wanted to come tell you to watch your ass," Rowely said. "There are some bloody tough spots along the way. We'll be close by, so shout if you need us to shoot some bastards trying to fuck with you."

"Doug, I think we really need the squadron safety officer in the convoy with us," I said, trying to hide the sarcasm. "Make sure we remain safe, you know?"

"I don't think so," Doug said. "I'll be right over the top of you. You know, keeping you safe from above."

"If you need anything, call *me*," Slifko said. "Doug will be eating trail mix or getting his ass chewed by the SCO. You know you can count on me. Now, Doug, on the other hand..." Slifko said, pausing for dramatic effect, "he's questionable."

"Screw you," Doug said and then paused. "Seriously, we just wanted to say goodbye and we'll see you on the radio."

In light of the situation, their playful jabs had a different feel to them. The loss of four good men still weighed heavy on my heart. Driving out of Iraq felt like the beginning of the end. I had been thinking about it a lot over the past few days. Once we arrived in Kuwait, we'd quickly load the ships, then begin flying home. Once there, we would each go our separate ways. Our lives would once again be segmented between family life and work life. It felt like part of me was slowly being ripped out. I hated the idea of giving up this bond we'd formed.

Doug stuck his hand out to shake. I fought off the urge to hug him. One by one, I shook their hands. "See you guys on the other end," I said and thought how lucky I was to have such friends. In just eight months' time, we had grown extremely close. There was something impossibly beautiful in that. It was beyond comforting to know that if I called, if I was in trouble, no matter the situation, they'd risk their own lives, do whatever was necessary, to get to me, to save me.

"Time to roll!" the first sergeant shouted.

At 7:00, twelve minutes before sunrise, we pulled out of Q-West feeling giddy. We drove to Highway 1 (MSR Tampa) and turned south. The road ran long and straight, four lanes in most places, two in others. Iraqis drove without regard for speed limits or no-passing zones. The highway was a free-for-all where drivers jockeyed for position, passed when they thought they could make it, and even drove the wrong way against oncoming traffic, trusting that other drivers would move aside and yield the road, like playing chicken on the highway was as natural as eating breakfast.

That morning, like a caravan of camels headed for the Persian Gulf, our long line of green and brown vehicles slowly crawled south on MSR Tampa. We tried to prevent Iraqis from separating our convoy, but inevitably they would pass a truck or two, then jet into our formation. We were certainly concerned about an attack from men in moving cars, but we felt that we could easily deal with a couple of guys wielding AKs. A car bomb is what we feared most, a vehicle-borne improvised explosive device (VBIED), another newly coined term.

Lauren had shown us pictures of a VBIED explosion at the gate of one of our compounds. I could not shake the image of bent and mangled steel from my mind. It was somewhat impossible to defend in a convoy. They'd drive a car into the middle of a convoy and then detonate the bomb.

We remained at full alert that day, constantly scanning the road, weapons at the ready. I rarely took my hands off my rifle. Sunset was at 5:30 on that first day. We made it to Combat Support Center (CSC) Warlion, unscathed, just before the sun fell below the horizon.

The facility was well established with sleep tents, port-a-johns, shower points, and a dining facility. No one cared to shower. We were exhausted from failing to rest the previous night and being on edge all day. We did enjoy a hot meal and then lay down to try to catch a few hours of sleep. I did not wake until my driver shook me.

"Time to go, sir," he whispered. I squinted through blurry eyes and pressed the light button on my Suunto watch—2:00 a.m. I laced up my boots, put my bedroll away, and quickly walked the line to check on the soldiers. It was eerily quiet. Hardly anyone spoke. I wasn't sure if it was fatigue or nervous anticipation. Baghdad lay ahead.

We departed CSC Warlion at 2:30 and slipped through Baghdad and Fallujah on a dark, moonless night, seemingly unnoticed. Initially, I feared that I might fall sleep as we drove. It was in my nature. When I was fourteen years old, I went on a road trip to Texas with a cowhand from Georgia to get a Brangus bull and work some cattle at ranches along the way. I was so excited to see Texas for the first time that I could hardly stand it, yet I slept 90 percent of the time we were on the road. The only part of Texas I saw were the parts when we were not driving. There was just something about traveling that turned the lights out for me, but Texans had not been trying to blow me up. As it turned out, I had no trouble staying awake on the roads in Iraq. We made it to CSC Scania, south of Baghdad, well after daylight. The movement had gone as smoothly as we could have hoped.

It seemed to take an eternity to refuel our entire convoy at CSC Scania. We were anxious to get back on the road. I could sense the soldiers' relief at having made it through Baghdad unscathed, yet one more dangerous stretch of road lay ahead. Morale was relatively high, but like me, the soldiers could not wait to get to Kuwait. As I walked back to my truck, Specialist Stephen Tubbs approached me.

We affectionately called him Tubby, which did not fit. Stephen Tubbs stood six feet, four inches tall and weighed a buck seventy soaking wet. I once asked Tubbs why he joined the army, and he told me that a member of his family had fought in every war since the Civil War. "I had just finished my associate degree when this war began," he'd told me. "So, it just kind of made sense."[1] Tubbs was a sharp soldier who made a super impression on everyone he met, sergeants and officers alike.

"Sir, you won't believe what I just saw," he said, with a broad smile.

"What's that, Tubby?" I asked.

"As soon as we stopped, I stepped off the side of the road to take a leak. This Iraqi dude in a white man-dress rushed up to me. He stunk like you would not believe," he added as a side note. "Anyway, he walked right up to me and reached inside his man-dress. I was about to draw down on him. I thought he might have a gun, but you know what he pulled out of his dress?" Tubbs asked excitedly.

"What's that?"

"He pulled out a stack of porn in one hand and two pints of whiskey in the other. You believe that, sir? Porn," he said, "which is banned in this country. And the whiskey? Not just any whiskey—Tennessee mash whiskey!" he said, with obvious appreciation. "I would not think a man could sell that stuff in Iraq, but I guess there are enough soldiers around that would sneak and buy it from him."

"I assume you made the correct decision, right, Tubby?"

"Sir," he said, rolling his eyes and slowly throwing his head back as if the question was silly. "Come on."

"I'm just messing with you, Tubby. He must have a good intelligence officer. He knew to present Tennessee whiskey to the 101st."

Suddenly, a sergeant yelled out, "Git your shit together. Let's go!"

"Time to go," I said to Tubbs.

It was well after noon when we finally pulled out of Scania.

Our next stop was CSC Kenworth, where we would remain overnight. Everyone knew that the leg from Scania to Kenworth was the last of the truly dangerous areas. If our thinly armored, sandbag-reinforced convoy was to be attacked, it would happen there. Every soldier in the convoy knew it, and the general mood in the convoy adjusted accordingly as we pulled onto the highway. Once at Kenworth, we would be able to relax a bit, but Kenworth seemed to be a thousand miles away.

CSC Scania had not even disappeared from the rearview mirror when we encountered our first issue, a flat tire. The call came from the rear of the march unit, letting everyone know that we would have to pull over and wait while the tire was changed. Vehicles stretched for a mile up and down the road as Lieutenant Matthew Wolfe swooped in with his team and changed the tire like a NASCAR pit crew. Everyone moved away from their vehicles and pulled security while we waited, other than those who required a latrine break. Men slipped into the bushes while women took turns holding ponchos up by their vehicles for privacy.

I could not help but chuckle to myself. Most young Americans could not imagine that scene. We were in the Sunni Triangle, a war zone, with twenty-year-old women, some just two or three years out of high school, squatting behind a poncho to pee. Afterward, they adjusted their body armor and resumed a position on the perimeter with their M4 machine gun.

Gray clouds hung low, threatening rain, as we pulled back onto the highway. As we crawled our way south, I keep repositioning my feet. Envisioning being blown up by an IED, I could not decide where my feet should be if I took a blast. Subconsciously, I was obsessed with the thought of losing my legs.

I had very little room to move inside the confined Hummer, yet I'd push my feet and legs to the inside console, hoping a blast would not affect them in the middle of the vehicle. Then I thought it would be better to lose my legs than get hit in the upper torso. *Which would be worse, losing a leg or an arm?* I wondered. These thoughts made their way around my mind over and over. Meanwhile, as I shifted my position in synchronization with my fears, I watched every Iraqi in sight. I inspected their expressions, tried to read their body language—friend or foe?

Thankfully, the next two hours of driving were quiet and uneventful. Despite being mentally and physically exhausted when we finally arrived at Kenworth, a soldier transmitted a loud *YEE HAW!* over the radio as we pulled in. His excitement and relief expressed what we all felt. We had driven for two days through some of the most dangerous territory in the world and, by the grace of God, had come out unharmed. Enemy activity from Kenworth to Kuwait had been relatively low. On some level, we felt like we'd made it.

All at once, it seemed as if we were *substantially* closer to home.

Kenworth had no sleeping tents, but they did have a dining facility. We'd arrived too late for dinner chow, but midnight chow was only a couple of hours away. I told the soldiers to prepare their sleeping gear so that we could get some rest right after dinner. I unfolded a cot beside my Humvee and rolled my sleeping bag out on it. It was already down into the forties and would likely drop to near freezing overnight.

I called for a quick huddle with the first sergeants and troop commanders. Everyone seemed to be doing well. We reviewed the time-line for the following day and then broke for chow. We rotated to eat in shifts. Some soldiers watched our gear while others ate.

I'm not sure if it was the stress or just several days of poor sleep, but suddenly I was exhausted. When my driver returned from chow, I slowly made my way to the dining facility. Midnight chow has always been a favorite of mine. "Western omelet, biscuits, and sausage gravy," I told the mess sergeant.

Captain Bob Jenkins, our battle captain and field artillery officer, ate with me. After chow, I put my tray away and picked up a banana on the way to the door. As I approached the door of the dining facility, I saw that an ancient-looking staff sergeant was standing in front of the doors. I nodded to him as we approached. "Sir, you can't take that banana out of the dining facility," he said.

"What?" I asked, confused at the comment.

"No food can be removed from the dining facility. I don't make the rules. I just enforce them," he said.

He was assigned to a National Guard unit that had been tasked with running CSC Kenworth. He looked to be at least sixty years old. I relaxed my expression. Certainly, he could reason with me. "So sergeant, we've spent the last year in combat. We have driven two days straight through the heart of Iraq. We've slept on the hoods of our vehicles, and we've got one day to go until we get to return to our families. The American taxpayers bought this food. I really don't think they care if I eat this banana inside this chow hall or if I take it with me to eat at sunrise on the road to Kuwait," I said.

The sergeant looked around as if to make sure no one was watching. Then he leaned into me to whisper in my ear. "I tell you what, sir. You just open your cargo pocket up there on your trousers. Drop that banana down into your pocket so I can't see it. I won't say a thing," he said and winked at me.

Following his instructions, I dropped the banana into my pocket, patted him on the shoulder, and said, "Have a good night, sergeant."

"Good night, sir."

When I got back to my truck, it had begun to rain. My sleeping bag was already wet. One last Iraqi slap in the face, I suppose. I quickly rolled my bag up and strapped it to my rucksack. After folding the cot and throwing it in the back of my Humvee, I crawled into the seat and struggled to get comfortable. For the next four hours, I drifted in and out of sleep.

Everyone was up and moving at first light. I sensed that no one had slept much, but I also knew that they didn't care. All three hundred of them were eager to get to Kuwait as soon as possible. It would be our longest day—365 kilometers (227 miles)—but 150 of it would be on the relatively harmless roads of Kuwait.

Slowly, mile by mile, what grass there had been disappeared. The terrain transformed into what I'd always imagined a desert looked like, endless brown sand with rolling dunes.

We made good time. By one o'clock, we were within a mile of the Kuwait border. I could see the boundary on the moving map displayed on my blue force tracker in the Humvee.

"Sir, let's pull over for a cigar once we cross the border into Kuwait," one of the first sergeants transmitted over the radio.

"Roger that," I said.

As I watched the icon of the trail vehicle cross into Kuwait, I spoke over the radio, "Go ahead and pull over, first sergeant."

We stopped on the side of the road, and those who had one lit a stogie. I could hear yips and shouts all up and down the road.

Schiller and Ken Hawley stood by the roadside as we rolled into Udairi. They beamed with smiles and waved as truck after truck made the turn into the parking area. As the vehicles came to a stop, Schiller began shaking hands and slapping backs. He walked down the line, stopping at each vehicle to welcome them to Kuwait and to tell them how proud he was of them. You could see the soldiers' pride in their faces. For all intents and purposes, our combat deployment was over.

Schiller worked them like a politician works a room of people, but it didn't feel that way. He was selfless. Not once did I see him put his own needs before those of his soldiers. Because all our troopers did not get to go home for R&R, Schiller did not go. He'd been severely wounded, yet he refused to leave his soldiers. He fought and assumed risk to try and make us more effective, and he never used the words *I, me,* and *my.* It was always *us, we,* and *ours.*

I'd grown extremely close to Schiller, rarely spending more than six hours away from him in nine months. He was demanding but fair. He never passed up a deficiency and he despised lack of discipline, yet he was never condescending or mean-spirited when he made corrections. Like Doug noted, he could chew a captain's ass, but it wasn't personal. We were at war, and Steve Schiller expected professionalism, commitment, and discipline. Cross those lines and he'd get emotional.

He was unquestionably the most tactically competent commissioned officer with whom I'd ever served, and he was about to return home from Iraq as the most decorated army aviator in the service at that time. For his actions in combat, Steve Schiller had earned the Silver Star, a second Distinguished Flying Cross to go with the one he'd earned during Desert Storm, the Purple Heart, and seven Air Medals, with one of those being for Valor.

REUNITED

I spent three days in Kuwait. Once we were clear of Baghdad and the likelihood of enemy attacks reduced, the SCO flew south with the helicopters. They arrived in Kuwait a day ahead of us. Once there, he and Ken Hawley pushed the soldiers hard to prepare our equipment for shipment home. When we arrived, all we had to do was clean the trucks and prepare them to be inspected and loaded onto the ship. Working around the clock, we finished the task in two and a half days and were ready to begin flying our troopers back to Fort Campbell.

The final inspection was for our personal gear. We laid out everything we owned on a poncho for a customs agent to inspect. Senior leaders were concerned that soldiers would try to take war trophies or unauthorized contraband back home with them. I just wanted to return to my family at that point. A Navy customs sergeant inspected my gear, then told me to pack it all back up. I was cleared for the flight home. *That was easy,* I thought.

A few hours later, a bus took us to Kuwait International Airport. Our carrier was a civilian contracted airplane. One final inspection checkpoint stood between me and the jet that would fly me home. I emptied my pockets and carry-on bag in front of a flight attendant at the checkpoint. "Sir, you can't have that," the lady said, frowning and pointing to my Gerber multitool.

"What do you mean?" I asked, clearly confused.

"You're not allowed to carry a knife on the plane. It's a new protocol, post 9/11, you know," she said.

I took a deep breath, determined to remain calm and civil. "Ma'am, let me get this straight. I have a rifle in my hand and a pistol on my hip.

341

I have been in combat for the past nine months, and you are concerned that I will hijack the plane that is taking me home to my family with a Gerber multitool?" I asked, trying to emphasize how truly absurd the idea was.

She grasped the logic. Her face softened. "Sir, I know it sounds crazy." Then she leaned in to whisper. "In fact, I think it's silly, but those are the rules, and it's my job to make sure we follow the rules."

I took a breath and relaxed. "Ma'am, I understand. I think this flight is worth the price of a Gerber," I said and placed it in the amnesty box.

Whether or not we realized it yet, our lives had changed on September 11, 2001. It would take years for the average person to fully comprehend it, but there was no point in time, no event, no "Victory" that would return us to a life that mirrored September 10, 2001. In fact, life would never quite be the same again.

We flew from Kuwait to Shannon, Ireland, and from there to Bangor, Maine. I had no idea what to expect upon return. In fact, I had not even considered what it might feel like to walk off an airplane on American soil after a combat deployment, so I was ill-prepared for what awaited me.

We walked through the jetway at Bangor like cattle being herded through corrals. Near the final turn, I could hear what sounded to be a crowd. We rounded the corner, stepped into the terminal, and were met with a shock. Hundreds of people erupted in cheers. Not expecting anyone to greet our plane, I was taken by complete surprise. World War II, Korea, and Vietnam veterans lined the corridor, shoulder to shoulder, all the way from the jetway to the waiting area. With tears in their eyes, they applauded and waved American flags. Shivers ran down my spine like a bolt of lightning. I felt an unexpected pride for which I was completely unprepared, and suddenly I found myself fighting back tears.

It was clear that America was determined not to repeat an ugly chapter from our post–Vietnam War history. Not everyone agreed with our invasion of Iraq, but the American people, particularly veterans, recognized that soldiers had no say in where they went. The overwhelming support and appreciation gave every soldier on that flight a deep sense of pride.

An elderly man sat in a wheelchair on the left side of the walkway. He reached out with his cell phone, begging any soldier to accept it. "Call your family," he implored. "Tell them you're back on American soil." A young soldier smiled, took the phone, thanked him, and hurriedly punched numbers. It was an incredible experience of overwhelming emotion that I will never forget.

After an hour in Bangor, we flew to Fort Campbell, where we did expect a huge crowd awaiting our return. As we began the approach, I felt the excitement welling up inside me. In a matter of minutes, I would get to see my wife and kids. The anticipation made me giddy, like a child again.

Meanwhile, Lisa had given herself an hour to drive to Fort Campbell and find a place in the crowd where she could watch me walk off the plane.

"Where are we going?" our daughter Kasey asked as they departed our neighborhood.

"We're going to meet Daddy," Lisa answered.

"There were signs posted all along the roadside directing me to the *Welcome Home* ceremony," Lisa told me later. "I followed the signs to the hangar, but when I pulled up, there was nowhere to park. A soldier standing in the road directing traffic told me to drive to the parade field and park. He said a bus would bring me over. I had been told that I would be able to park right by the ceremony since I was pregnant," she said.

Lisa was nervous. She was eight months pregnant and had three small children in tow, and I was due to land in a few minutes.

"I knew the parade field was a couple of miles down the road, but I was determined to not be *THAT* army spouse by pitching a fit," she said. "I would follow the rules just like every other soldier's wife."

As directed, Lisa drove to the parade field, parked, and rushed the kids out of the van. She boarded a bus, but it sat for several minutes before finally starting for the hangar.

My excitement grew as I heard the landing gear being lowered beneath the airplane. I could see cornfields below as we approached over southern Kentucky. Finally, I saw I-24 pass underneath the plane. As the wheels touched down on Campbell Army Airfield, a thunderous cheer erupted. The flight attendants beamed with joy, seemingly proud to be a part of delivering American soldiers back to their families. "Welcome home," a flight attendant announced over the intercom system, and the cheers rose again.

It seemed to take an eternity for the cabin door to open. Once it did, a sergeant appeared in the doorway. "You'll be greeted by General Cody at the bottom of the stairs," he said. General Richard "Dick" Cody was the Vice Chief of Staff of the Army, and a former commanding general of the 101st Airborne Division. "After you shake his hand, you'll walk straight to the hangar. The doors will be closed when you arrive. Form up in formation in front of the doors. Once you are in formation outside the doors, your families will be directed back inside the hangar. When they are seated inside, the doors will open, and you will march inside. General Cody will make a few brief remarks, and then you'll be released to greet your families. You will get ten minutes with them, and then you'll be directed to form back up and file out of the building. You'll then board the buses, which will take you back to your unit area to turn your weapons in at the arms room. Your families will pick you up at your unit area. Any questions?" he asked.

No one dared to ask a question for fear that it would prolong our wait on the plane. "Okay, let's go then," he said, and we began filing off the plane.

Families cheered and waved posters with their soldier's name printed on it as we exited the plane. I shook General Cody's hand at the bottom of the stairs, "Welcome home, Jimmy," he said. "We're proud of you."

As I walked toward the hangar, I frantically searched for Lisa and the kids, but there were hundreds of screaming people held back by a railing. They were crammed in tight against the barrier. I could not find her.

Just as the sergeant said, once we were in formation, they opened the hangar doors, and the 101st Airborne Division band began playing. We marched into the hangar to a deafening roar of cheers. Once again, chills shot up my spine. Keenly aware of the situation, General Cody spoke for less than two minutes, and then he told the families that they could join their soldier on the hangar floor. Children exploded from the bleachers like they were shot out of a cannon.

I saw several familiar faces, but I could not find Lisa. Iconic supporters of the 101st Airborne Division, TC and Bob Freeman, Hawk Ruth, Phil and Bill Harpel, Jack Turner, and others hugged my neck and slapped me on the back. Still, no wife and children.

Not knowing if she had seen me or not, I was hesitant to begin searching the crowd. My spirits began to fall as I watched families kiss, hug, and snap picture after picture. By the time the ten minutes expired, I found it hard to maintain a smile. *What happened?* I wondered. *Where are they?*

Meanwhile, Lisa's bus ride took an eternity. She grew more and more anxious as they approached the hangar. Finally, the bus pulled up in front of the building. Holding the two youngest, Austin and Madison, by their hands and Kasey tagging along beside her, she made her way inside. Family members filled the hangar floor, but she didn't see any soldiers. Colonel Greg Gass's wife, Val, approached her. "Lisa, did you find Jimmy?" she asked.

"No. I had to park at the parade field and ride the bus," she said. "We just pulled into the parking lot. Have you seen him?"

"No, but let me help you look for him," Val said.

Together, they searched the hangar floor from one end to the other, but it was too late. I was on the bus and headed for CAV Country. Realizing we had already departed, Val offered to call my unit. The sergeant on duty told her that we were on the buses headed for the arms room.

"I was devastated," Lisa later told me. "I was fat, pregnant, and dragging three kids all over Fort Campbell, trying to meet you. I was beyond excited to be there. Those ceremonies are so patriotic. They always make me feel so good inside, but I had missed the one that really mattered, the one in which I was to be reunited with my own husband. You were gone."

On the verge of tears, Lisa gathered the kids and walked back to the bus stop. Again, the ride to the parade field seemed to take forever. By the time she got back to her van, I had already turned in my rifle and pistol and gathered my bags. All I needed was my family, a ride home. I went to my office and called her cell phone. "Hello," she answered.

Her voice sounded so sweet to my ears. "Where are you?" I asked.

"You won't believe what I've gone through," she said. "I'm almost to CAV Country now."

"Okay, I'm in the office. I'll meet you on the street out back," I said.

"Okay, love you."

"Love you, too."

I quickly gathered my bags and shuffled to the street. A warm feeling filled my chest as I saw the van approaching. Lisa stopped the van and opened the door. I hugged and kissed her, squeezing as hard as one can safely squeeze a pregnant woman without hurting her. I didn't want to let go.

"Welcome home, love," she said, smiling.

"Daaadddy," Kasey and Austin squealed in unison.

"Hey, guys," I said, as they both freed themselves from their car seats and ran to hug my neck.

Madison stared at me from her car seat, a confused look on her face. I leaned into the van and kissed her on the cheek, but at three years old, it was clear that she didn't recognize me.

I heaved my bags into the van, and we headed for home. Lisa and I made small talk. Despite having been married for twelve years, it seemed awkward trying to suddenly reacquaint with one another after a year apart. The kids sat in the back staring at the guy up front.

That evening, as Lisa and I stood in the kitchen preparing dinner, I hugged her. She wrapped her arms around me and lay her head on my shoulder. The familiar smell of her hair was comforting. Then I heard her whimper. "When you left, I was thin and pretty," she said, her head still on my shoulder. "Now, I'm bloated and fat, eight months pregnant."

"I think you're beautiful," I said, pushing her back and kissing her forehead.

To be sure, the year I'd spent on the other side of the world had changed many things, but the way I felt about Lisa was undimmed by time and distance.

Madison stood against the wall, staring intently. Then, shyly, she asked, "Are you my daddy?"

"Yes, sweetheart, I'm your daddy," I said, heartbroken that she had forgotten me.

Seeing the disappointment in my eyes, Lisa interrupted. "Daddy's home, sweetheart. Daddy's home now."

Slowly, still somewhat unsure, Madison walked to my side, then gently hugged my leg. I rubbed her back and allowed a painful smile. "So, what now?" Lisa asked.

"I have to complete reintegration training; then I'll take a couple weeks of leave," I said. "Just hang out here at home with you."

"No, I mean when you do you have to go back to Iraq?" she said.

Not looking forward to answering her question, I described upcoming operations, and how the unit mission would ultimately lead up to the next deployment.

But as a veteran army wife, Lisa wasn't fooled by my half-hearted evasiveness. She persisted.

"So, how long?"

"Seventeen months," I said. "That's a long time, so let's enjoy it."

"That's seventeen months before you deploy again, but how many combat training center rotations at Fort Polk before you go?" she asked, keenly aware of the train-up requirements.

"Every brigade will want the CAV with them during their training, and there's only one CAV squadron," I said, not wanting to answer the question.

"Of course, they will," she said, then raised her eyebrows as if to say, just tell me.

"Five rotations," I answered. "Each of the four brigades in the 101st and also a brigade out of Alaska."

"Five months at Fort Polk, so that leaves twelve months filled with long hours and field training exercises at Fort Campbell," she said, then turned to the sink and began washing a cup.

I hugged her from behind. "With all the personnel turnover, we have to train," I said.

"Of course, you do. I know that, but that doesn't make it any easier, Jimmy. I'll have four children. It's not easy being left, you know," she said, then paused. "This isn't the army we joined."

She was right, of course. We'd joined during the Cold War, when training and exercises were predictable. After 9/11, military life had changed significantly.

I walked to the kitchen window and stared into the woods. A thousand thoughts flooded my mind. It had unquestionably been the most informative year of my career. I learned more during that year in combat than in the decade preceding it. The most profound lesson was not a tactic or a technical skill, but rather a way of thinking. In a hierarchical culture constrained by regulations, Steve Schiller had taught me that unless men like us constantly seek new, innovative solutions to the constantly changing problems we faced, the institution would never evolve and improve fast enough. A part of me was excited to go back to Iraq and continue this evolution that we'd begun.

I was also addicted to the brotherhood, drunk on the laughter and love. It was painful for me to accept that our team, my friends, would soon move on to other assignments throughout the army. Strangely, that made me eager to begin forging the next brotherhood, creating bonds that seemed to exist only in combat.

At that moment, I realized that I was torn between two worlds. For how long it would last, I had no idea. I hated the thought of leaving my family again, yet coming home made me feel like a part of me had been ripped out. It was the first of many times over the next decade that I would wrestle with that familiar old combination of guilt and excitement.

For the moment, with my family looking back at me, balance was easier. I'd be a father and a husband again, and I'd start right now.

MILITARY TERMS

ACR: Armored Cavalry Regiment
ADC-O: Assistant Division Commander for Operations
ADC-S: Assistant Division Commander for Support
ALSE: Aviation Life Support Equipment
ASE: Aircraft Survivability Equipment
ASR: Alternate Supply Route
AUSA: Association of the United States Army
Bastogne: 1st Brigade, 101st Airborne Division
BCE: Battlefield Coordination Element
BFV: Bradley Fighting Vehicle
BIAP: Baghdad International Air Port
BMP: Boyevaya Mashina Pekhoty (Russian Infantry Fighting Vehicle)
CAOC: Combined Air Operations Center
CCA: Close Combat Attack
CG: Commanding General
CGSC: Command and General Staff College
CIF: Central Issue Facility
CMOC: Civil-Military Operations Center
CP: Command Post
CSC: Convoy Support Center
CSH: Corps Support Hospital
Destiny: 101st Aviation Brigade

DMAIN: Division Main
DREAR: Division Rear
EOD: Explosive Ordnance Disposal
FAA: Federal Aviation Administration
FAA: Forward Assembly Area
FARP: Forward Area Arming and Refueling Point
FMQ: Fully Mission Qualified
GAC: Ground Assault Convoy
Glory: 101st Airborne Division Artillery
IED: Improvised Explosive Device
JSOC: Joint Special Operations Command
LMTV: Light, Medium Tactical Vehicle
LNO: Liaison Officer
LZ: Landing Zone
Marne: 3rd Infantry Division
MEU: Marine Expeditionary Unit
MKT: Mobile Kitchen Trailer
MMS: Mast Mounted Sight
MOPP: Mission Oriented Protective Posture
MRE: Meal, Ready-to-Eat
MSR: Main Supply Route
NBC: Nuclear, Biological, Nuclear
NCO: Noncommissioned Officer
NTC: National Training Center
NVG: Night Vision Goggles
OCD: Obsessive-Compulsive Disorder
OCS: Officer Candidate School
ORB: Officer Record Brief
POO: Points of Origin
PT: Physical Training
PZ: Pickup Zone

Rakkasans: 3rd Brigade, 101st Airborne Division

RPG: Rocket-Propelled Grenade

S1: Adjutant or Human Resources Officer

S2: Intelligence Officer

S3: Operations Officer

S4: Supply/Logistics Officer

SCO: Squadron Commander

SIMO: Systems Integration Management Office

SOAR: Special Operations Aviation Regiment

SOCOM: Special Operations Command

SOP: Standard Operating Procedure

STRAC: Standards in Training Commission

Strike: 2nd Brigade, 101st Airborne Division

TAA: Tactical Assembly Area

TAC: Tactical Command Post

TACOPS: Tactical Operations

TF: Task Force

Thunder: 159th Aviation Brigade

TIS: Thermal Imaging System

TOC: Tactical Operations Center

WMD: Weapons of Mass Destruction

ENDNOTES

Preface

1 Govtrack.us, H.J.Res. 114 (107th): Authorization for Use of Military Force Against Iraq Resolution of 2002, accessed June 29, 2016, https://www.govtrack.us/congress/votes/107-2002/s237.

2 Pew Research Center, "Public Attitudes Toward the War in Iraq: 2003–2008," dated March 19, 2008, http://www.pewresearch.org/2008/03/19/public-attitudes-toward-the-war-in-iraq-20032008/.

3 Soldiers are commonly called troopers in the cavalry.

4 Leo Tolstoy, *War and Peace* (New York: The Modern Library, 1994), Part 3, Chapter VII, 267–268.

Going to War

1 Stephen M. Schiller, email to author, September 22, 2015.

2 Old Abe was a bald eagle and the mascot of the 8th Wisconsin Volunteers during the American Civil War. He became the centerpiece of the 101st Airborne Division patch. Once a soldier serves in combat with a unit, they are entitled to wear the unit patch on the right sleeve of their uniform.

3 An MRE is an individual field ration. At one point, it consisted primarily of dehydrated foods, but by 2003 the variety of meals had expanded and many of the main courses were no longer dehydrated.

4 Kenneth Hawley, email to author, December 30, 2015.

Stogies and Stories

1 The TOC serves as the battalion's primary command and control hub (information management center), assisting the squadron commander in synchronizing operations. It is the location in the squadron where the majority of planning, staff coordination, plan execution, receiving/disseminating information, and monitoring of key events occurs. Since writing this book, the term TOC has been replaced by command post.

2 Stephen M. Schiller, email to author, October 25, 2015. General David Petraeus (Ret.) also told me about this flight.

3 Timothy Slifko, email to author, November 2, 2015.
4 Ibid.
5 Rick Atkinson, *In the Company of Soldiers: A Chronicle of Combat* (New York: Henry Holt and Company, 2004), 142–145.
6 Slifko was being funny. He was referring to the army-issue sand, wind, and dust goggles.
7 Ibid.
8 Douglas Ford, telephone interview with author, October 24, 2015.
9 Ibid.

The SCO

1 The *dishdasha* or *thawb* is an ankle-length garment, usually long sleeved, similar to a robe that is commonly worn by men in Arab countries.
2 The Mast Mounted Site contains a Thermal Imaging System, Day TV, and laser range finder/designator.
3 Cavalry units have held on to the tradition of wearing Stetson hats, but the hat is not officially authorized for wear in army regulations. Typically, they are only worn for specific ceremonies and formations.
4 Stephen M. Schiller, email to author, October 29, 2015.

The Storm: Udairi to An Najaf

1 Stephen Schiller's account of the initial ground war was derived from copious notes that he kept throughout the war.
2 A Ground Assault Convoy (GAC) was merely a convoy of military vehicles.
3 Curtis Phipps, email to author, December 5, 2015.

The Battle of Karbala

1 Johnny Rowell, email to author, December 3, 2015.
2 Schiller's notes.
3 Schiller's notes.
4 Schiller shared what ran through his head as he fought during a series of interviews with the author, February–April 2018.
5 Ibid.
6 Ibid.

Babylon: The Fight for Al Hillah

1 Curtis Phipps, email to author, December 5, 2015.
2 Joseph Anderson, interview with author, January 20, 2016.
3 Ibid.
4 Joseph Anderson, email to author, January 27, 2016.

The Locals: Stayla

1 Omar, video teleconference with author, February 22, 2016.
2 The *mukhtar* is the local village leader.

Improving the Foxhole

1 Richard Arnold, email to author, December 22, 2015.
2 Ibid.
3 Ibid.

At Last, Flying

1 Douglas Ford, telephone interview with author, November 23, 2015.

A Pair of Aces

1 Daily Mail.com, "Saddam's cousin 'betrayed sons,'" June 16, 2019, https://www.daily mail.co.uk/news/article-189745/Saddams-cousin-betrayed-sons.html.
2 Curtis Phipps, email to author, dated October 4, 2015.

Risky Business

1 Stephen M. Schiller, email to author, dated October 11, 2015.
2 Joseph Anderson, interview with author, January 20, 2016.

Brotherhood

1 Johnny Rowell, email to author, November 9, 2015.
2 Timothy Slifko, email to author, November 30, 2015.
3 Ibid.
4 Ibid.
5 Ibid.
6 Ibid.
7 Timothy Slifko, email to author, November 4, 2015. Tim and I had this conversation multiple times over the years. We re-created it from our memories, and the benefit of hindsight, on November 4, 2015.
8 Ibid.
9 Ibid.
10 Ibid.

The Changing of the Winds

1 These comments come from my recollection of conversations with Ken Hawley, notes, and multiple emails with Stephen Schiller throughout the writing of the book.
2 Ibid.

Anbar

1 Candy Smith, email to author, February 9, 2016.

Tender Mercies

1 David H. Petraeus, telephone interview, February 4, 2016.

2 Kate Blaise and Dana White, *The Heart of a Soldier* (Gotham Books, 2005).
3 Curtis Phipps, email to the author, November 28, 2015.

The Heat Is On

1 Field Manual 3-04.300, Chapter 5, paragraph 5-7 (August 12, 2008).
2 John Rowell often called infantry soldiers infanteers and grunters. There are many nicknames used for ground soldiers. The origin of grunt is hard to discern. Many say that it originated from the sound men make when laboring under a heavy load. The terms are then used in common vernacular, e.g., "That's grunt work."
3 Brian Pearl, telephone interview with author, June 15, 2016.

Miscreants

1 Ian Anderson, email to author, September 19, 2015.
2 Ibid.

Ramadan

1 Joseph Anderson, interview with author, January 20, 2016.
2 Christopher Lusker, interview with author, November 20, 2015.
3 Ibid.

Shrapnel

1 Stephen M. Schiller, email to author, September 30, 2015.
2 Kenneth Hawley, email to author, September 25, 2015.
3 Jeffrey Kelley, email to author, September 25, 2015.
4 Schiller, email, September 30, 2015.
5 Kelley, email, September 25, 2015.
6 Steve shared these thoughts with me as he recounted the event during numerous interviews.
7 Schiller, email, September 30, 2015.
8 Douglas Ford, telephone interview, June 15, 2016.

Weather

1 Daniel Hauf, email to author, October 8, 2015.
2 Adam Frederick, email to author, October 5, 2015.
3 Kate Blaise and Dana White, *The Heart of a Soldier* (Gotham Books, 2005), 289.
4 Kimberly Hazelgrove, email to author, January 8, 2016.
5 Eric Bucher, email to author, January 31, 2016.
6 Ibid.
7 Timothy Slifko, in discussion with author, October 31, 2015.
8 Kenneth Royar, email to author, October 7, 2015.
9 Frederick, email, October 5, 2015.
10 Slifko, discussion, October 31, 2015.
11 Ibid.

12 Ibid.

13 Royar, email, October 7, 2015.

14 The details immediately following Mike's crash were compiled from a multitude of sources, including my own recollection, as well as interviews with Adam Frederick, Steve Schiller, Jeff Kelley, Ken Hawley, and Kenneth "Todd" Royar.

15 Frederick, email, October 5, 2015.

16 Ibid.

The Long Drive

1 Stephen Tubbs, email to author, March 4, 2016.